The Architecture of the Italian Renaissance

Christoph Luitpold Frommel

The Architecture of the Italian Renaissance

Translated from the German by Peter Spring

With over 300 illustrations

Thames & Hudson

Für Sabine

Frontispiece: St Peter's, Rome, from the air.

Translated from the German by Peter Spring

© 2007 C. L. Frommel
English translation © 2007 Thames & Hudson Ltd, London

First published in 2007 in hardcover in the United States
of America by Thames & Hudson Inc., 500 Fifth Avenue,
New York, New York 10110

thamesandhudsonusa.com

Library of Congress Catalog Card Number 2005907161

ISBN-13: 978-0-500-34220-6
ISBN-10: 0-500-34220-2

Printed and bound in Singapore by C S Graphics Pte Ltd

Contents

1, 2 *Interior and exterior of the Baptistery of Florence Cathedral. This is a medieval structure, probably of the late eleventh century, but Renaissance architects believed it to be an ancient Roman building and took it as one of their models.*

Preface

This book is an introduction to the study and appreciation of one of the greatest epochs in the history of architecture. It focuses on buildings of the period between 1418 and 1580, and the some thirty-five key architects who designed them. In recent times the historical and cultural context in which they are set has tended to push works themselves into the background, but in order to appreciate them as they deserve this context has had to be reduced to a bare minimum. My primary concern has been to introduce readers to the basic principles of Renaissance architecture, to help them to understand its sometimes complex relations and developments, and to familiarize them with the more recent research.

For the fact is that our understanding of this period has fundamentally changed since the publication of Peter Murray's *The Architecture of the Italian Renaissance* by Thames & Hudson in 1963. The findings of this latest research on the period are summed up in three volumes on the Italian architectural history of the fifteenth and sixteenth centuries, published in Italian by Electa in Milan from 1998 to 2002. (For reasons of space I have had to dispense with detailed references to sources, but readers with specialized interests will find more extensive information in these volumes.)

The didactic nature of the publication entailed a selective and synthetic view. It has meant that the emphasis be firmly placed on the most influential masters. They and their most important works have been discussed in some detail, whereas the rest have been reduced to a representative selection. It begins with Brunelleschi's first, and ends with Palladio's last, building. No earlier architect distinguished himself by so unconditional a dedication to the revival of Antiquity as Brunelleschi, and not until the mid-eighteenth century were ancient monuments more faithfully imitated than by Palladio. The only really significant chronological dividing line in our period is, conveniently, the year 1500 itself, once Bramante had arrived in Rome and introduced a far-reaching alteration of the parameters within which architects worked.

In examining the individual buildings, the emphasis has been firmly placed on the reciprocity between function, construction and form that Vitruvius described and that have been the three fundamental constituents of all architecture since Antiquity. The distinction between them is especially fruitful for the Renaissance. Brunelleschi tried to combine the functions and building methods inherited from the late Middle Ages with those of Antiquity. Seldom did he literally take over the vocabulary and syntax of the ancient columnar orders. So the medieval tradition always remained present and its fusing together with the ancient heritage contributed decisively to the innovative richness of the new age.

Architecture does not narrate, in the way that painting and sculpture do. And yet it does have a content that goes beyond mere forms and functions. Florentine citizens may have felt the pointed arches, pinnacles, shafts and gables of their cathedral to be handsome and even devout forms without being able to describe them in any greater detail or understand them as part of the image of the heavenly Jerusalem as in northern Europe (fig. 4). But when Brunelleschi erected his Old Sacristy in San Lorenzo (figs 9, 11), they flocked to see it because there the architecture of their ancestors was experiencing a rebirth. To appreciate the proportions and the detail of the Corinthian order of the Old Sacristy, they must have compared it with the Florentine Baptistery, the presumed Temple of Mars (figs 2, 3). Perhaps some of them may even have looked at Vitruvius's treatise. There they could read that the colonnade originated from the primitive hut and that its columns and entablature were transformations of wooden trunks (Book I.1; III.5; IV.3). Cicero (*De oratore*, III. 180) too had implied that architecture owed its splendour and dignity to its wooden origin, even if parts of the orders had lost their original meaning. According to Vitruvius, the Doric order imitated 'the proportion of a man's body, its strength and grace', the Ionic 'feminine slenderness', and the Corinthian 'the slight dimensions of a virgin girl' (Book IV.1). There existed, in addition, the Tuscan order invented by the Florentines' Etruscan ancestors and the Composite order which Alberti would call Italic because it was invented by the ancient Italic peoples of the peninsula (Book II.1; IV.2). The correct use of the different orders soon became a criterion for architecture akin to the anatomically correct representation of the human body in the figural arts. No aspect of architecture was regarded with greater attention than the orders.

The 'content' of architecture, however, comprised not only the *ornamentum* of the columnar orders, their proportional relation to man, woman and girl, and their respective consecration to pagan gods or Christian saints. It comprised also the allusion to significant prototypes such as temple, basilica, mausoleum, triumphal arch or the antique house and their most spectacular examples. Even the theory of numerical proportions, by which musical harmony could be transferred to architecture, had a metaphysical background.

Architectural iconography in the narrower sense – the ability of a building to take on an iconographic form – only gradually gained ground in the Renaissance (for instance when the lantern of Brunelleschi's Old Sacristy alluded to the Holy Sepulchre in Jerusalem) and was mainly limited in the fifteenth century to such symbols as the Greek and Latin cross or simple geometric forms as the circle or sphere. Only in the sixteenth do we find plans in the form of a heraldic eagle as in Peruzzi's Rocca Sinibalda.

In Renaissance descriptions of architecture we will search in vain for the criteria familiar to us in modern architectural analysis. This is shown for instance by Raphael's description of the Villa Madama, by far the most important text by an architect of the period about one of his own buildings. Raphael does not describe the villa as we would do in architectural or structural terms. Following the example of such ancient authors as Pliny the Younger, he expatiates instead on its functions, climatic properties, position, character, and above all its proximity to the ancient prototypes. The return to the temple in religious architecture, and to the ancient house and villa in secular architecture, were the real concerns of architects and their patrons;

"pantheon"

3 *One of the best preserved of all classical buildings, the Pantheon in Rome was enormously influential in the Renaissance. This drawing by Raphael shows it before the upper level of decoration was altered in the eighteenth century, but diminishes the number of bays. Raphael copied it from a late fifteenth-century original.*

the rediscovery of the columnar orders was inseparably connected with this.

We shall appreciate the Renaissance architects only if we do justice to what it is that differentiates them from their predecessors. We shall appreciate those who rebelled against the rules only if we do justice to their violations and provocations. The buildings of the Renaissance need to be read primarily through the eyes of their contemporaries.

Since Burckhardt, Geymüller and Wölfflin, our capacity to analyse architecture has made enormous progress. Numerous criteria indispensable for the dating and attribution of a building and for the characterization of a master are indebted to the art-historical advances of modern times. Only those who have the patience to adopt them can really penetrate into the secrets of many buildings.

In the succession of individual building analyses that forms the bulk of this book, I have tried to describe, or suggest, the long, laborious, far from linear, and not always equally successful path that led from Brunelleschi to Michelangelo and Palladio and to the fusing together of the antique and the medieval traditions. Just as Brunelleschi always looked back to the Baptistery in his hometown, so the subsequent architects never lost sight of their origins. They copied the antique not only to equal but to surpass it, and measured themselves not only against their teachers, but also against the great founding fathers of the Renaissance. In their striving to achieve a new zenith in architecture, even the great architects of the seventeenth century – Borromini, Bernini and Cortona – continued to study and seek inspiration from Alberti, Bramante, Raphael, Giulio, Sangallo, Peruzzi, Serlio, Vignola, Michelangelo or Palladio.

To penetrate into this continuous and ever more complex dialogue, the formal qualities of each important building need to be described and their sources traced. So comparisons between them increase as the book advances. Without such a lasting quest for the *fil rouge* of tradition, the origins, birth and development of this new movement cannot be understood.

Only in the most exceptional cases do the written sources provide any real insight into the dialogue between architect and patron, so decisive for the way in which a building comes into being. How concrete, how specific were the ideas of the popes, the Medici, Gonzaga, Montefeltro, Chigi or Farnese when they commissioned their buildings? How did they interfere? Where did they get their way? Not even Clement VII's letters on the Biblioteca Laurenziana provide any clear picture of his intentions. So often our text must rest on suppositions about the patronage of architecture. Nor do the format and scope of this series permit any exhaustive analysis of the planning process, construction methods, choice of materials and colours, or the urban contexts in which buildings were set – to many of these important questions individual studies have been devoted to which the student is referred.

Like musical history, architectural history is dependent on a particular terminology. That terminology once formed an inseparable part of general education, but it now baffles, and even intimidates, many contemporaries. In the present book this terminology has been deliberately simplified: it is concentrated in little more than a score of key concepts which for the most part were already used in Antiquity and continued to be used in the Renaissance. They are briefly explained in a glossary at the end of the book.

My description of the individual buildings, and the characterization of the masters who designed them, condenses almost half a century of experiences and studies. This synthesis of a lifetime's experience necessarily places some demands on the reader. Despite that, the author hopes that this book will prove a useful guide and contribute a little to the enjoyment and appreciation of the works of art to which Jacob Burckhardt devoted his pioneering *Cicerone* a century and a half ago.

A book like this is the result not least of the circumstances under which it was written. Since my first longer period of residence in Italy as a 22-year-old student, it was granted to me to live in Rome and to work in the Bibliotheca Hertziana. To my gradual rise to the post of Director of that Institute I owe the fact that I have lived over half my life in this city and in close proximity to its monuments. No other city is so much a work of art in itself, or has in any comparable way grown and developed as a direct result of its architects' mutual influence and enrichment through the centuries. Rome has a further claim to fame: no city has as its disposal so many archives, libraries and research institutes. No city can claim to rival Rome as the city where all researchers who seek to elucidate the architecture of the last two millennia, both in context and in detail, inevitably come to study and meet.

I am grateful to the Max-Planck-Gesellschaft, its Roman Institute, the Bibliotheca Hertziana, and its ever-changing community of members and guests for the great privilege of being able to study this matchless legacy for so long and so undisturbed. The friendly exchange with colleagues of the host country, numerous congresses, exhibitions and shared visits to numerous centres of art in Italy, and not least the intensive exchange with my students and associates have helped me gradually widen my horizon and deepen my knowledge, and finally challenged me to write such a book as the one I am presenting here. I could hardly have written it before I had found in Sabine a partner whose predilections, interests and methods so closely coincided with my own and with whom I was able to cultivate, by daily exchange, a fruitful dialogue on the study of the Renaissance architecture to which we have both devoted our lives.

Peter Spring took upon himself the not easy task of translating my demanding text into English. He did not tire of penetrating into the complex subject through patient questions and discussions. He helped to make the text more easily comprehensible, enliven it with his own proposals for improvements, and give greater ease and perspicuity to analyses of architectural details not always easy to grasp.

The publisher, Thames und Hudson, and its staff have also displayed exemplary patience and understanding for the needs of an author whose thoughts constantly revolve around the Renaissance and its architecture, and have shown remarkable generosity and kindness in bearing with the long process of preparing this text for the press. Ian Sutton devoted himself to the editing of the text with unusual sensitivity; he and Alice Gillespie contributed valiantly to preparing the unusually generous corpus of photos that illustrate it, a large part of them from the photographic archive of the Bibliotheca Hertziana in Rome.

A book that arose from the constant dialogue with Italian Renaissance buildings and their masters is never really concluded, and the study of the period as a whole also alters the study of the individual monument: Is an idea, a motif really original? Is it a conscious continuation, an ingenious variant, or even a polemical correction, of what went before? Are there not layers of understanding that I have so far failed to penetrate? Is it indeed permitted to the historian at all to express judgements of a qualitative nature, and can these really do justice to the phenomena they seek to evaluate? These and many other questions lead inevitably to a constant revision of the text, and this lasting quest for what is appropriate, accurate and right is one of the few points in which the interpreter feels a sense of kinship with the creative artist.

Rome, July 2006

Publisher's Note

This book, translated from the German text of a leading scholar, uses a number of technical terms which have become normal in continental European architectural history but are less familiar to English and American readers. To replace them by explanations in English wherever they occur would be excessively cumbersome, and in fact they are in every case useful shorthand expressions to which the reader quickly becomes accustomed. The only cases where he or she is likely to be seriously puzzled are 'theatre motif', 'paratactical', 'rhythmic bays' and *Dorica, Ionica, Corinthia* (which are virtually self-explanatory, and form a convention that seems likely to be adopted in English).

With these, and any other problems of terminology, reference to the Glossary (p.218) is strongly recommended. It will make the book clearer and more enjoyable and, hopefully, even save time.

THE FIFTEENTH CENTURY

1 Brunelleschi, Donatello and Michelozzo

Filippo Brunelleschi (1377–1446)

The Renaissance had been anticipated for two centuries in Tuscany, in the southern Italy of Frederick II and elsewhere, but its birthplace was Florence and its founding architect was Brunelleschi. Yet while Gothic and *all'antica* elements were forged into an indivisible whole in the figurative arts, Brunelleschi aspired to golden Latinity. He was recognized even by his contemporaries as the reviver of antiquity, of the 'true' and 'rational' architecture. He regarded himself as the descendant and heir of antiquity and, as such, felt it was his responsibility to return to the origins of Italian art and replenish from that source the art of the present. So important was he for his hometown that Antonio di Tuccio Manetti (1423–97) dedicated to him the first extensive biography of an artist. Manetti was uniquely well qualified to write it: he had personally known Brunelleschi and as a civic official, author and architect was familiar in the best possible way with the circumstances of his hometown.

The son of an influential Florentine notary, Brunelleschi – he tells us – had learned the rudiments of Latin and mathematics. He had then decided to become a goldsmith and soon distinguished himself not only in *niello*, enamel and ornamental reliefs, but also as a sculptor. He exemplified the principles of central perspective in spectacular paintings of the Baptistery and the Piazza della Signoria, and so was also one of the fathers of Renaissance painting and of a highly visual approach to architecture. After his defeat in the competition for the bronze doors for the Baptistery in 1401, he travelled to Rome together with Donatello in order to improve his prospects by the study of ancient sculpture. Only there, Manetti suggests, did the ancient monuments open his eyes to architecture: 'He decided to rediscover the fine and highly skilled method of building and the musical proportions of the ancients and how they might, without defects, be employed with convenience and economy.' The following sixteen years he largely spent in Rome, supporting himself by his work as a goldsmith, in order to be able to measure in scale, and even disinter where necessary, the important buildings both inside and outside the city. He thus rediscovered the vaulting technique of the Romans, the forms and syntax of their orders, and acquired that incomparable mastery that prepared the way for his subsequent architectural career. In Manetti's words: 'He found among the beautiful and costly elements of buildings many differences, in the masonry and in the quality of columns, bases, capitals, architraves, friezes, cornices, pediments and volumes (*corpi*), and differences between temples and between the diameters of columns. With his subtle eye he clearly distinguished the characteristics of each type: Ionic, Doric, Tuscan, Corinthian, and Attic.'

Whether he ever returned to Rome after 1418 we do not know.

4 *Santa Maria del Fiore, the cathedral of Florence. The body of the church and the campanile date from the fourteenth century. Brunelleschi's dome was designed about 1418 and the lantern on the top not finished until after his death in 1446.*

But his studies and drawings of the antique, which doubtless comprised perspective views as well as the already highly developed representational methods of ground plans, surveys, sections and detail drawings, were to serve him as his lasting source of inspiration. He was certainly familiar, too, with Roman monuments elsewhere: even if he had not personally seen more distant buildings, such as the ruins of Split (Spalato) in Croatia or Orange in France, he must have known them at second hand. He must have seen drawings of these and other remote monuments, just as humanists since Petrarch and Boccaccio had obtained the manuscripts of Greek authors from distant places like Byzantium. Thus the humanist Ciriaco da Ancona brought back drawings from his extensive travels in the eastern Aegean, which, in spite of their amateurishness, provided contemporaries with inestimable insights into Greek architecture. Brunelleschi clearly privileged prototypes of the late imperial period and the following centuries, which were closer to the Baptistery and the local Florentine tradition than the Hellenistic antique. He also showed an undeniable interest in Justinianic and later Byzantine architecture.

Brunelleschi could not have identified the individual columnar orders, their vocabulary and their syntax and rediscovered their integer-based 'musical' proportions, without the help of Vitruvius, the only known architectural theorist of the ancient world. Vitruvius had been familiar, but only partly understood, throughout the Middle Ages. In 1415, during the period when Brunelleschi was still in Rome, the papal secretary Poggio Bracciolini brought a particularly precious copy of the *De architettura* back from the monastic library of St Gallen. The humanists, whom Brunelleschi befriended, may have introduced him to, and helped him to grasp, some of the indispensable passages, such as those on the columnar orders in the Third and Fourth Books.

As a goldsmith and sculptor by training, Brunelleschi had first worked in the late-Gothic style. Despite its incorporation of various antique motifs, his competition relief of 1401 is still imbued with that spirit. After his return to Florence from Rome, however, it must have increasingly seemed to him that the 'Teutonic' – i.e. Gothic – ornament of the city's most important public buildings was a betrayal of the Roman origins, the Latin identity, of his hometown. As already Dante, and later the humanists, so too did Brunelleschi see in the Baptistery the architectural centre of the city: in the words of Coluccio Salutati, 'a temple not of the kind of the Greeks or the Etruscans, but unmistakably of the Romans'. Churches like Santi Apostoli had, in the humanist view, been built much later, in the time of Charlemagne, but had preserved a remnant of the Roman tradition destroyed by the barbarians from the North.

It was not until relatively late that the Florentines had embraced the Gothic style, and typically more in vaulting technique and in decorative detail than in building types or proportions. The Cathedral of Santa Maria del Fiore, the guild church of Or San Michele and the Loggia dei Lanzi fundamentally differ from contemporary buildings in northern Europe: their proportions are more compact; their arches and vaults broader, more depressed, often hemispherical;

their Gothic elements, more restrained and combined with relics of the columnar orders. In c.1280 the builders of Santa Maria Novella looked back to the Romanesque style and recurred to the spacious bays and the pillars with engaged columns of San Miniato. And in the late fourteenth century, when work was proceeding on the marble incrustation of the exterior of the cathedral choir, the steep arches of the exterior of the Baptistery and its tall oblong panels were once again revived and even enriched with blind Diocletian windows. Columns also assumed growing importance in the pictorial backgrounds of Giotto, who could have seen equally elongated columns in Roman wall paintings. Yet Brunelleschi was the first, and for many years the only, architect who systematically banished the Gothic vocabulary from his buildings. Only under Brunelleschi's direct influence did other masters of his time do so, as in the classicizing tabernacles on the exterior of the guild church of Or San Michele.

During his years in Rome Brunelleschi must have repeatedly returned to Florence to carry out smaller architectural commissions. It was his vaulting of the dome of Florence Cathedral, however, that made his reputation as an architect. As early as 1367 the ambitious citizens of Florence had enlarged the crossing and planned a dome which was to become the largest after the Pantheon. Yet they still lacked the necessary technical skill to be able to turn their dream into a reality. In his model of 1418 Brunelleschi invented the suspended scaffolding technique, which was much cheaper and simpler than the traditional one. He combined the Roman vaulting technique, as he had studied it in the Pantheon, the Minerva Medica, the imperial *thermae* or Hadrian's Villa, with that of the Gothic, and thus paved the way to post-medieval dome construction. Brunelleschi did not have *carte blanche* in the enterprise: he may have preferred a hemispherical dome, but both in plan and section was bound to the projects of his predecessors. Yet he adapted himself brilliantly to circumstance, and the result was a miracle of engineering and boldness: a structure that, as Vasari says, challenges the heavens and forged the very image we have of the city. His fellow-citizens, indeed, came to regard the enormous dome as the landmark of their superiority and Brunelleschi, together with Cosimo de' Medici and Palla Strozzi, as one of the great heroes of Florence.

Spedale degli Innocenti

Brunelleschi began what is probably his earliest building, a foundling hospital, the Spedale degli Innocenti, in c.1419. The commission was given to him by the powerful silk-weavers guild (the Arte della Seta), to which he himself belonged in his role as a goldsmith. The guild had already erected other hospitals, all of them based on a similar type with central loggia, lateral wall blocks, squat upper storey and internal courtyard. Brunelleschi was thus faced with the task of translating a late-medieval type into the language of the Vitruvian columnar orders (figs 5–7).

The long arcaded portico of the Spedale was intended as a public concourse, thus giving Brunelleschi the opportunity to approximate the Piazza Santissima Annunziata, of which it formed one side, to an ancient forum. He raised it over a continuous podium of nine steps and made the column even more predominant than in any earlier post-antique building of Florence. The influence of the Baptistery's

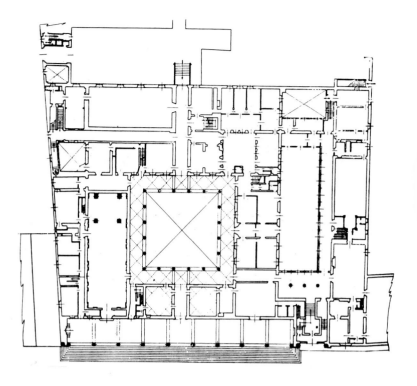

5, 6 *Brunelleschi's Spedale degli Innocenti, Florence, c.1419: plan and portico.*

inner system can be felt in every detail: in the upper storey of the Baptistery the arches are similarly framed by a colossal order of fluted pilasters. But only in the peristyle of the imperial palace of Diocletian at Split (Spalato) does a colossal order of pilasters frame a series of columnar arches in a similarly hierarchical way; this hierarchical thinking would appear even more commandingly in Alberti and Bramante. And only in the Pantheon were the arcades flanked by similarly closed wall blocks. These served as separate entrances for male and female visitors and were unfortunately later opened in broad arches: the balance between their vertical thrust and the horizontal movement of the arches was thus lost.

Such a composition could not have appealed to Vitruvius, and was only *a posteriori* justified by the *De re aedificatoria* of Brunelleschi's pupil Alberti. There he describes two fundamental qualities of the column: the column as fragment of the wall and the column as '*primum ornamentum*' (Book I, c.10; VI, c.13). Both pilasters with straight entablature and arches on columns are a sort of skeleton – *ossa* – of the wall. In the 'arched colonnade' – *columnatio arcuata* – of the arcades the architrave is represented by the arch (Book III, c.6; VII, c.15). The pilasters of the colossal order of the Spedale can be recognized in their square ground plan as *columnae quadrangulae*, as they were still called by Raphael and Serlio. They are 'affixed' – *affictae* – and partly hidden in the wall (Book VI, c.6). Whether the column really does act as a support and the entablature really does support a weight, or whether, like the colossal order of the Spedale, it only pretends to fulfil such a function, is not of prime importance. What matters is that the entablature seems to the eye to be supported by an order. The tectonic principle – as we call it – that is, the relation of load and support or its purely visual fiction, had been deduced by Vit-

ruvius from the wooden temple. It is this tectonic fiction we already find in the Colosseum where, instead of the columnar orders, the wall of pillared arcades takes over the load-bearing function. Brunelleschi would revive this tectonic fiction also in future buildings by using half-columns and pilasters as if they were round or square columns immured in the wall.

The column was also the *primum ornamentum*, the principal ornament of architecture. According to Vitruvius (Book III.1), the ancients had 'collected from the members of the human body the proportionate dimensions which appear necessary in all building operations': the column was thus 'anthropomorphic'. In contrast to Vitruvius Alberti accepted also arches on columns: in his typological hierarchy of the *ornamentum* the colonnade of a temple required a straight entablature, while the columns of a basilica could be slenderer and support arches (Book VII, c.4, 5, 14, 15).

Yet Brunelleschi still had a long way to go before he achieved the perfectly proportioned columns of antiquity or of his own Santo Spirito (fig. 18). The ratio between shaft width and height of the colossal order of the Spedale is 1:12 and that of the round columns

still *c*.1:11. They are considerably slenderer than recommended by Vitruvius and in Brunelleschi's later buildings and suggest how difficult it was for him at first to emancipate himself from late-medieval verticalism and give to the columns the weight they require in relation to the extremely broad arches. With their ratio of width to height of 2:3 these are proportioned similarly to the Baptistery's chancel arches. The Corinthian capitals are provided with the egg-and-dart of the Composite, but maintain two big inner scrolls (*helices*). This was probably no 'mistake', because Brunelleschi used normative Corinthian capitals for the colossal order and for most of his later buildings and could easily have copied the Composite capitals of the Baptistery. He may have enriched the capitals of the arches for similar hierarchical reasons as Alberti in the façade of Sant'Andrea (fig. 55).

As in the Baptistery, an impost block mediates between capital and arch: a late-Antique or Byzantine device. The arch is precisely hemispherical in form and incorporated into the tectonic system by

7 *Reconstruction of Brunelleschi's original elevation of the Spedale, showing the pilaster order intended for the upper storey.*

the archivolts. Above the capitals these are bent as in Split and should be read as a continuous architrave. Each of the nine arched bays is separately vaulted by an elegant umbrella dome. Their pure stereometric form was presumably discovered by Brunelleschi in late-Antique buildings and in the Veneto.

Manetti reports that Brunelleschi supervised the building workers of the Spedale only by scale drawings and did without a wooden model. But the area above the architrave was largely ruined during one of his longer absences from the site and was already censured by Brunelleschi's contemporaries. According to Manetti, the squat upper storey should have had its own order. In the peculiar right-angled bending of the architrave at the corners, the master-builder in charge of the construction clearly followed the upper storey of the Baptistery and the façade of San Miniato (figs 1, 42) – perhaps because not provided with sufficient instructions.

In subjecting the plan of the Spedale to the principles of symmetry and axiality Brunelleschi derived inspiration both from monastic cloisters in which the contemporary humanist Flavio Biondo found the most authentic survival of the ancient *domus*, and from secular buildings such as the imperial *thermae* in Rome. The principles of symmetry and axiality corresponded, like the tectonic logic of weight and support, to Brunelleschi's rational purism, but did not gain the upper hand in Florentine secular architecture till the Palazzo Medici in 1444 (figs 29, 30). In the Spedale degli Innocenti the Florentines could, in any case, for the first time admire a genuine revival of architecture in the antique style.

Cappella Barbadori

When Brunelleschi built a small funerary chapel in a right-hand corner at the end of the nave of Santa Felicita, presumably in the same year (1419), he again translated a late-medieval type into the language of the columnar orders (fig. 8). He connected the engaged columns of the two arches as in San Miniato with angular pillars. Though only their edges are visible inside the chapel, the fluted pilasters of the colossal Corinthian order can once again be recog-

8 *Reconstruction of Brunelleschi's original design for the Cappella Barbadori in Santa Felicita, Florence, 1419.*

nized as fragments of quadrangular columns immured in the wall. As in the Spedale, the arches of the arcades still rest on imposts from which also the saucer dome may have risen. The use of Ionic capitals as in the Baptistery, and of an architrave whose first fascia starts with an astragal, support a dating shortly before the Ospedale.

Old Sacristy

Giovanni di Averardo de' Medici belonged to the parish of San Lorenzo and already in 1417 had been appointed member of a commission which was responsible for the rebuilding of the church. According to Manetti, he first asked Brunelleschi to build only the sacristy and a chapel of the church, but then was convinced by Brunelleschi's projects to finance the entire church. In all this his son Cosimo, future *pater patriae*, may have played a decisive role (figs 9–11): indeed the rising structure was called '*I fondamenti di Chosimo*' (Cosimo's foundation) in 1422. By this time the Medici had already become the richest bankers of Florence and had entered into league with the *popolo minuto*, the less prominent of the guilds that then

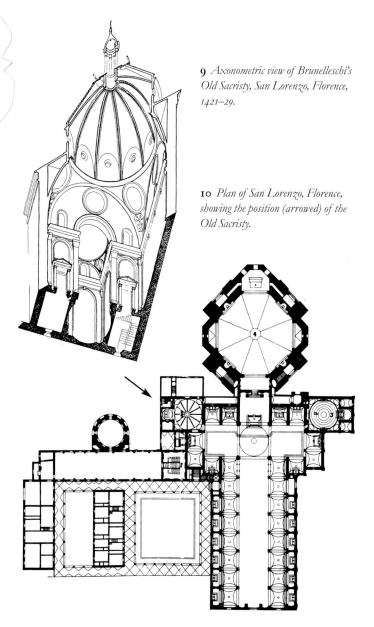

9 *Axonometric view of Brunelleschi's Old Sacristy, San Lorenzo, Florence, 1421–29.*

10 *Plan of San Lorenzo, Florence, showing the position (arrowed) of the Old Sacristy.*

11 *View of the Old Sacristy, looking towards the altar.*

12 *Reconstruction drawing of the twelfth-century baptistery of Padua, a probable model for Brunelleschi's Old Sacristy.*

13 *At the end of the transept of the church of San Lorenzo which Brunelleschi designed after the Old Sacristy, he used a very similar elevation.*

Instead, the eye of the visitor is immediately drawn to the façade-like altar wall. As in the baptistery in Padua, its central arch opens into the altar chapel while its lateral doors lead into small adjacent rooms. With its semicircular arch over the central bay this tripartite structure is a *serliana,* a variant of the Syrian arch and one of the most successful motifs of Renaissance architecture. As in the triumphal arch in Orange or in Pompeian mural paintings, the arch is separated from the entablature. Brunelleschi emphasized its triumphal character by repeating it on the transept walls of the church of San Lorenzo, through which the Old Sacristy is entered (fig. 13). This repetition of façade-like systems is characteristic of Brunelleschi's highly visual approach to architecture.

governed the Republic of Florence. By combining their funerary chapel with the sacristy of the church and subordinating its funerary role to a higher purpose, they were able to adopt more monumental dimensions than would otherwise have been acceptable to the Florentine guild-republic.

Neither Brunelleschi nor his patrons were satisfied with a sacristy of traditional type, like those of Santa Croce or Santa Trinita. They found instead a model for the combination of a public function and a funerary chapel with a domed, centrally planned building in the twelfth-century baptistery in Padua (fig. 12). Brunelleschi adopted the pendentives forming the junction between the cube-shaped square room and hemispherical dome, but eliminated the drum. The room is articulated by a Corinthian order which supports the archivolts of the four hemispherical lunettes. In the corners the pilasters are angled and not easily perceived as the vestiges of intersecting quadrangular columns immured in the wall. The entrance wall and the two side walls had to remain free for the sacristy cupboards. There the entablature rests on brackets as in triumphal arches. Their intervals are equivalent to the intercolumniations of a temple: according to Vitruvius, an entablature built of stone required a support at intervals of no more than four shaft-widths (Book III.3). These brackets alone make it clear that Brunelleschi understood the wall not as an empty space between the columns, but as the real load-bearing element of which the column is only a fragment, as later described by Alberti in his treatise.

The sarcophagus of Giovanni de' Medici executed by Brunelleschi's adoptive son is hidden below the sacristy table.

In the dome of the Old Sacristy Brunelleschi did not follow the prototype of Florence Cathedral or of the Pantheon, but combined the umbrella dome of Hadrian's Villa with Gothic ribs. The ribs of the dome, which lead the eye upwards, are not ornamental but the visible sign of reinforcing elements, set deep in the fabric. They converge on a ring which visually counteracts their vertical thrust – a system that recurs also in Brunelleschi's later domes. A corona of sixteen windows cuts into the lunettes of its small webs. As in the Baptistery, the dome is also lit by a lantern.

The central arch of the altar wall is conspicuously more slender and majestic than the arches in the Spedale or in the Barbadori Chapel. The proportion of 1:2.2 corresponds to the diagonal through two squares (1:root of five). Like other of Brunelleschi's proportions it could be easily translated by the craftsmen from the drawing into a larger scale without laborious calculations. While the height of the entablature of about a shaft width is still significantly lower than the Vitruvian norm, the proportion of the order of *c*.1:9.6 corresponds much more closely to it than in the Spedale. Vitruvius had differentiated the *Corinthia* by its higher capital from the *Ionica* proportioned 1:9 (Book IV.5). The fact that Brunelleschi would subject these proportions only to slight variations in his subsequent buildings suggests that he had already found the aesthetic norms of his architectural system.

On the exterior of the Old Sacristy he devoted particular care to the lantern, its only part visible from afar. Once again he took as his

model the Baptistery. But he transformed its octagonal lantern into a perfect rotunda and gave greater robustness to the six Corinthian columns, his first freestanding ones with an unbroken entablature, and enlivened them by the spiralling flutes of its pinnacle. Perhaps, as later in Alberti's Cappella Rucellai, the spiral was intended to recall the Holy Sepulchre in Jerusalem and hence the ascension of the soul to heaven (fig. 45). The dynamic circular movement of the lantern is reinforced by a concentric balustrade of sixteen Ionic colonnettes, as many as the round windows of the cupola, circling without axial relation round the six larger columns of the lantern itself. Their capitals are more normative than those of the earlier Barbadori chapel.

After having returned from exile in 1434, Cosimo asked Donatello to adorn the sacristy more lavishly with classicizing aedicules, bronze doors and reliefs, thus making it more obviously the funerary chapel of the Medici, but at the same time compromising Brunelleschi's design.

San Lorenzo

Already initiated in 1419, the renovation of the ancient basilica adjacent to the Palazzo Medici had begun with the brick pillars of a choir. But in the following years the building made little progress. Brunelleschi was presumably only involved in its design after Gio-

14 *Nave of San Lorenzo, Florence, looking east, begun by Brunelleschi soon after the Old Sacristy and still unfinished at his death.*

vanni de' Medici had commissioned him to build the sacristy and offered to fund the larger part of the church himself. When he died in 1429, Brunelleschi had completed only the lower part of the transept and the two Medici chapels in its left arm (figs 10, 13). Work was then interrupted.

In his design of the transept, however, Brunelleschi had established the system of the whole church: a cruciform basilica formed with a dome over the crossing, columnar arches and chapels all around. Its basic measurements of *c*.30 x 85 m were almost as large as the two great Florentine mendicant churches, the presumable prototypes of the 1419 project. While in his design of the choir his hand was forced by the existing walls, in the nave he could recur to the form and liturgical space of Early Christian basilicas (fig. 14). He also drew inspiration from the eleventh-century cathedral of Pisa, the only columnar basilica in Italy with a domed crossing, and distinguished the sanctuary area in a similarly hierarchical way. As later in Santo Spirito (figs 18, 19), it was intended to be the liturgical centre of the church. The cruciform pillars of the crossing are articulated by fluted pilasters of a giant Corinthian order. The inner ones continue upwards through the projections of the entablature into the arches. Their vertical continuity and their slender proportions of 1:16 are more reminiscent of medieval colonnettes than of interpenetrating columns with quadrangular section. As in the sacristy, their entablature runs round the whole interior and is supported by brackets. Only next to the crossing and in the corners of the transept are the brackets replaced by fragments of colossal pilasters springing from the lower order. These fragments and the brackets show once again that Brunelleschi regarded the continuous visual support of the entablature as indispensable.

He no longer concentrated the light on the choir, but increased it hierarchically from the chapels to the nave and transept. It would have reached its plenitude in the windows and lantern of a dome similar to that of the Old Sacristy. Basic geometric forms like the square and the cube, and arches with relatively large spans, had lent an unusual degree of spaciousness to much earlier churches, such as San Miniato, Santa Maria Novella and the Cathedral, and had differentiated them fundamentally from Early Christian and early medieval basilicas. In his quest for rational clarity and harmony Brunelleschi went a step further and developed a modular system. His basic module was a square, exemplified by the square of the crossing. He repeated it not only in the three cross-arms and in the sacristy, but combined four of these squares into the length of the nave. Thus the basilica would have comprised in all eight square modules of roughly the same width.

Brunelleschi continued the same square module in the elevation. The breadth, height and length of the nave without crossing are thus proportioned, according to a symmetrical scale of integers, approximately 1:2:4. So the church is not only geometrically, but 'musically' proportioned: its main measurements encompass two octaves and thus correspond to the most harmonious of the musical proportions described by Vitruvius (Book V.4) and Alberti (Book IX, c.5). The arches are proportioned as in the Old Sacristy. The columns are somewhat slenderer. The monolithic shafts far surpass those of the Spedale and show how Brunelleschi continuously strove to approach

perfection of form by successive corrections and adjustments of the same basic forms. Constantly seeking guidance from Vitruvius and the ancient prototypes, in detail, too, he came closer to the antique in each successive building. Since the columns of the nave belong to the same small order as the square columns of the transept, they necessarily support fragments of the entablature – as Brunelleschi had seen in the *natationes* of the Roman *thermae*, in the Basilica of Maxentius or on the exterior of the Baptistery (fig. 1).

Like Alberti (Book III, c.6), Brunelleschi understood the arches as curved architraves, but must have found those of the Baptistery and of the Spedale unsatisfactory. As in the Old Sacristy he added a frieze decorated with an acorn festoon and accompanied it with a broad cornice. He thus enlarged the curved architrave to a curved entablature. This solution meant, however, that two archivolts had to intersect over the entablature fragment placed over each column. The two entablatures of the exterior of the transept would probably have continued along the nave and unified the whole building. The never-executed façade would probably have followed the type of the façade of San Miniato (fig. 42). Pilasters corresponding to the giant order of the interior and a second order corresponding to the clerestory would have supported the entablatures and a similar pediment as on the transept façade. It would have been the first church systematically articulated by columnar orders.

It is enough to enter San Lorenzo to experience its light-filled spaciousness, the harmony of its proportions, the measured movement of its arcades towards the hierarchical centre of the crossing. As in hardly any earlier church, the column seems the *primum ornamentum* and the equivalent of the human figure.

It was not until 1442 that Giovanni's son Cosimo was powerful enough to transform the basilica into what was in effect his own mausoleum. After having failed to rebuild the Dominican church of San Marco, he concentrated his attention anew on San Lorenzo. Once he had been given permission to transform the crossing into his funerary chapel, he honoured his father's promise to finance the whole construction. Again it was to Donatello that he now entrusted the task of designing his tomb and reorganizing the sanctuary area itself. He gave instructions that he be buried in the upper part of the pillar which supports the floor of the crossing. As in tombs of saints, the four bronze grilles of the tombstone connect the altar area directly with Cosimo's bones, and, as in Early Christian basilicas, Donatello added two *ambones* to the side pillars of the crossing. As a result of these alterations the high altar had to be shifted backwards to the choir, while the dome now glorified the overweening patron.

Cappella Pazzi

Scion of a leading Florentine noble family, Andrea Pazzi had renounced his entitlements to nobility and during the 1420s worked his way up to becoming one of the city's most prosperous merchants and most influential politicians. Anything but an aesthetically minded humanist, he vied in wealth and power with Cosimo, and emulated him by planning a similar funerary chapel in the precincts of Santa Croce. Like Cosimo, he entrusted the commission to Brunelleschi

and associated its funerary with a more public function: namely, that of a chapter house. Brunelleschi seems to have planned the Cappella Pazzi as early as 1424–28 (figs 15–17). But political and financial problems, and perhaps also the patron's own vacillation, delayed its realization: it was not started until after 1442, its dome not vaulted until 1457 and its porch not completed until 1461 – perhaps by his follower Antonio Manetti Ciaccheri. In his planning of the chapel Brunelleschi was constrained not only by the type of the chapter house, with its precedent in that of Santa Maria Novella, but also by the site of the chapel itself, set between the large cloister, the *dormitorium*, and the campanile and chapels of the Franciscan church. In spite of that, he succeeded in giving the chapel a form even more perfect than that of the Old Sacristy. The diameter of the dome is only slightly smaller, the exterior slightly higher. He placed the tomb in an almost identical altar chapel, dedicated to Andrea's patron saint and lit by a window with the saint's image. To meet the needs of a chapter house, he expanded the domed cube-shaped space by the addition of two lateral barrel-vaulted arms surrounded with squat *pietra serena* benches for the monks to sit on during their assemblies.

The design of the column-supported porch, the first post-medieval colonnade with straight entablature in monumental scale, probably goes back to Brunelleschi too. The broader central arch,

through which the chapel is entered, projects upwards into the attic storey, thus approximating the whole composition once again to a triumphal *serliana*. Perhaps Brunelleschi, on one of his journeys to Rome, had seen the comparable cosmatesque porch of the cathedral of Civita Castellana. The squat upper storey of the façade has a structural function and is articulated by a delicate order of paired pilasters and a cruciform pattern of groups of four panels. Above the arch of the entrance bay rises a shallow dome, now hidden behind a provisional canopy roof; Brunelleschi may have wanted to conceal it behind a classical pediment. He also used pediments in the transepts of San Lorenzo and Santo Spirito, in order to make the approximation to the classical temple even more conspicuous. How much he strove to imitate antiquity here is again shown by the intercolumniations. They are *c.*3.5 shaft diameters broad and approximate to Vitruvius's *diastylos* (Book IV.3).

In the interior Brunelleschi could now project the system of the altar wall also onto the three other walls. The corner pilasters are reduced so that only one of the six flutes can be seen. By this device he ensured that the shaft width is exactly the same as that of the archivolt of the lunette that springs from the entablature above it; the barrel vaults of the lunettes thus remain symmetrically framed and their intrados corresponds to those of the altar chapel. Complete

15–17 *Cappella Pazzi, San Lorenzo, Florence, begun by Brunelleschi about 1442. Opposite: the interior and entrance front and (below) cut-away drawing.*

symmetry he also preserved in matching the four arched windows, which pierce the entrance wall of the portico, by the eight blind arched panels that articulate the other walls. Even the glazed terracotta busts of apostles, placed against a blue ground, in the medallions over the arches, seem to be looking through windows. This scheme is in close correspondence with the column-supported portico and strongly suggests that he planned both together. With their proportion of *c.*1:10.3, the columns and pilasters are slenderer than those of the Old Sacristy, while the entablature is slightly taller. The rich decoration of the frieze and archivolts and the brackets are comparable with those of San Lorenzo and suggest a dating to the immediately following years.

Santo Spirito

In 1434 Brunelleschi was commissioned by a group of wealthy citizens to renovate the Augustinian church on the Oltrarno. He was thus given a unique opportunity to erect a building of the same type, same functions and almost identical measurements as that of San Lorenzo and so correct everything that he had failed to achieve, or failed to complete, in his previous basilica (figs 18, 19). Perhaps his project for Santo Spirito was even influenced by a further journey to Rome. According to Manetti, he did not succeed in winning over his patrons to his original project in which he had aligned the façade with the Arno and preceded it with a piazza, with the aim of ensuring it a more prominent role in the fabric of the city.

The foundations were begun in 1434–36. But it was not until shortly before Brunelleschi's death, once the external walls and the chapels had been completed, that the first column could be raised. Probably he wanted to surround not only the three arms of the crossing and both sides of the nave, but also its entrance wall, with arcades. The nave would thus have retained the same proportion of 1:4 as in San Lorenzo. By continuing the aisles and the hemispherical chapels round the whole church, he may even have been trying to express a republican ideal. Altogether forty funerary chapels for potential sponsors of the new building were made available in Brunelleschi's plan – far more than in any other Florentine church. These chapels, and the continuity between aisles and ambulatory, concur to an extraordinary unification of the space, which expands stage by stage hierarchically up to the dome. Choir and transepts no longer have the same predominance as in Gothic churches, and as they still have in San Lorenzo, and thus the baldachin-like effect of the domed crossing is heightened: it dominates every part of the interior in a similar way. Indeed, seen from the nave, the basilica resembles a centrally planned building, and centralization corresponded to Brunelleschi's idea of perfection.

The Corinthian columns are even more genuinely antique and more perfect in form than in San Lorenzo. In the form of engaged columns they also recur on the aisle walls, where their convex volumes counteract the concavity of the narrow chapels. In the corners of the transepts three-quarters of their shaft even project: here they can clearly be recognized as full columns incorporated in the structure of the wall. The entablature fragments that mediate between the capitals and the arches are now stripped of any ornament and in detail resemble more closely those of the Pantheon (fig. 3)

18, 19 *Brunelleschi's Santo Spirito, Florence, begun 1436: interior looking towards the altar, and plan.*

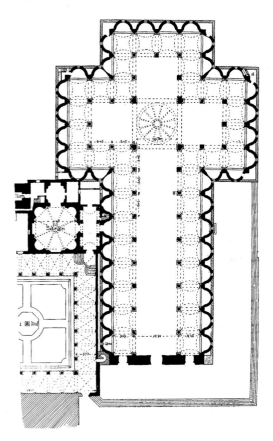

than in San Lorenzo. The archivolts too are now closer to the antique, for their mouldings correspond exactly to those of an architrave. As in the Baptistery, they do not intersect, but rise directly in pairs from the entablature over the columns. They are doubled not by a cornice as in San Lorenzo, but by a flat unmoulded strip of *pietra serena*, by which they reach the width of the columns. The cruciform pillars of the crossing of San Lorenzo are transformed into quadrangular columns. The elimination of their flutes and their proportion of 1:11.9 makes them resemble more closely the columns of the small order than in San Lorenzo. For the first time Brunelleschi gave the entablature a normative height. The elimination of the fragments of pilasters and brackets, and the flushness of the entablature with the wall, show that the weight is now unequivocally supported, not by columns or brackets, but by the wall itself. Approximation to antiquity in Santo Spirito is achieved not by too literal an interpretation of Vitruvius, but by unification, simplification and investing the classical orders with a more corporeal and sensuous quality than in his earlier buildings.

Paradoxically, however, other details betray his roots in the Florentine Trecento even more pronouncedly than before. He connected the semicircular chapels with the supporting wall, thus reducing it to a minimum. The chapels are extremely steep and, in the Romanesque fashion, only sparely lit by narrow lancet-like windows. At the corners of the crossing the chapels are only separated from each other by a narrow strip of wall (only on the exterior is this visible). The dynamically undulating profiles of the chapel arches are reminiscent of late-Gothic piers and intersected by the cornice of the entablature.

Santa Maria degli Angeli

In the same year, 1434, Brunelleschi began his first centrally planned building proper – an octagon with a sixteen-sided exterior – on the corner of the Via Castellaccio and Via Alfano (figs 20, 21). But the work was soon suspended and never reached beyond half the height of its chapels. It was an oratory to be funded from the bequest of the well-known Scolari family and was built next to an older church and a convent of Camaldolensians, who would celebrate masses for the souls of the donors. The superior of the order, the great humanist Ambrogio Traversari, certainly influenced the choice of the architect and his project. Once again a funerary function seems to have led Brunelleschi to opt for a centrally planned building. Nor is it by chance that he derived his basic inspiration from a mausoleum of the imperial period, now only known from ground plans, whose interior sides were similarly doubled on the exterior (figs 22, 23). As in this prototype and in the Baptistery, each side of Brunelleschi's interior is flanked by two unconnected pilasters of a Corinthian order with arches. As in the Old Sacristy, these arches open to chapels whose corner pilasters are reduced to a single flute. The chronological proximity to Santo Spirito is shown by the lancet-shaped windows and the widely splayed profiles which frame the niches of the chapels and are angled over their doors – this too a detail ultimately of Gothic origin. Instead of furnishing each chapel with its own saucer dome, Brunelleschi planned a series of barrel vaults, which connected the chapels far more directly and fluidly with the inner octagon. As in Santo Spirito, the expanding

20, 21 *Brunelleschi's church of Santa Maria degli Angeli, begun 1434: drawing of the interior by an unknown draughtsman, and plan by Giuliano da Sangallo.*

22, 23 *Plan and section of a Roman mausoleum known to Brunelleschi but now destroyed.*

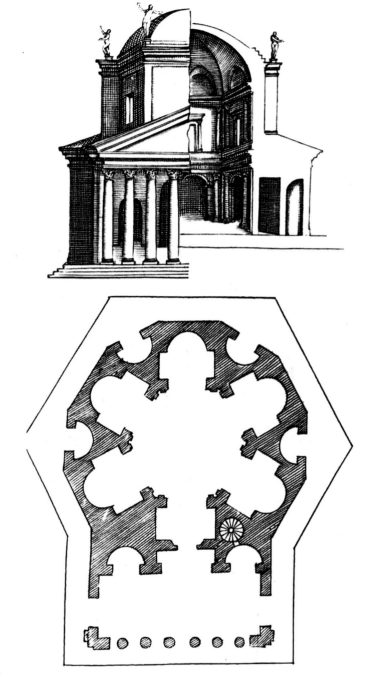

space, flowing freely from the octagon into the chapels, had become more important than the framing elements.

The drawings of the interior, presumably copied after Brunelleschi's project, show above the arcades an entablature similar to that in Santo Spirito. Above it rises the squat drum, its archivolts articulating large lunettes pierced by round windows. The eight webs of the dome, once again reinforced by ribs, rise, in a more tectonic way than in Brunelleschi's other buildings, over the entablature of the drum. Whether both the upper entablatures were to be supported by similarly fragmentary corner pilasters as in San Lorenzo, or – more probably – simply by the wall as in Santo Spirito, cannot be clearly determined from the later drawings. As in Santo Spirito, Brunelleschi reduced the supporting wall to a minimum by niches on both interior and exterior. The effect, however, is quite different from the imperial *thermae*, and the niches seem just as little hewn into the thickness of the wall as those in Santo Spirito. Roughly a quarter bigger than the Old Sacristy, the interior of the oratory would have hierarchically ascended from the niches to the chapels and thence to the dome and would have been abundantly lit from above. The horizontal forces would have been reinforced by the three heavy entablatures and the two rows of surrounding arches.

The sixteen-sided exterior, enlivened only by cylindrical niches, upright oblong wall compartments with a plain surrounding cornice and perhaps by triangular pediments, would have continued into the octagonal drum and dome: an interplay of stereometric forms that remains unique even in Brunelleschi's oeuvre. Brunelleschi apparently was asked to precede the adjacent garden of the monastary with a large portico over a stepped podium. A piazza in front would have stretched as far as the Via dei Servi. With a depth of *c.*7.50 m (24½ feet) and a width of *c.*41 m (134½ feet), the portico would have reached nearly half the length of that of the Spedale – a sort of vestibule as in Roman churches or in the Pazzi Chapel.

Palazzo di Parte Guelfa

Only the fragmentary Palazzo di Parte Guelfa permits an insight into Brunelleschi's ideas about a public palace (fig. 24). This seat of the most powerful political party in the city was enlarged in the early Trecento and further enlarged after 1415. In *c.*1430 construction began on a new audience hall, but it was only towards 1440, when the ground floor and the *botteghe* had been largely completed, that Brunelleschi became involved in the work. The ground floor, in spite of its late-medieval

24 *The Palazzo di Parte Guelfa, Florence, enlarged by Brunelleschi about 1440, later altered and recently restored: this photograph shows it before damage during World War II.*

forms, differs from Trecento precedents by its size, its more symmetrical ground plan and its regular window-axes. Brunelleschi terminated it with a tripartite entablature and let the *piano nobile* clearly rise above its surrounding buildings. He accentuated the corners of the *piano nobile* with a colossal order, and a powerful entablature, and made it a prominent sight in the townscape. The lower entablature supports the arched windows framed by archivolts and accompanied, as in medieval public buildings, by a second row of windows, circular like the niches in the Pazzi Chapel. The colonnette on the corner of the ground floor did not allow the corner pilasters to be unified into quadrangular columns, as in the crossing of Santo Spirito. Thus Brunelleschi replaced earlier symbols of worldly power such as battered basement, merlons and towers by humanistic urbanity, monumental dimensions, symmetry and a colossal order, though without lessening its powerful effect. He presumably wanted to reserve the colossal order for public buildings. Presumably, too, he wanted to articulate each floor of the palazzo he had planned for Cosimo de' Medici in front of San Lorenzo with its own order, as later Alberti did in the Palazzo Rucellai (fig. 35).

The 'tribune morte' of the cathedral dome

Brunelleschi's masterpiece remains the cathedral dome (fig. 4). He continued to work on its completion, both at the technical and formal level, throughout this life. His proposal to place half-cylindrical tribunes with conical roofs on the diagonals of the drum on the exterior was approved in 1439. The work, however, did not begin till 1443 and by the time he died had reached no further than the initial stages of the first tribune. This was not completed till 1449, so that details alien to Brunelleschi such as the squat proportions of the half-columns, the entablature fragments on top of their capitals or the rich decoration of the entablature are attributable to Michelozzo who succeeded Brunelleschi as architect of the cathedral. The cylindrical volumes of the tribunes, classical detail and all-encompassing white marble revetment counter the flat incrustation and polychrome fields of the polygonal exterior and invest it with the unmistakable stamp of Brunelleschi's late style. In the dialogue between half-columns and niches he drew on his experiences in Santo Spirito.

Lantern of the cathedral dome

Although the Opera del Duomo decided on Brunelleschi's model for the lantern in 1436, and ordered the first marble blocks for its construction in 1438, the actual work, as we have seen, did not begin until 1443, and the transport of the stone to the site only took place in March 1446, a month before Brunelleschi's death (figs 25, 26). His biographer Manetti nonetheless recognized the lantern as a work of Brunelleschi, though he attributed errors in its execution, such as the discrepancy between the arch and the jambs in the shell niches of the buttresses, to his malicious followers. The connection of a giant Corinthian order with arches on half-columns still recalls the Cappella Barbadori (fig. 8). But the columns are without entasis and, not least for static reasons, the arches are proportioned even more steeply than the chapel windows of Santo Spirito. This system is continued in the indispensable buttresses that surround the lantern. They are hollowed out by shallow shell niches and pierced by an ambulatory. The fragmentary flanking pillars look like fragments of polygonal columns. Their flutes are much broader than those of the big order and on each side reduced to two, thus providing deeper shadow lines. They support the lower spiral of the powerful S-shaped volutes that rise diagonally over the niches to join the big order. The tall and continuous entablature marks a second horizontal caesura and continues in a squat attic whose niches, alternating with baluster-crowned pedestals, lead into the steep pinnacle. The ridges between its cone-shaped segments seem to be hewn out of the same marble blocks. The vertical forces, which ascend in the pillars of the octagonal choir and drum and are channelled upwards by the marble ribs of the red tiled dome, converge in the lantern: they culminate in the huge golden orb.

Michelozzo was responsible for executing the greater part of the lantern until 1449. He may have adjusted the capitals of the half-columns, the S-shaped volutes, the entablature and the attic to his own more decorative vocabulary. However, so complex a conglomerate of *all'antica* forms can be attributed to no one but Brunelleschi himself. This is especially apparent from the ground plan of nearly

Gothic character. The load-bearing wall was again reduced to a series of thin pillars. Polygonal columns and half-columns, niches and volutes are fused together into a consubstantial structure. Thus Brunelleschi's last work testifies more eloquently than any other Renaissance architecture to the fusion of the antique and the medieval tradition.

Cappella Cardini in San Francesco in Pescia

Brunelleschi's adopted son Andrea di Lazzaro Cavalcanti, called il Buggiano, is confirmed as the architect of the Cappella Cardini in Pescia, completed in 1451. Following his master's designs, Buggiano had previously executed the sarcophagus and altar of the Old Sacristy, two lavabos in the cathedral of Florence and the pulpit of Santa Maria Novella. In the Cappella Cardini, he translated the architectural setting of Masaccio's *Trinity* into the more composed and more corporeal language of the late Brunelleschi. The engaged columns of the big order, their fluted shafts and their Composite capitals may already be influenced by Alberti (figs 36, 40). Only the small Corinthian colonnade which carries the barrel vault is provided with an architrave. Under the intrados of the arcade the columns are quadrangular and paired, but then extend to two round columns and a final pilaster on each side.

From Alberti and Filarete to the early twentieth century Brunelleschi was justly celebrated as the founding father of the Renaissance and the rediscoverer of ancient architecture. More recently, reacting against this interpretation, architectural historians have tended to underline his medieval roots. Brunelleschi did not repudiate those roots and they are no less important than the ancient prototypes for his buildings. He would hardly have been successful if he had totally broken with the Trecento tradition of his hometown, but his ideal was Roman Antiquity. After he had convinced his fellow-citizens about the technical and financial advantages of his model for the cathedral dome, he was given the opportunity in the Spedale and in the Barbadori and Ridolfi chapels to translate tried and tested architectural types into the *latinitas* of the Florentine Baptistery. He thus convinced Giovanni and Cosimo de' Medici to commission the Old Sacristy and San Lorenzo from him. In the following years they helped him to push through his new style in Florence. From *c.*1434 onwards he modelled himself even more directly on the antique. Within a small range of building types he continually strove to come ever closer to his ideal – in a similar way to the architects of the ancient temple, or more recently Mies van der Rohe. The closer he came to this goal, the freer he felt to draw on his Gothic legacy. Characteristically, he did so only in mode of composition and not in vocabulary. In the economy of their tectonic framework, in the almost abstract rationality of their proportions and especially in their spatial effect, his buildings differ fundamentally from all prototypes. Through unconventional inventions like his cathedral lantern, he opened up to the following generations the chance to fuse together both traditions and thus to develop innovative and forward-looking forms and systems.

Brunelleschi, ever since his first buildings, must have aspired to the ideal of a new Florence with forum-like piazzas, classicizing basilicas, centrally planned buildings, monumental palaces and villas articulated and adorned with the classical orders. He therefore only

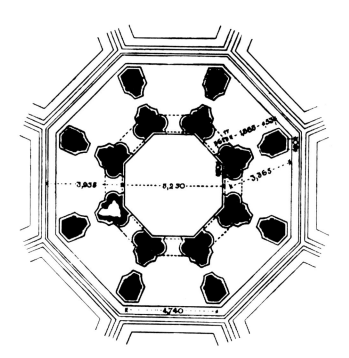

25, 26 *Brunelleschi's last work was the lantern of the cathedral, probably not built (by Michelozzo) exactly to his design after 1546.*

took on those commissions that were compatible with this ideal. But these commissions became fewer and fewer after 1434, when Cosimo became the leading figure of Florence. Cosimo now gave his preference to Donatello and Michelozzo – perhaps because they were less purist, more tractable, and more amenable to his own ideas. Brunelleschi's only known commissions during this late phase are those for the cathedral. He was also active as an engineer and military architect and highly esteemed as an adviser to the courts of northern Italy. As such he was often travelling, and may have designed the extraordinary plan of Belriguardo, the *delizia* of the Este near Ferrara.

Donatello (1386–1466)

When he was little more than sixteen, Donatello had accompanied Brunelleschi to Rome. There he mainly studied Roman sculpture. Unlike Brunelleschi, what he sought in architecture was not prescriptive norm, but dazzling richness, variety, breadth of variation and originality. Nonetheless, architecture – architecture reduced, that is, to the frame of sculpture or the background of figural reliefs – played an unusual and influential role in his works. His decorative approach proved prescriptive for the further development of Renaissance architecture.

27 *Donatello's Annunciation in Santa Croce, Florence. The frame shows how he adapted the classical vocabulary of column, frieze and cornice to a personal language of his own.*

The fact that he still adopted Gothic forms for the tabernacles of *St Mark* (c.1411) and *St George* (1417) on the exterior of the guild church of Or San Michele suggests that his journey to Rome (unlike that of Brunelleschi) had not revolutionized his architectural conceptions. Yet the latter tabernacle is distinguished by an exceptional tectonic logic. In his later pedimented tabernacle for the bronze statue of *St Louis* (c.1422), he showed his indebtedness to Brunelleschi by basing himself on the model of the Barbadori Chapel. He opened the elegant arch flanked by Ionic columns to a deep shell niche, elongated the proportions of the columns and pilasters, and lavished rich classicizing ornament on every possible surface.

In 1434, after his return from a second trip to Rome, he was commissioned by Cosimo de' Medici with the decoration of the Old Sacristy in San Lorenzo (fig. 11). There Donatello behaved – says Manetti – in so high-handed a manner to his erstwhile mentor, Brunelleschi, that the friendship between them was ended. In the classicizing simplicity that differentiates the door-aedicules so fundamentally from the tabernacles of Or San Michele, or in the lapidary and nearly abstract architectural settings of the terracotta roundels, one can sense the effect of a renewed and direct encounter with the Roman antique.

Only in about 1435 did Donatello find his own architectural style in the *Annunciation* in Santa Croce (fig. 27). Now he translated the prototype into his own language. He transformed the round columns into elongated quadrangular ones with entasis and their flutes into laurel leaves; he adorned the bases with volutes, the capitals with masks, the frieze with a monumental egg-and-dart, and the cornice with shells. He terminated the curved pediment in volutes, a motif to be imitated by Michelozzo and many others (fig. 33), flanked it with putti, and adorned it with garlands. In short he countered Brunelleschi's normative and usually spare vocabulary with the extravagant richness of a hedonistic antique, his golden Latinity with a more colourful vernacular. That Donatello later derived inspiration from Roman monuments such as the Basilica of Maxentius, or from ancient temples and theatres, in his scenes from the *Life of St Anthony* in the Santo in Padua in c.1449 and in his *Scenes of the Passion* in the pulpits of San Lorenzo in c.1460–70, was probably also due to his dialogue with Alberti. In his architectural vocabulary, however, he never returned to the classicizing simplicity of the Old Sacristy aedicules.

Michelozzo (1396–1472)

Brunelleschi and Donatello long stood alone in their boundless and uncompromising dedication to antiquity, while Michelozzo only hesitantly eliminated Gothic elements from his vocabulary. He too began as a sculptor, and assisted in the building of the sacristy of Santa Trinita, where Ghiberti started to fuse together late-Gothic and antique forms. From the very beginning Michelozzo must have distinguished himself as a virtuoso in architectural ornament, so much so that Donatello enlisted his help in the decoration of the tabernacle of *St Louis*. There Michelozzo had occasion to study and imitate Brunelleschi's architectural system. In succeeding works such as the funerary monument of John XXIII and the pulpit in Prato Michelozzo became the partner responsible for the architectural frames of Donatello's sculptures.

28 *The Palazzo Comunale at Montepulciano by Michelozzo, begun 1440, was clearly based on the Palazzi Vecchio of Florence.*

In contrast to Ghiberti, Michelozzo drew a sharp distinction between Gothic and *all'antica* elements, but cannot at first have found any contradiction between them. Thus he topped the Composite columnar order of the Brancacci funerary monument in Sant'Angelo a Nilo in Naples (1426–33) and the portal of Sant'Agostino in Montepulciano (*c.*1437/38) with a crocketed pediment that he took almost verbatim from the Gothic windows of Or San Michele.

After the death of Giovanni de' Medici he became Cosimo's architect, and built for him the little church of San Francesco in Mugello (1429/30). It is characterized by squat proportions and a still rather archaic vocabulary. After Cosimo's return from exile he constructed the convent of San Marco with the Ionic arcades of its famous three-aisled library, the *vestibulum* and *atrium* of the Santissima Annunziata, and probably also the Medici villa in Careggi. His Palazzo Comunale in Montepulciano, begun in 1440, follows the Palazzo Vecchio so closely that it could until recently be dated to the Trecento (fig. 28). After Brunelleschi's death, Michelozzo also assumed the post as architect of the *Opera del Duomo* and emerged as the city's leading architect. For unknown reasons, however, he was replaced both as architect of the Medici and of the cathedral by Antonio Manetti Ciaccheri in the early 1450s and never reconquered his former Florentine glory.

Palazzo Medici

When Cosimo began to build his family palace in 1444, he passed over Brunelleschi, just as he had done in the decoration of San Lorenzo, and gave his preference to the tried and tested Michelozzo instead. Like the exterior of the Palazzo Comunale in Montefiascone, that of the Palazzo Medici is clearly placed in the tradition of the Tuscan late-medieval palazzo, but is shorn of the more eye-catching symbols of civic power such as tower and merlons, which would hardly have been compatible with Cosimo's role as *primus inter pares* and *pater patriae* (fig. 29). In other respects, too, it is archaic: its exterior is not articulated by Vitruvian orders, nor are the big arches of its ground floor aligned with the windows of the upper storeys. Miche-

29 *Michelozzo's Palazzo Medici, Florence, begun 1444. The three storeys display contrasting types of ashlar. The corner arches of the ground floor, originally open, were given windows designed by Michelangelo.*

30 *Courtyard of the Palazzo Medici, where Michelozzo follows the model of Brunelleschi's Spedale.*

lozzo privileged, instead, the contrast between surface textures: between the natural rustication of the ground floor, the flat ashlared courses of the *piano nobile* and the smooth masonry of the upper storey. The side front facing San Lorenzo shows how thin and spurious these ashlared courses are. The exterior differs from the palazzo in Montepulciano not only in its sheer size and more urbane character, but also in its massive classicizing cornice, the first of any post-medieval palace. In its succession of dentils, egg-and-dart and consoles, Michelozzo directly followed the Temple of Serapis in Rome.

He took over Brunelleschi's new language only with some hesitation. He thus held fast to the late-medieval *bifora*-windows. In the arcades and entablature of the courtyard he followed the model of the loggia of the Spedale degli Innocenti – symptomatically Brunelleschi's earliest and also most un-Vitruvian building (fig. 30). The symmetry and the dominance of entrance axis also presuppose the lesson of the Spedale. This particular combination of traditional and progressive elements may have contributed to the fact that the Palazzo Medici paved the way for the rapid development of the Central Italian palazzo type.

Choir of the Santissima Annunziata

The centralized choir of this church was commissioned by Lodovico Gonzaga, new lord of Mantua and general of the Florentine troops, in commemoration of his father and for the celebration of masses for his soul (figs 31, 32). Continuing Brunelleschi's idea of a forum *all'antica*, Cosimo de' Medici had already commissioned Michelozzo with the construction of the *vestibulum* and *atrium* of this church and seems to have encouraged Lodovico to invest part of his Florentine

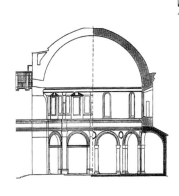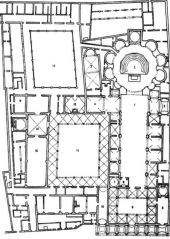

31, 32 *Plan of the Santissima Annunziata, Florence, with a section of the circular choir that Michelozzo added about 1444.*

income in this building. The architect was once again Michelozzo. In the choir of the Santissima Annunziata he tried to revive the ancient circular temple and give it a new lease of life, just as Brunelleschi had tried to do in Santa Maria degli Angeli ten years before (figs 20, 21). In the ten-sided exterior, in the deep, over-semicircular chapels and even in the diameter of *c*.25 m (82 ft), Michelozzo followed the model of the so-called Minerva Medica in Rome which was then thought to be a temple or a mausoleum. But he made the inner plan round and the dome hemispheric as in the Pantheon. He also adopted squatter proportions than in Santa Maria degli Angeli, and opted for a drum and a dome without ribs and coping which was intended to be much more clearly visible from outside than it is now. Clearly, Michelozzo's concern was to surpass Brunelleschi on his very own ground, the faithful imitation of antiquity, and in this he may have been already assisted by Alberti. But a comparison of the two ground plans suffices to show how utterly superior Brunelleschi's is; Brunelleschi, indeed, had severely criticized Michelozzo's design. Alberti would later, in the last years of his life, propose to broaden the entrance to the rotunda.

Michelozzo's architectural detailing

Michelozzo owes a good deal of his fame to his ingenious detailing. Already in the tomb of Cardinal Brancacci erected in Naples (*c*.1428) he tried to imitate Composite capitals with two rows of acanthus leaves topped by egg-and-dart and flanked by Ionic scrolls. He could have copied them from the exterior of the Baptistery, but Brunelleschi's influence was still so strong that they are more similar to the capitals of the Loggia degli Innocenti. In the magnificent Composite capitals of the courtyard of Palazzo Medici he reduced the acanthus leaves to one row and enlarged both the egg-and-dart and the four diagonal volutes in an unconventional and highly tri-dimensional way. Only in the capitals of the tabernacle of San Miniato of *c*.1450 did he reach the level of his antique prototypes (fig. 33). One of them was immediately imitated at the Arco dei Cavalli in Ferrara, maybe even after a design of Michelozzo's. Already in *c*.1440 he had imitated in the pergola of Cosimo's Villa at Trebbio the ancient Composite capital with flutes. It was another important rediscovery which he developed to perfection in the tabernacle of San Miniato and which would then be varied and widely disseminated by Alberti, Bernardo Rossellino, Francesco di Giorgio and their followers.

A similar evolution can be observed in his variations of the Corinthian capital. In the pulpit of Prato (1433) he probably still followed the design of Donatello, who shortly before had brought back from Rome varied forms of Corinthian capitals. Donatello conceived the capitals less and less as normative, but as decorative features which could be altered at will. On the façade of San Agostino in Montepulciano (1437/38) and in the *atrium* of the Santissima Annunziata (*c*.1448) Michelozzo imitated another antique prototype: on each side of the capital two large volutes flank a flower or palmette and are supported by single acanthus leaves in the corners. This type found its classical formulation only on Alberti's Holy Sepulchre of Christ (fig. 45) and became the most successful capital for the rest of the fifteenth century, from the courtyard of Palazzo Piccolomini in Pienza to Urbino and the late Roman Quattrocento (figs 62, 66, 125).

33 *Michelozzo's tabernacle of San Miniato, Florence,* c.*1450.*

In *c*.1445 Michelozzo designed the aedicule of the cloister of Santa Croce, the prototype of the windows of the Palazzo Ducale in Urbino, and the tabernacle of the Santissima Annunziata; and in *c*.1448/49 the tabernacle of San Miniato. In the former tabernacle Donatello's influence can still be felt, but the latter comes closer to Alberti (fig. 35). In both the form alters from capital to capital; variants of Corinthian and Composite capitals are placed under the same entablature, just as Alberti would do in the façade of Santa Maria Novella (fig. 43). Not only the various capitals but also the entire tabernacle of San Miniato, whose scroll-like endings of its archivolt are reminiscent of Donatello's aedicule (fig. 27), would become exemplary for the following decades. No one, indeed, contributed so much to the gradual rediscovery of ancient architectural ornament as Michelozzo, and this would hardly have been possible without Alberti's help. He had in 1438 returned to Florence and was in close contact with the Medici. Since Brunelleschi was more inclined to perfect than enlarge his vocabulary, and Donatello was intent on pursuing his unorthodox fantasies, it is likely that Michelozzo and Alberti worked increasingly together, a collaboration which may have been promoted by the Medici and continued even after 1444, when Alberti occasionally returned to Florence for short visits.

2 Alberti and his Contemporaries

Leonbattista Alberti (1404–72)

Brunelleschi had led architecture to new heights. He had developed it into a scientific discipline that demanded the skills of a painter, sculptor, engineer, mathematician, philologist and archaeologist, in other words a universal culture of just the kind that Vitruvius had prescribed for the architect (Book I.1–3). That Alberti, his only congenial follower, was not a craftsman but a humanist by training therefore comes as no surprise.

Born in Genoa in 1404, the illegitimate son of an exiled Florentine noble banker, he had been given a humanistic education at the University of Padua. Probably it was not until 1430, after he had studied jurisprudence in Bologna and after the ban exiling his family had been lifted, that he got to know Florence. By then Masaccio was dead, but he forged friendships with Brunelleschi, Donatello, Ghiberti and probably also Michelozzo, who had already laid the foundations of the new style. At first Alberti devoted his attention to the principles of painting such as central perspective, to the secrets of which Brunelleschi had no doubt introduced him and which he described in his first theoretical work on the arts, his treatise on painting (1435). He dedicated the Italian translation of this work to Brunelleschi and praises him in its introduction as the first of that small group of artists who had again equalled, indeed surpassed, the art of antiquity; and this, moreover, by his own innate talent, without teachers or precursors.

By 1431–33, Alberti had become secretary of the patriarch of Grado and an official in the papal Curia with a prebend in San Martino at Gangalandi near Florence. He thus achieved the material independence that permitted him to devote himself to his humanistic and artistic interests. Though his illegitimate birth prevented his ordination as a priest, he became a member of the papal Curia and a canon of Florence Cathedral. He left Rome for Florence with the Curia in 1434, and travelled from Florence to Ferrara in 1437 for the Council that began there. After the Council had moved to Florence in 1438, he spent the following period in that city and was thus able to follow the creation of the works of Brunelleschi, Donatello and Michelozzo.

Portal of the Palazzo Vitelleschi in Tarquinia

Even before 1440 Alberti may have contributed to the palazzo that the powerful Cardinal Vitelleschi, governor of Rome and general of Pope Eugenius IV, built in his hometown of Tarquinia in *c.*1436–39. Most of its portals, its large traceried windows, its ashlars, betray the Angevin Gothic style. By contrast, significant elements of the left wing of the main façade are built in a more classicizing style unparalleled in Lazio during these years. Vitelleschi had wished to erect an equestrian monument on the Campidoglio in Rome in 1436; perhaps already on that occasion he had sought Alberti's advice. In any case, not only the colonnade of the belvedere and the colonnettes dividing the windows of the staircase tower, but especially the magnificent portal with its pediment-entablature supported by volute-brackets, are closer to the spirit of Alberti than to that of Donatello and

Michelozzo, who had clearly inspired its rich decoration, or to that of Filarete, who was then active in Rome. As in Alberti's Palazzo Rucellai (fig. 35), the portal is Ionic and the colonnettes of the windows are a sort of Corinthian as recommended in Alberti's *De re aedificatoria* for noble palaces (Book IX.3). The documents show that it was being constructed in 1439. In spite of all its inconsistencies, it comes far closer to the antique prototypes than any earlier portal.

Palazzo Rucellai

Even before he returned to Rome in 1444, Alberti may have met his only known Florentine patron, the prominent merchant Giovanni Rucellai, for whom he was to design three of his six securely attributed buildings. A man of mercantile origins, Rucellai forged ties, by

34 *Plan of cellar and ground floor of Alberti's original five-bay project of Palazzo Rucellai, Florence, largely the result of the ad hoc acquisition of adjacent properties. The section on the left shows the cellars.*

35 *Façade of the Palazzo Rucellai, built piecemeal by Alberti from about 1447 onwards, and enlarged after 1458. There was clearly an intention to add another bay on the right, making it symmetrical.*

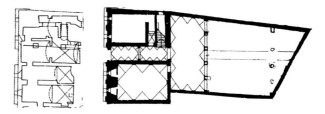

intermarriage, with the city's leading families. He married the daughter of the powerful Palla Strozzi, Cosimo's enemy, while his son Bernardo was groomed as a Medici protégé: his godfather was Piero de' Medici, and he married in turn the granddaughter of Cosimo de' Medici, Nannina, in 1458.

In 1445/46 Giovanni bought two houses and a plot to the north of his old house on the corner of the Via della Vigna and Via dei Palchetti. Soon afterwards Alberti may have designed a three-storeyed five-bayed palazzetto for the site.

The first three bays of the façade (fig. 35), comprising the long *andito*, a narrow staircase and the huge rear loggia, were probably finished in 1451 (figs 34, 36). Rossellino, to whom 'the model' of the Palazzo Rucellai was attributed by an anonymous writer in *c*.1540, may have directed its execution before leaving for Rome in the summer of 1451. The slight divergence between the axis of the main portal and the axis of the *andito* is explained by the western wall of the house of Rucellai's mother, which had to be respected and where Giovanni may have lived during this first phase of construction. This house, which corresponded to the fourth and fifth bays of the original façade, was integrated into the new building soon after 1451.

Alberti took as his starting point Michelozzo's Palazzo Medici. He translated it into a smaller scale, distinguished the entrance bay by widening it and gave the ashlars of all three floors the same smooth form as in the *piano nobile* of Palazzo Medici, but calculated their horizontal and vertical rhythm in a far more methodical and coordinated way. He also integrated the wall openings into the façade system in a more strictly symmetrical way than in the Palazzo Medici and provided the columns of the *bifora*-windows with an entablature.

As in the Palazzo Medici the ground floor is vaulted and the windows of the two upper floors rise only from the entablature, *c*.1.70 m (5½ ft) above the floor, thus funnelling the light diagonally into the rooms. The ground floor of the façade is thus proportioned to each of its two upper floors in a ratio of roughly 4:3, as described by Vitruvius for the Forum (Book V.1). When discussing the *ornamentum* of a prominent town house in his treatise (Book IX.4), Alberti speaks of façades with three storeys of a kind he could hardly know from antiquity. These storeys should decrease in height from bottom to top. Each storey is distinguished by a colonnade. If there are many windows, they follow the system of Roman theatres with pillared arcades (Book VIII.7; IX.7). The ornamentation of the main portal should be Ionic and that of the windows Corinthian (Book IX.3). Alberti worked on the treatise at the time when he was planning the Palazzo Rucellai. This building in fact follows the prescriptions of the treatise more precisely than any of his later buildings. As on the exterior of Roman theatres, the orders are combined with the arches of the windows. The impost cornice of the famous *theatre motif* (as in the Colosseum) is lacking. The ashlars represent the wall (a role prescribed for the wall in Alberti's architectural theory); above the window arcades they are lengthened and narrowed as if to provide additional support to the unbroken entablature of the wide intercolumnations. The ashlars seem almost as if added to the skeleton of the colonnade as an afterthought.

The capitals of the colonnettes which divide the windows of the *piano nobile* are Corinthian. The portal is Ionic, though it looks much

36 *Palazzo Rucellai courtyard. Only the entrance loggia was planned by Alberti.*

more archaic than its counterpart ten years later in San Sebastiano (fig. 47).

In contrast to the exterior of Roman theatres, Alberti adapted the superimposition of the orders to the hierarchy of the three floors. He furnished the *piano nobile* with Composite or 'Italic' capitals, which the treatise praises as the most magnificent because they combine the beauties of Ionic and Corinthian (Book VII.8). Their classical form was represented at the Baptistery (fig. 2), but Alberti chose those of the mausoleum of Hadrian as his model, which Michelozzo had already rediscovered (fig. 33). The lesser importance of the upper storey is expressed by a more modest Corinthian order and by a bracketed frieze, both directly inspired by the upper storey of the Colosseum. The brackets recall their origins from wooden buildings, as described in the treatise (Book VII.9). An attic above the upper cornice – the first regular example of its kind – opens in an Ionic colonnade reminiscent of the lantern of Brunelleschi's Old Sacristy. The Doric order of the ground floor is placed over a squat marble bench and pedestals with flat cornices, the first case of a radical abstraction in Alberti. The egg-and-dart and fluted neck of the capitals betray again the influence of Michelozzo's decorative richness. A pattern of *opus reticulatum* is incised as mere ornament between the pedestals.

Alberti showed his indebtedness to Brunelleschi and followed the precepts of his treatise by reducing the orders to the flat strips of the 'affixed colonnade' – *columnatio afficta* – which projects only slightly from the continuous ashlar courses and whose pilasters appear as quadrangular columns only at the left corner. Thus, in spite of all its learned detail, the façade of the Palazzo Rucellai is further removed from the rich and sensuous plasticity of the Antique than the later façades of San Francesco, Santa Maria Novella and the Campanile of Ferrara cathedral (figs 40, 43, 38). The pilasters seem as thin as pasteboard and the profiles of pedestals, entablature and archivolts are either abstracted or not yet distinguished by the strength of Alberti's later buildings. One feels that he started out here from the flat wall and only gradually discovered the third dimension.

Only the entrance loggia of the courtyard was planned by Alberti. Its archivolts were only painted without any profile. The central bay is on axis with the portal. As on the façade, it is wider than the other four bays and hierarchically distinguished by a coat of arms. Though not as rich, its Composite capitals are similar to the slightly earlier Composite one of the tabernacle of San Miniato (fig. 33). The four other capitals lack the egg-and-dart and the astragal. Both the flat archivolts and the hierarchy of capitals betray again Alberti's tendency towards abstraction. By combining all these heterogeneous elements in a quite new and unconventional way, he opened the way to future generations of architects.

In 1458 Rucellai was able to buy the adjacent house from his cousins and to add two further bays and a portal to the façade wing, though without achieving the intended symmetry of eight window-axes. The right side of the façade thus remains unfinished. Despite this, Rucellai succeeded in transforming what began as a modest palazzetto into a genuine patrician residence. Simultaneously he must also have planned the triangular piazza on which it faces and the arcaded loggia on its eastern side (perhaps designed by Rossellino).

Palazzo Pitti

Luca Pitti's monumental garden-palace on the other side of the Arno was built in the immediate aftermath of the Palazzo Rucellai (fig. 37). Pitti had purchased the site, including most of the Boboli hill, in 1454. Work on the building seems to have started in the same year, from 1455 onwards under the direction of Bernardo Rossellino. It had reached its third storey by 1472, but had still not been completed by the mid-sixteenth century.

With its three storeys of roughly equal height, the Palazzo Pitti is about 10 m (33 ft) higher than the Palazzo Medici. Originally the ground floor opened with three portals onto a spacious piazza and each of the two upper storeys comprised seven arcaded wall apertures. The irregular ashlars, the keystones of the arches and the rectangular windows of the ground floor are reminiscent of the Palazzo Medici. But, as on the back wall of the Forum of Augustus in Rome, the powerful rustication is now continued in all three storeys. The axial alignment and regular rhythm of the wall apertures and the deliberate irregularity of the ashlars of the two upper storeys come far closer to the Palazzo Rucellai. The windows are also separated by regular pillars from which the arches of the windows rise. The pilasters of the window jambs, their abstract capitals akin to those of the façade of Santa Maria Novella (fig. 43), were no doubt planned also to support straight entablatures of *bifora*-windows. The Ionic colonnettes of the balustrade that runs below the windows are

37 *Façade of the Palazzo Pitti, Florence, executed* c.*1455. The guiding spirit was probably Alberti.*

reminiscent of the Old Sacristy and the attic of the Palazzo Rucellai (fig. 9), and contribute, like the unbroken succession of window arcades, to the predominance of the horizontal forces. The windows, however, are set much deeper in the wall than in previous Florentine palaces and start at floor level. They give to the façade, as does the continuous rustication, a robustness, a muscular three-dimensionality, unprecedented for the time.

Not only the symmetrical ground plan and the opening to the landscape, but also the classicizing monumentality are easier to associate with Alberti than with Rossellino, the architect of Pienza (figs 60–62), who participated in its execution, while the stylistic difference from the Palazzo Rucellai may be due simply to its much later date.

Campanile of Ferrara Cathedral

Alberti had got to know Ferrara as a member of the curial entourage as early as 1437. Later, in 1443, he accepted an invitation from Lionello d'Este to give his advice for the equestrian monument of Lionello's father, Niccolò III. He may also have had some influence on the design of its *all'antica* pedestal, for which payment was made in June 1451. Lionello must have esteemed Alberti as a leading expert on ancient architecture of his time and asked him for a commentary on Vitruvius during this visit. Thus Alberti was stimulated to write his treatise on architecture, the *De re aedificatoria*.

Alberti could also have designed the campanile of Ferrara Cathedral (fig. 38). Its particular plan was conditioned by the pedestal zone begun in 1412. The first floor was completed in 1454. An attribution to him is suggested not only by its detail, but also by its system

38 *The lowest storey of the campanile of Ferrara Cathedral, plausibly attributed to Alberti.*

indebted to Brunelleschi's last works. As in the lantern of Santa Maria del Fiore in Florence (fig. 25), slender columns without entasis and entablature support the arches of the arcades and are flanked by a colossal order of squat quadrangular columns. As in the crossing of San Lorenzo (figs 13, 14), the entablature is supported by fragments of recessed pilasters and is projected over the corner pillars. As on the exterior of the Baptistery of Florence, the latter are layered in white and green blocks and form the outer layer of the stratified wall. The archivolts and the entablature itself are reminiscent, on the other hand, of the Palazzo di Parte Guelfa (fig. 24). The abstracted capitals of the giant order recur on the ground floor of the façade of Santa Maria Novella in Florence and in the windows jambs of the Palazzo Pitti (figs 37, 43). The capitals of the round columns have only one row of acanthus leaves, but a more articulate egg-and-dart than in the courtyard of the Palazzo Rucellai (fig. 36). The tondi in the spandrels are similar to those on the façade of San Francesco at Rimini (fig. 40). Not only the detail, but also the compressed plasticity of the articulation finds its stylistic parallel closer to San Francesco in Rimini than to the Palazzo Rucellai. Before 1454 no other architect would have been capable of so complex a design.

San Francesco at Rimini (Tempio Malatestiano)

Sigismondo Malatesta, the despot of Rimini, started in 1447 to enlarge the nave of the thirteenth-century church of San Francesco, the ancient burial place of his family, with two lateral chapels. He wanted to glorify himself and Isotta, his mistress and later wife. Having won a battle against the king of Naples in 1448, and in fulfilment of his vow to embellish the church if victorious, he added further chapels which required a new articulation of the exterior. He asked Alberti for a project which is known from the foundation medal struck in *c*.1451/52 (fig. 40). It shows a two-storeyed façade with segmental pediment and a dome with squat drum rising behind it.

Alberti seems to have been in Rimini in 1453/54 and supervised the making of a wooden model. Work on the remodelling of the church was then in progress. From Rome he gave Matteo dei Pasti, who superintended the building's execution (and cast its foundation medal), precise written instructions which show his technical expertise. When Sigismondo fell from power in 1462, the façade had scarcely risen above the ground floor and the dome area was never begun.

In the basilica façade system Alberti followed the eleventh-century model of San Miniato (fig. 42). Already Brunelleschi seems to have taken it for a late and somehow corrupt testimony of ancient architecture. Alberti's other important source, the nearby Arch of Augustus, alluded to Sigismondo's victory (fig. 41). The system of the arch is continued in a slightly smaller scale into the side bays of the façade. Reduced to simple arcades, an unbroken entablature and even smaller scale, this system is adjusted, in the form of pillared arches, to the Gothic windows of the new chapels placed along the sides of the unaisled nave. As in the campanile of Ferrara, these arches form the first layer of a stratified wall and, as in the Colosseum, the widely projecting impost cornice surrounds the whole pillar, and the upper entablature is unbroken. Classicizing sarcophagi containing the ashes of humanists admired by

39, 40 *In 1447 Sigismondo Malatesta decided to transform his church of San Francesco at Rimini into a dynastic mausoleum, the Tempio Malatestiano. Alberti was commissioned to encase the old fabric in a classical disguise (right). It was never finished, but the foundation medal (below) shows that it would have had a huge dome over the east end.*

41 *One of Alberti's models for the Tempio Malatestiano was the nearby ancient Roman Arch of Augustus.*

Sigismondo were placed in the deep arcades. These arcades, however, correspond to the theatre and not to the temple of Alberti's hierarchy of building types (Book VII. 4; VIII, 7).

The rich ornamentation of the façade surpasses even that of the Arch of Augustus. The classicizing letters of the dedicatory inscription (first of its kind) adorn the frieze; flowers and festoons with Sigismondo's *imprese*, the unbroken *basamento*; and oak-leaf-wreathed porphyry medallions, the spandrels. Two heavy festoons are suspended from the portal pediment. The capitals of Brunelleschi's lantern (fig. 25) are transformed into 'Italic' ones by corner volutes combined with the wings of cherubim that recall the church's spiritual purpose. Cherubim recur in the projections of the frieze.

Alberti wanted to cover the nave with a single roof, thus ingeniously fusing together the exterior into a uniform plastic block. In the upper storey of the project illustrated on the foundation medal, columns with fragments of entablature support a semicircular arch, like that of Michelozzo's tabernacle of San Miniato (fig. 33). This upper arch encloses an inner arch; it is pierced by a small colonnade opening up to the planned wooden barrel vault inside the church; segmental half-pediments conceal the sides of the roof. In his letter to Matteo of November 1454, Alberti considered replacing these with twin S-volutes which would have topped the triangular walls in

42 *Alberti remembered the articulation and the green-and-white marble cladding of the Romanesque church of San Miniato, Florence, when he came to the façade of Santa Maria Novella.*

Florence (figs 1, 2), a fourteenth-century master had clad its ground floor with a stratified marble incrustation of slender and narrow arcades decorated with Corinthian capitals and pierced by pointed-arch funerary niches below. Alberti replaced the Gothic with a classical portal. As on the Tempio Malatestiano (fig. 40) its sheltering arch represents the Corinthian *porticulum* described in the treatise (Book VII.12). But in the paired pilasters of the jambs he now followed the pronaos of the Pantheon. The portal's detail and festoons also seem incomparably more antique and triumphant in spirit.

Alberti, however, continued to adopt the Baptistery as his main model for the articulation of the ground floor. The engaged columns are thus also hewn from dark green stone from Prato, have Corinthian capitals, are placed on high pedestals, project in the entablature and seem even more elongated than their extremely slender proportion of *c.*1:13 (ratio of shaft width to height). As in the campanile of Ferrara (fig. 38), the corner-reinforcing quadrangular pillars are layered in white and green blocks and are much thicker and sturdier, attaining a proportion of only *c.*1:8. As in Ferrara, their capitals are revealed as a *Composita* by the concave abacus and the egg-and-dart. Their necks are now fluted, as in the tabernacle of San Miniato (fig. 33). Clearly, in elongating the engaged columns, Alberti wanted to achieve consonance – the *concinnitas* of his treatise (Book IX.5) – with the fourteenth-century blind arcade. Already in his earlier buildings he had started out less from orthodox rules than from a specific situation.

By displacing the side portals from the axis of the aisles, the fourteenth-century master had renounced any precise correspondence between the façade and the interior of the church. Alberti was obliged to follow suit. Inspired by the proto-Renaissance façade of

43, 44 *Façade of Santa Maria Novella, Florence. Alberti follows the earlier precedent of marble veneer, but provides Vitruvian orders, a Pantheon-like portal (opposite) and assimilates the upper storey to the façade of a temple.*

front of the roof. As in the medal, the pillars were to continue in an arch, the fluted pilasters in entablature fragments and a pediment, and the pilasters to the back of the deeply shadowed window embrasure in a colonnade. This superstructure would have risen like a thin slab over the lateral bays as later in Santa Maria Novella (fig. 43), and in no way reflected the structure of the interior.

The foundation medal speaks of a *templum*. Alberti, indeed, may have understood the planned round choir as a temple-*cella* comparable with the interior of the Pantheon. Its *c.*30 m (98 ft) diameter would have been even greater than that of the Santissima Annunziata (figs 31, 32) and its centre may also have been intended for the stalls of the Franciscans. Thus Alberti tried for the first time to combine church, temple and triumphal arch to the despot's glory and the victory of his soul over death.

The façade of Santa Maria Novella

In the Palazzo Rucellai and in the Tempio Malatestiano Alberti had combined medieval and antique prototypes. A few years later Giovanni Rucellai entrusted to him a similar task by commissioning him to complete the façade of the Florentine Dominican church of Santa Maria Novella (figs 43, 44). In the tradition of the Baptistery of

the Collegiata of Empoli, he topped the ground floor with an attic. It alludes to the triumphal arch, as do the arch of the portal and the projections of the entablature. At the same time it neutralizes the unequal bays of the lower storey. Thus Alberti separated the upper from the lower storey and allowed it to stretch widely beyond the existing structure of the church not only in breadth but also in height. He abandoned any coordination with the Gothic interior and made the façade look like a temple front. As on the corners of the ground floor, the quadrangular pillars are layered in white and green blocks, but are much slenderer (*c.*1:12) and support a heavier and unbroken entablature and a massive triangular pediment. Thus for the first time the temple front is predominant. Rucellai followed Sigismondo Malatesta in the self-glorifying inscription of the frieze as not even the Medici had dared.

The oblong panels that fill the outer bays of the marble incrustation intensify the vertical forces of the façade and counteract the weight of the huge rose window at the centre, so massive that its lower circumference seems almost to break into the attic below. At the same time, however, the rose window is firmly anchored in the façade on all sides by the medallions in the pediment and lateral volutes and by the arch of the portal. Even in ornament Alberti tried to link his *all'antica* forms with typically Florentine and late-Gothic décor. For the sake of *concinnitas* he was more willing to make compromises than Brunelleschi.

The work on this ambitious and (due to its rich marble incrustation) highly expensive undertaking seems not to have been begun before 1458, but the ground floor may have been planned before, and continued even after 1470, the date of the inscription. The façades of Santa Maria Novella and the Tempio Malatestiano are the first known in the long row of post-medieval façades that really deserve this name.

Cappella Rucellai in San Pancrazio

Already in *c.*1440 Giovanni Rucellai had expressed his intention to erect 'a chapel with a tomb similar to that of Christ in Jerusalem' either in Santa Maria Novella or San Pancrazio. So, as in the Old Sacristy in San Lorenzo and the Pazzi Chapel, he wanted to combine his own funerary chapel with a higher purpose and thus give it a more monumental form (fig. 45). In none of its many imitations had the founder so closely linked the sepulchre of Christ with the salvation of his own soul as Rucellai did in the inscription over the door to the *sacellum*. In the prominent inscription that runs round the frieze, on the other hand, he proclaims that Christ had risen and was no longer to be encountered in the place of his burial.

In order to make the tomb visible also from the interior of the church, Alberti opened up the right wall of the chapel into a colonnade that continued the orders of the chapel as well as the inner articulation of the old church; in the nineteenth century, this was closed and the two columns transferred to the façade of the church. The chapel's *columnatio afficta* – engaged colonnade – is here freed from the wall to which it corresponds in height and thickness. Concealed arches, which aroused Vasari's admiration, relieved its extremely broad intercolumniations and may have been understood by Alberti as a hidden part of the skeleton of the wall.

The older, slightly irregular chapel has a rectangular ground plan

45 *The Cappella Rucellai in San Pancrazio, Florence, contains the symbolic Holy Sepulchre of Christ with Rucellai's tomb.*

of only *c.*6.15–6.40 x 12.25 m (20 ft 2 ins x 40 ft 2½ ins), and a height of *c.*10.40 m (34 ft 1½ ins). Alberti covered it with a barrel vault with transverse arches and articulated it far more modestly than the Medici and Pazzi Chapels. The fluted Corinthian columns and pilasters, proportioned *c.*1:10.5, the reduced corner pilasters and the strigilated frieze with the Rucellai coat of arms, come closer to Brunelleschi than in Alberti's previous buildings, but the entablature is heavier.

This austere setting helps to make the Holy Sepulchre, set like a casket at the centre of the chapel, even more brilliant in effect. It too is barrel-vaulted and its ground plan with apse approximates even more closely to the chapel in type. Its width and height are proportioned to the chapel approximately 1:3. Its outside is articulated in a similar rhythm with an order of fluted pilasters again proportioned *c.*1:10 and topped by a tall unbroken entablature. The capitals with high volutes and only two acanthus leaves follow the antique type revived by Donatello and Michelozzo. The intercolumniations are narrower than those of the *pietra serena* articulation, but, as in all Alberti's buildings, still much wider than those recommended by Vitruvius and the treatise. All this heightens in a very suggestive way the three-dimensional relation of chapel and sepulchre. In contrast to the honey-coloured marble of the tectonically active elements, more 'passive' elements, such as the surrounding moulded base, the frieze and the intercolumniations, are in lighter marble. In the detail of the order, in the dark green frames of the oblong panels and in the heraldic, geometric or floral motifs of the circular marble inlays, the incrustation coincides almost exactly with that of the upper storey of the façade of Santa Maria Novella (fig. 43), and so seems to have been executed by the same workshop at roughly the same time. The Holy Sepulchre is topped by a prominent acroteria frieze of Florentine lilies: here motifs of Etruscan temples and of late-medieval funerary monuments are combined. As in Brunelleschi's Old Sacristy, the spirally fluted coping of the tall lantern, supported on a circular colonnade, formerly placed over the shrine's only source of light, was probably intended to allude to the Holy Sepulchre in Jerusalem.

The De re aedificatoria

Alberti presented his treatise on architecture to Pope Nicholas V in 1452. Its spirit comes closest to his early projects. After 1452 he may have altered it only in details. Medieval manuscripts of Vitruvius, which were heavily corrupted and unillustrated, provided him with his starting point. Vitruvius was then thought such a bad writer, he says, that the Latins took him for a Greek and the Greeks for a Latin (Book VI.1). Like the first version of his earlier treatise on painting, Alberti wrote in Latin and hence for a small circle of humanists and enlightened patrons such as Lionello d'Este or Nicholas V.

As in his 1454 letter to Matteo de' Pasti, Alberti distinguishes himself in his treatise by a considerable knowledge of building techniques and building materials which he must have acquired already during his Florentine years and in great part must have owed to his friendship with Brunelleschi. The influence of the *De re aedificatoria* on subsequent architecture can only be demonstrated in the circle of Lorenzo de' Medici, who promoted its *editio princeps* in 1485. Some generations later Vasari could say that 'it is no marvel if the famous Leon Battista is known more for his writings than for the work of his hands'.

In the treatise Alberti speaks almost exclusively of ancient types and forms of building. He too saw the origins of Italy in the antique and hoped, like so many humanists, that it could reacquire its lost identity in all fields of life. After he had returned to Rome in 1444, he had an even better chance to study the principles of ancient architecture. He assembled all other available passages of ancient literature that treated of architecture and studied all major monuments. So he perfected his knowledge and gained a better understanding of antiquity. Like Brunelleschi, he must have drawn and reconstructed the ancient monuments in ground plan, section and elevation – longstanding methods of architectural representation, whose precision he preferred to the deliberately distorting means of perspective.

Vitruvius's treatise on architecture was imbued with the spirit of Hellenism: it was in essence a treatise on the principles of Greek, not Roman, architecture. Though he had worked under Augustus, Vitruvius had not described the buildings of the early imperial period and ignored, or spurned, such basic elements as the arch and vault, engaged and quandrangular columns: precisely those elements on which the architecture of the Early Renaissance, and Alberti's in particular, was to be based. In his treatise Alberti tried to establish rules which were also valid for the architecture of the Roman Empire and of his master Brunelleschi.

Even when Alberti, in his vision of the new city, again and again allows experiences of his own time to shine through, he always follows the model of antiquity. His ideal city is thus crystallized around the raised central temple with column-supported pronaos. The forum is surrounded with arcaded porticoes. The basilica of the law courts, theatre, circus, amphitheatre, palaestra, curia, schools, libraries and baths are situated in its immediate proximity. The city gates resemble triumphal arches, and the commemorative and funerary monuments, the royal palace or the many-storeyed town house and one-storeyed country house are inspired by antique prototypes. Characteristic post-antique building types, such as hospitals or monasteries, are only perfunctorily described.

The beauty of a building, according to Alberti, rests on its harmony, its *concinnitas*. As musical harmony, it can be expressed in the ratio of small, not fractioned numbers. Ornament plays only an auxiliary role and helps to distinguish the rank in the hierarchy of building types. Like Aristotle, Alberti saw the highest beauty achieved when the well-proportioned building was so decorated that nothing could be added to it or taken away from it except for the worse.

The temple is characterized by a colonnade, the *columnatio*, with straight entablature and pediment and its *cella*, if possible, by a centralized ground plan and a vaulted ceiling – a type directly inspired by the Pantheon (fig. 3). Columnar arcades, the *columnatio arcuata*, and flat roofs are permissible in basilicas, pillared arcades decorated with orders in triumphal arches and theatres. Private buildings should take second place to public and princely buildings.

Structurally the column, Alberti taught, is an integral part of the wall: 'a row of columns was nothing but a wall open and discontinued in several places' (Book I.10). In actual fact, the freestanding columns that had played so central a role for Brunelleschi rarely occur in Alberti's own buildings: only in the early rear courtyard of the Palazzo Rucellai and in the entrance to the Cappella Rucellai did he use them: altogether only six round columns occur in his entire work. In Alberti's later Mantuan buildings the stratified wall becomes the surface of the three-dimensional body or shell, a sort of visualization of its structural skeleton, while the order is reduced to mere decoration of its stratified surface; it can be present in abstracted form or absent altogether. In its narrow interrelation with the wall the autonomy that the column still had in Roman antiquity and in Brunelleschi is more and more diminished. This interpretation of the order was to become fundamental for Bramante, Raphael, Michelangelo and the further history of architecture.

Column and entablature descend from the tree trunks of the primitive hut. They were then translated into stone and assumed beautiful everlasting form. Structurally, says Alberti, an architrave is a horizontal column and an arch a round architrave (Book III.6).

At the same time the column is the principal ornament of all architecture (Book VI.13) The column could be round or square. It could also be partially concealed in the wall, and appear as half-column or pilaster. The capital, originally a structural member between the wooden column and its architrave, became its principal ornament. The most successful capitals are Doric, Ionic or Corinthian, but even more beautiful is the combination of Ionic and Corinthian by which the ancient Italians produced Composite capitals. What is decisive, however, is less the ornament of the column than its proportions; here too Alberti paved the way for an abstracting interpretation of the classical orders.

According to Alberti, the diameter of the column does not correspond to the ratio of the foot to the height of the human body, as

Vitruvius said (Book III.5; IV.3, 7). It corresponds instead to the ratio of the mean proportion of the depth (1:6) and width (1:10) of the waist of the human body to its height which is 1:8 (Book IX.7) and in this Alberti may have been influenced by the entasis. Thus the ratio of 1:8 of the Ionic column is the result of a rather abstract three-dimensional calculation – and not of visual analogy as in Vitruvius. Nor can the ratio of the Doric column (1:7) be directly derived from the relation of the foot to the height of the male body and the Corinthian (1:9) from the girl's, as Vitruvius had propounded. Alberti based the Doric column, instead, on the ratio of the mean proportion between the depth of the waist (1:6) and the diameter of the Ionic column (1:8) to its height; and the Corinthian column (1:9) on the ratio of the mean proportion between the width of the waist (1:10) and the diameter of the Ionic column to its height. These different proportions of the three orders concern not only the colonnade, but the whole building. Though the three orders are, as in Vitruvius, autonomous entities, they depend mainly on proportion, while detail and ornament are secondary.

In the noble image that he paints of the architect, Alberti bases himself on Vitruvius, but also, no doubt, on the exemplary personality of Brunelleschi. The architect, he taught, is a key figure of any enlightened community life. Through his buildings he forms and guides society and ensures its fame among posterity. Like a demiurge, he conceives his buildings in the mind and transmits them to the craftsmen responsible for their execution through drawings and models, which contain all his ideas and are easily reproducible (exactly the process he had followed in planning the Tempio Malatestiano). Although a follower of Aristotle, Alberti thus prepared the way for the conception of *disegno* as the father of all the arts, a conception that would dominate theory from Michelangelo on.

San Sebastiano in Mantua

Alberti had built mainly for Giovanni Rucellai and Sigismondo Malatesta up till 1460. During the last twelve years of his life he was given the opportunity by Lodovico Gonzaga, lord of the little margravate of Mantua, to design his two most original buildings and those most prescriptive for the further development of architecture.

In 1459 Alberti had come to Mantua, where Pius II hoped to prepare a crusade against the Turks. In December Lodovico Gonzaga asked him to lend his edition of Vitruvius to the pope. So it is clear that by then at the latest the three must have exchanged ideas on the renewal of architecture. The margrave then commissioned Alberti to build two churches, San Sebastiano and San Lorenzo, a loggia and a monument to Virgil. The foundations of San Sebastiano were already in progress in March 1460 (figs 46, 47). The death of Lodovico in 1478 led to the suspension of the work. Not until decades later was it continued, but never finished.

Lodovico had dreamt of a threatening plague and dedicated the church to the appropriate saint. But probably he also wanted to provide himself with a funerary church that could rival the Tempio Malatestiano and Cosimo de' Medici's San Lorenzo.

For the first time Alberti had no pre-existing building to adjust to or incorporate. He could plan freely here and fuse together his ideas

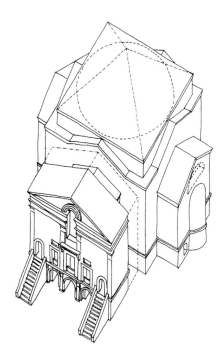

46 *Alberti began the church of San Sebastiano in Mantua in 1460, but it was never finished and in this reconstruction drawing some parts remain conjectural.*

47 *San Sebastiano, Mantua, as it exists today.*

with a wealth of heterogeneous, mainly antique prototypes and motifs into a new invention. As in some ancient mausolea, he designed the upper storey as a centralized temple and reserved the lower church for tombs, entered probably by a portal in the centre of the large staircase-podium. He divided the lower church into square cells by massive pillars with a plain but prominent impost cornice, cross-vaults and broad transverse arches. The hemispherical apses of its transepts and chancel would have housed altars for masses for the dead.

The upper church is preceded, as in the Pantheon, by a massive block-like porch, which can be recognized as the pronaos of a temple by its monumental order and pediment. Clearly Lodovico's limited resources forced Alberti to be satisfied with the closed walls of the entrance porch as in another Roman mausoleum, the so-called Tempio del Dio Redicolo. As in the ground floor of the façade of Santa Maria Novella (fig. 43), the central bay with the main portal is much smaller than the lateral ones; and as in the façade of San Miniato (fig. 42), a window cuts through the entablature. This interruption is linked above, as on the side front of the triumphal arch in Orange, by a small arch in the tympanum. The façade may also have been inspired by the peristyle of the imperial palace in Split (Spalato), with which he – like Brunelleschi – must have been familiar. There the similarly pedimented main façade is opened up in a Syrian arch leading into a vaulted circular room, which Alberti may have interpreted as a *cella;* and there too a staircase between the two halves of the staircase-podium similarly leads into the cross-vaulted pillar-supported hall of the lower storey, though this was largely hidden at the time.

The lower half of the square columns of the façade, which rests without base on a strap-like cornice, was executed still under Alberti's direct control. With their flat relief and their over-slender proportions of *c.*1:11 their effect is even more insubstantial than in Santa Maria Novella. Presumably Alberti had planned the whole order in

stone, but with similar abstract capitals to those in some of his earlier buildings. The relation of the small central intercolomniation to the wide lateral ones is also similar to the façade of Santa Maria Novella. Even without being forced by an earlier articulation and following his trend to simplification and abstractioin he renounces intermediate pilasters. With its height of more than 3¾ shaft widths, the entablature is as heavily proportioned as that of the Holy Sepulchre in San Pancrazio (fig. 45), but its cornice, which continues directly into the tympanum, differs from other cornices of Alberti by its more prominent denticulation and its lesser projection.

Alberti no doubt planned a barrel vault for the squat *vestibulum*. Its proportions are reminiscent of the porch of the Cappella Pazzi. The main portal leading into the interior of the church from inside the porch corresponds to the exterior one of the façade and was executed still under Alberti's control in 1461/62. The reconstruction of the *porta ionica* is much more Vitruvian (Book IV.6) than that of the Palazzo Vitelleschi and Palazzo Rucellai (fig. 35), and in its monumentality, measurements and forms comes even closer to ancient prototypes than the *porticulum* of Santa Maria Novella.

The interior of San Sebastiano follows that of the Roman mausoleum of the Cercenii near the Via Appia. Instead of a cross-vault supported by corner columns, Alberti planned a hemispherical dome, some 16 m (52½ ft) in diameter with a drum and lantern. It is the dome that hierarchically would have dominated the squat barrel-vaulted arms and turned the space into a genuine church. Presumably Alberti wanted to decorate the interior with economic means similar to those familiar to him from ancient monuments. While the three apses would have housed altars of Sebastian and two other saints, Lodovico himself could have claimed a magnificent tombstone under the dome like that of Cosimo de' Medici in San Lorenzo. Eschewing orders and other ornaments, and following the principle of *concinnitas*, Alberti made both the exterior and the interior of the *cella* ascend hierarchically from the semi-cylindrical apses to the dome and the lantern. When Lodovico, six years after Alberti's death, asked his son Cardinal Francesco Gonzaga to contribute to the funding of the building, the latter expressed his misgivings about it: he declared that its classicizing character was as bizarre as Alberti's face and wondered whether it was supposed to serve as a church, mosque or synagogue.

Badia Fiesolana, Villa Medici in Fiesole and Antonio Manetti Ciaccheri (1405–60)

Alberti was probably associated with a group of Medici buildings near Fiesole, highly innovative in type but of controversial attribution. The huge convent of the Badia was erected by Cosimo de' Medici for the Canonici Lateranensi near Fiesole in *c*.1455–60 (figs 48, 49). It combined a monastic complex with a little apartment where Cosimo could spend some time in the company of the learned friars. This may have been the reason why the staircase and the *sala* are reminiscent of a palace and why its two loggias connect it more closely with nature and landscape than Cosimo's villas in Careggi, Caffagiolo or Trebbio.

The church may have been planned at the same time as the convent, but was only erected in 1461–67 by Cosimo's son, Piero de' Medici (fig. 50). The prototypes for its Latin-cross plan, section proportioned 1:2, saucer dome, barrel vaults, square chapels, and even individual forms such as the over-slender Corinthian quadrangular columns of the crossing, chapel arcades, window frames, and the ornament of the arches of the crossing, are without exception to be found in buildings designed by Brunelleschi. The most likely architect is Antonio Manetti Ciaccheri, who was awarded all the Medici architectural commissions during the 1450s. He began his career as Brunelleschi's carpenter in the dome of Florence Cathedral, but later

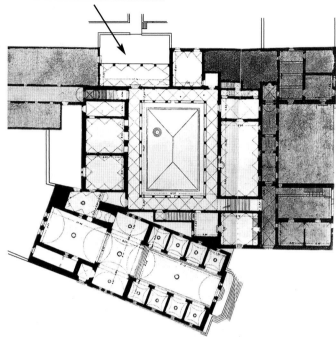

48 *The rear garden loggia of the Badia Fiesolana (left, arrowed on the plan) led into a spacious cloister.*

49, 50 *The Badia was commissioned by Cosimo de' Medici, probably with advice from Alberti. The church (below right), placed diagonally to the cloister, may have been designed by Manetti Ciaccheri, then the Medici's favourite architect.*

51, 52 *The Villa Medici, near Fiesole, built by Cosimo's son Giovanni. Its loggia is comparable to that of the nearby Badia. Both were part of a comprehensive Medici project, probably inspired by Alberti and realized by Manetti Ciaccheri.*

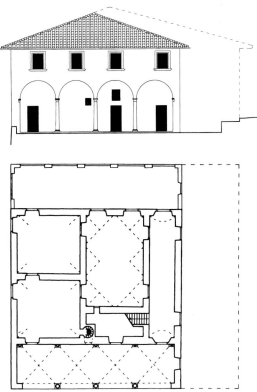

came to rival his master by presenting an alternative design for its lantern. He designed the sacristy intarsias in the cathedral in 1438, replaced Michelozzo as architect of the lantern in 1452, and rose to become the city's leading architect. Cosimo commissioned him to execute the dome and finish the nave of San Lorenzo in Florence and also gave him work in San Marco and in the Santissima Annunziata. In the convent of the Badia he seems to have translated Cosimo's ideas into the vocabulary of his mentor Brunelleschi. But the type of the unaisled church, barrel vault and chapels anticipates Sant'Andrea so closely that Alberti may have had some part in its planning, and also reminiscent of Sant'Andrea is the entablature without architrave (fig. 56).

An inspiration by Alberti is even more likely for the nearby Villa Medici which Manetti Ciaccheri probably constructed for Cosimo's second son Giovanni in *c.*1452–55 and which cannot be separated from the adjacent convent of San Girolamo and the Badia (figs 51, 52). This highly sophisticated Medicean programme combined two monasteries with two suburban residences.

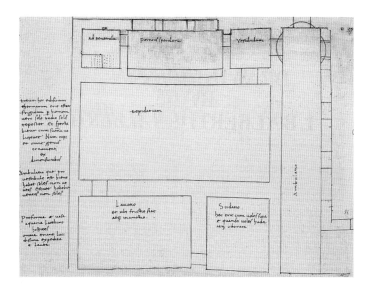

53 *An outline plan for a bath-house in Alberti's hand and probably intended to be part of a villa.*

Giovanni's villa was a primarily utilitarian building without central axis, symmetrical apertures, orders or other exterior decoration. Originally it was much smaller than today and had a square plan. Its eastern front opened in four columnar arches and continued in the upper garden terrace cut into the hillside. The exclusion of all defensive elements and of an inner courtyard made it the first true villa since antiquity. In the simplicity of its *concinnitas*, integration with the landscape, and subservience to the amenities of garden, climate and nature, it came as near to the ideas of the *De re aedificatoria* as the Palazzo Rucellai. These are strong arguments for attributing the general idea of the villa to Alberti and for dating the treatise no later than 1452.

When writing his treatise Alberti may have produced the U-shaped plan for a bath-house *all'antica*, obviously the fragment of a villa project (fig. 53). Like the Villa Medici, the small *porticus specularium* overlooks the landscape. As Alberti explains in his accompanying note, the *ambulatio* of the open courtyard is climatically oriented, while the beauty of the exterior is exclusively based on proportion, the *concinnitas* of his Ninth Book.

Shortly before his death Manetti designed the chapel of the Cardinal of Portugal in San Miniato, which was then executed by Rossellino. A spirit akin to the Badia at Fiesole and the chapels of the nave of San Lorenzo can be felt in the slender proportions of the arcades and angled corner pilasters. The sumptuous decoration and the cosmatesque inlays of the floor were added by Rossellino and others.

Sant'Andrea in Mantua

After a period of reflection lasting over a decade, Alberti presented his last project in *c.*1470 (figs 54–56). It far surpassed all his previous ones. He had heard that Lodovico wanted to reconstruct the Mantuan church where the relic of the Holy Blood was venerated, and was able to reconcile his ideas with those of both the margrave and the sceptical Cardinal Francesco Gonzaga, to whom control over Sant'Andrea had recently been handed over. Alberti proposed first a *templum etr-*

uscum, of the kind described by Vitruvius (Book IV.7), which would, he said, be 'more spacious, more enduring and joyous, worthier, brighter and cheaper' than the project presented by Antonio Manetti Ciaccheri, the presumed architect of the Badia Fiesolana, whom Lodovico had previously invited to produce a design. Clearly Alberti believed he had rediscovered Vitruvius's Etruscan temple in the Basilica of Maxentius, which he interpreted as the Templum Pacis and thus reconstructed with a columnar pronaos. Lodovico may have liked the idea of a Tuscan temple in a town founded by the Etruscans.

In his definitive project Alberti extended the single-nave interior into a choir with a dome over the main altar which was to be situated above a crypt with the relic of the Holy Blood. He transformed the exedras of the Basilica of Maxentius into the chapels of the nave, the round columns topped with entablature fragments into quadrangular pillars with a continuous entablature and the semicircular cross-vaults into an uninterrupted barrel vault. All this is reminiscent of the Badia (fig. 50), but the monumental width of 18.60 m and the squatter proportions of the section of the nave (2:3) are far more similar to the Basilica of Maxentius. The illumination is now concentrated on a big rose window in the entrance wall and rather small ones in the walls of the nave and chapels. Probably the lighting would have been only marginally improved by the dome and windows in the choir. Alberti was convinced that subdued lighting was favourable to meditation.

In spite of all its deviations from ancient prototypes and norms, Sant'Andrea comes incomparably closer to the spirit of antiquity than all Alberti's previous buildings. Once again he differentiated the porch from the *cella*, the temple interior, and combined the temple front with the triumphal arch. This is most clearly visible in the monumental deep barrel-vaulted arch at the centre of the façade and the narrow flanking bays where niches separate the pilasters of the colossal order. Here for the first he succeeded in seamlessly combining the dignity of sacred architecture with triumphal majesty. Lodovico Gonzaga, unlike the Malatesta and Rucellai, seems to have eschewed dedicatory inscriptions and coats of arms on both church façades. But this triumphal arch certainly glorified the patron no less than it did the *preziosissimo sangue*.

The effect of the central barrel-vaulted porch, a monumental *porticulum*, is produced not least by its slender Brunelleschian proportions of *c.*1:2.2 and by its eminently three-dimensional and hierarchical structure. Its spaciousness is further enhanced by vestibules in the form of transverse barrel-vaulted arms, which give access to the side doors, and from which the orders and arches gradually rise to the central arch and the colossal order.

During the Quattrocento only three bays of the nave were realized. Their triumphal system and their dimensions correspond to the façade. As in the main axis of the Pantheon, arches are flanked by 'pillars' articulated with an order of square columns and panels. But both arches and pillars are much slenderer and the doors and the windows make it obvious that the pillars are not what they seem: they have been reduced

54 *Axonometric view of Alberti's last work, Sant'Andrea at Mantua, showing the cross-arms enlarged by Giulio Romano and Juvarra's cupola.*

55, 56 *Sant'Andrea's façade was the first to be based on the combination of a triumphal arch and a temple front, which Alberti extended into the elevation of the nave.*

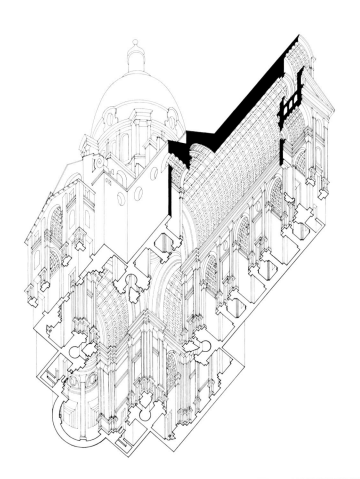

to thin walls, behind which square chapels are concealed. Though on a higher hierarchical level, the relation of the nave to the chapels is similar to that of the porch and its transverse vestibules. This eminently three-dimensional effect is still further increased by the rose windows above, which alternate with those in the rear wall of the chapels. The square columns of the order are integrated in the massive pillars which are reduced to thin walls above the impost.

Alberti may have planned a coffered barrel vault like that in the Temple of Venus and Rome. But he supported it, as in the Basilica of Maxentius, with triangular buttresses and hollowed out the wall between them in niches. He therefore concentrated the pressure of the vault on a few load-bearing walls, as he had learned to do from Roman and Gothic monuments and from Brunelleschi (figs 20, 21).

How carefully he composed is also shown by the subtle differences between interior and exterior. Alberti also calculated the façade to be visually effective from some distance away. So the colossal central arch is given far greater emphasis than those of the interior by the more plastic detailing of its order and its archivolt is accompanied by a sort of cornice. The vertical thrust is even more palpable in its two side bays; here the narrow intercolumniations are hollowed out with superimposed doors, niches and windows. In the side bays he ingeniously avoided any projection of the entablature of the small order over the shafts of the colossal pilasters.

In the interior of Sant'Andrea, with its tunnel-vaulted nave, the effect of flushness is even stronger: the flat wall, and not the projecting order, is here the protagonist. Alberti eliminated the aisles, broadened the nave and gave it a character of joyous festivity by articulating the side chapels with a sequence of triumphal arches, the first of its kind: blueprint for the future development of the aisleless church. By pressing arches and square columns closer to each other, he also weakened the vertical impulse and made even clearer how directly the chapel follows the system of the Arch of Titus.

Giulio Romano enlarged the project for the eastern part of the church after 1524: he reinforced the pillars of the crossing, to bear the weight of a dome with drum, and elongated the three cross-arms which, as in Alberti's project, were to end in lateral porches.

Alberti had promised Lodovico a large but economical building. So he limited himself to using stone only for the capitals and bases and mainly used brick for the rest of the building, placing his trust in such excellent experts as Luca Fancelli and his Lombard bricklayers. In detail, however, he created an atmosphere of sumptuousness by a hitherto unrivalled wealth of classicizing ornamentation. The capitals with which he topped the pilasters of the central bay of the façade are Corinthian, but he fused them nearly invisibly with two eggs of the Composite. The capitals of the outer pilasters differ from the Corinthian ones of the fluted small order again by their egg-and-dart. While the Composite capitals of the big order of the nave are rather canonical but fluted, those of the small order are are reminiscent of the quadrangular corner pillars of Santa Maria Novella. The columns of the small order have no bases. Their continuous entablature is even reduced to a wave-scroll frieze and a cornice with astragal and egg-and-dart.

In the nave of Sant'Andrea Alberti's architectural career attained its high point. So it is no surprise that it was imitated countless times right down to the nineteenth century, long after its descent from the

templum etruscum had been forgotten. In spite of all its antique borrowings, however, its fundamental difference from the interior of the Pantheon or the great public concourses of Roman imperial *thermae* can be felt at first glance. Of ultimately medieval origin is not only the elongated nave and its combination with a crossing, but also the systematic coherence and *concinnitas* by which the façade and interior and the elements of the nave are both vertically and horizontally interlinked. Even more clearly than in his treatise and in his earlier buildings, Alberti demonstrated that he imitated the ancient monuments not literally, but in such a way that they would be compatible with the functions, technical standards, financial resources and the taste of his time and his patrons. He despised any literal copy of a prototype and in Sant' Andrea even avoided the direct citation of antique motifs we still find in San Sebastiano. He tried instead to create new inventions by the combination of ancient, medieval and contemporary principles.

The triumphal arch of the Castel Nuovo in Naples

Alfonso of Aragon's arch in Naples cannot be separated from Alberti's vision of triumphal architecture (fig. 57). The king of Naples erected it in 1453–58 over the main entrance of his fortress-

57 *The new classical entrance to King Alfonso's castle in Naples, added in stages between 1453 and 1471. The ground floor and its attic were designed or at least inspired by Alberti.*

residence (Castel Nuovo) to commemorate his victory over the Angevins in 1443. In the project of a minor artist of c.1452 the composition is already similar and shows the equestrian statue of the king in the upper arch, but the detail is still in part Gothic.

Only the ground floor and the attic were executed before Alfonso's death in 1458. Only in 1465–71 his son and successor Ferrante adopted a new project and added the two upper floors and the inner arch.

The ground floor, with its entablature powerfully projected over the paired columns of the side bays, and its relief-decorated attic follow the example of ancient triumphal arches more closely than the façade of the Tempio Malatestiano. So Alfonso may have asked Alberti to revamp the earlier project and give it a more authentically classicizing character. The architecture of the ground floor was executed by Pietro da Milano, Francesco Laurana, Paolo Romano and the Spaniard Pere Johan in 1453–56. Two highly talented assistants of Donatello, Isaia da Pisa and Andrea dell'Aquila, joined the team in 1455/56 and were responsible for much of the figural sculpture. The architectural background of the attic relief, with its triumphal procession of Alfonso I and its isocephalic figures packed into a shallow stage, is clearly inspired by Roman reliefs. This masterly composition far outstrips the capacities of the sculptors mentioned in the documents and their authenticated works. It is also far superior to Ferrante's additions, realized under Pietro's direction. Pietro was still under Alberti's influence when he designed the medal of René and Jeanne d'Anjou in 1462. So it is possible that not only the architecture of the ground floor, but also the relief of its attic is inspired by Alberti. The arch of the Arsenal in Venice, started only a few years later, is clearly influenced by that of Castel Nuovo.

Nicholas V, Pius II and Bernardo Rossellino (1409–64)

From 1444 right down to his death in 1472 Alberti mainly lived in Rome as an employee of the Curia. He was personally attached to Popes Nicholas V and Pius II. Yet he left not one building in Rome.

Clearly he only accepted those commissions in which he could realize his ideas in as free and unobstructed a manner as possible, and this was even harder in the Vatican than elsewhere. Nonetheless, he must have exerted some influence on the popes as an interlocutor and adviser, and also (indirectly) on the architects they employed. So it is not implausible to assume that Alberti contributed to Nicholas V's vision of the new Rome.

Nicholas's biographer Giannozzo Manetti describes the pope as a princely architect who wanted to re-establish the authority of the Church and convince the illiterate crowd of the faithful by impressive buildings, a new Solomon whose ideas were to be realized by his Hiram, Rossellino. As the guiding principles of his vision he cites piety, security, ornament and salubrity. The city walls, churches and aqueducts were to be restored, St Peter's and the Papal Palace adjusted to meet their altered functional demands, and the Vatican quarter (the Borgo) renovated with a new and regular town plan comprising two piazzas and three streets lined with seignorial houses, taverns and shops (fig. 58).

The programme for the Vatican grew only slowly. It was determined by three overriding concerns: security, ceremonial and proximity to nature. In adopting it, Nicholas V followed, on the one hand, the model of the Papal Palace in Avignon, which had already differed from earlier papal residences by its more courtly character, and, on the other, the contemporary tendencies of Medicean architecture. The sparely decorated, groin-vaulted rooms suggest, however, that the pope's primary concern was functional.

Antonio da Firenze, who had arrived in Rome in September 1447, built the north wing of the Papal Palace in 1450–54. It contained three apartments, each for a different season in the year: the Appartamento Borgia, the set of rooms we now know as the Stanze, and the rooms in the storey above it; they faced onto an extensive garden to the back, the later Cortile del Belvedere. The library, stables and kitchens were to be erected north of this garden. The programme for the Papal Palace remained binding for the following century.

The Florentine architect Bernardo Rossellino was called by Nicholas V in 1451. Both Alberti and Giovanni de' Medici, who had replaced his father Cosimo as papal treasurer, had no doubt recommended him to the pope as one of the technically most experienced and formally most progressive architects of the time. In the preceding years Rossellino had perhaps executed Alberti's project for the Palazzo Rucellai and may therefore have been in close contact with

58 *Reconstruction of Pope Nicholas V's plan for the Vatican area, probably reflecting Alberti's ideas.*

him. Certainly he progressively absorbed Alberti's influence and, as a consequence, gradually assimilated classical antiquity. When Rossellino built the upper storey of the façade of the Confraternity of the Santissima Annunziata in Arezzo in 1433–35, he still combined Gothic and classical forms in a way similar to Ghiberti and the early Michelozzo. Soon after, in *c*.1435–40, he drew on a more classicizing vocabulary in the Chiostro degli Aranci of the Florentine Badia, but still held fast to the vertical continuity of the Gothic by linking the columns of the lower loggia to those of the upper loggia with dwarf pilasters. In works of the late 1440s, such as the portal of the Sala del Concistoro of the Palazzo Pubblico in Siena or the tabernacle of Sant'Egidio in Florence, he unreservedly followed the style of Donatello and the late Michelozzo. Rossellino's growing affinity with Alberti's ideas is much more obvious in the tomb of Leonardo Bruni in Santa Croce in Florence (started before 1458), which is reminiscent of Alberti's portal of Santa Maria Novella (fig. 44). It is also palpable in the palazzetto he began for the curial official Pietro della Luna in Viterbo in about 1452. The stumpy columns of the courtyard support a straight entablature, which also serves as a parapet for the *piano nobile* and is correspondingly high. The decoration of the frieze with four rows of smooth ashlars shows how undogmatic he was in conforming to the Vitruvian syntax. The fluted Ionic capitals and columnar arches of the upper loggia are Michelozzian in style and akin to the buildings of Pienza.

Soon after entering the service of Nicholas V, Rossellino built the round tower for the papal treasury on the north-eastern side of the Papal Palace in 1453. A fortified corridor was to connect it with the Castel Sant'Angelo in a straight line and thus extend the Borgo northwards. But only the two stretches of wall leading from the round tower (the Torrione) to the old walls to the west and to the atrium of St Peter's were executed. A triumphal-arch-like portal was to provide access to the lower courtyard of the palace, the later Atrium Helvetiorum. From there a staircase ascended to the Pope's private garden, in what is now the Cortile San Damaso. This garden-court was to be flanked to the north by a conclave hall and dining rooms, to the south by a palace chapel, and to the west by a so-called *theatrum*, perhaps the predecessor of Bramante's Logge whose pillared arcades could be compared with the exterior of ancient theatres. They opened up to the garden and the wide panorama in a way similar to the contemporary Villa Medici in Fiesole.

St Peter's

According to Manetti, Rossellino translated the pope's ideas for the new choir of St Peter's into a feasible architectural project. With its new choir the basilica was to surpass the temple of Solomon. Mattia Palmieri, a friend of Alberti who made him the executor of his will, writes in his chronicle that Alberti had not only shown the pope his treatise on architecture in 1452, but also convinced him to base the plans for St Peter's on antique prototypes.

Work on the choir started in June 1452. During the three years of construction the colossal walls of the new choir advanced only *c*.7.60 m (25 ft) above ground level. But this was enough to exert a decisive influence on Bramante's later plans for St Peter's. As in Brunelleschi's San Lorenzo, the crossing was to be topped by a hemispherical dome

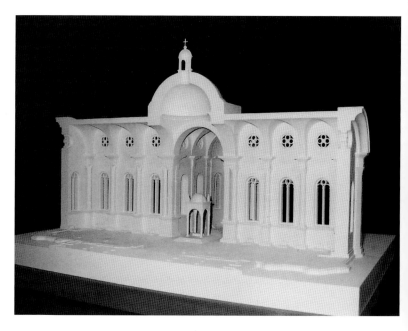

59 *Nicholas V also proposed to rebuild the choir of St Peter's on a larger scale, represented in this modern model of Rossellino's project.*

and continued in the three arms of a Latin cross, a symbol of particular importance for Nicholas (fig. 59). As in Gothic cathedrals, huge stained-glass windows would have flooded these arms with direct light and, as in Santa Maria sopra Minerva in Rome, the cross-vaulting would have been supported by columns. But the slender Gothic colonnettes would have been replaced by colossal columns as in the imperial *thermae*. These had to be matched on the outside by polygonal pillars, which would probably have been provided with the capitals and entablature of a columnar order.

Rossellino must also have followed the ideas of the pope when, in 1453, he restored San Stefano Rotondo, the largest of the Early Christian central-plan churches to which Nicholas V gave precedence in his restoration of Rome. The '*cella*' of the rotunda is preceded by a vaulted *atrium* and sober, but well-proportioned twin doors. By placing its high altar in the centre of the Latin cross formed by four minor altars, Nicholas V transformed the well-lit inner circle of the rotunda into a huge choir probably intended for magnificent papal masses.

Pienza and Siena

With Pius II (1458–64), of the Sienese Piccolomini family, another great patron of architecture ascended the pontifical throne. When he travelled to Mantua in 1459, he stopped off at his birthplace in Corsignano, south of Siena, and commissioned Rossellino to embellish the miserable little town with a palace and a cathedral 'so that he might leave a lasting a memorial of his birth' (as he himself put it in his autobiography) (figs 60–62).

The situation, in terms of patronage, was much the same as it had been eight years earlier in Rome: the pope had his own ideas and looked for an architect who would realize them. Again he chose Rossellino. No doubt he also asked Alberti for his advice. Pius wanted (as he also explains) to have a cathedral of the three-aisled kind he had admired during a journey through southern Germany and Austria. Both the ground plan, characterized by square bays in the nave, oblong bays in the aisles and polygonal choir, and the tall traceried windows come closer to a true *Hallenkirche* like Sankt Jakob in Wasserburg than to an Italian version of this type like San Giacomo degli Spagnoli in Rome, with which Rossellino must have been familiar (fig. 63). The Gothic traceried windows are reminiscent of those that Nicholas V had ordered for the nave of St Peter's in 1449. But the church they illuminate presents a complete classical order, its capitals inspired by the Palazzo Rucellai.

The splendid façade dominates the new piazza. Here Rossellino was much freer to follow his classicizing ideas. In contrast to the façade of Michelozzo's Sant'Agostino in Montepulciano, he connected the four pillars with two-storeyed arcades – a motif probably inspired by the inner façade of the *natatio* of the Baths of Diocletian. The four pillars rest on the same pedestals as the columns and break through the entablatures; they even continue in shallower and more decorative form in the tympanum. The Baths of Diocletian also inspired the pedimented shell niches placed in the lateral arches. The articulation of the façade mirrors the structure even in details such as the archivolts over the three portals which double the relieving arches.

The neighbouring Palazzo Piccolomini is clearly subordinated to the Cathedral. Its dimensions, courtyard and inner layout follow the Palazzo Medici, while the system of its exterior follows that of the Palazzo Rucellai, both of them patrician and not papal palaces. Pius no doubt saw both when passing through Florence in 1459. In erecting it, it may be presumed that he was thinking not only of his own glory but also of the future status of his family.

To adapt the system of the Palazzo Rucellai to the greater scale of the Palazzo Medici, Rossellino widened the bays and raised the

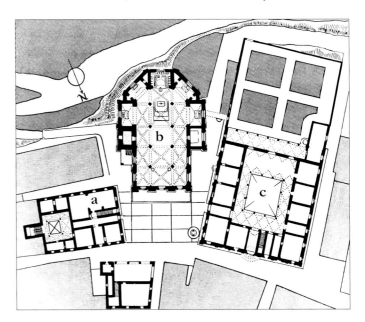

60 *The refoundation of his hometown by Pope Puis II Piccolomini under the name of Pienza was supervised by Rossellino, one of Alberti's most faithful disciples.*

a *Episcopal palace*
b *Cathedral*
c *Palazzo Piccolomini*

61 *Façade and section of Pienza Cathedral, by Rossellino. The interior of this hall church is heavily influenced by German and Sienese Gothic architecture.*

62 *The central piazza of Pienza, with the Cathedral on the left and the Palazzo Piccolomini on the right, both by Rossellino, c.1460.*

window arcades to the entablature. He thus blurred Alberti's allusion to the Roman theatre motif, weakened the tension between aperture and columnar order, and reduced the autonomy of the lower order by integrating it into the rustication. Perhaps he even wanted to characterize this rusticated order as Tuscan and thus allude to the Pope's origins.

Although Rossellino could plan freely, he could only ensure the symmetry of the exterior by abandoning its correspondence with the interior. This means that some doors and windows are blind; the three-storeyed garden-loggia is concealed behind the first bay of the façade on the piazza. As in the Vatican and in the Badia Fiesolana, the column-supported arcades of the garden loggia overlook a rectangular terraced garden and a landscape stretching to Monte Amiata far in the distance.

When the Pope returned to Corsignano, or Pienza as he had renamed it, in the summer of 1462, he saw the Cathedral and the Palazzo Piccolomini already in large part completed. Only now did he order the other buildings that surround the piazza of the little town: a bishop's palace opposite the Palazzo Piccolomini; a town hall

with an arcaded portico and a traditional machicolated campanile opposite the Cathedral; a house for the canons to the left of the Cathedral; and a row of houses for the poor. Each of these buildings received its proper size and form – a hierarchy to which greater importance was attributed than to the symmetry of the piazza itself. Although Pienza was situated in Sienese territory, Pius financed all these buildings with the revenues of his private treasury, the same source with which Nicholas had financed the choir of St Peter's. He did not hesitate to have a large part of the old town demolished and encouraged his cardinals, not always successfully, to build further palaces. He tried to justify all this by the consideration that the Curia was better off spending the summer months in a healthy malaria-free refuge like Pienza.

Rossellino must also have planned the monumental Palazzo Piccolomini for Pius II's brother in Siena. It was presumably intended to stretch as far as the Piazza del Campo and symbolize the re-won power of the Piccolomini. In its exterior he now followed the model of the Palazzo Medici in Florence, but again tried to achieve a stricter symmetry and adopted a similar kind of ashlar as in the Palazzo Piccolomini in Pienza. The Palazzo delle Papesse comes even closer to the ashlars of the Palazzo Medici, but the patron, Pius's sister, seems to have insisted on typically Sienese pointed *bifora*-windows.

3 Francesco del Borgo and Roman Architecture from Pius II to Sixtus IV

Francesco del Borgo (*c.*1420–68)

San Giacomo degli Spagnoli

Under Nicholas V's successor, the Spaniard Callixtus III (1455–58), the only church to be begun in Rome was the national church of the Spanish community (fig. 63). Its design thus slightly preceded that of Pienza Cathedral, but its construction proceeded far more slowly. In 1498 the church was realigned, elongated with a basilica choir to face onto Piazza Navona, and enlarged with wider aisles. Yet even in its original form it was a typical *Hallenkirche*, of a kind that was far more widespread in Spain and in Germany than in Central Italy. In San Giacomo, however, the type is already translated into the language of the columnar orders; it was clearly under the influence of Alberti and Nicholas V's project for St Peter's.

As in the Cathedral of Pienza, the cross-vaulted bays were divided into single bays by broad transverse arches. As there, the

63 *Interior of the old part of San Giovanni degli Spagnoli, Rome, attributed to Francesco del Borgo.*

cloverleaf pillars betray their descent from Gothic basilicas like Santa Maria sopra Minerva. Although the details of the order were reworked by a drastic restoration in the 1920s, old photographs show the same type of capitals that Alberti had used in the Holy Sepulchre in San Pancrazio (fig. 45) and entablature fragments significantly more classical in form than in Pienza. Even the absence of entasis could be justified by the orders of the Colosseum. The only architect active in Rome in the late 1450s to whom this classical order can be attributed was Francesco del Borgo, though he is documented as an architect only after 1461.

Pius II's Loggia delle Benedizioni

In Pienza and Siena, Pius II had mainly sought inspiration from Florentine and Gothic prototypes. But, after his return to Rome, he decided for the first time to embark on a truly imperial project. No doubt with Alberti's encouragement, he commissioned a classicizing Loggia delle Benedizioni to be built in front of the atrium of the old basilica of St Peter's. The architect to whom the commission was given, Francesco del Borgo, was a humanist and geometrician from Borgo San Sepolcro, a kinsman of Piero della Francesca. He had begun his career in the Curia in 1447 as an accountant responsible for administering Nicholas V's extensive building activities.

A Loggia delle Benedizioni had already been planned by Nicholas V, not in front of St Peter's but close to the Torrione and probably similar to the single-bay one at the Lateran. But now the whole width of the atrium of St Peter's was to be preceded by an imposing eleven-bayed, two-storeyed loggia of open arcades. Deliberately classical in style, it took as its model the ancient Tabularium. The massive pillar-supported arcades on two storeys which originally overlooked the Forum Romanum are, like the Colosseum, decorated with superimposed orders of engaged columns. Since the Middle Ages they have supported the rear façade of the Palazzo Senatorio.

Francesco, like Alberti, was not satisfied with a literal copy. He replaced the engaged columns with costly marble shafts from the Porticus Ottavia, raised them over pedestals on the ground floor, furnished them with Corinthian capitals, and projected the entablature above them as in Roman triumphal arches. He thus lent the entablature a triumphal character similar to the Tempio Malatestiano; indeed the accounts for the building describe the architrave explicitly as '*architravis triumphati*'. But the ambitious original project was never realized, and the loggia never extended beyond four bays in width. Under Paul II and Alexander VI, it was continued to include the second storey. Under Julius II und Bramante, it was even given a third storey, before being demolished entirely by the remodelling of the piazza by Paul V.

Francesco is securely identified by contemporary sources as the architect of the Loggia. He might therefore have been Alberti's only direct pupil. In the tabernacle that he erected close to the Ponte

Milvio in 1461 in commemoration of the translation of the relic of the head of St Andrew, he also followed an antique prototype, not least in the detail of the Ionic capitals with their diagonal volutes.

Palazzo Venezia and San Marco

The nephew of Eugenius IV, the Venetian Pietro Barbo (future Pope Paul II), had, as a cardinal, already built an imposing palace for himself next to his titular church of San Marco in Rome. The elevation represented on the foundation medal of 1455 – a twin-towered machicolated structure – suggests that he still laid relatively little value on the new *all'antica* architectural language of the Florentines. Even after he had ascended the papal throne, he at first preferred to employ a traditional master-builder. Only after a year's hesitation or so did he finally commission Francesco del Borgo to transform his palazzo into a modern papal residence (figs 64, 65). His ambitious plan was to transplant the papal seat, and the many offices of the Curia, into the very heart of ancient Rome.

Paul's private quarters were situated in the area of the former cardinal's palazzo incorporated into the southern half of the new east wing of the complex. To the west they continued in the two-

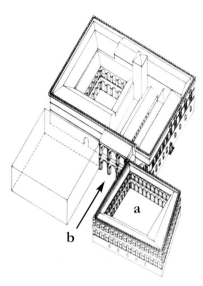

64 *Axonometric view of the Palazzo Venezia, Rome, as it was before the Palazzetto at the bottom (**a**) was shifted to make way for the present Piazza Venezia. The façade of the church of San Marco functioned as the Loggia delle Benedizioni (**b**).*

65, 66 *The Palazzo Venezia was conceived as a papal residence by Francesco del Borgo. In this photograph (below) the Loggia delle Benedizioni (opposite) appears on the far left, now freed from the buildings that once hemmed it in.*

storeyed Loggia delle Benedizioni in front of the church of San Marco (fig. 66). The church was transformed into a genuine papal chapel by the extension of its choir. To the south an overhead passage linked the apartment with a cloister-like terraced garden. To the north lay a suite of ceremonial rooms and the grand staircase. Presumably, a western wing would have closed a concentric courtyard surrounded by two-storeyed five-bayed arcades on all sides. A piazza in front of east wing was to be decorated by the equestrian statue of Marcus Aurelius and the Quirinal *Horse-Tamers* and formed the point of arrival of the ancient Via Flaminia, the present Via del Corso (as it soon came to be called due to the annual carnival horse races run along it). Further piazzas were to be laid out in front of the north wing with the official entrance and in front of the basilica with its Loggia delle Benedizioni (looking towards the Capitol). The whole complex was to be surrounded by the buildings of the curial administration and prominent members of the papal entourage. In this way Paul II combined the essential parts of Nicholas V's programme for the Vatican Palace into an incomparably more functional and systematic layout than had been possible in the Vatican.

In the exterior of the so-called palazzetto, the adjoining arcaded building that surrounded the *hortus conclusus* and which could be planned more freely than the large palazzo itself, Francesco took the upper storey of the Palazzo Vecchio as his model. Paul II and his successors still sought to express their secular power through the signals that the heavily fortified *palazzi comunali* of the later Middle Ages were able to transmit, but that the Florentines had already ceased to employ thirty years previously in the Palazzo di Parte Guelfa (fig. 24). The combination of a defensive exterior with a square hanging garden surrounded by loggias is still reminiscent of Nicholas V's secret garden in the Vatican (fig. 58).

The Loggia delle Benedizioni erected in front of San Marco, with its three pillar-supported arches, half-columns and triumphally projected entablature of a Composite order, is both formally and materially far more modest than the project for the loggia in front of St Peter's. It directly follows the Colosseum in its cylindrical shafts, its simplified Composite capitals, even its measurements.

Francesco del Borgo also transformed the columns of the nave of San Marco into half-columns by reinforcing the wall towards the aisles and immuring the rear part of their shafts in quadrangular pillars. In the lower storey of the palazzetto with the inner garden he combined arcades on octagonal 'columns' of a Corinthian order with an entablature inspired by Brunelleschi. Above it he built a loggia of Ionic columnar arches, whose terminating entablature is once again inspired by the Colosseum.

He comes closest to the antique, however, in the coffered barrel vault of the entrance vestibule (or *andito*) of the east wing. Like the coffering of the Pantheon, it was executed *in situ* by pouring liquid concrete into wooden shuttering: an important revival of the building practices of imperial Rome, though one that had never been completely forgotten. The vestibule provided access to the church and to the pope's private rooms and connected them with each other. The fragmentary arcaded *loggiato* in the courtyard may have been planned by Francesco, but was only begun after Paul II's death by his nephew Marco Barbo and differs in its slenderer pillars, steeper proportions and superimposition from the Loggia delle Benedizioni. The same master who built it may also have designed, shortly after 1471, the magnificent pedimented portal (with Paul II's coat of arms in the tympanum) on the Via del Plebiscito; the detail of its *Composita* comes even closer to the antique than the architecture of Francesco del Borgo.

Marian basilica in Loreto

As a cardinal, Pietro Barbo, the future Paul II, had accompanied Pope Pius II on a pilgrimage to Loreto. He was particularly devoted to the Madonna of Loreto and attributed his recovery from an illness to her intercession. He then vowed a monumental basilica to her in thanksgiving. It was begun in 1469 and intended to protect and enhance Mary's legendary house (the Santa Casa), the most important goal of pilgrimage in Italy after Rome.

In its ground plan and elevation the project for the new basilica was directly inspired by Florence Cathedral. To maintain the Santa Casa as visible as possible from all sides, however, the octagonal crossing was only supported by fragile pillars, as in San Petronio in Bologna. As in Santa Maria del Fiore, engaged shafts occupy the corners of the quadrangular columns, but these do not continue in a second storey; they flow, instead, into the ribs of the Gothic vaulting, thus weakening the vertical forces; the proportions thus approximate more closely to Renaissance taste. As in Florence Cathedral, the choir, with its surrounding chapels and ambulatories, could be expanded to give it the semblance of a central-plan building. The high dome on a drum that Giuliano da Maiano began and Giuliano da Sangallo completed in *c*.1500, however, had negative repercussions on the choir itself: it made a reinforcement of the pillars of the crossing by Antonio da Sangallo the Younger necessary, and thus the transparency of the interior of the church was sacrificed to the genuinely Florentine effect of the fortified exterior. It was further reduced by the massive marble incrustation of the Santa Casa and the restorations of the nineteenth and twentieth centuries. Before the chapels of the nave were added, the pointed traceried windows may also have continued in the aisles, as in Florence Cathedral.

The choir is now most impressive from the outside when seen from afar. Semicircular sacristies mediate between the equally round bastion-like apses of the three arms of the cross. And here instead of rich incrustation a colossal pilaster order with a tripartite entablature was planned. But this never progressed far and in *c*.1487 Pontelli replaced it by an arcaded sentry walk carried on corbels. Its purpose was to protect the basilica from a possible Saracen incursion. Pontelli (an expert military architect) also protected the whole basilica precinct with walls and bastions.

Curiously the name of the first architect, who must have been Florentine, is not recorded. The geometric forms of the traceries are also closer to the Florentine than the Sienese, Milanese or Venetian Late Gothic. Even more systematically than Pius II in Pienza, Paul II must have insisted on a Gothic system and Gothic vocabulary that was still the fashion in his hometown of Venice and that clearly corresponded more closely to his religious sensibility than the *all'antica* style of Francesco del Borgo. Among the prominent Florentine masters of these years, such an overriding recurrence to the tradition of the Florentine Trecento can only be attributed to Giuliano da Maiano (1431–90); but his presence in the area of Loreto cannot be documented before 1477.

Giovannino dei Dolci († 1486)

Santa Maria del Popolo

Since the pontificate of Nicholas V papal architects had come exclusively from Tuscany, birthplace of the new architecture. But under Alberti's growing influence, Rossellino, Francesco del Borgo and their followers had created an unmistakable Roman school. Francesco died prematurely in 1468, after he had in the space of a few years pointed Roman architecture in a new direction, indeed had helped it to find a new identity. Paul II was satisfied with a traditional follower. Sixtus IV (1471–84) even made do with jumped-up building workers: had he accorded as much value to the artistic as to the functional character of his buildings, a carpenter like Giovannino dei Dolci or stonemasons like Meo da Caprina and Giacomo da Pietrasanta would have had difficulty in assuming the mantle of Rossellino and Francesco del Borgo.

As the former superior general of the Franciscans, Sixtus IV showed quite particular devotion to the Madonna. To her he erected – instead of continuing the choir of St Peter's – a total of four shrines and approved the building of a fifth, all of them relatively small. The first object of his patronage was a church situated next to the city gate, the Porta del Popolo, leading into the Via Flaminia (the main approach for pilgrims and visitors from the north) (fig. 67). The Pope was so attached to this church, in which an icon of the Virgin Mary attributed to the Evangelist St Luke was venerated, that he, rather like Paul II in San Marco, had its choir re-adapted for papal masses and repeatedly visited it on festive occasions or for personal devotion. He transferred the maintenance of the church to the Augustinians, for whom he erected next to the church an extensive

67 *Interior of Santa Maria del Popolo, Rome, built under Sixtus IV by Giovannino dei Dolci, begun 1471.*

convent with two cloisters, whose gardens stretched up to the Pincio. The Augustinian Fathers were also given the job of looking after the throngs of pilgrims expected to arrive in Rome, especially for the Holy Year in 1475, and providing accommodation to prominent guests, before they made their entry into the city and were received by the pope. The Augustinians were also expected to celebrate masses for all the kinsmen and leading members of the Curia whom he encouraged to erect their funerary chapels and monuments in the church.

These various functions were combined by Giovannino dei Dolci (from 1471 on) in a basilica with a nave and two aisles divided by pillar-supported arcades and polygonal side chapels. In the three arms of the square crossing below the dome, and in the pillars of the nave, the influence of Rossellino's project for St Peter's is unmistakable. As there, the systems of the Roman imperial baths and of Santa Maria Novella are seamlessly fused together. The half-columns are thus provided with entablature fragments topped by elongated imposts that support the groined vaulting. In the squat proportions, plastic wall relief and Rossellino-influenced detail, Giovannino follows instead the model of his former master Francesco del Borgo: the ground-floor loggia of the Palazzetto Venezia.

In the church's slightly later façade, closely coordinated with its interior, Giovannino simplified the system of Santa Maria Novella (fig. 43) and gave it a flatter wall relief comparable with Alberti's late style (figs 46, 47, 54, 55). It has similarities with the upper storey of the Loggia delle Benedizioni at San Marco and the garden courtyard of the Palazzo della Rovere at Santi Apostoli, which Giovannino seems to have built during the same years.

Santa Maria della Pace

Sixtus IV had vowed to erect a further church over a miracle-working icon of the Madonna, if God were to grant him peace. After his victory over the Neapolitans in August 1482, he then attached the epithet of *pace* to the church and started its construction. The interior is dominated by the octagonal choir under the dome, which is far larger and wider than the truncated nave. Modelled on the octagonal choir in the Cathedral of Florence, it permitted an even more splendid realization of papal ceremonial than in Santa Maria del Popolo. Its hierarchical importance is expressed by colossal pilasters of a Corinthian order, placed on tall pedestals. The short nave, flanked on both sides by two hemispherical chapels and articulated with a simpler *Dorica*, could only have accommodated a limited number of the faithful. The Doric order also recurs on the tower-like exterior of the octagon and formerly on the pedimented façade. The tectonic clarity of these orders and the flat wall relief are reminiscent of the façade of Santa Maria del Popolo, and so the project can safely be attributed to Giovannino.

Giovannino can also be recognized as the architect of the Sistine Chapel, the *cappella magna* or palace church of the Vatican, and of the funerary chapel of the pope in the outer left aisle of the old St Peter's. Both are characterized by a similarly austere pragmatism.

Ospedale di Santo Spirito, Meo da Caprina (1430–1501) and Turin Cathedral

The measures preparatory to the Holy Year in 1475 also included the building of a bridge (Ponte Sisto) and a spacious hospital for pilgrims (Ospedale di Santo Spirito), which Sixtus IV himself numbered among his most important achievements.

68 *The Ospedale di Santo Spirito, Rome, was built to serve pilgrims in the Holy Year of 1475.*

69 *The octagonal chapel of the Ospedale stands in the centre of the long main ward, with another such ward at right angles to it.*

begun to assimilate classical elements but who had not yet wholly jettisoned the Gothic tradition.

Perhaps this master was Meo da Caprina, who gave a similar form to the exterior of Turin Cathedral in 1490. But there he followed the most recent developments in his native Tuscany by articulating the pedimented three-bayed façade with paired pilasters of a *Dorica*, as in Santa Maria delle Carceri in Prato. In its interior he followed the model of Santa Maria del Popolo, but once again revealed his more archaic approach by transforming the engaged columns into over-slender colonnettes.

Similar octagonal pillars and comparable archaic details as in the Ospedale also recur in the Madonna della Pietà adjacent to St Peter's, the only quincunx (domed Greek cross with four secondary cupolas) church of the Roman Quattrocento. It was founded by a German confraternity that devoted itself to the care and the burial of pilgrims.

Sant'Agostino and Giacomo da Pietrasanta (†c.1499)

The powerful and affluent Cardinal Estouteville from Rouen had begun to renovate the church adjacent to his Roman residence soon after 1450 when its ground plan and the position of its pillars were defined. Then it was also decided to incorporate the apse of the previous building into the left transept. Towards the end of his life he commissioned Giacomo da Pietrasanta to finish and enrich the project. As the dedicatory inscription on the façade affirms, the church was completed in the year of Estouteville's death, 1483.

It too was entrusted to the Augustinian Fathers, and Pietrasanta's project is clearly modelled on its sister church of Santa Maria del Popolo and its convent. The pillar-borne arcades of the interior, no doubt begun before 1470, were however far narrower and squatter than there. This meant that Giacomo could only face every second pillar with half-columns topped with projecting entablature fragments. He continued them in a second order of square half-columns, whose entablature fragments once again stretch right up to the foot of the vaulting. The north French patron clearly preferred steeper proportions and richer lighting than in Santa Maria del Popolo, and Pietrasanta may, like Rossellino in Pienza, have derived inspiration for his double order from the superimposed columns of the *natatio*-façade of the Baths of Diocletian. However, he failed to connect the individual parts of the building and handle the principles of tectonics and uniformity as systematically as Giovannino in Santa Maria del Popolo.

The imposing façade, as a temple raised over a flight of steps, and its inscription reflect the particular claims of the cardinal. With its gigantic S-shaped volutes, which connect the central bay with the lower side bays and conceal the massive buttresses that rise from the chapels in a way similar to Alberti's Sant'Andrea (fig. 54), it comes even closer to the façade of Santa Maria Novella (fig. 43) than that of Santa Maria del Popolo. However, Pietrasanta let the chapels stretch beyond the width of the façade in order to ensure the axial alignment of the side portals with the aisles. Alberti's direct influence can also be felt in the well-proportioned pedimented *Porta Ionica* at the centre of the façade. The numerous blind panels evince a certain *horror vacui* and may have been intended to be filled with paintings.

With its octagonal crossing and three diverging wings, the hospital follows a type already adopted in Florence and Milan (fig. 68). The simple forms betray, on the other hand, the style of the Palazzetto Venezia. Only the two visible sides of the exterior are articulated. Both look symmetrical. The crossing, which served as the hospital's chapel (fig. 69), is distinguished by a prominent octagonal *tiburio* and lit by large traceried windows, still of Gothic type and corresponding to the religious function of the crossing. The section is reminiscent of a basilica church. But the porticoes are open to the exterior and undoubtedly intended both for the convalescence of patients and as a public concourse.

A Doric pilaster order adorns the octagonal pillars of the arcades. Both on the main and side fronts a *vestibulum* with a giant order distinguished the entrances to the interior. In the upper storey pilasters of a second Doric order flank the *bifora*-windows and are precisely co-ordinated with the beams of the ceilings of both the long hospital wards. In a similarly Vitruvian way the triangular pediment is coordinated with the ridged roof (and does not rise above it like the façades of Santa Maria Novella and of so many subsequent churches). The colossal Doric order of the vestibules and the *bifora*-windows of the adjoining hospital recur in the impressive campanile of the adjacent church.

The octagonal pillars, the marble traceried windows of the drum, the steeply proportioned marble portal, all point to a master who had

4 Florentine Architecture under Lorenzo de' Medici

Giuliano da Sangallo (c.1445–1516)

When the twenty-year-old Lorenzo took over the Medici bank and the reins of Florentine policy from his father Piero in 1469, he had at his disposal the most magnificent palazzo in the city, numerous country estates, modern villas like the one in Fiesole and the monumental church of San Lorenzo for the funerary monuments of his family. But he still had no architect in his employ whose service Federico da Montefeltro might have envied. Although Lorenzo was not necessarily set on new buildings, and although the Medici still had to beware of the mistrust of their fellow citizens, he nonetheless introduced a new phase in Italian architecture. Perhaps it was even Alberti who had recommended the services of the Florentine Giuliano da Sangallo, one of the great talents of the younger generation. Like the brothers Giuliano and Benedetto da Maiano and Pontelli, Giuliano had been apprenticed to Francione, who had been famous for his fortifications and marquetry. Giuliano made the stalls for the Palazzo Medici chapel. He travelled to Rome to study the ancient monuments in 1465. There he presumably came into contact with Alberti and

Francesco del Borgo. Alberti must in any case have fostered his passionate interest in the antique; his influence is already visible in Giuliano's earliest buildings.

Palazzo Scala and Palazzo Cocchi

In *c.*1472/73 Bartolomeo Scala, Lorenzo's chancellor and close aide, commissioned Giuliano to erect a suburban palazzo in Florence (fig. 70). Lorenzo himself may have had a hand in its design, even in the choice of the site. In its placement of the reception rooms on the ground floor and their proximity to the garden, it corresponded to Alberti's ideas of the ancient house (Book 5, c.14) and combined the advantages of urban with rural life. The rectangular ground plan differed, however, from that of the Villa Medici in Fiesole (fig. 51) by its axial-symmetrical organization, of a kind that hitherto could only

70 *For the first time in Florentine architecture, the courtyard of Giuliano da Sangallo's Palazzo Scala (c.1472/73) uses the 'theatre motif', a combination of arcades and a Vitruvian order exemplified by the Colosseum and the Palazzo Venezia, but the treatment, with reliefs by Bertoldo, is richer and more sculptural.*

have been found in churches and in a few fortresses and would be immediately taken up by the Casa del Mantegna in Mantua and in the projects of Francesco di Giorgio. In the forms of the Palazzo Scala, Giuliano based himself less on Roman models than on Alberti's Sant'Andrea (figs 55, 56). That goes not only for the chapel and for the predilection for barrel vaults, but also for the panelling of the pilasters and pedestals, the abbreviated architrave and the capitals.

The arcades of the courtyard are, however, stockier in proportion than Alberti's. The corner pilasters remain separated, as in the interior of Santa Maria degli Angeli (figs 20, 21), and the impost cornice is very narrow. The architrave and frieze of the entablature are projected above the pilasters, but the projection ends (as in some ancient prototypes) below the cornice, which is smooth and continuous and runs unbroken round the whole courtyard. Following the model of the triumphal arch, which also plays a prominent role in his drawings after the antique, Giuliano continued the projection into the tall attic-like pedestal zone of the upper storey. The pedestals separate the sequence of oblong Bertoldo reliefs and would no doubt have continued in a colonnade. Such decorative magnificence had hitherto been reserved for churches. It fundamentally differs, no less than the ground plan, from the sobriety of buildings like the Badia and the Villa Fiesolana, and would shortly after make its entrance into Urbino and Milan.

In the Palazzo Cocchi on the Piazza Santa Croce Giuliano was faced by the task of incorporating parts of the pre-existing ground floor with shops and rusticated pillars (fig. 71) into a new façade. He ingeniously linked the unequal pillars into three arches. To gain added residential space he made the corner pillars of the two upper storeys broader and supported the overhang on both sides with elegant S-shaped volutes. He doubled the pilasters on the broader corner pillars, but left the real corner naked, even cut back its entablature, and thus embraced Alberti's more decorative, rather than Brunelleschi's tectonic, interpretation of the order. In the articulation of the two upper storeys Giuliano started out from the façade of the Palazzo Rucellai. He combined the arches of the ground floor with the colonnade of the third storey to produce the dominating theatre motif of the *piano nobile*. He thus showed how well he had understood the heterogeneous roots of that motif: Roman (arcaded) bays on the ground, Greek (trabeated) bays on the top floor. He therefore tried to break through the traditional monotony of uniform wall apertures.

The arches of the *piano nobile* are blind and its large windows are supplemented with smaller square ones – perhaps the earliest example of a genuine mezzanine window. The two lights of the oblong windows of the upper storey are separated with colonnettes, a reduced variant of the paired *bifora*-windows of the late-Gothic tradition, reminiscent of Alberti's *fenestra accubans* (Book IX, c.3). The panelling of the pilasters of the Palazzo Scala has disappeared and the entablatures are now far more normative in form. The richly decorated capitals are also inspired by the Palazzo Rucellai, but the theatre motif is now provided with an impost and is thus a step closer to the antique.

'Domus Nova' in Mantua

Pilaster orders also reappear in *c.*1480 on the garden wing of the 'Domus Nova', a never-finished addition to the Gonzaga residence in Mantua, which overlooked a huge formal garden and the adjacent lake. The project was designed by Luca Fancelli (1430–95), a former assistant of Alberti and long-standing architect of Lodovico Gonzaga. Fancelli, however, had to leave the design of the windows to Mantegna. The two colossal pilaster orders that articulate the façade are easier to derive from Brunelleschi and Alberti than from the Palazzo Ducale in Urbino, the plans for which the patron, Lodovico's son and heir Federico Gonzaga, had wished to see during the planning. The tower-like projections of the corners of the block and the monotonous rhythm of the pilaster order and of the fenestration recall, on the other hand, the façades of Filarete's ideal city *Sforzinda* and suggest that Fancelli made less use of the latest architectural tendencies than his younger compatriot Giuliano.

Panel paintings in Berlin, Urbino and Baltimore

Only in Giuliano's oeuvre do the types and forms of three famous panel paintings of urban perspectives recur. They have been variously attributed to Piero della Francesca, Luciano Laurana, Francesco di Giorgio, Baccio Pontelli and Cosimo Rosselli (among others). The earliest of the three is no doubt the one in Berlin (fig. 72). Here we look through the open colonnade of a *vestibulum* onto a piazza. Similar colonnades and capitals are anticipated by Brunelleschi and Alberti, and would play an increasingly important

71 *Façade of the Palazzo Cocchi, Florence, where Giuliano uses blind 'theatre motifs'.*

role in Giuliano's buildings. As in Alberti's description of a harbour (Book V, c.12), the piazza overlooks a bay with ships and a hilly peninsula in the distance. The harbour is guarded by a waterfront fortress, reminiscent of the Castel Sant'Angelo. The palazzo in the right foreground is articulated by three pilaster orders. In the small square windows of its ground floor, arched windows of the two upper floors, and its terminating bracketed entablature, it follows again the model of the Palazzo Rucellai. Yet its regular ashlars, window arches now freed from Gothic *bifore* and crowning balustrade are closer to Giuliano than to Alberti. The opposite building in the left foreground has (like the Palazzo Medici) a garden surrounded by a high merlon-topped wall

annexed to its rear. An arcaded loggia, communicating with the piazza, is opened up on its ground floor. Its quadrangular columns are only mirrored at the corners on the inner wall. As in Rossellino's Chiostro degli Aranci, they continue without any intervening entablature fragments into half pilasters, which rise to the entablature that terminates the ground floor; this is a solution that is no longer conceivable in Giuliano after 1480. On the other hand, the pedimented window-aedicules look more advanced than the windows of the Palazzo Cocchi, and so the panel may have been painted *c*.1480.

The rotunda in the centre of the panel of Urbino (fig. 73) is characterized by its Corinthian colonnades and aedicules in both storeys as a

Three fantasy paintings of ideal cities, now in Berlin, Urbino and Baltimore, whose design can be attributed to Giuliano da Sangallo.

72 *Berlin: we look through a double colonnade into a piazza whose palaces still recall Palazzo Medici and Palazzo Rucellai.*

73 *Urbino: both the rotunda in the centre and the flanking buildings correspond to Giuliano's style of c.1485.*

74 *Baltimore: with the opening of a large space and the even more classicizing and complex articulation of the buildings, this panel is by far the most mature one.*

temple in the Albertian sense (cf. Book VII). A similar type would later recur in Giuliano's Codex Barberini. The *opus reticulatum* of the podium zone and the buildings in the background are still reminiscent of those in the Berlin panel and of the Palazzo Rucellai. But the palazzo in the left foreground is now opened up on both ground and third floors into a trabeated portico, whose columns are mirrored by answering pilasters on the inner wall. As in the Palazzo Cocchi, the building in the right foreground has an arcaded loggia on the ground floor and blind theatre motifs pierced by tall rectangular windows in the floor above. As there, the corners between the pilasters are left naked. A Doric order on the ground floor is topped by an order of Corinthian half-columns on three storeys, all of them with fluted capitals. Comparable vestigial pediments and pedestal-like terminations on the rooftop can be found in some ancient triumphal arches in Giuliano's sketchbooks.

Even more progressive in the richness and variety of its architectural language is the panel in Baltimore (fig. 74). The higher viewing point, spatial expanse and perspective depth, motifs such as the triumphal arch and the octagonal church, and the animation of the scene with minuscule figures seem inspired by Perugino's fresco of the *Christ's Charge to St Peter* in the Sistine Chapel (1481). The panel is also more progressive in the varied rhythm of its façade articulation, ranging from the triads of corner pilasters of the octagonal church to the paired columns of the triumphal arch and the triumphal-arch blind arcading of the palazzo to the left. These triumphal-arch motifs once again go back to Alberti's Sant'Andrea and would recur in simplified form in the Cancelleria in Rome in *c.*1489. The amphitheatre presents, in its four storeys, a similar superimposition of *Dorica*, *Ionica* and two kinds of *Corinthia* to the Colosseum.

The tiny scale of the figures is hardly compatible with a set design. And even if Alberti's temple and basilica are lacking, the scene is clearly intended as the vision of an ideal city – just like the panels in Berlin and Urbino. Giuliano, who is unlikely to have painted these panels himself, probably produced the designs on which they are based. Perhaps he even designed them on commission from Lorenzo de' Medici as a gift to a foreign prince, such as the model of a palace he would give to the king of Naples in 1489. Giuliano, as a pupil of Francione (famed also as a virtuoso in the art of perspective), was well equipped for such perspectival views.

Santa Maria delle Carceri in Prato

In the spring of 1485 the citizens of Prato had commissioned Giuliano da Maiano to erect a pilgrimage church as a shrine over a miracle-working icon of the Madonna painted on the wall of a former prison. Two surviving ground plans probably express his project; they suggest that he wanted to emphasize the corners of an octagonal building with columns with projecting entablature – quite similar to the earlier pulpit of his brother Benedetto in Santa Croce.

Clearly, however, Lorenzo de' Medici wanted a building more in the Albertian style. Only two days after the work had begun, he ordered it to be suspended. In August he asked Luca Fancelli, architect of the Gonzaga in Mantua, for a drawing of Alberti's San Sebastiano in Mantua. He must have esteemed San Sebastiano as an adequate type for such a church and Alberti as the leading architectural oracle of the age. Indeed, in the same year he patronized the

75, 76 *Santa Maria delle Carceri, Prato, by Giuliano da Sangallo, 1485, a Greek-cross design with a dome over the centre. While the interior and the cupola still largely follow Brunelleschi, the exterior order and the altar, 1509, are more classical than even Alberti.*

printing of the *De re aedificatoria*. The affinities of the church as built with San Sebastiano are, however, slight. Instead of its naked cube, rudimentary arms and separate portico, a true Greek-cross plan was chosen (figs 75, 76). Filarete had already identified the Greek cross as the ideal form for a church, and only a few years earlier the Marian church in nearby Bibbona had been built on such a plan. Lorenzo now commissioned Giuliano da Sangallo with the project.

In the interior Giuliano combined the system of the Pazzi Chapel with that of the crossing of Santo Spirito. He remained faithful to Brunelleschi right down to the ribbed cupola, the ornament of the arches and the form of the window-aedicules in the lunettes. Yet by hiding the impost from which the blind drum springs by a balustrade and by cutting the round windows directly into the base of the hemispherical dome, he showed his predilection for simple geometrical forms and new spatial effects.

On the exterior, as in the churches of the Urbino and Baltimore panels, he contrasted the white marble panelling of the order, the aedicules and the large blind panels of the walls with the dark-green marble framing, and did so in a far more tectonic way than Alberti in the upper storey of the façade of Santa Maria Novella or the Holy Sepulchre in San Pancrazio. Even the triads of pilasters are reminiscent of the church of the Baltimore panel.

Already Giuliano may have planned to place above the *Dorica* of the ground floor an Ionic order in the squat upper storey, behind which the barrel vaults of the arms of the cross are concealed. The Doric pilasters of the exterior bind the arms of the cross together, but are not coordinated with the angular fluted Corinthian pilasters demarcating the corners of the interior to form ideal quadrangular pillars. Here again it becomes clear that Giuliano was more receptive to Alberti's decorative, than to Brunelleschi's tectonic, interpretation of the order.

Presumably Giuliano wanted to terminate the ridge roofs with corresponding triangular gables. In this way he would at least have approximated the arms of the cross to the porticoes of a temple. As so often in Florence, the exterior is thus invested with greater significance than the interior. Lorenzo de' Medici too must have laid the greatest value on so clear-cut a form of the pilgrimage church, and its effect when seen from afar.

The proportions of the plan follow a system of small whole integers. They are therefore 'musical' like those of Brunelleschi and Alberti. With its slender relation of *c.*1:9.6, the *Dorica* comes closer to Brunelleschi's *Corinthia* than to Vitruvius. Its column bases are modelled on those of the Colosseum and its capitals for the first time furnished with two annulets. With their flat profiles, high Florentine

fleur-de-lys-decorated neck and reduced echinus, they are, however, more decorative in effect than most ancient prototypes. But like the Ionic bases and the glazed terracotta frieze of the interior, they show how much more precisely Giuliano based himself now on the detail of ancient monuments than Alberti or than he had himself in his previous buildings. In the interior he decorated the capitals with the symbols of the evangelists and thus varied an ancient prototype. Only in the courtyard of the Palazzo Pazzi, Florence, can such figurative capitals be found before this date; just for this reason they have sometimes been attributed to the young Giuliano.

Villa Medici at Poggio a Caiano

An even more exact insight into the intentions of Lorenzo and his architect is afforded by the two Medici villas of Lorenzo's time, both country seats in the midst of extensive agricultural estates which Lorenzo had bought during the preceding decades as a financial investment (figs 77, 78).

The more monumental one he began in 1485 at Poggio a Caiano some 20 km (12½ miles) west of Florence. In the centralized ground plan Giuliano continued along the path that he had begun in the Palazzo Scala and that increasingly approximated the profane with the sacred in architecture. But he still drew a sharp distinction

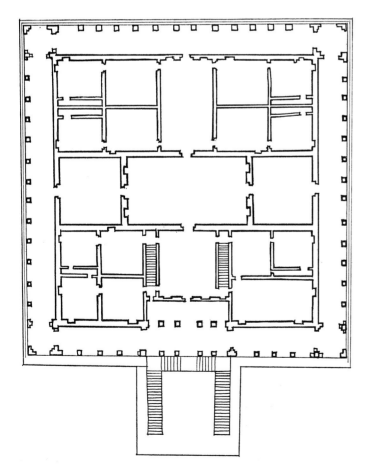

77, 78 *Façade and ground plan of the Villa Medici at Poggio a Caiano by Giuliano do Sangallo, 1485.*

between villa and palace. Formalization is restricted to the two antique elements, the *podium villae* and the *vestibulum*. The undecorated exterior ends without any cornice below the wooden rafters, and differs from the villa in Fiesole mainly in the more regular rhythm and classicizing framing of the window-aedicules. Their sill and their cornice are supported by brackets, which had first appeared in the Badia Fiesolana and on the garden front of the Palazzo Piccolomini in Pienza.

Forming a compact stereometric block, the two main storeys rise impressively over the broad podium opened up with arcades all round which isolate the building from the surrounding courtyard and gardens. These arcades are widened in the corner bays and emphasized by squat pilasters of the Doric order with partially projecting entablature. They match the isolated windows in the outer bays of the façade. The other windows are concentrated in the central bays, once again creating a more complex rhythm than in earlier façades.

A double-ramped staircase, once placed in front of the centre of the podium, provided axial access to the *vestibulum*, on which the articulation of the exterior is concentrated. Its temple front, topped with a triangular pediment, is reduced to four round and two corner columns. Its central bay is wider. The column neck of its slender *Ionica* is once again fluted and the frieze decorated with figural relief as in the Palazzo Scala. The tympanum is adorned with the Medici arms and the barrel vault with richly decorated coffering.

The longitudinal axis leads to the salon at the centre of the building, which is illuminated by circular lunette-windows in the recessed side walls and surrounded by four square apartments like the towers of a castle. Its barrel vault, built with concrete poured into wooden moulds in the ancient technique, is lavishly decorated with a complex system of stuccoed coffers with Medici *imprese* like those of the

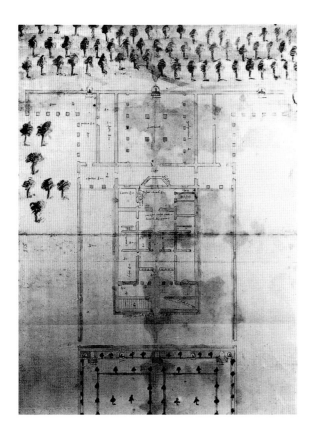

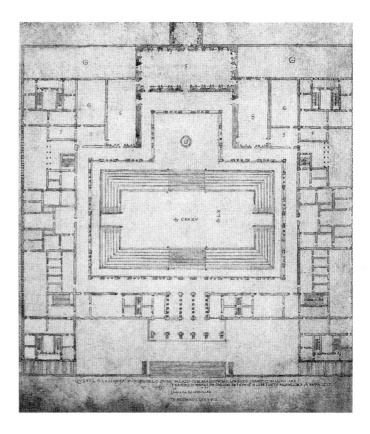

79 *Giuliano da Sangallo's plan for Lorenzo de' Medici's villa at Agnano near Pisa, c.1490, was only partly realized.*

80 *Giuliano also made a more elaborate plan, with a wide transverse salon and a large number of apartments, for the king of Naples.*

vestibule. Thus the dominance of the *piano nobile* and of the longitudinal axis seem to be more important than the opening to the gardens and to the landscape. They make the building look more like a princely residence than a real villa. From a distance one first sees the side front with its deeply recessed and dark-shadowed central part. These deep indentations of the side faces, one on either side, were necessary to provide lighting for the oblong, traverse-placed central *sala*.

In *c.*1490 Giuliano da Sangallo may also have begun Lorenzo's far more modest villa at Agnano near Pisa; it was continued much later but drastically altered in plan (fig. 79). Cut into the hillside, it probably comprised, in origin, only the ground floor and a *piano nobile*. As in Poggio a Caiano, the two-ramped staircase ascended to the colonnade of the *vestibulum* overlooking the formal garden and fish-pond. This entrance loggia led into a *sala* and other living rooms. The tripartite and strictly symmetrical plan was imitated in many sixteenth-century villas.

Project for the king of Naples
In his sketchbooks Giuliano da Sangallo distinguished two projects as inventions of the 'M[agnific]o L[orenz]o'. In the less developed of the two, symmetrical staircase ramps are placed in front of the *podium villae*, as in Poggio a Caiano and as was usual in ancient villas. They similarly ascend to the columnar portico of a *vestibulum* that leads into the central *atrium*, whose octagonal form and cupola with skylight are clearly inspired by imperial *thermae*. On the rear side a portico leads into a corresponding *vestibulum* at the same level. Loggias of different

form, connecting four square apartments, are placed in front of the two other sides. In the second, significantly more professional project, the exterior is articulated with projecting wings, containing the apartments. In the corners of the entrance portico two similar staircases ascend to the central *vestibulum*. Columns divide the *vestibulum* into three aisles forming altogether twenty-four square compartments. It was undoubtedly intended to be distinguished by a pediment, as Alberti had recommended. The transverse salon, illuminated by windows in the narrow side walls and connected with porticoes with the terrace outside, is reminiscent of the villa at Poggio a Caiano too. But it may also prepare the project for the palace of the king of Naples, also identified by letters as Lorenzo's invention (fig. 80).

Lorenzo de' Medici had commissioned the wooden model: to Giuliano was entrusted the mission of delivering it to the king in person at the end of 1488. The project was not only far more ambitious and costly than all his villa designs, but also formed for the first time the complete entrance sequence of the Vitruvian house. A broad flight of steps cuts into a high podium and leads to the *vestibulum*, a pillar-supported loggia, with a colonnade placed in front of it, as in the Loggia delle Benedizioni of Pius II. This would have been triumphally topped by a projecting entablature and probably also by a pediment. The three barrel-vaulted aisles of the atrium, into which it leads, are divided by colonnades and lead in turn into the huge square *peristylium*. This is surrounded by pillar-supported arches – every second one screened with colonnades – and opens up into the auditorium of the *cava aedium*. The centre of the rear wing is recessed and opens to the three doors of the ceremonial hall, again placed transversely (as at Poggio a Caiano) and the whole complex culminates in the octagonal chapel. The side wings each comprise three square apartments, separated by gardens and smaller rooms.

No project of the Quattrocento comes closer to Vitruvius and the antique. None prepares the way, in so many features, for the villa and palace architecture of the next decades. Clearly, however, it was too far removed from the functions of a traditional royal residence, indeed far too grand and utopian in scale, to be actually built.

The king's son, Alfonso of Aragon, decided to build a reduced version in Poggio Reale in the following year. This was executed by Giuliano da Maiano, but was clearly based on Giuliano's ideas. According to a contemporary source, it was actually planned by Lorenzo de' Medici single-handed. Lorenzo, a keen student of architecture, had also planned the fortress of Pisa.

Four tower-like apartments surround the oblong courtyard, which was also used as a theatre (with steps leading down to it doubling as seats). The villa is continued by terraced gardens, a fish-pond and a loggia. Transmitted by Serlio's treatise, this type was to survive into the seventeenth century.

Sacristy of Santo Spirito

Lorenzo de' Medici's patronage of Giuliano da Sangallo also extended to the commission given to him in *c.*1488/89 to design a sacristy for Santo Spirito in Florence (fig. 19). Like Brunelleschi in San Lorenzo (fig. 10), Giuliano took as his starting point the dimensions of the crossing of the adjoining church. But he also seized the opportunity to take over the type of octagonal halls with diagonal corner niches in Roman imperial *thermae* (as in the Baths of Diocletian): a type that already appears in his projects of the preceding years (fig. 80). In contrast to Brunelleschi's Santa Maria degli Angeli or Michelozzo's Santissima Annunziata (figs 20, 31), the Corinthian order of the lower storey supports no arches, but is combined with the arcades of the niches to form a series of separate theatre motifs.

Even more antique in spirit, and more volumetric in effect, is the *vestibulum* that leads from the left aisle of the church to the sacristy (figs 19, 81). It is related in type to the porch of the Pazzi Chapel and, as there and in Alberti's Mantuan churches, it is to be understood as the portico of a Christianized temple. The barrel vault, which Giuliano did not design till 1493 and executed together with Cronaca, is no less magnificent, even if more severely coffered than in the salon at Poggio a Caiano. It is supported by a Corinthian order of columns, six on either side, placed in front of the side walls, no doubt the finest in Giuliano's oeuvre. As in the porch of the Pazzi Chapel, the Vitruvian intercolumniations of the side bays are widened in the broad portal bay.

In his design, only in part executed, for the church of the Madonna dell'Umiltà in Pistoia of around 1492 Giuliano recurred to the type of the sacristy articulated with paired pilasters and theatre motifs, and preceded by a barrel-vaulted *vestibulum*.

He might also have lent a helping hand in the domed Greek-cross system of Santa Maria delle Grazie in Pistoia and contributed to its *all'antica* colonnade and pendentive dome without drum. The church was begun in *c.*1469, but clearly had not progressed much beyond its foundations before 1484. Its decorative detail is, however, far below

81 *The monumental vestibule between the church of Santo Spirito in Florence and the new sacristy is the work of Giuliano da Sangallo and Il Cronaca, 1488–93.*

Giuliano's level. Step by step Giuliano da Sangallo came ever closer to the antique, far closer indeed than Francesco di Giorgio or Bramante in their buildings of the same period.

Atrium of Santa Maria Maddalena dei Pazzi

In the same spirit Giuliano designed in 1491 the atrium of an unassuming Cistercian church, whose nave he had perhaps reconstructed in *c.*1481 (fig. 82). The single-storey, portico-surrounded forecourt of the church comes even nearer to the atrium of St Peter's or that of San Clemente than Michelozzo's previous atrium in the Santissima Annunziata. As in the Urbino panel, he replaced the arcades by a colonnade supporting a straight entablature and showed himself once again the most systematic pioneer of the Vitruvian orders. As in the vestibule of Poggio a Caiano, the order is Ionic and the intercolumniations are relatively broad. As in the Pazzi Chapel, only the intercolumniations of the entrance axis are expanded into broader arches. They rest on square columns which also recur in the corners, where they are now joined together to form L-shaped pillars. And while the square columns support saucer domes, the entablature of the colonnade supports an *all'antica* barrel vault. This entablature is limited both outside and inside to a three-fascia architrave; it is consonant with the frugality and austerity of the Cistercian Order. The

82 *Giuliano's atrium of Santa Maria Maddalena dei Pazzi, Florence, with a colonnade bearing a straight entablature dates from 1491.*

voltes of the capitals hang downwards to the fluted neck, as in an antique prototype found in Florence. Like the corner capitals in the façade of Santa Maria Novella, they are reduced at the corners to fluting, egg-and-dart and astragal.

Palazzo Gondi and Palazzo Strozzi in Florence and Palazzo della Rovere in Savona

When Sangallo designed a town house for the rich Florentine merchant Giuliano Gondi close to the Piazza della Signoria in 1490, he must at Gondi's express wish have followed the type of the Palazzo Medici and Palazzo Pitti (figs 83, 84). Here he could come closer to the antique only in detail. The palazzo as planned was significantly smaller than either of these two precedents and, moreover, Gondi managed to acquire only part of the site. Giuliano was therefore able to execute only five window-axes of the façade and a fragment of the courtyard; he was forced to insert its staircase into one of the courtyard loggias, as in late-medieval precedents. Presumably Giuliano's original plan envisaged eleven window-axes and a courtyard with surrounding loggias of three arcades on each side, as in the Palazzo Medici.

In his system of ashlars for the façade, Giuliano follows the model of the Palazzo Medici: projecting pillow-shaped rustication on the ground floor, courses of smooth ashlars in the *piano nobile*, carefully coordinated with the voussoirs of the arched windows (the cruciform ashlars between the window arcades alluding to the cross of the Gondi coat of arms), and flat blocks in the upper storey. On the other hand, the strict symmetry, the three portals and the rectangular grated windows of the ground floor, the narrower arches of the wall apertures with their cruciform mullions and the carefully calculated ashlared courses of the upper floor presuppose the Palazzo Rucellai and Palazzo Pitti. Giuliano achieved his closeness to the antique here not by classical orders, but by hierarchy of stonework and by the greater composure of the proportions. Also antique in spirit are the architrave-like fasciae of the door- and window-frames and the upper cornice inspired by the temple of Augustus in Pozzuoli.

The columnar arcades of the courtyard, the bending archivolts, the exaggeratedly high frieze and the low imposts also reveal their closeness to the Palazzo Medici. Giuliano's hand is unmistakable in the slenderer proportions and in the magnificent detail of the Corinthian capitals, the staircase and the fireplace in the main reception room on the first floor.

The wooden model of the slightly earlier and more monumental Palazzo Strozzi was made in Giuliano's workshop, and once again Lorenzo de' Medici contributed decisively to its realization. But the shorter blocks of the rustication, the denser sequence of windows, the *bifore* without entablature and old-fashioned relieving arches are easier to associate with Benedetto da Maiano than with the architect of the Palazzo Gondi. The frieze and the massive terminating

83, 84 *Palazzo Gondi, Florence: façade and courtyard with staircase, designed by Giuliano in 1491, but never finished. He translates Palazzo Medici into more classical forms, but the lack of space forced him to put the staircase in the right courtyard loggia.*

cornice, not begun till *c.*1491, as also the two upper courtyard storeys, are attributable to Cronaca (fig. 87).

After the death of Lorenzo in 1492, Giuliano da Sangallo entered the service of Cardinal Giuliano della Rovere and moved to Rome. There he was commissioned by Pope Alexander VI to create the magnificent *all'antica* coffered ceiling for the basilica of Santa Maria Maggiore with its Ionic colonnade that Giuliano had revived but could not surpass.

In June 1494 he accompanied the cardinal to France. On the way, both of them stopped off at Savona, birthplace of Giuliano della Rovere, and discussed the building of a family palace, whose dimensions were to be similar to those of the Cancelleria (figs 130–32). But also the Palazzo della Rovere never extended beyond five window-axes and a barrel-vaulted *andito*. On the façade Giuliano recurred to the ancient orders, but held firm to a paratactic succession of the bays and even adopted the type of the upper order of the Palazzo Cocchi for the capitals.

Cappella del Soccorso in the Cathedral of Naples

Only Giuliano can have designed for Cardinal Oliviero Caraffa the magnificent *all'antica* colonnades below the choir of the Cathedral of

85 *Soon after 1497 Giuliano paid a brief visit to Naples, where he may have designed the Soccorpo under the cathedral.*

Naples (fig. 85). By dividing the squat room into three aisles of the same width with columns, he combined the type of a crypt with that of the *vestibulum* of one of his villa projects. The side aisles continue the steps leading down to the chapel from the cathedral. The central aisle leads to the chapel's high altar. The side walls, articulated with pilasters lavishly decorated with candelabra panels, are opened up into shell niches containing further altars. The rich decoration recalls that of the slightly earlier stairwell of the Palazzo Gondi and the colonnade the *vestibulum* of the sacristy of Santo Spirito (fig. 81), even though the execution does not achieve the same high level and betrays the fact that Giuliano's visit to Naples can only have been brief. He could have designed the chapel soon after his return from France in the spring of 1497.

Giuliano da Sangallo left his distinct stamp on the Florentine Quattrocento just as Brunelleschi and Alberti had done before him. In his reconstructions of the ancient house, his colonnades and in his detail he came even closer than they to the antique. Even if he did not create any comparable masterpieces, he was, together with Francesco di Giorgio and Bramante, the most important pioneer of the Roman High Renaissance.

Simone del Pollaiuolo called Il Cronaca (*c*.1457–1508)

Vasari hailed Cronaca as one of the founders of the High Renaissance and the most excellent Florentine architect of his time. Cronaca, like Brunelleschi and Giuliano, had spent many years studying the Roman monuments. His surviving drawings after the antique concentrate on details and are laid out in a rigorously orthogonal fashion, as Alberti had prescribed.

86 *San Francesco al Monte, Florence: the nave looking towards the entrance. The church had been begun in 1470 by an unknown architect. Cronaca took over some twenty years later.*

Cronaca was the leading stonemason on the building site of the Palazzo Strozzi from 1489 onwards and its master-builder from 1490. His masterpiece, the Franciscan church of San Salvatore or San Francesco al Monte, in Florence, had evidently been begun in the mid-1470s by an unknown architect (fig. 86). By transforming the single nave into the language of his master Giuliano, Cronaca may have drawn inspiration from the typologically comparable interior of the Augustinian church near the Porta San Gallo, begun by Giuliano in 1488 but destroyed in 1527.

The appearance of this latter church is probably transmitted by two later drawings. Its flat-roofed nave was articulated with theatre motifs of a plain Doric order that opened up into square chapels with saucer domes and balustrades at ground level. The chapels were also continued round the entrance wall. As in the Old Sacristy, the triumphal arch formed a *serliana* and its central arch widened into the altar chapel – all these motifs are more plausibly attributable to Giuliano than to a later architect.

In San Francesco al Monte the side walls are similarly articulated with theatre motifs of a Doric order with fluted capitals. The almost square chapels are barrel-vaulted. Cronaca had to be satisfied with blind and partly asymmetrical arcades, where this was forced on him

87 *Il Cronaca continued Benedetto da Maiano's project of the Palazzo Strozzi in Florence, but the courtyard seems to be due entirely to him.*

by the former building. The pilasters are squatter and the entablatures heavier than in Giuliano's previous buildings. The corner columns and groin vault of the tomb chapel to the right of the choir are again inspired by the mausoleum of the Cercenii.

Cronaca's tendency to classicizing weight and monumentality is even more evident in the *serliana* of the triumphal arch. Its depressed arch achieves not only the same breadth but nearly the same height as the order. The window aedicules are articulated with slender pilasters, abbreviated entablature and alternating pediments and float as freely in the wall surface as in the sacristy of Santo Spirito. On the exterior the articulation is even more austere: it is reduced to the window-aedicules and the small arched windows of the chapels – probably under the influence of Savonarola, who was preaching against all forms of luxury at the time and had a strong influence on Cronaca.

In the interior of the narrow and elongated Latin cross of San Pietro in Scrinio, a church only known from drawings, Cronaca varied the elevation. It was adorned with an Ionic order and round niches.

Cronaca's squat and powerful *all'antica* language is also unmistakable in the Palazzo Strozzi. He terminated the exterior with an abbreviated entablature, directly inspired by the Temple of Serapis in Rome. The ill-conceived idea of an upper storey with pedimented aedicules, only transmitted by the wooden model, perhaps goes back either to him or to Giuliano. In the courtyard Cronaca supported the four-sided arcades with traditional round columns with Corinthian capitals. These he topped with quadrangular Doric columns on simplified bases in the relatively squat arcades of the *piano nobile* (fig. 87). As in the ground floor, their brackets support a tripartite entablature. On the two closed sides the arcades are pierced by large cruciform and small round windows. The colonnade of the upper storey stands on pedestals, connected – perhaps for the first time – by balustrades.

5 Luciano Laurana, Francesco di Giorgio and Architecture under Federico da Montefeltro

Luciano Laurana (1420–79)

Federico da Montefeltro had, at the age of eighteen, taken over the duchy of Urbino in 1444 after the early death of his brother. A decade or so later be began the modernization of his modest residence in the little hill-town in the Marche. His first architect was Maso di Bartolommeo, the master of the portal of San Domenico. Maso's hand is also detectible in the elegant *bifora*-windows of the east wing of the Palazzo Ducale and in the decoration of the Sala di Iole, where he gave proof of his mastery of the language of Donatello and of his master Michelozzo.

As the victorious *condottiere* of the pope and his allies, Federico acquired such wealth that he could afford to transform his palazzo

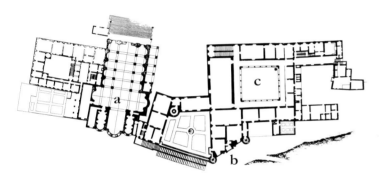

into a genuine princely residence. Contemporaries praised his architectural talent. If Alberti really visited him in 1464 (as has been claimed), he could have discussed preliminary plans with him. At much the same time Federico could have got to know the man who was to become his court engineer and architect. The Dalmatian-born Luciano Laurana had worked for Federico's brother-in-law Alessandro Sforza in neighbouring Pesaro in 1465/66 and may have played a part in the articulation of the *piano nobile* of the Palazzo Ducale (Sforza) with its magnificent aediculated windows, entablature and crenellated roofline. The stocky rusticated arcades, the portal and the *salone*, as well as the earlier part of the nearby Villa Imperiale, had already been built before 1457 by an unknown, perhaps Florentine architect.

Federico justified Laurana's official appointment as court engineer and architect in 1468 with the circumstance that there was no architect of comparable erudition in Tuscany: Michelozzo was old, Antonio Manetti Ciaccheri and Rossellino were dead and the exponents of the younger generations had not yet risen to prominence.

Like Pius II in Pienza and Paul II in Rome, Federico was not interested just in remodelling his residence: he wanted to leave his stamp on the whole town over which it presided. Laurana was ordered to demolish both the old cathedral and a part of the city walls in order to create space for the piazza, the new cathedral and the Palazzo Ducale (fig. 88). Its new suite of rooms stretched from the Sala di Iole to the

88, 89 *The palace of Federico da Montefeltro at Urbino is due to two architects, Luciano Laurana up to 1474 and Francesco di Giorgio after that date. Laurana conceived the basic layout with the domed cathedral (**a**) to the left in the photograph, and the two-towered façade of a suite of rooms (**b**) that includes the* studiolo, *behind which is the courtyard (**c**).*

imposing twin-towered façade on the western declivity and comprised a monumental staircase, a huge saloon and the private apartments of Federico and his wife, as well as its adjacent hanging garden. The result was that the surface area of the complex was more than quadrupled in size.

Both Federico and Laurana must have been familiar with the Badia laid out, probably by Antonio Manetti Ciaccheri, below Fiesole in accordance with the ideas of Cosimo de' Medici in 1455–60 (figs 48, 49). Like no previous building of the period, it opened up views on the landscape. Its external loggias, central courtyard, refectory and staircase, axially aligned with the courtyard loggia, provided important precedents for the Palazzo Ducale and no doubt influenced Laurana, who was Manetti Ciaccheri's rather than Alberti's follower.

In the rectangular – almost square – area of the courtyard, as also in the layout of the rooms round it, Laurana must have been inspired by the Palazzo Medici and Palazzo Piccolomini (figs 30, 62). As there, access was given to the *sala* through *andito*, loggia and staircase, and, as in the Vatican and the Palazzo Venezia (figs 64, 65), the rooms became progressively smaller. A second apartment for the warmer periods of the year was laid out at garden level. Perhaps Laurana was also inspired by the Badia in the ingenious way he built the famous *studiolo* and loggia into the unavoidable triangular space between Federico's apartment and the splayed new valley façade, which had to be adjusted to the irregular topography of the hilltop site (fig. 89).

Laurana transformed one tower of the old city walls, the Castellare, into the centre of the duchess's apartment, which was connected not only with Federico's apartment but also with the planned cathedral. Below the hanging garden lay the extensive service rooms and in the substructures on the valley side, the stables and bathroom. Similar hanging gardens had already been created in the Villa Medici in Fiesole (figs 51, 52) and in the Palazzo Piccolomini in Pienza.

The façade with its slender twin cylindrical towers identifies the building, even from afar, as the seat of a prince. The towers conceal spiral staircases and have less a defensive than a scenic connotation and thus seem to be inspired not only by the Castel Nuovo in Naples but also by medieval prototypes such as the church of San Claudio near Macerata. Three arcaded loggias, one above the other, are opened up between them. They are a further signal to the visitor that this prince had no need to barricade himself behind defensive ramparts. He could look out from his loggia and view the land whose benefactor he was.

In opening up the building to the landscape, in the distribution of the rooms, in the virtuoso exploitation of parts of the existing fortifications, or in the axial alignment of the entrance of the staircase with the courtyard loggia, Laurana surpassed not only all previous city palaces, but all residences of European princes of the time. He showed himself to be one of the great pioneers of the renewal of secular architecture. In the priority he gave to function rather than symmetry he stood closer to Michelozzo and Manetti Ciaccheri (figs 48, 51) than to Alberti. He modelled the lower window-aedicules of the valley front on Michelozzo's Porta del Noviziato at Santa Croce in Florence; perhaps it was he who had already done something similar

in the *piano nobile* of the Palazzo Ducale in Pesaro. But Laurana's strength lay less in *all'antica* vocabulary than in functional and structural innovations. This may be one of the reasons why he was dismissed, after only five years' activity, when the Palazzo Ducale was very far from having been completed.

Francesco di Giorgio (1438–1502)

Debut in Siena

The rich Republic of Siena enjoyed its greatest artistic flowering in the early fourteenth century. It thus embraced the Gothic style more wholeheartedly and more enduringly than did Florence, its great Tuscan rival, situated just a few hours' journey away. The new Renaissance style of architecture was first introduced into Siena by the Florentine Bernardo Rossellino, who had erected exemplary buildings for Pius II both in Siena and in neighbouring Pienza since 1459 (figs 60–62). Through him this style was learnt not only by stonemasons, building workers and carpenters, but also by emerging architects and sculptors like Antonio Federighi, Vecchietta and Francesco di Giorgio.

The Palazzetto Calusi in Siena may have been one of Francesco's first buildings. Though it is entirely built of brick, its ground floor is characterized by its regular ashlars as a subordinate basement podium and its first floor by classicizing window-aedicules as the *piano nobile*. Perhaps inspired by Giuliano's Palazzo Cocchi, both storeys are closely linked together by flanking fluted pilasters with abbreviated entablature and by the framing of all the wall apertures with uniform arcades. The austere but harmonious brick façade of Santa Caterina in Fontebranda (1466–74) (see further below) shows a comparable sensibility for light and shadow and the changing textures of wall surface.

In the brick church of the Osservanza in Siena, begun in the summer of 1467, Francesco likewise fused together several prototypes (fig. 90). He translated the type of the Sienese monastic church of Santa Maria degli Angeli, begun in 1457, into Brunelleschi's language. He thus topped the two bays of the nave with shallow saucer domes on pendentives and distinguished the dome of the sanctuary by a blind drum. He also followed the Cathedral of Faenza, begun by Giuliano da Maiano in 1474, by opening each bay in two squat arches framing barrel-vaulted chapels on either side.

What is remarkable about the Osservanza is Francesco di Giorgio's reduction of the Vitruvian order to pillars and entablature, as on the exterior of the *duomo* in Pienza (figs 61, 62). He stripped the order of those 'anthropomorphic' proportions and ornaments that had been so essential for Brunelleschi but that had made architectural planning so difficult. He used pillars instead, which were bound to no detail and no proportions. The round or quadrangular column as 'the principal ornament in all architecture', as Alberti had taught (Book VI, c.13), he reserved for especially festive occasions. The elimination of columns and pilasters enabled him to develop an essentially abstract architecture that was to prove influential for the following centuries. As in Gothic architecture and in Pienza Cathedral, he made the pillars appear also on the exterior and thus expressed the correspondence between outside and inside, between form and structure.

90 *Francesco di Giorgio was Sienese. His early church of the Osservanza in that city, begun in 1467, looks back to Brunelleschi but with cupolas on the nave and barrel-vaulted chapels.*

The same principle was followed in the exterior of the church of Santa Maria in Portico a Fontegiusta in Siena, built by an unknown master from Como in *c.*1479–84. The quincunx divided in nine almost equal cells with cross vaults and the combination with an upper church are reminiscent of San Claudio near Macerata. Even more faithfully than in Pienza Cathedral, the unfinished façade reflects the interior of a *Hallenkirche*-type in its lower, and a single-nave *oratorium* in its upper storey. So the idea for the church could go back to Francesco.

Palazzo Ducale in Urbino

The worldly aspirations of Federico da Montefeltro further increased in 1474 thanks to his elevation as duke, nomination as *gonfaloniere* of the Church, and the marriage of his only son to the niece of Pope Sixtus IV. In *c.*1476 he finally found a suitable replacement for Laurana both as military and civil architect in Francesco di Giorgio, who may have been recommended to him by his natural son Alessandro, commander of the Sienese troops.

The parts of the Palazzo Ducale built by Francesco di Giorgio can be clearly identified by the monogram 'FD', *Federicus Dux*, which

Federico began to use after his promotion in 1474, whereas the parts attributable to Laurana, and dating to the period before 1474, are identified by Federico's previous monogram 'FC', *Federicus Comes*. The façade overlooking the piazza, the upper loggia of the valley façade, the two chapels, the bathroom and the courtyard loggias were presumably designed by Francesco (figs 89, 91, 92).

The subtle differences of the upper loggia of the valley façade from the lower ones reveal Francesco's deeper knowledge of the antique and the latest Florentine developments. He thus rendered the detail of the Corinthian order in an incomparably more *all'antica* way, replacing Laurana's railing with a classicizing balustrade, and (as in the upper storey of the Pantheon) allowing the cornice of the door to intersect the fluted pilasters. The outside of the loggia is topped with a tripartite entablature, volute-decorated pediment, and a colossal Donatellesque baluster on which Federico's heraldic eagle is perched.

Francesco di Giorgio's first concern was to transform the piazza front into a genuine façade with a lavish marble decoration of *opus isodomum*, huge aedicules and corner lesenes. These are approximated to an order by their bases and proportion. Their shafts are richly adorned with double guilloches. They have no capitals, but are projected instead in an abbreviated entablature. The frieze too is lavishly ornamented with palmettes and acanthus scrolls. Like the corner pilasters of the Palazzetto Calusi in Siena, these lesenes are purely decorative and probably should have been continued in the upper storey.

91, 92 *In about 1476 Francesco di Giorgio took over the palace of Urbino. The piazza side is unfinished except for the marble facing of the lower storey and the classical aedicules (above), but behind it lies one of the most exquisite of Renaissance courtyards (below), its inscribed frieze proclaiming the duke's fame.*

Even more clearly than in the Palazzetto Calusi, the upper storey is unmistakably distinguished as the *piano nobile* by its marble window-aedicules supported by fluted pilasters, a more monumental variant of Michelozzo's and Laurana's aedicules; their consoles, framing Federico's monogram and *impresa*, are integrated into the marble frieze of the ground floor. In order to lend some semblance of symmetry to the façade, Francesco continued the eccentrically situated portal leading into the courtyard by two further blind portal-aedicules, so that three ground-floor portals alternate in syncopated rhythm with the four windows of the *piano nobile*. On the west wing, where the windows stand directly over the portals and this syncopated rhythm is intermitted, he also tried, by further blind portals and windows, to produce a symmetrical façade articulation. In the aedicules of these portals he repeated the rich décor of the corner lesenes, but completed the order by a tripartite entablature. The walls between the portals are only partly clad with *all'antica* marble ashlars, since the work was interrupted by Federico's death in 1482.

Laurana had presumably planned a courtyard with smaller bays and larger loggias. Francesco enlarged the corner pillars and planned to separate the corner bays by transverse arches as in Giuliano's atrium of Santa Maria Maddalena dei Pazzi. The Composite capitals of the columns are directly inspired by those of the Domus Flavia in Rome and betray the same hand as the upper loggia of the valley façade and of the interior of the church of San Bernardino outside Urbino (fig. 95).

The giant order of the corner pillars frames the columnar arcades of the courtyard in a way similar to Brunelleschi's San Lorenzo (fig. 14). But these pilasters are clearly separated, and so it seems as if the four walls of the courtyard are only loosely joined together – as in Giuliano's Palazzo Scala, which Francesco certainly knew (fig. 70). In *c.*1480 Francesco would repeat the same system in the courtyard of Federico's Palazzo Ducale in Gubbio.

As on the façade of the Palazzetto Calosi, he continued the giant order above the projecting entablature into the upper storey, which is squatter in proportion. The continuation of the lower order is emphasized by the projecting corner pilasters which are distinguished from the others by their broader shafts and fluted capitals and thus reminiscent of those of the façade of Santa Maria Novella (fig. 43). Both Alberti and Francesco may have understood them as the Attic order described by Raphael.

The duke's self-glorification went so far that he wanted to be buried in a *tempietto* in the garden-court behind the Palazzo Ducale. Its form is perhaps transmitted by a painting of the Barocci school. It seems to follow the temple of Portumnus in Ostia: a model influential for Francesco's drawings of centralized *tempietti*.

Urbino Cathedral

An essential part of the enlarged piazza was the renovation of the Cathedral (fig. 93), which had been planned since 1435. It may have been started by Laurana and was continued by Francesco at much the same time as his work on the Palazzo Ducale. It flanks the south side of the piazza, while its triple apses rise, like the valley front of the palazzo, over the substructures of the western declivity. By reducing the cathedral to an unassuming brick building and concentrating all the magnificence on the Palazzo Ducale, Francesco and his patron reversed the hierarchy of the piazza of Pienza (figs 60, 62).

The type of the three-aisled pillar-supported barrel-vaulted basilica with octagonal dome over the crossing, square transepts and chancel and hemispherical side chapels derived from the church of the Badia Fiesolana and perhaps also from San Marco in Rome (figs 48, 50). Yet, as in the Osservanza (fig. 90), Francesco eliminated columns and pilasters and furnished the pillars of the arcades with a tripartite entablature, on the model of Brunelleschi's Santa Maria degli Angeli (fig. 20). The arches of the dome were supported by two storeys of lesenes that, in contrast to the Osservanza, recurred only in the corners of the nave and arms of the cross, as Brunelleschi too must have planned in San Lorenzo (fig. 13). As in late Gothic buildings of Siena such as the courtyard of the Palazzo Pubblico or the exterior of the Loggia della Mercanzia, the lesenes were to be understood as reduced pillars. Like pillars, they did not carry, but intersect, the projecting entablature.

The colossal order and the triumphal rhythm of the façade were inspired by Alberti's Sant'Andrea. Both entablatures were to be continued round the whole exterior; the lower one even to cut through the blind arcades. Probably Francesco wanted this façade, as in Pienza Cathedral and in the Madonna di Fontegiusta in Siena, to be

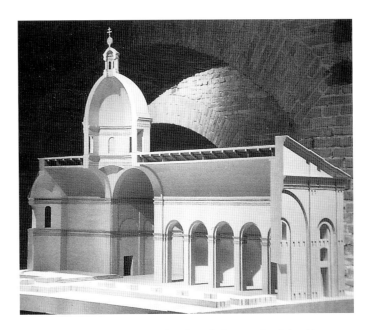

93 *Model of Urbino Cathedral, perhaps begun by Laurana but designed by Francesco and inspired by the Badia Fiesolana and Alberti's Sant'Andrea.*

topped by a pediment. In the delicate layering of the architectural articulation of the façade – we can distinguish all five different layers – and the subtle play with light and shadow he once again showed himself a virtuoso of brick technique and a precursor of Bramante, Raphael and Giulio Romano.

San Bernardino outside Urbino

Federico's funerary church, begun in 1482, was annexed to a convent, like precedents in Florence, Rimini, Milan, Rome or Sinigallia (figs 94, 95): the Franciscan community was a guarantee of the continuing celebration of masses for the dead. As in the Santissima Annunziata (figs 31, 32) and the project for the Tempio Malatestiano (fig. 39), the building combined a centralized choir with an unaisled nave. And as in the mausoleum of the Cercenii, four corner columns support the arches of the vault, a domed structure without a drum. The entablature over the corner columns, with its magnificent inscription in praise of the titular saint in the frieze, is continued round the whole interior. The squat columns on high pedestals, the arches of the dome, the niches, and above all the thickness of the walls, visible behind the columns and in the window embrasures of the barrel-vaulted nave, invest the interior with a robustness characteristic of Francesco.

The rectangular window of the entrance wall with a central column again seems inspired by Giuliano da Sangallo's Palazzo Cocchi (fig. 71), while the aedicules with alternating triangular and segmental pediments are directly inspired by the Pantheon and the Baptistery and cannot be matched even in Florence before 1485. The high altar was formerly adorned by Piero della Francesca's altarpiece (now in the Brera, Milan), in which the martial duke, kneeling in adoration before the Madonna, is praying for the salvation of his soul. Federico's tomb (now in a wall monument) was perhaps originally planned to be placed under the dome, like that of Cosimo de' Medici.

94, 95 *The small church of San Bernardino outside Urbino was designed by Francesco di Giorgio and begun in 1482 to serve as the funerary chapel of Federico da Montefeltro, whose tomb probably was originally to be placed under the dome.*

The exterior of the church is reduced to elementary volumetric shapes which only produce their full effect when seen from afar. It is reinforced by corner lesenes, like Pienza Cathedral, and horizontally demarcated by string courses and entablatures. The thickness of the masonry made it impossible to place the window triads on the exterior of the nave as symmetrically as in the interior; on the exterior they are displaced closer to the choir than to the entrance wall.

Francesco's tendency to robustness is expressed even more bluntly in the unusually squat and sturdy brick pillars of the austere cloister. They carry a simple entablature and support the huge weight of the tall, sparely fenestrated wall without any intermediate arches or cornices.

Convent of Santa Chiara in Urbino

As a pendant to San Bernardino, Francesco di Giorgio began the construction of another brick-built convent at much the same time (fig. 96). Commissioned by Federico and his daughter Elisabetta, the convent of the Poor Clares is situated on the north-western edge of the town; the ground falls away sharply below it. Federico's wife, Battista Sforza, who had died in 1472, was buried in the later remodelled round chapel.

Not only the middle of the valley front, as in the Badia Fiesolana (figs 48–50), but all three wings of the façade open in an imposing sequence of fourteen tall brick arches. The façade wing overlooks a hanging garden supported on a massive six-arched substructure and, beyond it, the distant landscape; it thus comes even closer to a villa in type. As in the cathedral, the sturdy pillars of the arches are topped by the entablature of an order and continue in lesenes. These extend to the narrow cornice separating the two storeys and continue in a

96 *The brick-built convent of Santa Chiara (Poor Clares) was also commissioned from Francesco by Federico, whose wife Battista Sforza had died ten years earlier and was buried there. The loggias of the valley front recall the Badia Fiesolana and anticipate future villas.*

second order of lesenes articulating segmental arched arcades. Even more than in the façade of the Cathedral, the tectonically active pillars of the ground floor are dissolved into the more passive layers of brickwork in the upper storey. Presumably it was to be terminated by a projecting entablature (as in one of Pontelli's intarsias in the Palazzo Ducale). The same system is varied in the convent's cloister, now incomplete but no doubt planned as rectangular. Francesco was inspired by Roman aqueducts and viaducts to design sequences of identical arcades on two storeys, as on the valley front of the convent of Santa Chiara. But in the continuity he sought to establish between pillar and lesene, a motif that also recurs in the courtyard of the Palazzo Luminati in Urbino, he deferred more visibly to Rossellino and to the late Gothic architecture of his native Siena. The undecorated brick technique encouraged him to emphasize the vertically ascending forces more clearly than was permitted by the orders in the courtyard of the Palazzo Ducale.

Santa Maria del Calcinaio in Cortona

In 1484/85, when he was once again mainly living in Siena, Francesco designed his last masterpiece as a shrine for a miraculous icon, the pilgrim church of Santa Maria del Calcinaio below Cortona (figs 97, 98). As already in San Bernardino, in Urbino Cathedral, or in his fortresses, he once again gave proof of his talent for placing a build-

ing in a lapidary manner in the open landscape, where it is visible from afar. He also followed Urbino Cathedral in the Latin-cross plan, drum and octagonal dome, nave proportioned almost 1:2, hemispherical chapels and barrel vault supported on an entablature that runs unbroken round the whole interior. As in San Bernardino, the pedimented aedicules, both inside and outside, stand on a narrow impost cornice. But this is now tectonically supported by lesenes which continue in an order of Ionic pilasters. As in Florence Cathedral, the upper order continues through the projection of the heavy entablature into the arches of the smooth barrel vault. Thus a continuity is created with the two orders on the opposite wall and a sequence of four gigantic arches spans and articulates the entire nave – another example of Francesco's hidden affinity with medieval architecture. The last arch ends in the crossing, where its supporting members can be recognized as square, as in Brunelleschi. This two-storeyed system is repeated in the three single bay cross-arms and in the tall octagonal drum.

The effect of the interior is, however, quite different from that of the two churches in Urbino. The tectonically active members, as in other Tuscan churches, are articulated in dark *pietra serena* and contrast with the white-stuccoed walls. The hemispherical chapels are wider than the shadow-creating *pietra serena* arches by which they are framed and thus partly lit, partly left in shadow – another example of Francesco's refined play with chiaroscuro effects. Equally original is the way he bends the profile of the archivolts and lesenes of the niches inwards at the top and bottom and thus adds tectonic emphasis to the corners of their mouldings.

The church is flooded with light from a total of eighteen windows, and yields nothing in this respect to Brunelleschi's basilicas.

97 *In 1484/85 Francesco di Giorgio designed the pilgrim church of Santa Maria del Calcinaio, near Cortona, a Latin-cross plan with octagonal dome.*

By restraining, or even abstracting the classical order, Francesco, as in San Bernardino, privileged geometrical purity of form and unbroken vertical lines at the expense of Vitruvian detail.

Again he was forced by the thickness of the wall to abandon symmetry of articulation in the cross-arms and on the exterior where these irregularities are less visible. It is all the more understandable why many architects avoided aisleless churches.

98 *As in Brunelleschi's churches, Santa Maria's interior is articulated by lines of dark* pietra serena *standing out against the whitewashed walls.*

Palazzo Comunale in Jesi

In 1486, after having returned to his hometown, Francesco di Giorgio designed a further public building, the Palazzo Comunale in Jesi. Its massive unified block is even more volumetric in effect than Rossellino's comparable bishop's palace in Pienza. The ground plan is divided into the courtyard, two side wings for ancillary rooms and two relatively steep staircases and the back part with the two aisles of its huge hall. The proportions of this hall, and its system of pillars and cross-vaults, are again reminiscent of the lower church of San Claudio near Maecerata, but it has two aisles like the audience hall of the Palazzo Vecchio in Florence; this suggests that it was originally intended for the same purpose. It was used as a salt-depot, as the Renaissance inscription over its richly decorated door proclaims.

The courtyard directly connects with the piazza front. Each side of its ground floor is framed by elegant triads of arches supported on square columns. The arches in the central bays are broader and their arches flatter, thus giving the entrance axis a quite extraordinary emphasis, even if it stops dead at the rear wall of the courtyard. The slender columns of the *piano nobile* of the courtyard were added by Andrea Sansovino only in *c.*1509. Francesco would probably have repeated the square brick columns there. The ground plan of an unexecuted project for a university building in Siena is comparable, despite differences in function.

Even earlier than Giuliano da Sangallo and Bramante, Francesco developed into one of the pioneers in fifteenth-century architecture and exerted a long-standing influence. That influence should be sought, above all, in the close correspondence – inspired both by the Gothic tradition, by Brunelleschi, Alberti and Rossellino – between interior and exterior and in the reduction of the Vitruvian orders to shallow layers of brickwork. Francesco's many-sided qualities extended to technically innovative fortifications and technical appraisals for the cathedrals of Milan and Pavia, and intensive studies of the antique, for which his various journeys through the peninsula, even into the *terra incognita* of southern Italy, provided him with several opportunities. Despite his extraordinary archaeological knowledge, his acuity in the interpretation of ancient buildings remained, however, far behind that of Giuliano da Sangallo.

The various versions and fragments of his theoretical writings date for the most part to the period after Federico's death in 1482, when he was less overloaded with commissions. He was penetrated by the teachings of Vitruvius and Alberti and tried also to derive the proportions of a building, and especially the columnar order, from the human body. A transcript of the *De re aedificatoria* is known to have been in Federico's extensive library. In the masterly drawings of his treatise Francesco introduced a broader and more complex repertoire of building types and forms than Filarete, from whom he took over the ascending hierarchy of buildings types from the simple house to palace and church: a hierarchy that Serlio, a pupil of his pupil Peruzzi, would later develop in a more exhaustive manner in his Sixth Book. In his predilection for centralized profane buildings with atrium Francesco showed his affinity with Giuliano da Sangallo, whose influence right from the start can be felt a good deal more directly than that of Alberti.

6 Bramante and Lombardy

Antonio Filarete (*c.* 1400–69)

As in Rome and Urbino, so too in the Duchy of Milan architects were mainly called from Florence to introduce the new Renaissance style. That style arrived soon after Brunelleschi's innovatory buildings: as early as 1432 Cardinal Branda Castiglioni ordered the parish church in his hometown of Castiglione d'Olona to be erected on the model of Brunelleschi's Old Sacristy. Yet eleven years previously he had held firm to the Lombard late-Gothic style in the Collegiata in the same town where he is buried next to the choir.

After he became duke of Milan in 1450, Francesco Sforza also deferred to Florence, even seeking architectural advice direct from the Medici. He called their architect Antonio Manetti Ciaccheri to his court, and commissioned the Ospedale Maggiore from another Florentine, Antonio Filarete, though Giovanni de' Medici had recommended Bernardo Rossellino instead. This charitable institution was planned on an immeasurably larger scale than Brunelleschi's foundling hospital in Florence, or even the hospital of Santo Spirito in Rome; it was intended to perpetuate the duke's magnanimity and Christian charity to future generations.

Filarete, like Michelozzo, had begun as an assistant in Ghiberti's shop. He lived in Florence until he received the commission to produce bronze doors for St Peter's in 1433. The *all'antica* architectural settings of the narrative scenes show indeed that he was a follower of Ghiberti and Donatello, but give no presentiment of the future architect.

In its rigorous symmetry, columnar arcades and tripartite entablature on the ground floor, the Ospedale Maggiore takes Brunelleschi's Spedale degli Innocenti and the courtyard of the Palazzo Medici as its models. But local tradition gained the upper hand in the detailing and the squat proportions.

Not until 1462, when the chapel of the Florentine banker Pigello Portinari was begun behind the apse of the church of Sant'Eustorgio, did Brunelleschi's vocabulary really begin to take hold in Milan. The architect, perhaps once again Filarete, followed the Old Sacristy not only in type, but also in the tectonic system of the interior, which is decorated in the most magnificent way. The influence of the local late-Gothic tradition is still manifest in the pointed traceried windows and pinnacle-crowned corner pillars of the exterior, but the classical orders dominate in the drum, lantern and even in the pinnacles themselves.

Florentine influence is also manifest in the Certosa of Pavia, the mausoleum of the dukes of Milan. As in Brunelleschi's later basilicas, the Latin-cross plan is composed of a regular grid of large and small squares. Only in 1450–73, once Francesco Sforza had come to power, did the architects Giovanni and Guiniforte Solari alter the late-Gothic project for the choir. The three cross-arms are prolonged by additional square bays, each of which opens into three semicircular chapels. Their interior follows the Gothic scheme of the nave, but their exterior is characterized by similar plastic volumes and verticalizing towers to the Cappella Portinari; it must have inspired Bramante, who placed his first *serliana* there.

Filarete's Sforzinda

Filarete met Alberti in Rome and was certainly familiar with his architectural treatise. Reacting to Alberti's ideas of the city, far removed from the Italian reality, Filarete presented his own ideal city in his *Trattato d'architettura* in 1461–64 (fig. 99). He called it *Sforzinda* (after the reigning house), and dedicated it to the duke. In this diverting combination of treatise, fiction and dialogue, he wrote in the vernacular, in a plain Italian which everyone could understand, and illustrated his text with numerous drawings. In it, the architect, clearly a self-portrait, gradually convinces the duke to build Sforzinda as his capital city. It is circular and fortified by a castle and city walls. Churches, public and private buildings, markets, hostelries, banks, even a brothel, are grouped round elongated piazzas, reminiscent of those of Santa Croce and Santa Maria Novella in Florence. Convents, hospitals and open-air theatres, on the other hand, are transferred to the outskirts. The buildings are symmetrically laid out and adorned with Vitruvian columnar orders, though Filarete was still little *au courant* with their principles. He was satisfied with the monotonous repetition of column- or pillar-borne arcades, paratactically articulated orders or the theatre motif in several storeys mechanically

99 *Antonio Filarete's architectural treatise was inspired by Alberti's example, but his ideal city of Sforzinda is more influenced by the structure and functions of contemporary towns.*

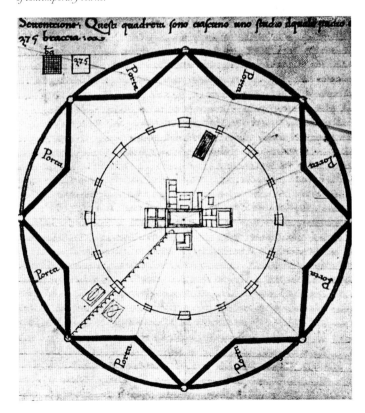

stacked on top of each other. He privileged centralized buildings. In planning them he started out from a basic grid. In his representation of the House of the Virtues he even made use of a perspectival section – all this undoubtedly in Brunelleschi's and Alberti's footsteps. But he fundamentally differed from both – as for instance when he recommended the cruciform plan for churches and not the circle of the pagan Pantheon, or gave greater importance to charitable establishments than to the evocation of ancient monumentality.

Giovanantonio Amadeo (1447–1522) and the Cappella Colleoni in Bergamo

In c.1471, long after the funerary churches and chapels of the Medici, Gonzaga, Malatesta, Rucellai and Portinari had been started, the Venetian *condottiere* Bartolomeo Colleoni also decided to erect a monument to his own piety, glory and wealth (fig. 100). Although his hometown of Bergamo was situated in Venetian territory, he chose as his architect a precocious young Milanese: the twenty-four-year-

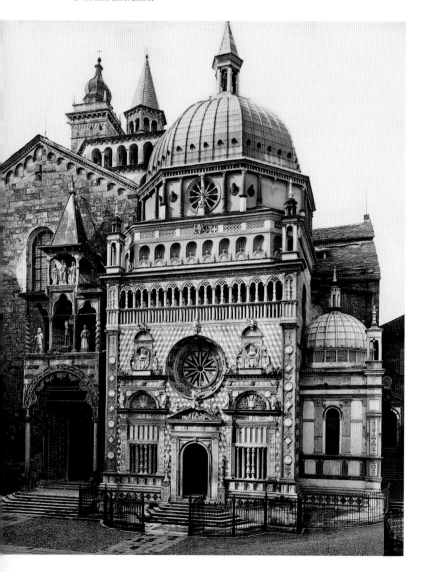

100 *The Cappella Colleone in Bergamo by Giovanantonio Amadeo, c.1471, combines the typology of Brunelleschi's Old Sacristy with Donatellian and Urbinate decoration.*

old Giovanantonio Amadeo, who was related by marriage to the Solari, the most powerful family of architects in Milan. Even as a twenty-year-old sculptor in the Certosa of Pavia Amadeo had distinguished himself as an inventive connoisseur of classicizing decorative motifs, which he had learnt from Donatello and no doubt also from Filarete.

The chapel again follows the type of Brunelleschi's Old Sacristy, and was also intended to serve as the sacristy of the neighbouring church of Santa Maria Maggiore. Colleoni, however, laid the main emphasis on the exterior and its programme, intended to perpetuate his fame. The chapel dominates its own piazza. It surpasses all previous chapels in its lavish decoration of polychrome marble incrustation.

Amadeo may have also been inspired by Donatello to flank the façade with a colossal order of over-slender pilasters and to decorate it with portrait medallions, arabesques and candelabra. He eschewed Gothic forms, reduced the Ionic capitals to scale-patterned volutes and opened the frieze in one of those high-arched galleries that had been common in Lombardy since the Middle Ages. The portal and the window-aedicules seem already influenced by the portal of San Domenico in Urbino and the ground-floor windows of the adjoining Palazzo Ducale (fig. 91). The rectangular window openings are far smaller than the framing aedicules and suggest that Amadeo had originally planned a more traditional façade and that a part of the chapel's incrustation arose only after 1476.

Amadeo's capricious, sometimes even downright humorous, fantasy was absorbed less by the Vitruvian norm than by minutiae of *all'antica* details, such as the variety of colonnettes with which he 'mullioned' the window-aedicules, the central rose window and balustraded gallery. During the following decades he would contribute decisively to the dissemination of Donatello's forms and a 'vernacular' interpretation of antiquity through Lombardy. He would become the most dangerous rival of his contemporary Bramante; indeed he would assume control of and so drastically alter two of Bramante's most important projects that they are hardly recognizable as his work.

Donato Bramante (1444–1514)

Bramante's origins are still shrouded in mystery. Born in Castel Durante in the duchy of Urbino, he could have followed at close hand the gradual growth of the Palazzo Ducale in the *capoluogo*. There he may also have come into contact with Laurana and Alberti and, as his biographers report, studied painting and especially perspective under Piero della Francesca and Fra Carnevale. Perhaps the *Miracles of St Bernardino of Siena* that formerly decorated a niche in the saint's church in Perugia are his first surviving work. The scenes with their elaborate architectural settings betray the influence of Alberti, Piero, Francesco di Giorgio and above all Fra Carnevale. Perhaps he could find no further work in Central Italy. Perhaps he was drawn to Mantua by Alberti's buildings and by Mantegna, who is also mentioned as his master, and to Milan by the Gothic cathedral, as Vasari tells.

Whatever the case, he moved to Lombardy, where he painted the façade of the Palazzo del Podestà in Bergamo, his earliest authenticated work, in c.1477. The pillars without capitals are reminiscent of

Francesco di Giorgio; the partial projection of the entablature, of Giuliano da Sangallo; the small colonnade with varying capitals in the over-high frieze, of Amadeo; and the pillars ending in brackets, of Mantegna's great altarpiece in San Zeno. These numerous stimuli are in themselves proof of the eclecticism with which he absorbed the most disparate influences.

The Prevedari engraving

In his contacts with Mantegna's *atelier*, Bramante saw how a broader public could be reached through the new technique of copperplate engraving. So he had an architectural fantasy engraved in 1481 (the so-called Prevedari engraving) (fig. 101). It permits a much more precise insight into his architectural formation than the frescoes in Bergamo.

A perspective view is opened up into a ruined building: a deep enfilade of pillared arches leads into an apse. The crossing is topped by a polygonal dome without mediating pendentives and drum. It continues in the right arm of the transept which is flanked by a lower corner room. Just enough is shown to be able to restore the 'temple'

101 *Bramante's early Prevedari engraving, in which a classical ruin is apparently used as a church, foreshadows his later architectural style.*

as a quincunx. The cross on top of the candelabrum-shaped monument in front of the crossing (with Bramante's signature on the pedestal), the kneeling monk in the foreground, and the altar in the deep apse on which the central perspective's vanishing point converges, show that the building was used as a church. But centaurs and other antique figures in the rich décor, as also its ruinous condition, imply that it had originally served for pagan purposes. Bramante could have got to know the quincunx in the Marche, in Venice and, first of all, in the little church of San Satiro in Milan, on whose enlargement he was then working (fig. 102). As late as 1521 his pupil Cesariano still reconstructed ancient temples in the form of a quincunx in his commentary on Vitruvius. Bramante too must have seen in it a type of the ancient temple.

This type of an interior space hierarchically ascending from the chapels through the arms of the cross to the dominating central dome was far more compatible with Christian liturgy than the circular or deep rectangular *cella* of the Vitruvian temple and corresponded so exactly to Bramante's spatial ideas that he raised it to the leitmotif of his whole oeuvre. By this emblematic transformation of a pagan temple into a church he sought to fuse the ancient and the Christian traditions.

The round windows and ribs of the dome are reminiscent of Brunelleschi (figs 9, 11, 17). Other aspects of the print, the square crossing, the rosette-decorated arches and the deep apse with shell niche, betray the influence of Piero della Francesca's *Pala di Montefeltro* (painted, we recall, for San Bernardino in Urbino). In the squat pillars, their narrow entablature-shaped impost cornice or the two-part capital type of the pilasters, Bramante's familiarity with the repertoire of Francesco di Giorgio can be felt (figs 93, 94), while in the lavish figural decoration he may already have drawn inspiration from the courtyard of the Palazzo Scala (fig. 70). Lastly, the figures reveal the influence of Mantegna, while the wheel-window, central baluster, *oculi* piercing the groined vaulting and over-lavish décor reflect his indebtedness to Amadeo and the Milanese Early Renaissance. The high viewpoint, the asymmetrical section and the distribution of the figures in space are anticipated in *St Bernardino's Miracle of the Stillborn Child*. But direct citations from the antique can hardly be identified.

Thus the many sources from which Bramante drew in Bergamo four years previously are now further enriched with the quincunx. In this print Bramante proved himself a visionary of expanding spaces and founded a new tradition of spatial representation.

Santa Maria presso San Satiro

A few months later Bramante proceeded to enlarge a chapel, which he himself had erected as a shrine for a miracle-working icon, into what was to be his first church (figs 102–4). In its Latin-cross plan, square crossing, barrel-vaulted nave and semicircular chapels he followed the model of Urbino Cathedral (fig. 93). He even anticipated the Madonna del Calcinaio in the continuation of the entablature-projected pilasters into the transverse arches (fig. 97). He formed the pillars of the arcades into a separate order, in the way that Alberti had already done in Sant'Andrea. In the *all'antica* coffering of the barrel vault and the hemispherical dome raised over a high entablature and lit by windows cut into the lowest row of its coffers, he also came far closer to Sant'Andrea than in the Prevedari engraving. The spatial constraints of the site (abruptly curtailed by a street to the rear) inspired him to a design that makes the church unique in Renaissance architecture and produces the convincing illusion of a third cross-arm forming the chancel. It hardly projects beyond the rear façade but is sufficient for three ingeniously foreshortened arches and seven equally foreshortened rows of coffers in the barrel vault. At the same time he made the vanishing point coincide with the Holy Sacrament on the altar (just as Raphael would do in the *Disputa*). He replaced the aisles with niches on the choir wall of the transepts. In this way he was able not only to elongate the nave, but also to link the left arm of the cross axially with the adjoining Carolingian chapel of San Satiro. In the shell niches, with which he surrounded the whole interior, as also in the asymmetrically angled corner pilasters, he showed again his close knowledge of Brunelleschi's buildings.

102–5 *The church of Santa Maria presso San Satiro, Milan, was commissioned from Bramante as an extension of the tiny Carolingian chapel (below right), which he transformed into a rotunda and attached to the transept of the new church, as shown on the plan. The cramped site, however, meant that there was no room for a chancel (top of plan) since the Via del Falcone ran past its east end (below). So Bramante cleverly supplied one in* trompe-l'oeil *(opposite) which from the nave gives a convincing impression of a whole fourth arm of a cruciform church.*

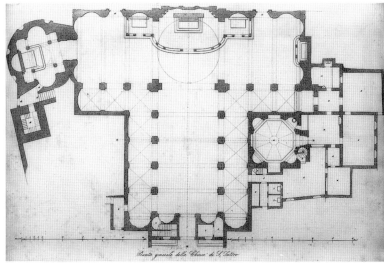

Like the façades of Sant'Andrea and Urbino Cathedral, the impressive rear façade prepares the visitor for the interior. Its central pedimented temple-front (one shaft-width deep) represents the central cross-arm and the flanking colossal order, the four quadrangular pillars of the crossing. The miniature pilasters of the small order mirror that of the nave and transepts. They alternate with blind panels in rapid rhythm at the centre of the façade, but in the side bays corresponding to the transepts the rhythm is slackened. Inspired by ancient triumphal arches, Bramante reinforced the corners by preparatory half-pilasters and pilaster triads, with the entablature projected over them. The rear façade, in its volumetric outward projection and condensed and dynamic articulation, surpasses any earlier Renaissance architecture. Its direct correspondence with the interior seems to be directly influenced by Gothic examples. Bramante combined it, however, with the single-storeyed character of the ancient temple and, in its complex rhythms, went beyond even Sant'Andrea. As in so many of his later buildings, he balanced the vertical forces of the colossal order in the dominating centre with the horizontal forces of the transepts. As in the Prevedari engraving, his detailing is not yet bound by Vitruvian norms: he elongated the Corinthian capitals with a cornucopia-decorated neck, provided the upper fasciae of the architrave (as in some antique prototypes) with egg-and-dart orna-

106 *Bramante articulates the octagonal sacristy of Santa Maria presso San Satiro with alternating niches and a verticalizing order which continues into the Lombard gallery and the ribs of the cupola.*

ment, exaggerated the height of the frieze, and enlivened it with decorative panels.

Bramante also transformed the exterior of the adjacent Carolingian quincunx of San Satiro into a rotunda. Its components hierarchically ascend from the cylinder of the ground floor to the broken gables of the attic, the octagonal *tiburio* and the tapering lantern. In the contrasting volumes of the two churches, Bramante showed the same scenographic ingenuity as the Prevedari engraving: the church and its circular *tiburio* are thus contrasted with the rotunda and its polygonal *tiburio*.

Bramante also plays with rhythms in both storeys of the adjacent sacristy (fig. 106). He evidently followed early Christian prototypes in its steep octagon and its diagonal semicircular niches. They alternate with rectangular niches and their pillars are once again topped by a complete entablature that runs round the entire octagon. The niches are combined, as in the transept, with the pilaster order to form theatre motifs. The pilasters are richly decorated and angled in the corners of the octagon. They are continued through the projecting entablature and the miniature order of the gallery into the rib-like strips between the panelling of the dome, whose lower *oculi* are pierced like the vault in the Prevedari engraving.

In this vertical thrust and rigorous tectonic system Bramante comes even closer to the Gothic. In the gallery the heavy entablature is supported by squat pilasters which alternate with abstract panels and volutes. Bramante follows here Vitruvian norms far less than either Brunelleschi or Alberti, but uses the antique forms far more tectonically than Amadeo. The frieze is magnificently decorated with oblong terracotta medallions and mythological scenes, as in the courtyard of Giuliano's Palazzo Scala.

Pavia Cathedral

The success of Santa Maria presso San Satiro must have prompted Cardinal Ascanio Sforza, the brother of Lodovico il Moro, to commission Bramante to design his episcopal church in Pavia in 1487/88 (figs 107–9). The Pavians wanted a building modelled on Hagia Sophia in Constantinople, and indeed some of the elements of the cathedral executed under Bramante, such as the vault of the crypt or the two-storeyed pillars of the octagonal crossing under the dome, come extraordinarily close to that model. Bramante must have seen elevations of Hagia Sophia like those present in Giuliano da Sangallo's Codex Barberini, and presumably also envisaged a round dome.

A domed crossing flanked by exedrae in the longitudinal axis as in Hagia Sophia would have been unsuitable for the functional demands of a modern cathedral; it would also have contradicted Bramante's spatial conceptions. He therefore fused the prototype of Hagia Sophia with that of the basilica of Loreto. Like Brunelleschi in Santo Spirito, he surrounded the nave and the three arms of the cross with semicircular chapels, which similarly intersect each other in the corners.

He showed himself once again a master of flexible rhythms by the way he decorated the pillars of the interior with bundled and overlapping pilasters of a Corinthian order, like bundled Gothic piers, and connected them with corresponding pilasters on the opposite piers. In the detail of the order he comes far closer to the antique than in his previous buildings.

107–9 *Bramante's design for Pavia Cathedral (exterior reconstructed above) was inspired by both Gothic cathedrals and Hagia Sophia in Constantinople. It was modified by Amadeo who succeeded him in 1495. In Bramante's pillars and crypt (above right) the Byzantine prototype is still recognizable.*

Just as the interior was to ascend from the chapels and transepts to the light-filled dome, so Bramante planned the exterior as a hierarchical sequence rising from the cylindrical and hemispherical volumes of the chapels, sacristies and apses to the pedimented arms of the cross and the central dome – a complex, spatially expansive organism branching out in all directions that would not find its congenial follow-up until Bramante's projects for St Peter's. This fusion of Byzantine and Gothic elements with the heritage of Brunelleschi and Alberti made Bramante the most progressive architect of his time.

In 1495, when the crypt was finished and the area of the dome and choir had barely risen above the entablature of the lower order, Bramante was supplanted by Amadeo. As on the façade of the Colleoni Chapel, Amadeo decided to open up the frieze zones of the entablatures into high galleries and to articulate the brick exterior in the Lombard style with rhythmically ascending buttresses, volutes, pinnacles, gables and an octagonal dome over a high two-storeyed drum.

Santa Maria delle Grazie in Milan and Leonardo's centralized building projects

In *c*.1492, during his period of activity in Pavia, Bramante received the commission to transform the choir of the late-Gothic Dominican church of Santa Maria delle Grazie, built by the Solari, into a mausoleum for the duke of Milan, Lodovico Sforza, and his wife, Beatrice d'Este (fig. 110). With its semicircular chapels the new crossing seems inspired by the cross-arms of the Certosa, but it now has the same breadth as the whole nave and is continued into the deep chancel. The choir thus achieves a monumentality akin to that to which Alberti must have aspired in the rotunda of the Tempio Malatestiano (fig. 39). The triumphal elevation was once again based on Brunelleschi's Old Sacristy and, as in the crossing of Brunelleschi's basilicas, the slender Corinthian order continues through the projecting entablature into the arches. The wheel-like roundels painted on the extrados of the chancel arch are a kind of playful homage to Brunelleschi, multiplying the lunette-windows of the Old Sacristy (fig. 11). They confer on the earlier master's repetition of the circle a new, more dynamic and playful quality which is continued in the ascending roundels of the dome.

The foundation stone was laid on 29 March 1492. But the building was soon removed from Bramante's control and transferred by

110 *Interior of Santa Maria delle Grazie, Milan, begun by Bramante in 1492 but finished by Amadeo.*

111, 112 *Sketches by Leonardo da Vinci for centralized domed churches were the result of an intense dialogue with his friend Bramante, who knew him in Milan since the 1480s.*

the duke to Amadeo, who was to place his unmistakable Lombard stamp on the executed building, both outside and in the drum and details of the interior.

Bramante's project for the exterior of Santa Maria delle Grazie must have resembled Leonardo's contemporary projects for domed central-plan churches (figs 111, 112). It is possible, therefore, that he envisaged a hemispherical dome for the exterior and a colossal order for its four supporting pillars.

Leonardo had arrived in Milan only in 1483. So he must have seen Giuliano da Sangallo's first Florentine buildings and been stimulated by Bramante to produce his own projects, perhaps also for Pavia Cathedral and Santa Maria delle Grazie. Translating the plasticity of Florence Cathedral into Bramante's language, he reinforced the corners with pilaster triads, combined large and small orders, lent far more emphasis to the vertical continuity of the members than Brunelleschi, Alberti or Giuliano, and even occasionally recurred to the quincunx. At the same time he held fast to archaisms such as the Gothic *bifora*-windows, which never appear in Bramante. Only several years later would Leonardo experiment with interiors; like Bramante, he let the individual spatial cells grow out of each other.

Bramante, in turn, seems to have been influenced by Leonardo's sculptural moulding of the exteriors of buildings; Leonardo may even have drawn his own project for Pavia Cathedral. Indeed the influence of Leonardo's unexecuted projects was to persist. It can still be felt in Battagio's Santa Maria della Croce in Crema, in the cathedral choir in distant Sebenico, in the central-plan Santa Maria

della Consolazione in Todi (fig. 134), or in Bramante's centralized project for St Peter's (fig. 143).

The cloisters of Sant'Ambrogio in Milan and the triumphal arch of Abbiategrasso

In the Canonica, the canons' residence of Sant'Ambrogio, begun in *c.*1492, Bramante combined a cloister with the canons' cells and an atrium that provides access to the medieval church (figs 113, 114). In this he followed the model of Michelozzo's atrium in front of the Santissima Annunziata and especially Giuliano da Sangallo's atrium in front of Santa Maria Maddalena dei Pazzi (fig. 82). After Lorenzo's death in 1492, Giuliano had come to Milan, in order to win the patronage of Lodovico il Moro with a palace model and hence as a potential rival and may have shown his drawings to Bramante. It is also possible that Bramante revisited Florence shortly before.

Much more intensely than in the central arches of Giuliano's colonnades, but in a way similar to the rear façade of Santa Maria presso San Satiro, Bramante emphasized the hierarchical dominance of the entrance bay by a colossal order. Its entablature, on which the windows of the cells of the canons were to rest, would have run above the arcades as in Brunelleschi's basilicas and the columns are also provided with fragments of a tripartite entablature (figs 11, 18).

113, 114 *Bramante began the Canonica of Sant'Ambrogio, Milan, a combination of an atrium and a cloister, about 1492. The large central arch gives access to the church. Far right: one of the corner columns imitating the knots of a tree trunk.*

115 *Bramante's portal of Santa Maria Nascente at Abbiategrasso, commissioned by Ludovico il Moro before 1497.*

On the other hand, Bramante showed himself a pupil of Francesco di Giorgio by the thin outward-projecting layer of brickwork that ascends from the entrance arch to the terminating upper cornice, further underlining the predomination of this triumphal arch at the centre of the portico. Bramante still holds firm here to Alberti's simplified version of the Corinthian capital and to Francesco di Giorgio's two-part version of its decorated neck (figs 45, 94), but varies it like Giuliano in the contemporary courtyard of the Palazzo Gondi (fig. 84). The knobbed shafts of the corner columns, intended to look like knotted trees – actually an ancient conceit described by Alberti (Book IX, c.1) – allude to the Sforza.

Even more monumental and sumptuous in decoration is the arch of the portal of Santa Maria Nascente in Abbiategrasso (fig. 115). It was commissioned by Lodovico il Moro and the date 1497 is inscribed in the lower storey. Once again Bramante surrounded the atrium with squat arcades and provided it with an even more dominating central triumphal arch. Here it is a deep Corinthian porch as in Alberti's Sant'Andrea. The large barrel vault of the porch rests on paired columns on two storeys. Even more organically than in the rear façade of Santa Maria presso San Satiro (fig. 102) and in the entrance arcade of the Canonica, the horizontal movement of the small order gives way to the vertical movement of the large arch. A similar tendency can also be detected in the painted triumphal arch that links the three arches at the entrance to the central piazza of Vigevano.

In the arch of Abbiategrasso the influence of Giuliano da Sangallo can be felt in Bramante's new predilection for the column. Giuliano may also have inspired him for his only Milanese colonnade with straight entablature, the *ponticella* of the Castello Sforzesco, which he erected over an old bridge in c.1495.

Bramante seems even to have been familiar with Giuliano's Urbino panel (fig. 73): so much is suggested by the engraving of his perspective stage set of a scene (fig. 116). It is the first known stage set in central perspective and Bramante may have designed it for the production of a comedy at the Milanese court. Like later Renaissance stage sets, it is divided into a shallow forestage, a foreshortened but accessible area flanked by two palaces and a painted backdrop with a

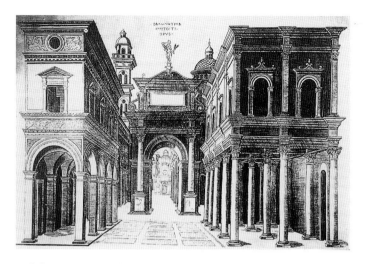

116 *Perspective stage set by Bramante, probably for a Milanese court comedy.*

triumphal arch, churches and bell-tower. As in the Urbino panel, one palace opens in a colonnade, the other in pillared arcades. Even the church façade is similar. The detail is, however, much less Vitruvian and Bramante's predilection for projecting entablatures and vertical continuity is very different from the calculated balance of Giuliano's buildings.

In 1497, once again on commission from Ascanio Sforza, Bramante designed the two cloisters of the Cistercian monastery adjacent to Sant'Ambrogio in Milan in 1497 (fig. 117). But their construction in large part postdates his removal to Rome. As already in the Canonica, he followed Brunelleschi by placing entablature fragments above the columns and thus completing the order in the Vitruvian manner. Though it is difficult to recognize Bramante's hand in the capitals, much suggests that he had already planned one Doric and one Ionic cloister and thus came a step closer to Giuliano's more classicizing language. Bramante replaced the round columns at the corners with quadrangular ones, as Giuliano had done in the atrium of Santa Maria Maddalena dei Pazzi (fig. 82). Bramante may even have derived inspiration from Giuliano's drawing of the Crypta Balbi for the blind theatre motifs of the upper storeys of both cloisters. So it was through Giuliano's mediation, and only a few years before the Tempietto in Rome (fig. 137), that he drew closer to the Vitruvian orders.

Bramante's contribution to Lombard secular architecture has still largely to be elucidated. The Palazzo Beccaria in Pavia is undoubtedly reminiscent of the one palace of Bramante's design for a stage set and clearly derives from a master in his circle. With its two storeys articulated with orders, it follows a type that perhaps Fancelli had already introduced into Mantua. It would later spread over wide parts of Lombardy, Emilia and Romagna and find its most magnificent form in the Palazzo dei Diamanti and Palazzo Costabili which were built as part of Ferrara's expansion under Ercole d'Este (the *Addizione Erculea*) after 1492. In the pilaster-flanked diamond-pointed rustication – the diamond was a symbol of the Este family – of the façade of the Palazzo dei Diamanti the influence of Francesco di Giorgio can also be felt, while the columnar arcades of the Palazzo Costabili and especially its corner solution are reminiscent of Pontelli's cloister of Santa Maria delle Grazie in Sinigallia.

During his two decades' activity in Lombardy Bramante experimented with the most varied types and formats and altered them according to his own quite unique and inimitable ideas. His influence on Lombard masters can especially be felt in the buildings of the highly talented Giovanni Battagio. An early admirer of Bramante in Lombardy, Battagio had derived inspiration since 1488/89 from the sacristy of Santa Maria presso San Satiro and no doubt from Leonardo's projects for the central-plan buildings of the Incoronata in Lodi, Santa Maria della Passione in Milan and Santa Maria della Croce in Crema, though without repudiating his Lombard identity.

Bramante's influence is also unmistakable in the order of the ground floor of the Palazzo della Loggia in Brescia, executed after 1492, with three corner pilasters and two-part capitals. In type and in its projecting full columns this façade follows, on the other hand, the Palazzo del Podestà in Bologna.

Yet it was not until the emergence of Cristoforo Solari (*c*.1468–1524) that Bramante found a genuine disciple in Lombardy. Solari's datable buildings, however, fall into the period after the turn of the century and already presuppose knowledge of Bramante's Roman buildings. Cristoforo may have executed both of the cloisters at Sant'Ambrogio and formed the capitals in a yet more *all'antica* way than Bramante had planned.

117 *Bramante designed two cloisters for the Cistercian abbey of Sant'Ambrogio in Milan, one Doric, the other (below) Ionic.*

7 The Venetian Early Renaissance

Venice, the centre of the richest, most expansionist and best-governed Italian state, had for much of the Quattrocento remained attached to the Gothic style more wholeheartedly than other Italian cities. Thanks to its wise policy, it could long dispense with the kind of bristling domestic fortifications behind which the nobility and the rich in other Italian city-states continued to immure themselves. The Palazzo Ducale and the palaces of the patricians of Venice, facing directly onto the canals, were opened up with ever-larger windows and loggias. Their marble columnar arcades, often on two or three storeys, were enriched with ever more elaborate traceries, as in the lavish façades of the Ca' d'Oro or the Ca' Foscari. But although Venetian patricians had appealed to their Roman roots as early as the thirteenth century, the Doge's Palace with its double arcade continued to exert its influence on palace architecture well into the late fifteenth century: in this centre of republican power the city's medieval identity still reigned supreme. In 1438 Giovanni and Bartolommeo Bon had built the Porta della Carta in Gothic forms. But when Bartolommeo designed the Arco dei Foscari some years later, he eschewed Gothic and was inspired instead by the façade of San Marco. He thus approached the Renaissance, and mediated the rediscovery of classical antiquity, through pre-Gothic forms in a way rather similar to Brunelleschi in Florence. It was only in the Ca' del Duca on the Grand Canal that the Corner brothers began to respond to the Central Italian prototypes of the Early Renaissance style: the column-supported loggia was to be flanked by towers with giant corner columns and diamond-pointed rustication, as in Francesco Sforza's castle in Milan. Neither the architect of the Ca' del Duca, nor that of the roughly contemporary triumphal arch of the Arsenal Gate, is known. The arch was begun in 1457. Its paired Corinthian columns, projecting entablature and pedimented attic seem already influenced by the arch of the Castel Nuovo in Naples and come even closer to the common prototype, the Roman arch in Pola.

Mauro Codussi (*c.*1440–1504)

San Michele in Isola and San Zaccaria

Not until the arrival of an outsider, Mauro Codussi, who came from the area of Bergamo, did Venice acquire an architect perfectly familiar with the most recent developments in Italian architecture, from Lombardy to Naples. Codussi embraced the new ideas with a sure instinct. The influence of Michelozzo, Alberti and Rossellino is thus predominant in his façade for San Michele (on the island of Murano). After San Marco, it is the first Venetian façade to be entirely clad in marble (fig. 118). Begun in *c.*1468, its orders reflect the structure of the basilica interior, as slightly later in Santa Maria del Popolo in Rome. As in the Palazzo Piccolomini in Pienza (fig. 62), the pilasters of the ground-floor order are incorporated in the ashlars. But these are now cut of precious marble and their alternating sequence of shorter and longer blocks is completely regular. The capitals of the pilasters are adorned with fluted Ionic capitals and their projecting

entablature with an inscription. The line of the pilasters breaks through the entablature into the squat upper order with another inscription and thence into a semicircular pediment. Codussi knew all these features from the tabernacle of San Miniato (fig. 33) and from the façade of San Francesco in Rimini (fig. 40). The richly fluted decoration of the pediment is echoed in the quarter segments that conceal the roofs of the aisles. The way that these half-gables intersect the quadrangular corner columns is still reminiscent of the Frari and Santi Giovanni e Paolo, the two Venetian churches of the Mendicant Orders. Justifiably the patron of this façade could hail it as the first in Venice to be built in the antique style.

Even more elaborate, though similar in scheme, is the façade of San Zaccaria, the completion of which Codussi took in hand fifteen years later. Codussi was constrained by the squatness, narrow bays and four projecting pillars of the pre-existing ground floor. He continued it ingeniously in an equally low storey, which he exclusively articulated by a continuous row of slender shell-niches, topped by an entablature and projected outwards above the pillars. Only in the side bays are two of these niches pierced to form windows. In the three upper storeys Codussi already showed his indebtedness to Bramante's sacristy of Santa Maria presso San Satiro and the arch of Abbiategrasso (figs 106, 115). He transformed the pilasters of the niches into a Corinthian order and combined its pilasters with the windows to form steep theatre motifs. Above the pillars the pilasters become paired columns. As in the gallery of Bramante's sacristy, the

118 *Mauro Codussi's San Michele in Isola, begun about 1468, was the first Venetian church to be fully alive to the Renaissance.*

abbreviated entablature of the lower fourth storey is supported by abstract panels that permitted him to incorporate the lateral half-gables into the façade system more organically than in San Michele. In the simple alternation of arches with paired columns of the equally squat fifth storey, the only one whose bays exactly correspond in width to those of the storey below, he comes closest to the Palazzo Loredan (fig. 121). The vertical thrust of the central pillars ends in the semicircular pediment, a more classicizing variant of that of San Michele (fig. 118). The evidence suggests that the façade must have taken several decades to complete.

San Giovanni Crisostomo

In the early 1490s Codussi and his patrons also began to reflect on Venice's architectural origins. Perhaps inspired by Bramante's Prevedari engraving and the churches in Pistoia and Orciano di Pesaro (fig. 124) (on which see below) he recurred to the quincunx. He, like Bramante, must have understood its system as that of the ancient temple.

Condussi adopted the domed quincunx scheme, in a version congenial to Venice, in the church of San Giovanni Crisostomo, begun in 1497. There he could have supported the vaults, as in San Giacomo al Rialto, his medieval prototype, with four massive columns and given them added tectonic force, as in the church of Orciano, by topping them with entablature fragments. But instead he preferred to adopt as his model the undecorated system of the crossing of Urbino Cathedral (fig. 93) and the Madonna del Calcinaio in Cortona (fig. 97).

119, 120 *Codussi's later church of San Giovanni Crisostomo, 1497, uses a domed quincunx plan, though the façade (right) follows the model of San Michele.*

As there, there are two superimposed orders. The lower one consists of slender square columns with bases and pedestals but without capitals. From this lower order also spring the small arches opening into the domed side chapels. The smaller upper order, supporting the arches of the dome, by contrast, has no bases but is topped by Corinthian capitals and projections of the surrounding entablature. The detailing of the orders thus contradicts the tectonic thinking of Francesco di Giorgio. The correspondence of the façades with the interior, however, is wholly in the spirit of Francesco. The main façade resembles in type that of San Michele in Isola; the curving archivolts of the half-gables intersect the quadrangular corner columns in a similar way.

Palazzo Lando and Palazzo Loredan-Vendramin

In the Venetian palaces of some more progressive patricians Codussi succeeded in introducing the new style even more rapidly than in Florence or Rome. He thus limited the plain rustication on the façade of the Palazzo Lando, as in the Palazzo Calusi in Siena, to the subservient ground floor (containing the service areas) and flanked it with orders (fig. 122). They continue in the two upper storeys, forming continuous vertical strips. The syncopated rhythm of the windows on the ground floor and the form of their frames seem inspired by the Palazzo Ducale in Urbino, as also does the fusing of the entablature with the pedestal zone of the pilasters. The connection of the entablature with the balustrades, on the other hand, is reminiscent of the courtyard of the Palazzo Strozzi. In the balustrades of the later and more progressive Palazzo Loredan-Vendramin, Codussi used

archaic colonnettes, and since comparable convex outward-curving balustrades cannot be substantiated elsewhere in Italy before a project of Sangallo for the Palazzo Farnese in 1514, they may be later in date. Even in the monumental paired *bifora*-windows Codussi drew on Central Italian and not Venetian prototypes, such as Michelozzo's oratory of the Santissima Annunziata in Florence; only in the trefoils does a vestigial echo of Venetian Gothic ornament survive.

Only shortly before his death did Codussi begin, though not complete, his masterpiece: the Palazzo Loredan (fig. 121). Like Bramante in his last Milanese buildings, and perhaps even encouraged by Bramante's Palazzo Caprini in Rome (fig. 136), he raised the columns into the most important decorative element of the façade. The ground floor is squat and articulated by a modest order of pilasters. But in the two upper storeys the pilasters become full columns, a luxury anticipated only by the triumphal arch of Naples (fig. 57). In the *piano nobile* the columns are also fluted, raised over a pedestal, and set behind a balustrade, so that this floor is even more clearly predominant than in the Palazzo Lando. The high entablature of the top floor, whose widely outward-projecting cornice is decorated, as in the Palazzo Medici, with dentils, egg-and-dart and consoles, is clearly related to the whole façade.

All three storeys now follow the same rhythm, and to this vertical hierarchy a horizontal one corresponds. So the three central arches, still filled in the traditional manner with paired *bifore*, are only divided by a single column, while the corners are flanked with paired columns – an ingenious translation of the Venetian façade type into Bramante's new language. Codussi now eliminated every Gothic

detail and already prepared the way for the three-dimensional corner solution of Sansovino's Libreria. In the beauty of the over-slender marble columns, their magnificent detail, polychrome marbles and trophy-like décor, he followed tendencies similar to Giuliano da Sangallo. The capital-shaped consoles of the upper storey conform to the narrow rhythm of Vitruvian intercolumniations; they are reminiscent of Giuliano as also are those of Santa Maria dei Miracoli.

The influence of Bramante's arch in Abbiategrasso can also be felt in the paired columns of the staircase of San Giovanni Evangelista. Francesco di Giorgio's projects may have inspired him in the two-ramped type. Thus Codussi is remarkable for the eagerness with which he embraced every innovation, integrated it into his own architectural repertoire and transfused it into the Venetian tradition.

Pietro Lombardi (*c*.1435–1515) and Santa Maria dei Miracoli

The name of another leading architect tells us that he too came from Lombardy. In *c*.1481 Pietro began to erect a magnificent church for a convent of nuns over a miraculous image of the Madonna (fig. 123). It is the one church of the Venetian Quattrocento whose splendour

123 *Pietro Lombardi's church of Santa Maria dei Miracoli, begun about 1481, exemplifies the Venetian fusion of local styles with those of Lombardy and Central Italy.*

can withstand comparison with that of palaces of the period. Like Codussi, Pietro had worked as an assistant in the Palazzo Ducale in Urbino and started out from Florentine prototypes in his Venetian funerary monuments. The stereometric block-like character of his only church, Santa Maria dei Miracoli, a plain oblong box, its surrounding orders and the correspondence of the hemispherical pediment with the wooden barrel vault of the single nave, and of the blind arches of the choir with its lunettes, presuppose again Central Italian prototypes. As in the Roman Ospedale di Santo Spirito or in Pontelli's Sant'Aurea in Ostia, not just the façade, but the whole exterior is articulated by orders. As on the Florentine Baptistery, the presumptive Temple of Mars and Brunelleschi's most important source of inspiration (fig. 1), the lower storey is articulated by a pilaster order, from which the portal projects; as there, the order continues through the pronounced horizontal caesura of the entablature into the blind arcade of the upper storey; and as there, the upper storey ends with a robust surrounding entablature from which the monumental semicircular pediment rises. Even the large panels of marble incrustation and surface patterning with tondi and cruciform ornaments are reminiscent of Florentine incrustation. The magnificent capitals recall Giuliano da Sangallo (figs 76, 84).

Though the marble-panelled incrustation of the nave echoes that on the exterior, the correspondence is less exact than in Codussi's churches. The nave is also less organically connected with the altar chapel. A central flight of steps leads up to the sanctuary and high altar, distinguished, as so often in Venice, by its autonomous position and its hemispherical dome.

Thus Pietro Lombardi was less intent on tectonic coherence than Codussi, but superior in the lavish décor of his wall surfaces – also magnificently displayed in the entrance arch of the Scuola di San Giovanni Evangelista.

In another masterpiece, the façade of the Scuola di San Marco, one of the most powerful of these charitable confraternities so typical of Venice, Pietro used the scheme of the preceding church façades, but gave it steeper proportions and added a third floor. In the aedicules on the first floor, on the other hand, he recurred to prototypes he had seen in Urbino and in the marble-encrusted perspective arcades on the ground floor even derived inspiration from the choir of Santa Maria presso San Satiro.

The architecture of the Venetian Early Renaissance was thus developed from the fusion of the local tradition with the most varied prototypes of Central Italy and Bramante's Milanese works. In each of the larger buildings, secular or religious, this fusion took place in a different way. And since the patrons who commissioned them could hardly claim such comparably broad and detailed knowledge of contemporary developments in architecture, the decision regarding what sources to draw on must largely have been left to the two masters to whom the Venetian Early Renaissance is most heavily indebted. Clearly they were more open to outside influences than native Venetians. But they were also creative in their assimilation of the native Venetian tradition. They thus helped the city to achieve a new architectural identity, in a way that is scarcely paralleled elsewhere in Italy outside Florence, Rome or Milan – neither in Turin, Ferrara, Bologna, nor in Naples, Palermo and the smaller towns.

8 Architecture under Innocent VIII and Alexander VI

Baccio Pontelli (1449–before 1500)

The religious architecture of Sixtus IV in Rome, in spite of all its formal shortcomings, had been distinguished by a greater variety in type than in most other centres. A good deal more monotonous and slower was the development of secular architecture. This was mainly represented in Rome by the palaces of Sixtus IV's nephews, who imitated and varied, but never really equalled, the Palazzo Venezia. This situation did not change until the arrival on the scene of Baccio Pontelli, active in Rome since roughly 1480. Like the slightly older Giuliano da Sangallo, he had only gradually found his way to architecture. From 1478 to 1482 he was working as the most trusted assistant of Francesco di Giorgio in Urbino and absorbed much of his architectural language. Yet at the same time he preserved his Florentine identity, and in some of his own *tarsie* in the Palazzo Ducale he came astonishingly close to the architectural perspectives in the panels in Berlin und Urbino (figs 72, 73).

Santa Maria in Orciano di Pesaro

Pontelli's first datable commissions came from the brother of Cardinal Giuliano della Rovere, Giovanni, son-in-law of the duke of Urbino and lord of Sinigallia. For him he erected the Marian church

124 *Baccio Pontelli: interior of Santa Maria in Orciano di Pesaro, 1482, a domed quincunx.*

of Orciano near Senigallia in 1482 (fig. 124). The church is a domed quincunx in type. The drum and the dome rest on columnar arches, as in the medieval San Giacomo al Rialto, and not on pillars as in Bramante's Prevedari engraving (fig. 101). Even the rectangular ground plan and the three chapels on either side are reminiscent of San Giacomo. Though the dome in Orciano is illuminated by a low drum with four round windows, it seems that the system of the crossing was also prepared by the domed area of San Bernardino outside Urbino (fig. 95); its corner pillars likewise stand on tall pedestals and its arches similarly intersect each other. The detail too is close to Francesco di Giorgio and resembles that of the *stufetta* of the Palazzo Ducale in Urbino. A good deal richer are the trophy-decorated pilasters of the chapels, and especially the side portal of the unfinished façade. In this portal Pontelli surpassed in magnificence the portals of the Palazzo Ducale and prepared the way for his Roman portals. Only in the pilasters, which mirror the Doric columns, may have been inspired by his countryman Giuliano da Sangallo.

The repertoire of forms of the Palazzo Ducale in Urbino also lives on in the Rocca of Sinigallia and in the adjacent convent of Santa Maria delle Grazie, which Pontelli erected as a funerary church for Giovanni della Rovere during the same period.

Sant'Aurea in Ostia and San Pietro in Montorio

Shortly afterwards Pontelli was commissioned by Cardinal Giuliano della Rovere to complete the Rocca in Ostia and erect its nearby episcopal church (fig. 126). Under the powerful impression made on him by the ancient monuments of Rome, Pontelli, in the design of this church, now liberated himself from the influence of Francesco di Giorgio, and sought more direct inspiration from ancient prototypes such as the so-called temple of the Dio Redicolo. As in ancient temples, and already in the Ospedale di Santo Spirito (fig. 68), the Corinthian pilasters correspond to the beams of the open roof truss, and the pediment, to the ridged roof. Also in the high pedestals, powerful pilaster shafts, capitals of Albertian type, non-projecting entablature, or the window arches reinforced with traceries, he comes closer to the Roman school than to Francesco di Giorgio.

The portal of the fortress, which he even signed, as also the related portals of the convent of Grottaferrata and of the Vatican Palace (now lost), still betray, however, their origin in the Palazzo Ducale in Urbino. Both the portal of Grottaferrata and the pedestals of Sant'Aurea are adorned with similar trophies as in the church of Orciano, whose dissemination in Rome is above all attributable to Pontelli.

Pontelli's apprenticeship to Francesco di Giorgio is especially unmistakable in the exterior of the Franciscan church of San Pietro in Montorio (figs 127, 128). He must have taken over as architect of the building in *c.*1488, after the Spanish royal house had promised to finance a more expensive building. But by the time he left Rome in the spring of 1492 not even the capitals were being carved, for their pomegranate emblems allude to the Battle of Granada and the expulsion of the Moors from Spain in 1493.

The aisleless nave and the chancel, for which a flat wooden ceiling may originally have been planned, were entirely remodelled by Pontelli. He furnished them with cupola-like groin vaults placed a saucer dome over the crossing and half an umbrella dome over the polygonal apse; this succession of domical bays vaguely recalls Francesco di Giorgio's early Osservanza church in Siena (fig. 90). As there, but in contrast to Roman churches, the individual bays are separated by powerful pilasters of a Corinthian order, which are continued above

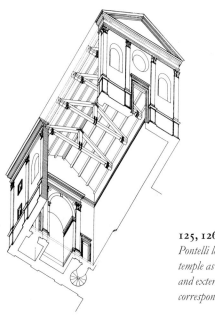

125, 126 In Sant'Aurea in Ostia Pontelli looked to the ancient Roman temple as a prototype: axonometric and exterior. Note how the pilasters correspond to the beams of the roof.

the projecting entablature into the transverse arches and doubled in the crossing. The two bays of the nave are each divided into two parts, as in the Osservanza and Sant'Agostino in Rome. Even the relatively flat pilasters that separate the hemispherical chapels have entablature projections above them – necessarily so, as the entablature is flush with the wall as in Cortona (fig. 97). In this highly unusual differentiation between more powerful and narrower pilasters Pontelli may also have derived inspiration from the upper storey of the courtyard of the Palazzo Ducale in Urbino (fig. 92). Even the problematic miniature order of the impost zone may go back to Pontelli, although the possibility cannot be excluded that he wanted to lower the imposts to the entablature as in many churches of the Roman Quattrocento (fig. 67). The lighting through the rose window and the lunettes was originally supplemented with windows in both exedrae of the transept.

The exterior forms a foursquare lapidary block. Formerly uniform with the feigned travertine of its side walls, the façade occupies a commanding position on the edge of the Janiculum, rather like the Madonna del Calcinaio near Cortona (fig. 98). It is rather more lightweight and dynamic in effect, however, thanks to its podium, slenderer proportions and small rose window, but has, like Sant' Aurea in Ostia, absorbed something of Francesco's volumetric power. As in Cortona, the lower storey of the façade is articulated with quadrangular columns without capitals that carry projections of an abbreviated entablature. And as in Cortona, this abbreviated order supports the real order, a variant of the *Corinthia*. On the side fronts, on the other hand, giant lesenes reach to the top of the wall and the

127, 128 *Façade (left) and nave of San Pietro in Montorio, Rome, begun by Francesco di Giorgio in c.1480 and taken over about 1488 by Baccio Pontelli, who failed – or deliberately chose not – to make the orders of exterior and interior correspond.*

129 *Pontelli's Belvedere of Pope Innocent VIII (c.1485) is the first Roman Renaissance villa. Its fortified exterior corresponds to all papal buildings of the fifteenth century.*

surrounding entablature is projected over them. Neither on the façade, nor on the sides of the church, does this order correspond to that of the interior: Pontelli uses individual motifs of Francesco di Giorgio, without unifying them into an equally coherent system.

Belvedere of Innocent VIII

As a patron of architecture Pope Innocent VIII Cybo (1484–92) is especially famous for his Belvedere on the northern hill of the Vatican (fig. 129). It dates to the same years round 1485 as Lorenzo de' Medici's villa at Poggio a Caiano (figs 77, 78); Lorenzo's daughter later married the pope's son. This only genuine villa of the Roman Quattrocento is directly inspired by the convent of Santa Chiara in Urbino (fig. 96). The three wings of its valley front similarly rest on high substructures, enclose a terrace and partly open up in arcades on the extensive landscape.

The villa's forms once again reveal the hand of Pontelli, who was soon after confirmed as papal military architect. The lesenes of the convent of Santa Chiara have now become two complete orders. At the corners the pilasters are broadened and, as in San Pietro in Montorio, reinforced by a second layer. The lower entablature is directly comparable with the upper one of the façade of San Pietro in Montorio (fig. 127). The segmental arches of Santa Chiara have been transformed into semicircular ones. In the upper entablature, consoles and a massive crenellation appear in place of frieze and cornice and once again represent the militant character of papal power. The fact that the side wings are of different sizes is explained by the functions of the papal apartment. The principles of symmetry

and axiality are even less in evidence here than in Roman palaces of the period before 1485.

In contrast to the exterior, the inside of the loggia is far more carefully calculated than any profane interior of the Quattrocento. The theatre motif of the exterior is here mirrored in bundled lesenes and blind arcades. As in the façade of Urbino Cathedral, but in contrast to the similarly articulated loggias of the Farnesina, the impost cornice intersects the arcades. All this is hardly attributable to anyone but Pontelli in Rome in the years around 1485.

Palazzo della Cancelleria

As papal architect, Pontelli was subordinate to the Cardinal *camerlengo* Raffaele Riario, the nephew of Giuliano della Rovere. In the summer of 1489 Riario had won a large sum of money in gambling from the nephew of Innocent VIII. Thanks partly to this stroke of good luck he seems to have commissioned Pontelli to build his new residence in Rome, but he must also have involved other masters such as Andrea Bregno, Mantegna and Melozzo da Forlì in the planning. Riario, who had a lively interest in Roman antiquities, had made a decisive contribution to the renaissance of the ancient theatre, one of the aspirations of the humanistic circle of Pomponio Leto. Shortly before the beginning of the building of the Cancelleria he had also promoted the first printed edition of Vitruvius. In his dedication the editor, Sulpizio da Veroli, a pupil of Pomponio, encouraged Riario to

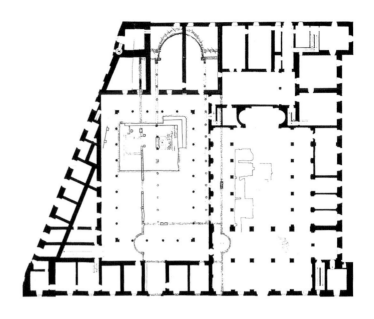

130–32 *The first phase of the huge palace of the Cancelleria was started in 1489, probably by Baccio Pontelli. In its scale (right: plan), façade (opposite) and courtyard (below) it begins a new era in Roman architecture that was to come to fruition in Bramante. The courtyard was started only in 1496, possibly under Antonio da Sangallo the Elder.*

restore one of the ancient theatres or to build a new one; he would, Sulpizio suggested, have sufficient time to build churches once he eventually became pope! Even Riario's contemporaries believed that the Cancelleria lay over the theatre of Pompey and that it had been intended for dramatic performances. No doubt Riario tried to live up to these expectations.

The Cancelleria was, however, erected on the site of the early Christian basilica of San Lorenzo in Damaso (figs 130–32). The building work thus had to be phased in such a way that a new church was available for worship before the old basilica was wholly demolished. The first phase was the building of the entrance wing, which, as its large inscription proclaims, was completed in 1495, three years after Pontelli had left Rome in mysterious circumstances.

Like the Domus Nova in Mantua, the façade is flanked by shallow corner-block projections, one shaft width in depth, but exceeds it by far with its total width of fourteen bays. Both in system and in detail the façade comes far closer to Francesco di Giorgio and Giuliano da Sangallo. Like the Palazzo Ducale in Urbino (fig. 91), it is clad with regular ashlars of light-coloured travertine. Only the two upper floors are distinguished by Corinthian orders as the residence of the cardinal and his court. On these floors the purely paratactical sequence of single pilasters as in the Palazzo Rucellai and Palazzo Piccolomini (figs 35, 62) is jettisoned in favour of a system of simplified triumphal arches. Such triumphal arches in sequence had been exemplified by the interior of Alberti's Sant'Andrea (fig. 56), but arched windows here replace the arches.

The architrave of the entablature of the ground floor is replaced by a small astragal, as in San Pietro in Montorio; and, as in the Palazzo Ducale in Urbino, the pedestals on both upper storeys link the pilaster order with that of the window-aedicules. On the *piano nobile* the window-aedicules follow the prototype of the Porta dei Borsari in Verona. The more modest windows of the third storey, where the entourage of the cardinal lived, can be compared with those of the Palazzo Comunale in Jesi.

The slight projection of the lateral bays reinforces the four corners of the irregular layout. These projecting corner blocks can be recognized as urbanized towers in vestigial form and thus identify the building as an urbanized fortress. On the side and rear fronts of the complex both the rhythm of the orders and the detail of the aedicules and entablature are simplified. The left front facing onto the busy Via del Pellegrino accommodates the shops of the goldsmiths on its ground floor. In order to avoid the acute angle, the southeastern corner block is polygonally bent; and to ensure symmetry, both the polygonally bent corner block and the adjacent large stairwell window are repeated at the left (southwestern) corner. On the right side-front the corner blocks project further outwards, to ensure better lighting in the rooms overlooking this once relatively narrow street. Only the bays of the garden wing, which comprised the cardinal's private apartment, are less regular in fenestration. In no previous palace are the hierarchical and functional differences between the individual wings so clearly expressed as here.

The layout of the plan is also axially organized and leads from a new street and the entrance vestibule – or *andito* – through to the entrance portico of the arcaded courtyard. There one turns left to the ceremonial staircase that leads to the upper portico and thence to the flat-ceilinged *sala*. A sequence of ever-smaller rooms follows beyond it. It ends in the private apartment of the cardinal with chapel and bathroom, to which the garden and the stables were annexed. The ceremonial layout of the Palazzo Venezia (fig. 64) is thus combined here with the more courtly and refined layout of the Palazzo Ducale in Urbino.

Only in 1496, after the completion of the façade wing, was the courtyard begun. The private apartment in the rear wing, in which Bramante may have been involved, may be later in date. The courtyard follows, even in dimensions, the columnar arcades of the Palazzo Ducale in Urbino (fig. 92). But it surpasses this model, since it has loggias on two storeys, and each of its long sides is one bay longer. The central arch of the entrance loggia is somewhat broader and distinguished with pinkish granite columns with more complex bases. The upper loggia is distinguished as the *piano nobile* by its Ionic bases and the doubling of the neck of the Doric capitals. Also richer in the upper loggia is the decoration of the marble bands that connect the two granite blocks of the L-shaped square columns. The entablatures correspond to those of the façade and are only supported by an order on the third floor.

When the building of the courtyard began, four years had already elapsed since Pontelli's departure from Rome. Giuliano's brother Antonio da Sangallo the Elder was now acting as architect to the pope and to the Camera Apostolica. Antonio seems to have taken over the supervision of the building of the Cancelleria and remodelled some details of the project, perhaps even with Giuliano's help. The surviving accounts of the building work mention a single architect by the name of Bernardino, presumably the author of the Codex Coner who belonged to the Sangallo circle and was also born in Florence. Antonio the Elder presumably delegated to him the task of supervising the building of the courtyard.

Giuliano had already adopted, and based on ancient prototypes, the Doric capital decorated with heraldic motifs in the Madonna delle Carceri (fig. 75). The corner pillars and the slenderer proportions of the arcades may also be attributable to Giuliano's invention. The courtyard as a whole is more spacious and majestic than any earlier known courtyard and the antique granite shafts, some of them hewn from granite from the Baths of Diocletian, contribute to its Roman grandeur.

The new church is concealed behind the last six of the fourteen bays of the façade wing overlooking the piazza. It has low pillared, instead of columnar, arcades dividing the nave and aisles. These were no doubt begun under Pontelli. The church's tall nave, its short cube-like shape reminiscent of the Curia in the Forum, is encapsulated by the upper storeys of the Cancelleria on three sides; the arcades of its double porch support the *salone* and the right aisle and its chapels the *sala seconda*.

Even before he moved to Naples, Pontelli could have designed the chapel for the humanist and royal chancellor Giovanni Pontani in Naples, erected in *c.*1490–92. It is a synthesis of funerary chapel and ancient mausoleum. While the ground plan and the paratactic pilaster order are reminiscent of Sant'Aurea (fig. 126), the Ionic capitals with

their fluted neck and the projection over them of the entablature immured in the wall are far closer to the Madonna del Calcinaio (figs 97, 98). It is probable that the original design for the chapel envisaged a different upper termination and not the unsatisfactory existing attic, and other windows than the *oculus* clumsily intersecting the cornice.

Antonio da Sangallo the Elder (*c.* 1460–1534) and the Rocca of Civita Castellana

In little less than a decade Pontelli and a few patrons in the Curia had succeeded in raising Rome once again to a centre of European architecture. And if Pontelli did not possess the power and originality of Francesco di Giorgio, he was still one of the few architects who laid the foundations of the High Renaissance by fusing the innovations of Alberti, Francesco di Giorgio and Giuliano da Sangallo with the style of the Roman school.

In Giuliano's younger brother, Antonio da Sangallo the Elder, the Borgia Pope Alexander VI found a practised architect who was well acquainted with the latest achievements of both Florentine and military architecture. Antonio revealed his affinities with Cronaca's squat proportions in his arched gateway set into the fortifications of

133 *Antonio da Sangallo the Elder's courtyard of the Rocca of Civita Castellana, 1499, bears witness to the influence of his brother Giuliano.*

the Vatican, the Porta San Pietro, completed in 1497, the first Roman façade with quoining.

In 1499 he began the Rocca of Civita Castellana. In the huge courtyard he followed the model of the two lower storeys of the Colosseum not only in system but also in superimposition (fig. 133). At the same time he held fast to the flat relief of the late Alberti, which Giuliano had already privileged in his Florentine buildings. Though much coarser, the detail shows how indebted he was to Giuliano.

Then, around 1501, he presumably designed the Palazzo Castellesi-Giraud on the new Via Alessandrina (named after the pope) close to the Vatican. As on the left side front of the Cancelleria, the triumphal-arch motif is there reduced to paired pilasters and the window-aedicules simplified. The Sangallesque training of the architect is plain from the ornament with which the upper spandrels of the aedicules are decorated, while the smooth pillar-supported arcades of the courtyard are reminiscent of those of the *piano nobile* of the Palazzo Strozzi. Perhaps it was also intended to be continued in a columnar portico (fig. 87).

THE SIXTEENTH CENTURY

9 Bramante and his School

Seldom does the start of a new epoch coincide so exactly with that of a new century as the High Renaissance. In 1568 Vasari regarded it as a time of unrivalled flourishing of the arts and differentiated it from the two preparatory phases inaugurated respectively by Giotto and Brunelleschi. Its centre was Rome, its most important patron Julius II. Instead of Brunelleschi and Alberti, from whom the architects had sought guidance and inspiration right down to the 1490s, now it was Bramante and his pupils who became the leading exponents of European architecture.

Alexander VI Borgia (1492–1503) had plunged the papal state into one of its worst crises. Only in a few building projects could he vie with his predecessors. Architects like Pontelli or Giuliano da Sangallo had abandoned Rome, and Giuliano's brother Antonio, Alexander's only reputable architect, remained permanently resident in Florence and mainly devoted himself to fortifications and military architecture. If Michelangelo and Bramante went to Rome in the 1490s, they did so not just because major commissions were to be expected from Raffaele Riario, Oliviero Caraffa, Bernardino Carvajal and other powerful cardinals in the Curia, but also because they wanted primarily to study the antiquities.

Bramante's Roman years (1499–1514)

Bramante arrived in Rome soon after Lodovico il Moro's fall and was immediately entrusted with several commissions on the eve of the Holy Year. Vasari's report that he contributed to the planning of San Giacomo dei Spagnoli, the Cancelleria and Santa Maria dell'Anima is plausible: Bramante's hand is still evident in the two latter buildings. Like San Giacomo dei Spagnoli or Pienza Cathedral, Santa Maria dell'Anima – the German national church in Rome – is a *Hallenkirche*, then one of the favourite types in Germany. Slender pillars decorated with a Corinthian order divide the nave from the aisles. Steep exedra-shaped chapels are opened on either side and deepen the closer they come to the choir, thus widening the space and brilliantly overcoming the irregularities of the terrain. This is a stroke worthy of Bramante's genius.

Bramante's removal to Rome speedily led him to a radical transformation of his style. The affinity with his last Milanese building (fig. 117), can barely be recognized in the cloister of Santa Maria della Pace, which he began to erect for Oliviero Caraffa in the summer of 1500 (fig. 135). The cloister is entered through an

134 *The centralized church of the Madonna della Consolazione at Todi, begun 1508, was executed by Cola da Caprarola, a collaborator of Antonio da Sangallo the Elder, who may have designed the two lower storeys.*

135 *In the cloister of Santa Maria della Pace, which he began in 1500, soon after arriving in Rome, Bramante continued the complex play with vertical and horizontal forces of his Milanese period, but brought his language closer to that of the Sangallo brothers.*

unassuming portal at the side. The visitor's first impression of the diagonal view is of the contrast between the cloister's finely articulated structure and the massive octagon of the adjacent church. Without yet imitating the antique directly Bramante combined the flat theatre motifs of the courtyard of Civita Castellana (fig. 133) with Giuliano's open colonnade, which had already inspired him in Milan, and more elegant proportions (figs 73, 77, 79, 82, 116). Here he not only adjusted his style to monastic frugality, but still regarded the antique with the eyes of the Sangallo brothers. The arcades are cut into the bare wall without archivolts and the capitals of the Ionic pilaster order reduced to their basic element, the volutes. As in the cloisters of Sant'Ambrogio, the bays of the upper floor are divided (fig. 117). Slender columns alternate with broader pillars that are clearly identified by their capitals as quadrangular columns. They support the bracketed entablature, based on that of the Colosseum and the Cancelleria (fig. 131). Their Composite capitals can be recognized as a fusion of the Ionic of the ground floor with the Corinthian of the round columns – a synthesis comparable to that of colonnade and arcade in Giuliano's Palazzo Cocchi (fig. 71). In the quadrangular columns, the rapid horizontal movement of the short bays is intersected with the vertical movement of the pilasters with which the columns are faced and the paired consoles above them. This virtuoso interplay between the basic forces of architecture goes far beyond Bramante's earlier work.

Palazzo Caprini

Bramante succeeded in an even more radical renewal of an older type in the (long-demolished) Roman residence he built for a prominent curial official, Aurelio Caprini, and his brothers in *c.*1501 (fig. 136). It was situated on the Via Alessandrina, newly laid out for the Jubilee in 1500, which now provided a direct road link between the Papal Palace and the Castel Sant'Angelo. Presumably the building was intended to stretch over the whole west side of the Piazza Scossacavalli. Presumably, too, it was not to remain below the minimum height of *c.*15.60 m (51 ft 2 ins) prescribed by the pope, but was to be furnished with a third storey like most palaces of this period. Caprini, however, failed to acquire all the necessary real estate. The palazzo remained

136 *The rusticated basement and Doric order of Bramante's Palazzo Caprini (Raphael's future house), started in 1501 but never completed, became a highly influential model for the future.*

fragmentary. The fragment, however, that did survive became one of the most influential prototypes of the Renaissance.

Bramante revived here the ancient technique of brick faced with stucco. This meant that he could build far more cheaply than Cardinal Adriano Castellesi in his nearby palazzo. Yet he succeeded in developing an incomparably more antique alternative. Now under the influence not only of the Sangallo brothers, but also of the antique, he designed a ground floor incorporating shops in the form of an arcaded podium, built in the antique style with irregular rusticated blocks and radial voussoirs above the imposts. This *basamento* was hierarchically contrasted with the residential *piano nobile*, where the paired members of the order alternate with the windows. Here Bramante transformed the delicate pilasters of the Palazzo Castellesi into more volumetric half-columns, the flat aedicules into balustraded balcony windows, and the decorative *Corinthia* into a monumental *Dorica* with triglyph frieze. In no previous palazzo had the patron's self-glorification found more fitting expression. The triglyph frieze, aligned with the paired columns, invests the order with a particular dignity. It was the first triglyph frieze of the Renaissance to be executed: Alberti had only described it, Francesco di Giorgio only drawn it and erroneously called it Ionic.

Despite the smooth cornice that clearly demarcates the two floors, the vertical movement is continued through the voussoirs of the rusticated podium into the paired pedestals and engaged columns right up to the triglyphs in the frieze of the entablature. The half-columns look far slenderer in proportion than the canonical *Dorica* in Vitruvius (Book IV.3). Their slenderness is further emphasized by their divided pedestals, and complemented by the elongated window apertures. These vertical impulses, comparable to the vertical alignment established by the projecting entablature in the cloister of Santa Maria della Pace, would probably have been balanced by a compensating horizontal emphasis in the projected but never-executed third storey, no doubt Ionic, and in the broader format of a seven-bayed façade.

The Tempietto

Even more astonishing is Bramante's breakthrough to the antique in the Tempietto, whose foundation stone was laid by the powerful Cardinal Bernardino Carvajal in 1502 (figs 137, 138). The memory of what was presumed to be the place of martyrdom of St Peter on the site of San Pietro in Montorio drew pilgrims to the church of the Spanish kings on the Gianicolo. But it would also – so he hoped – help the cardinal in his bid to ascend the papal throne and become the *papa angelicus*, whose imminent election had been prophesied by the Blessed Amadeo da Silva in the grotto over which the Tempietto was built.

Both the extremely narrow site (a small cloister between the church and a bigger cloister) and the function of a *memoria*, a commemorative chapel, suggested a central-plan building. Bramante transformed it into a peripteral temple. The circular *cella* is surrounded by a peristyle, of a kind described by Vitruvius and

137 *Opposite: Bramante's Tempietto, begun in 1502, marked the site of St Peter's martyrdom.*

Alberti and still to be seen in ancient examples in Rome and Tivoli. The influence of Giuliano was once again decisive; for he more than anyone had propagated the return to the colonnade. But even more crucial was the influence of Francesco di Giorgio, who had already, in his drawings, reconstructed ancient circular temples with a comparable drum. Only through the uncanonical drum did the Tempietto receive the steep proportions and the intensive lighting of a chapel and thus fused together a pagan with a Christian sanctuary. The *Dorica* may have alluded to the heroic martyr, but its choice was also dictated by Bramante's growing interest in this hitherto humble order. The columns are proportioned *c.*1:8.6, i.e. less slender than in the Palazzo Caprini, but still more than the prescriptions of Vitruvius. The deviation from the norm could be justified by two other Vitruvian rules that ought to take precedence. First, the columns should be proportioned 1:8 in intercolumniations of medium size, but should be slenderer in smaller, and stockier in larger, intercolumniations (Book III.3). Second, irrespective of the size of the intercolumniations, or of the chosen order, Vitruvius recommended the ratio of 1:10 for the columns of a round temple (Book IV.8).

If Bramante had followed some antique prototypes and diminished the bays radially from exterior to interior, the bays would have been far too narrow for the doors and niches. Only on the exterior of the *cella* did Bramante repeat the order of the portico in the form of slightly diminished pilasters. Between the shafts he squeezed small niches and windows whose frames are cut into the thickness of the wall. He severed the inner order from the exterior, placed it on high pedestals, and followed the rhythm of the triumphal-arch motif. In this way he gave appropriate expression to the victory of the prince of the Apostles over death. By opening up four large and four small niches with windows in the interior of the *cella* and eight small niches in the external wall he reduced the thickness of the wall to the statically necessary pillars, as he had learnt from Roman imperial *thermae*.

Serlio transmits a ground-plan project in which the Tempietto is surrounded by a concentric cloister. Bramante may have derived inspiration for such a scheme from the Teatro Marittimo, a circular island surrounded by a concentric colonnade he had seen at Hadrian's Villa. But the ambitious project remained unexecuted: Carvajal may have rejected it because it would have entailed, if any, a central altar. Bramante clearly intended to continue the symmetry of the concentric exterior into the interior: the visual axes would have remained open. But during the execution, i.e. during his lifetime, three of the four large niches, and thus the two visual axes that would have connected the *cella* with the circular court, were closed. The monstrous altar we now see can hardly be associated with Bramante: it conceals the steep flight of steps leading down to the grotto of Amadeo da Silva, but is ill-adjusted to the exedra to the rear and to the cosmatesque pavement.

The visitor, on entering the little cloister, is immediately confronted with the circular peristyle of sixteen grey granite columns with a stepped travertine stylobate and a travertine entablature. The circular movement is continued by the surrounding balustrade, drum and the once slightly lower hemispherical dome.

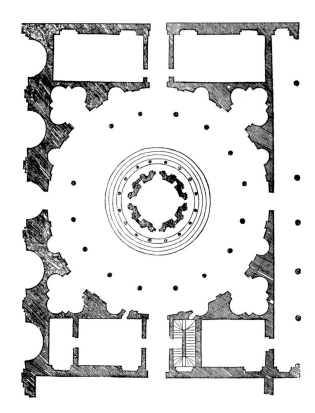

138 *Serlio included the Tempietto in his treatise, showing how it was intended to be surrounded by a circular cloister.*

At the same time the volumes rhythmically decrease from the colonnade to the drum to the dome and its formerly volute-supported terminal, the 'flower' described by Vitruvius (Book IV.8). The composition therefore follows once again the hierarchical principle, and the horizontal forces are once again balanced by the vertical ones in the most organic way. In spite of its steep proportions, drum and panels still reminiscent of the sacristy of Santa Maria presso San Satiro, the Tempietto was praised by contemporaries as the first building congenial to the spirit of antiquity, and indeed no earlier master had succeeded in designing a building so close to the antique.

Cortile del Belvedere and Vatican

When Cardinal Giuliano della Rovere returned to Rome after a nineteen-year-long exile and ascended the papal throne as Julius II on 1 November 1503, he must already have known who could best translate his imperial utopia into stone. He lost no time in commissioning Bramante to extend the old Papal Palace into a princely residence (figs 139, 140). Bramante connected it with the Belvedere of Innocent VIII on the northern hill of the Vatican, a villa in which Julius often resided and to which he annexed his most beautiful antiquities (fig. 129). The inscription of the foundation medal explicitly alludes to Suetonius's description of Nero's Domus Transitoria, which connected the imperial palaces on the Palatine and Oppian hills.

The project was ambitious: two corridors over 300 m (984 ft) long were to encompass an enormous court that was to terminate in the steps of an outdoor auditorium and then continue at a higher

139 *Reconstruction of Bramante's second project for the Cortile del Belvedere. We are looking away from the papal apartments. In the foreground is the lower court with its two-storeyed corridor; behind that an intermediate and upper garden flanked by porticoes.*

140 *The Cortile from the east, about 1588; the old papal palace on the left. Beyond the Cortile is Ligorio's Casino (see p.192).*

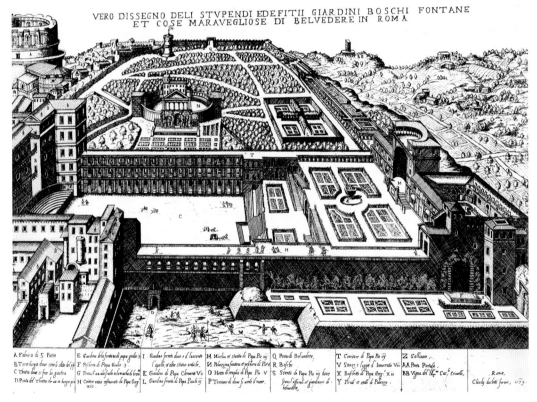

VERO DISSEGNO DELI STVPENDI EDEFITII GIARDINI BOSCHI FONTANE ET COSE MARAVEGLIOSE DI BELVEDERE IN ROMA

level in two garden terraces. The first of these terraces, which corresponds to the ground floor of the old palace, ended in a central nymphaeum, from which two staircase ramps ascended in a zigzag to the upper garden, surrounded on three sides by porticoes and culminating once again in a central niche-like exedra, the *point de vue* of the huge layout. The pope would have been able to take it in at a glance from his residential quarters in the Appartamento Borgia situated at the level of the upper garden: in its extensiveness and axial-symmetrical organization, the enormous layout was also a mirror image of his political plans. This system of stairways and terraces was inspired on the one hand by the Temple of Fortuna in Palestrina, then thought to be palace of Julius Caesar, and on the

other by the projects for the palace of the king of Naples and the villa at Poggio Reale (fig. 80).

The porticoes in the lower storey of the Cortile were opened by theatre motifs with a Doric pilaster order on pedestals. Bundled pilasters of a squat *Ionica* alternated with pedimented aedicules flanked by statue niches in the unarcaded upper storey. Bramante thus varied here the system of the cloister of Santa Maria della Pace (fig. 135) in a far more monumental form, and was no doubt encouraged to do so by the personality and ambition of Julius II. The *Dorica* is now more powerful and more genuinely antique in form than in the slightly earlier Tempietto. The *Ionica* is without ornament, though with capitals whose volutes diagonally extend into space as in antique prototypes and Francesco del Borgo's tabernacle of St Andrew.

Like the interior of the Tempietto, the porticoes of the upper garden are articulated with a series of triumphal arches. So when the pope had crossed the Ionic storey of the Cortile, he entered a kind of *via triumphalis* worthy of the Pontifex Maximus. The convex steps of the central exedra are continued in the concave rows of seats of a kind of Odeion, no doubt conceived for the recitation of poetry.

Bramante designed the spiral staircase, erected in a tower annexed to the east wall of the Belvedere, in an equally ingenious way (fig. 141). It was intended to provide a direct link between the papal apartment in the Belvedere and the northern exit road. A continuous spiral ramp winds upwards. It was perhaps intended to be topped by a wooden dome. It comprises four complete spirals. Each spiral is equivalent to one storey. Each is supported by eight columns and each corresponds to a different columnar order: the lower *Tuscanica* develops into the slenderer *Dorica*, which in turn

141 *The spiral ramp at the north-east corner of the Belvedere, with the first superimposition of four Vitruvian orders.*

develops into the even slenderer *Ionica*. Only the terminating *Composita*, the *ordo italicus* praised by Alberti (Book VII, c.6), which Bramante still conceived as a variant of the *Corinthia*, corresponded to the residential floor of the pope.

Such a superimposition of four Vitruvian orders, as introduced by Bramante in the Court, garden and spiral staircase, had only one Quattrocento precedent, painted, not built: the amphitheatre in the panel in Baltimore (fig. 74). Bramante was now systematically engaged with the ancient prototypes, with Vitruvius and Alberti. In contrast to Alberti, whose *De re aedificatoria* preceded and partly contradicted most of his own buildings, Bramante achieved an unrivalled mastery of the huge repertoire by both systematic and pragmatic experiment and thus by the constant dialectic between theory and practice. While grasping that without Vitruvius and Alberti he would never be able to understand the laws of ancient architecture, he had at the same time realized that their prescriptions in no way demanded a dogmatic application. Ever since his Milanese exordium he had experimented with the endless possibilities of varying the rhythms of his wall systems. Now for the first time he combined the hierarchy of the orders with the rhythms of wall articulation by assigning the *Dorica* to the theatre motif, the *Ionica* to the bundled pilasters, and the *Corinthia* to the triumphal-arch motif. In a similar way he varied the forms and rhythms of steps, ranging from the broad seating of the auditorium to the zigzag ramps, from the convex and concave steps of the exedra to the spiral staircase of the Belvedere.

In the spring of 1505, when the execution of the eastern corridor with auditorium, nymphaeum and parts of the exedra and spiral staircase had been begun, but less than half of the planned layout completed, the impatient pope turned his attention to the reconstruction of St Peter's. After having laid the foundation stone of the new basilica in April 1506 and decided on the necessary demolition of the old buildings, he commissioned Bramante with the comprehensive renovation of the old Papal Palace. Already in the planning of the Cortile del Belvedere and St Peter's Julius II had recalled the ambitious building programme of his fellow countryman Nicholas V (fig. 58). Now he turned it into the blueprint of the further planning of the palace, as confirmed by a fragmentary drawing by Bramante. He now left the apartment of his hated predecessor and moved into the suite of rooms on the second floor – the so-called Stanze, which were frescoed by Raphael. From these rooms he again wished to be able to reach the Belvedere without the effort of going up and down stairs. This meant that Bramante had to raise the Cortile one storey in height. But since the level of the Stanze lay well above that of the upper garden, no wholly organic connection between them was possible. And although Bramante built the third courtyard storey in lightweight peperino and opened it in colonnades, the foundations were too weak and parts of the east wing collapsed less than two decades later. Like the Arch of Jupiter Ammon in Verona, the columns of this new storey were to support blind panels instead of an entablature. Only the eastern wing of the project was realized by Bramante. Drastically changed by later architects, only small fragments still transmit an idea of this gigantic project.

The new Cortile was now to be prepared also by a gigantic forecourt. A conclave hall of the size of the nave of St Peter's was planned in its southern wing, and a huge stable block with the library above it in its northern wing. The tower of Nicholas V was to be crowned with a colonnaded conclave chapel, a more monumental variant of the Tempietto, on its south-east corner. Lastly Bramante started to replace the fragmentary loggias of Nicholas V with a thirteen-bay layout on four floors, the so-called Logge, which formed the only façade of the palace. They overlooked the secret garden, the later Cortile di San Damaso, the Piazza San Pietro, the city and the landscape towards the Alban hills. The numerous horizontal links between the various part of the complex were complemented by a series of staircases, most of them negotiable by horses too, so that even the old palace could better respond to the needs of the papal residence. By far the most important staircase, the Scala Regia made famous by Bernini's spectacular remodelling, connected the atrium of St Peter's with the Sala Regia, the audience hall in which the popes received princes now better illuminated by a triumphal *serliana* above the papal throne.

St Peter's

The Constantinian basilica was dilapidated. Nicholas V had decided (as we have seen) to preserve much of the nave, but to add a larger choir. This scheme, translated into architectural terms by Rossellino, is often overlooked, but shows that Julius's decision to rebuild the entire basilica is not entirely unprecedented. Nicholas V, indeed, was Julius's great model. But when Julius decided to have the whole of the old basilica swept away, and a new one built in its place, he also had other ideas in mind. An important role in this decision was played by the Pope's wish to link his tomb with that of the Prince of the Apostles and his name with the first church in Christendom. If it may be doubted whether the plan to rebuild St Peter's was really prompted by Michelangelo's project for the funerary monument of Julius II, as Michelangelo's biographers claim, Bramante's projects for the basilica can hardly be separated from it. In the earliest of these projects Bramante started out from Rossellino's foundations, but he transformed the choir into a domed quincunctial system (fig. 142). Thus he recurred to the type believed to be that of the ancient temple that he had already disseminated in the Prevedari engraving (fig. 101). Michelangelo probably wanted to place the wall monument, as he had first planned the papal tomb, in one of the broad niches near the apse.

Bramante proposed to widen the crossing over Peter's tomb by splaying the dome pillars well beyond the width of the nave. He wanted to top the crossing with a fenestrated drum and a dome probably similar to that of the Pantheon and prolong it with a nave modelled after that of the Basilica of Maxentius, then thought to be the Temple of Peace. He thus wanted to fuse three different types of the ancient temple together.

But soon afterwards, in April 1505, the Pope authorized the project presented by Michelangelo for a monumental freestanding funerary monument comprising forty over-lifesize statues, on such a colossal scale that the choir envisaged in his first project would have been far too small to accommodate it. Bramante was therefore

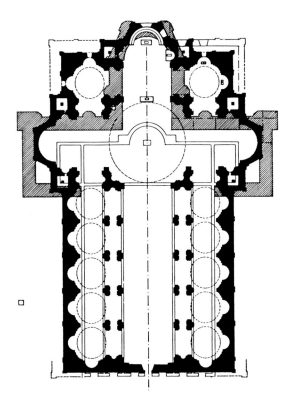

142 *Conjectural reconstruction of Bramante's first project for St Peter's. It shows the outline of Old St Peter's (in line), the foundations of Rossellino's new choir for Nicholas V (shaded), and Bramante's proposal (in black), the altars and Julius's wall tomb.*

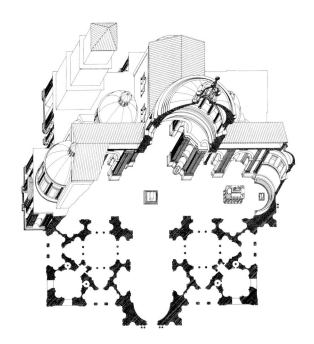

143 *Bramante's centralized St Peter's, based on the so-called 'parchment plan' and the foundation medal.*

obliged to enlarge the four arms of the Greek cross in his famous parchment plan, in order to create a huge choir in which the freestanding funerary monument would find its ideal place (fig. 143). In the squares between the four arms of the cross he placed all the chapels, vestibules and sacristies, thus transforming the basilica into a perfect central-plan building. He further enlarged the area of the

144 *The foundation medal for the new St Peter's issued in 1506 shows the external elevation of the same plan (fig. 143).*

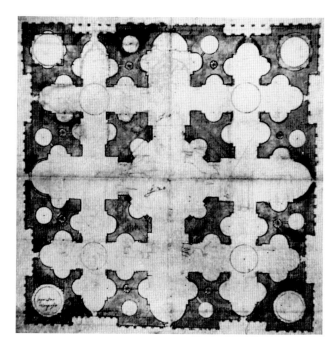

145 *Giuliano da Sangallo's proposal for a centralized St Peter's. Giuliano had become second architect to St Peter's.*

crossing under the dome and reduced the load-bearing skeleton to a minimum by exedras and niches. The ground plan is a masterpiece in itself: as in the Baths of Diocletian, which Bramante had studied thoroughly, the walls, hollowed out with arches and niches of varying size and depth, are thinned, thickened, compressed, expanded, moulded as a plastic material. Naves and chapels, vaults and domes would have been unified into a quite unique spatial continuum enlivened by the skilful distribution of light and shade. As in the Baths of Diocletian, rooms of different shape were to be united by visual axes and separated by screens of columns.

The most reliable image of the exterior is that presented by the foundation medal (fig. 144) which shows a centralized building. As in Leonardo's variations of Florence Cathedral and Bramante's project for Pavia Cathedral (figs 107–9), the new St Peter's was to grow organically from the corner domes to the hemispherical domes of the apses to the great hemispherical dome of the basilica. It was to be articulated by two superimposed orders, and its entrance front emphasized by two slender bell-towers with rhythmically diminishing storeys.

After having authorized the project by sending the foundation medal to the ruling monarchs and princes of Europe, the pope had second thoughts. For Giuliano da Sangallo, who had become his second architect in 1504, had warned him of the project's static risks. In his counter-project Giuliano started out from Bramante's parchment plan, but reinforced the pillars and in doing so deprived the interior of its expanding sense of space (fig. 145). By continuing the crossing into an octagonal drum-supported dome he returned to the model of Florence Cathedral, and by enclosing the whole organism in a block-like exterior he also reduced its hierarchical structure.

Presumably it was during a joint discussion with the pope that Bramante sketched an entirely new project on the back of Giuliano's project. He had to take over Giuliano's massive pillars, but continued them in the four aisles and three-bayed nave of a basilica plan and in the ambulatories of the cross-arms. Bramante justified this project on the same sheet by the ground plans of two Milanese churches, i.e. the domed octagon of San Lorenzo, then thought to be the Temple of Hercules, and Milan Cathedral, the most Gothic of all Italian cathedrals, which he also considered exemplary. No doubt on commission from the pope, he then worked out these new ideas more precisely in the famous *sanguigno* (red-chalk) plan (fig. 146).

The project was now even larger and more costly than the parchment plan, and so the pope, after costing it more precisely, insisted that it be drastically reduced. Bramante was forced to jettison not only the ambulatories, but also his domed quincunx (fig. 147). He was also obliged to incorporate the beginnings of Rossellino's choir arm and to use relatively cheap building materials like uncut tufa and as little brick and travertine as possible in the execution.

In the series of triumphal arches and in the barrel vault of the three-bayed nave he returned to the prototype of Alberti's Sant' Andrea in Mantua (figs 54, 56). By projecting the entablature over the pilasters and continuing their line in broad transverse arches, he underlined even more forcibly than in his Lombard buildings the plastic strength of the pillars and the vertical continuity of the members – still faithful to the legacy of Francesco di Giorgio. He continued this system in three arms of the cross which are much longer than those planned by Alberti for Sant'Andrea and thus recurred to his first church, Santa Maria presso San Satiro (figs 102–4). No doubt the lessons of Giuliano's counter-projects also contributed to this building's compactness.

In spite of Herculean efforts, the work, spread over seven years, never extended much further than the four pillars supporting the dome, fragments of the first pillars of the nave and the choir arm (fig. 148). Vaulted in Bramante's lifetime, it was in great part demolished after Michelangelo had returned to the quincunx.

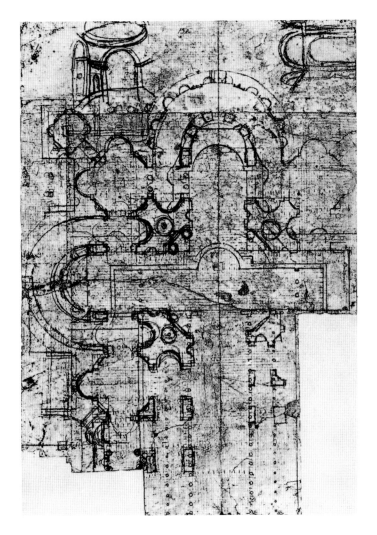

The interior of the executed project was planned some 3.30 m (10 ft 10 ins) higher than today and its nave some 5.40 m (17ft 8ins) narrower and one bay shorter. Its series of triumphal arches surpassed in majesty and monumentality by far the *via triumphalis* of the upper Belvedere. Equally the Cappella Magna under the cupola with its lower diameter of *c.*48 m (157 ft) its enormous dome and its height of *c.*100 m (328 ft), would have been much more magnificent than in Florence Cathedral. Drum and dome would have been simpler in form than in the projects of Leo X, but presumably would also have followed the model of the Pantheon and allowed the light to flow in through separate groups of columns. Ten windows in all, on the other hand, would have illuminated the choir and its monumental tomb. Shortly before his death Julius II christened the choir arm 'Cappella Iulia' and gave instructions that it be decorated with marbles and mosaics. An altar dedicated to the Birth of the Virgin was to be placed in the shell-niche of the apse. The choristers of the newly founded Cappella Iulia were to be installed in the *serliane* of the arcaded windows, which were to be supported with columns from Old St Peter's.

The articulation of the exterior, only executed in the area of the choir arm, reflected the interior with the same coherence as in the rear façade of Santa Maria presso San Satiro (fig. 104). The *Corinthia* of the interior was, however, transformed into a higher *Dorica*, as in

146 *A later proposal by Bramante in which the centralized crossing is combined with a conventional longitudinal nave and ambulatories.*

147 *Axonometric projection of Bramante's revised project of 1506.*

148 *The crossing of St Peter's as built, including Bernini's later baldacchino.*

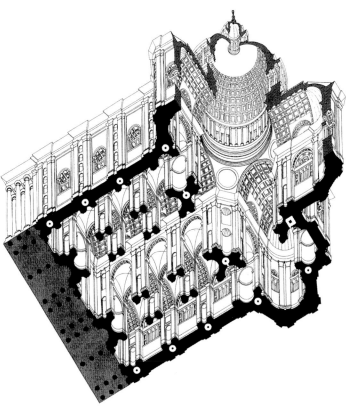

the Madonna delle Carceri (figs 75, 76). The triumphal arches of the nave would have continued into the aisles and their rhythm been mirrored on the exterior walls. On the exterior Bramante clearly wanted to contrast the broad horizontal bays with the vertical impulse of the over-slender bundled pilasters proportioned *c*.1:12. Five portals, corresponding to the nave and four aisles, would have been opened in the porch of the huge vestibule, which would have been flanked by slender bell-towers and culminated in a pediment corresponding to the ridge roof. The entrance to the basilica would thus have been transformed into a temple portico.

Not to be separated from Bramante's projects for St Peter's is the chancel of Santa Maria del Popolo, the funerary chapel of Cardinal Ascanio Sforza and soon after also of Cardinal Girolamo Basso della Rovere (fig. 149). Its remodelling was commissioned from Bramante by Julius II in the autumn of 1505. The central mausoleum is distinguished by Andrea Sansovino's funerary monuments in the lateral flat niches,

149 *Choir of Santa Maria del Popolo, Rome.*

Pinturicchio's *Coronation of the Virgin* in the vault and original stained-glass *serliane* in the lateral walls. The placing of the mausoleum in the chancel meant that the choir of the Augustinians had to be displaced to the right transept. Both sides of the cross-vaulted centre of the chancel were flanked by short bays with huge niches and coffered barrel vaults. The chancel terminates in a semicircular apse decorated with a giant shell-niche and illuminated from an open coffer of the adjacent barrel vault; it was probably meant to have a proper altar. Nowhere else is Bramante's expanding sense of space so authentically to be felt.

Palazzo dei Tribunali and Via Giulia

The Sacra Rota, the highest papal court, like the Camera Apostolica which was responsible for the administration of the Papal State, had been installed by Innocent VIII in a new building in the right wing of the atrium of Old St Peter's. This was earmarked for demolition when it was decided in 1507 to destroy the Loggia delle Benedizioni and to enlarge the piazza up to the new façade of St Peter's. The pope then commissioned Bramante to unite all the tribunals of the Holy See under a single roof. This new 'palace of justice' was to be erected opposite the seat of the vice-chancellor, the later Palazzo Sforza Cesarini in Via dei Banchi, and separated from it by a piazza. It was to be an administrative centre of unprecedented monumentality. It was to be situated on a new street named after the pope, the Via Giulia, an 11 m (36 ft) thoroughfare that led in a straight line from the Ponte Sisto at one end to the ancient Ponte Trionfale (which Julius intended to rebuild) and the Banchi at the other. A little later Bramante lengthened and straightened the Via della Lungara on the other bank of the Tiber as a parallel axis leading from the Porta Settignana to the Porta Santo Spirito, so that Rome could now boast of two magnificent new streets.

Julius II wanted at first to give the Palazzo dei Tribunali the form of a fortress with towers, crenellations and battered basement as shown in the foundation medal. Bramante must have convinced him to change his mind and opt for a more urbane building, closer in type to the Cancelleria, which he adapted to its specific functions and his own increasingly plastic and monumental style (fig. 150). He there-

150 *Reconstruction of the façade of Bramante's Palazzo dei Tribunali, Rome, 1508, of which only parts of the base were executed.*

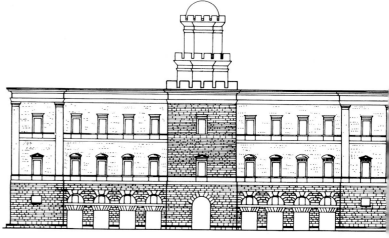

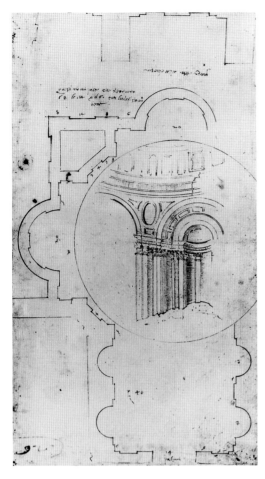

151 *At the end of the courtyard of the Palazzo dei Tribunali was to stand the church of San Biagio, a centralized choir and a short nave flanked by semicircular chapels.*

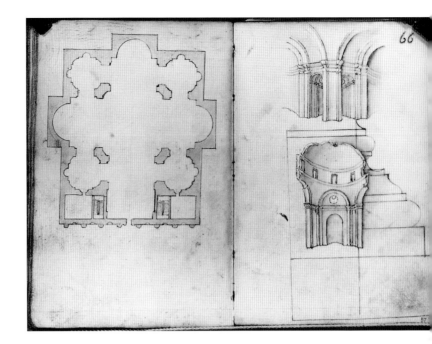

152 *Plan and interior of San Celso, a return by Bramante to the domed quincunx economically expressed.*

fore planned to clad the basement podium and the central tower with massive rusticated blocks, and to unify the two upper storeys of the projecting corner blocks with a colossal order, of the kind that had already signalled a public or civic function in Brunelleschi's Palazzo di Parte Guelfa (fig. 24). In the superimposition of the three orders of half-columns of the courtyard, which was to comprise 5 x 5 arcades, he would have followed the Colosseum.

The entrance axis was, in Bramante's project, to culminate in the central-plan church of San Biagio (fig. 151). As in Santa Maria della Pace in Rome, its short nave, flanked by semicircular chapels, would have continued into an octagonal choir. On the rear wall the pilasters and the apse of the chapel would have been connected to form a kind of *serliana* and culminated in a hemispherical drum-supported dome. Hierarchically placed between the projecting corner towers of the Palazzo dei Tribunali, the church would have formed the centrepiece of the Tiber front.

San Celso and the church at Roccaverano

The renovation of the church of San Celso was a result of the remodelling of the late-medieval city centre (fig. 152). It bordered on the Piazza di Ponte and the present-day Via di Banco Santo Spirito, which, according to the proud inscription of 1512, was straightened by Julius and ever since has provided an axial continuation to the Ponte Sant'Angelo. The site for the church, surrounded by shops,

was approximately square: it permitted Bramante to recur to the domed quincunx type. The patron of the church was the papal master of ceremonies Paris de Grassis, who clearly insisted on extreme economy. Bramante therefore articulated the interior simply with slender lesenes that knit together the individual parts of the interior and break through the two surrounding entablatures, as in Urbino Cathedral (fig. 93): it is the most mature and at the same time most abstract of the numerous variations of this type that was so congenial to him. The central crossing under the dome even more clearly predominates over the corner chapels here than in his quincunx projects for St Peter's.

153 *Façade of the church of Santa Maria del Popolo, Roccaverano. The giant order reflects the nave section, the smaller lateral orders the corner chapels.*

A further central-plan church was built, after a plan by Bramante, for the papal treasurer Enrico Bruni in the same period, around 1509, at Roccaverano, Bruni's Piedmontese birthplace (fig. 153). Here, by contrast, the crossing under the dome and its pillars are reduced in favour of the arms of the cross and the corner chapels, and the niches are very shallow. The hierarchical spirit thus gives way to a more basilica-like space. The façade, the only one from Bramante's Roman years ever to be executed, is articulated in a way that clearly expresses the basilica section: as such, it stands in the long tradition that leads back to the churches of Codussi, to the panel in Urbino, to Santa Maria presso San Satiro, to Francesco di Giorgio, Alberti and Brunelleschi and ultimately to the façade of San Miniato in Florence (figs 40, 42, 43, 55, 73, 104, 120). But Bramante now produced an even more exact correspondence between façade and interior. The colossal order of Corinthian pilasters corresponds to the pillars of the dome, the central arch to the nave, and the small order and arcades to the corner chapels. As in Urbino Cathedral (fig. 93), the arches of the vaults are projected as blind arches on the façade, but only in the lateral arches does the entablature continue above the doors.

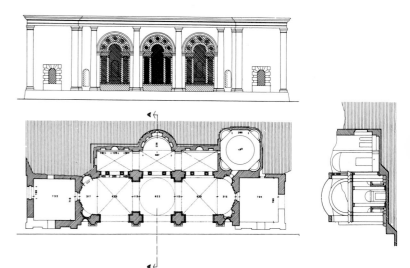

154 *Plan and elevation of Bramante's Nymphaeum at Genazzano, the building of a villa near Rome. The small door on the right leads into an octagonal bath-house.*

Nymphaeum at Genazzano

Bramante began the villa below the Castello Colonna of Genazzano in eastern Lazio, perhaps never completed and now ruined, in *c.*1508/09 for the young Pompeo Colonna, who had shortly before been appointed bishop of Subiaco and Rieti (figs 154, 155). The volumetric exterior betrays its chronological proximity to the Palazzo dei Tribunali. The three arches in its centre are separated by niches

from the projecting corner bays, where the engaged columns are transformed into square ones. The three arches open on a big loggia. Its central bay is hierarchically distinguished by a saucer dome. Its side bays are covered by cross-vaults and extend into semicircular exedras which, as in St Peter's and Santa Maria del Popolo, are deco-

155 *All that is left of the Nymphaeum is a picturesque ruin.*

rated with huge shells. A small door in the right exedra leads to the octagonal bathhouse situated to the rear of the complex, a direct imitation of the imperial baths. Its round basin at the centre was lit (as in the Pantheon) by an *opeion*. The rear arches of the loggia are supported by slender *serliane* reminiscent of the windows of Bramante's St Peter's. They open up onto the actual nymphaeum, situated at a slightly higher level. Thus the hierarchy grows from the niches and the small order of the exedras through the larger order of the exedras to the even larger one of the exterior and culminates in the central bay. With its three Tuscan orders, the building can be recognized as an *aedes tuscanica*, just as the Tempietto can be recognized as an *aedes dorica*.

Only the mouldings of the orders are carved from travertine, the walls and the vaults are built of unhewn tufa. The stucco preserved in the large shells of the exedras was no doubt intended to cover the entire building, a technique that was even more economical than the brickwork of the Palazzo Caprini (fig. 136).

As in Antiquity, and as postulated by Alberti (Book V, cc.17–18), this villa for the first time comprised only one storey. It thus became the prototype for Sanmicheli's La Soranza and the villas of the young Palladio. In the space of a few years Bramante had come so close to the antique that the typologically comparable Belvedere of Innocent VIII seems light years away (fig. 129).

The cylindrical gallery that surrounds the dome of the church in neighbouring Capranica Prenestina is reminiscent in type of the *tiburio* of Santa Maria presso San Satiro. It is opened in a central Pantheon-aedicule and a series of *serliane* framed by rusticated quoins like the inner arcades of the Colosseum. Even with the completed balustrade they are more steeply proportioned than in the nymphaeum, but this can hardly be an argument against an attribution to Bramante.

Bramante's last project for St Peter's

Giovanni de' Medici, the son of Lorenzo the Magnificent, who had been one of the most illustrious patrons of his time, ascended the pontifical throne as Leo X in March 1513. Financial problems had hitherto prevented him from commissioning any large-scale architectural works. But now he wanted to surpass his great predecessor Julius II through even more ambitious plans. This meant that Bramante had to integrate the already executed fragment of St Peter's into a substantially larger and richer project.

Bramante's final project for Leo can only be reconstructed from the few executed fragments and from the competing projects of Giuliano da Sangallo and Raphael (figs 159, 171). From this evidence we can deduce that he wanted to lengthen the nave to five bays, close the inner aisles with enormous niches, extend the outer aisles into square chapels, and recur to the ambulatories of the red-chalk plan (fig. 146). On the exterior the ambulatories would have projected as segments beyond the chapels of the aisles. The triumphal arches would have been continued in the ambulatories and their arches screened by colonnades of a small order. Bramante clearly wanted to retain the long choir arm and therefore continued the *Dorica* of the Julian basilica also on its exterior. In the huge drum groups of four columns would have alternated with closed wall blocks as in the ambulatories.

The portico of the façade would have surpassed the forest of columns in the pronaos of the Pantheon. St Peter's would thus have been much more monumental and spacious in effect than in any of the earlier projects.

This megalomaniac project, whose exterior was now to be executed entirely in expensive travertine, demanded a considerably longer building time. In order to enable papal masses to be celebrated in St Peter's once again after a seven-year intermission, Leo commissioned Bramante to protect the high altar by erecting over it a temporary shrine in stuccoed peperino. Its appearance is known from contemporary drawings. Erected directly in front of the old apse, it was articulated with blind theatre motifs, three on the main front and one at each side. The shafts of the Doric order came from the demolished parts of the old nave and were embedded into the pillars as in Pius II's Loggia delle Benedizioni (fig. 66). Bramante provided this order with a triglyph frieze and reinforced each of the corners once again with three columns. In the decoration of the capitals and the entablature he modelled himself on the magnificent prototypes of the Basilica Aemilia.

Santa Casa in Loreto

The tendency to *all'antica* magnificence, to a more normative articulation of the orders and to more compact plasticity is even more manifest in the Santa Casa, the marble shrine built round the House of Mary, which had been venerated in the crossing of the basilica of Loreto since the Middle Ages (fig. 156). Even though the figural reliefs and a part of the rich decoration were only executed by Bramante's followers, there can be no doubt that the triumphal rhythm

156 *The lavish decoration of the shrine Bramante built round the House of Mary at Loreto was in great part added by his successors.*

of the marble *Corinthia* and the corner triads of its fluted columns are due to Bramante. They are the last testimony of his indefatigable striving to come ever closer to the antique. Only Brunelleschi and Alberti had so fundamentally transformed architecture in so short a time, and none had come so close to the antique. This is all the more astonishing since in the period before 1500 Bramante's imitation of the ancient monuments had been less wholehearted than that of Giuliano.

Giuliano da Sangallo during the pontificate of Julius II: 1500–13

Between Alberti's death and Bramante's move to Rome there was no more expert connoisseur of the architecture of antiquity than the Florentine Giuliano da Sangallo and none that translated his knowledge so directly into architecture. At the same time he continued the tradition of the first half of the fifteenth century. He was thus able to produce buildings both in the traditional and in the antique style on demand: for the same Giuliano Gondi, for whom he had designed a palazzo of the type of the Palazzo Medici in Florence in 1491 (fig. 83), he would build a funerary chapel in the *all'antica* style ten years later.

On the altar wall of the Cappella Gondi in Santa Maria Novella in Florence he used a triumphal arch for the first time. He encrusted it with polychrome marbles and adopted an undecorated *Dorica*, with the entablature projected over it and continuing in the attic. The central arch rises to the architrave and dominates the narrow side bays, opened up with niches. The balusters that support the altar table are bound systematically into the pedestal zone of the order, as in the courtyard of the Palazzo Strozzi (fig. 87). On the side walls colonnettes of a small *Dorica* support a projecting entablature. The lateral benches cover the black sarcophagi and are supported on paired volutes. Thus Giuliano succeeded in evoking both in form and material an atmosphere of classical magnificence, of a kind that would be surpassed only by Raphael in the Chigi Chapel.

Only in the spring of 1504, when Bramante had already planned the Cortile del Belvedere, did Giuliano come to Rome, and even if all the major projects went to Bramante, he was no doubt immediately involved in them. His first independent commission for the pope was the belvedere-loggia on top of the Castel Sant'Angelo, which he began very soon after his arrival. There he returned to his favourite motif, the colonnade. In the slender columns, broad intercolumniations and decorative capitals of the *Dorica* he continued the style of the Cappella Gondi and, in supporting the vault above the walls only with small brackets, showed that he had not yet absorbed Bramante's new *all'antica* style.

In his project dated 1505 for the never-realized Loggia dei Trombettieri in St Peter's Square (fig. 157) he came even closer to the triumphal arch than in the Cappella Gondi. The attic with the large dedicatory inscription is flanked by its own squat order and topped by a pediment. The figural decoration is concentrated, as in antique prototypes, in the relief panels above the impost cornice, the arcade spandrels and the frieze between the capitals, but the order still lacks Bramante's plasticity.

157 *Giuliano da Sangallo's project for the Loggia dei Trombettieri in St Peter's Square, 1505, is virtually a Roman triumphal arch.*

In the same year, the planning of the new St Peter's led to his first direct confrontation with Bramante. Giuliano countered Bramante's complex domed quincunx project (fig. 143) with a simplified structure with octagonal drum-supported dome and projecting temple pronaos, corner towers and *vestibula* (fig. 145). He thus produced a fundamental reorientation of Bramante's plan. Shortly after, he again reacted critically to Bramante by producing his own variant of Bramante's red chalk plan. There he even took over Bramante's ambulatories and the splayed pillars of the dome, but held fast to the paratactical sequence of the members of the order.

Giuliano was then commissioned to enlarge the papal hunting lodge at La Magliana, outside Rome. The previous buildings by Innocent VIII and the utilitarian requirements imposed on him hardly explain why he failed to profit there from Bramante's innovations, either in the inner courtyard or in the stairs, reception rooms and loggias. The executed loggias, with their stumpy *Dorica*, their exaggeratedly high frieze and the massing of the statue niches in the corner of the papal apartment, are equally old-fashioned.

Only in three contemporary façade projects did Giuliano really succumb to Bramante's influence. Their della Rovere coats of arms point to his Roman years before 1510. The earliest of these was presumably intended for a secular building. Here the high pedestals, paired half-columns and triglyph frieze are undoubtedly inspired by Bramante's Palazzo Caprini (fig. 136) and by the energetic projections of the members on the exterior of St Peter's (fig. 147). The *Dorica* has an *Ionica* above it, also with a projected entablature. As in the Basilica Aemilia, quadrangular pillars at the corners reinforce the half-round columns. In the upper storey the central Pantheon-aedicule grows

158 *Giuliano's project for a church façade combines the basilican section with the triumphal arch.*

out of the Ionic order, so that the articulation is dynamically condensed in the centre. The small side windows are adorned, as in the Cortile del Papagallo, with shouldered frames. The size of the windows and the high position of the central one suggest that the façade was rather small and intended for an ephemeral piece of festive architecture.

Giuliano comes even closer to Bramante's verticalizing dynamic in two projects for church façades he would propose again in 1515/16 for San Lorenzo in Florence (fig. 158). In these two drawings he develops the basilica façade type that already crops up in the Urbino and Baltimore panels (figs 73, 74). In *c.*1492 the Florentine sculptor Benedetto Buglioni, no doubt on the basis of a project of Giuliano, had already combined the basilica-section scheme with the triumphal arch in the façade of Santa Cristina in Bolsena for the future Pope Leo X.

In *c.*1510, after his return to Florence, Giuliano varied the type of the Pantheon-aedicule in the magnificent pedimented marble high altar for the Madonna delle Carceri in Prato (fig. 76). He gave the columns slenderer proportions, fluted their shafts and decorated the frieze with acanthus and palmette. He also coordinated the predella with the pedestals and their bases with the altar. He thus continued the Gondi Chapel in an even more systematic way.

Giuliano must have begun the Roman residence of the bishop and later cardinal Andrea della Valle in *c.*1508. Its three-storey façade is articulated only by simple cornices and elegant Ionic marble aedicules with long brackets and pulvinated frieze. The arcaded ground floor of the courtyard is clearly indebted to that of the Cancelleria (fig. 132), but differs from it in its polychrome marble incrustation, decorative Doric capitals and exaggeratedly high entablature, which again serves as a windowsill: all characteristics of

Giuliano's style (fig. 84). Its frieze was decorated with reliefs, as previously in the Palazzo Scala (fig. 70), in this case ancient reliefs from Andrea della Valle's famous collection of antiquities. The niches between the windows of the *piano nobile* were filled with statues: a motif that Raphael would adopt in the façade of the Palazzo Branconio dell'Aquila (fig. 167). In the rather stumpy pillar-supported arcade of the attic Giuliano followed a Roman tradition, but betrayed his closeness to the antique in the abbreviated entablature of the upper cornice. The staircase opens axially into the portico of the courtyard. The four walls of its first landing are distinguished by marble theatre motifs of the Doric order. Also worthy of Giuliano is the Ionic fireplace of the Sala Grande with its splendid frieze decorated with griffins and acanthus rinceaux.

Giuliano's work for Leo X and the Medici (1513–16)

Giuliano had already known the new pope as Lorenzo the Magnificent's son. In July 1513 he presented him with a project for the transformation of the fifteenth-century Palazzo Madama into a papal palace. He placed in front of it a three-winged portico, a monumental *vestibulum* that would open onto the Piazza Navona and also serve as theatre courtyard. He thus alluded to the imperial palaces in Rome and Constantinople that had both overlooked a circus. Giuliano further underlined this implicit imperial claim by the colossal statues of the *Horse-Tamers* from the Quirinal, which were to flank the entrance of the portico. The inner arrangement of the rooms, by contrast, still seems archaic, as in the project for the papal hunting lodge at La Magliana. Equally archaic is the roughly contemporary project for the Torre Borgia, which he wanted to articulate with a colossal and a small order as in the right-hand palace of the Baltimore panel (fig. 74).

The plans for the remodelling of the Palazzo Madama into a papal palace were authorized by its owner, Leo's sister-in-law Alfonsina Orsini. But she then decided to commission Giuliano instead to build a dower house for herself in its immediate environs, the Palazzo Lante-Medici. She died in 1520, when the building under the direction of Baccio Bigio had reached the *piano nobile*. The façade is as simply articulated as that of the Palazzo della Valle. But now the ground floor is adorned with monumental aedicules, whose tectonic clarity and decorative magnificence eclipse all previous window frames. Equally magnificent are the courtyard porticoes with their columns of polychrome marble. No doubt the same excellent stonemasons, perhaps even including Jean de Chenevières, the later architect of San Luigi dei Francesi, sculpted the Doric capitals in the most splendid way with the coats of arms and heraldic devices of the Medici and Orsini. Presumably the columns of the upper loggia with the pronouncedly downward-hanging volutes of the Ionic capitals also go back to Giuliano's project.

When on 1 January 1514 Leo X appointed him second architect of St Peter's, then under construction, Giuliano once again remained in a subordinate role. After Bramante's death in April of the same year, Raphael succeeded him as architect in charge on 1 August, and Giuliano thenceforward exerted little more influence on the planning process. But his three independent projects for St Peter's dating to 1514/15 remain the most important source for these two years so

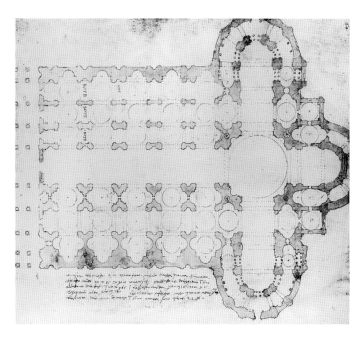

159 *In his last project for St Peter's Giuliano provides an ambulatory completely encircling the chancel and transepts.*

160 *In his proposal for the façade of San Lorenzo in Florence, 1515, Giuliano translates his earlier façade design into the style of the late Bramante.*

problematic for the further history of the basilica. In presumably the earliest of the three (GDSU 9A) Giuliano takes Bramante's Leonine project as his starting point. He extends the nave to at least seven bays, transforms the side chapels into two additional aisles, eliminates the ambulatories, but retains the long choir arm and Bramante's articulation of the interior and exterior. In the second project (GDSU 7A), by contrast, he takes over the chapels, but prolongs the ambulatories of the transepts by two bays, so that they extend in semicircular projections beyond the exterior. On both sides of Bramante's chancel he repeats octagonal sacristies of the kind he had already built in Santo Spirito (fig. 18). He recurs to the flanking bell-towers and varies the forest of columns of Bramante's pronaos. In the most mature of the three projects, which he included, not by chance, in his *Libro* (fig. 159), he comes closest to Raphael and now surrounds the chancel too with an ambulatory, eliminates the towers and reduces the columns of the pronaos. In all this he identified with the world of Bramante and Raphael, though without making any substantial innovation of his own.

In the summer of 1515 the now seventy-year-old Giuliano, embittered by not having been given larger commissions, worn out by his labours and crushed down by old age and illness (Vasari), returned to Florence. When the pope visited his hometown in the following winter, Giuliano must have presented to him his project for the still-unfinished façade of San Lorenzo, presumably at first only the elaborated façade projects from the period before 1510 (fig. 158). Criticisms may then have prompted him to complete three further projects (fig. 160).

A comparison between both series shows in what direction his style had moved. In his later series he eliminated pedestals, projecting entablatures and blind arcades, and designed a porch with its own balustrade-protected terrace. Instead of figural reliefs, he now decorated the wall surfaces with *all'antica* marble incrustation and inscriptions. In this way he helped the classicizing character and the

horizontal forces to gain the upper hand. One can feel the influence of Bramante's rich and normative late style, as well as Raphael's rival project, only a few months earlier in date (fig. 165).

In the third project, which he even signed, but which seems to have been drawn by his brother Antonio, he countered the horizontally focused façade with vertical flanking bell-towers. He knits them to the façade by repeating their entablature projections on the corners. But how unsystematically he planned even in his last projects is shown by the *bifora*-windows in the bell-towers, to which also Leonardo always held firm.

In *c*.1515/16 he also designed the project for a Medici residence to the north of the Spedale degli Innocenti in Florence (fig. 161). There he recurred almost literally to the rear half of his project for the king of Naples of 1489 (fig. 80). Stimulated however by the Cortile del Belvedere (figs 139, 140), he now opened up the courtyard

161 *Plan by Giuliano for a magnificent Medici residence, never built, combining a palace and a spacious garden.*

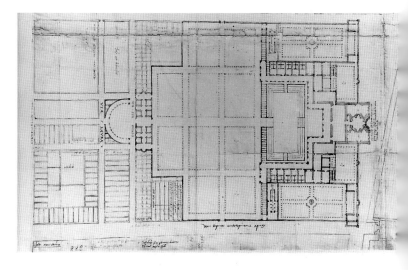

to an extensive garden, through which the slightly raised building would have been entered. Clearly the city-centre residence of the nephews of the pope was to yield nothing to those of the pope or the king of France.

Giuliano da Sangallo cannot be dissociated from the architecture of Bramante's High Renaissance. But he contributed far less to its major developments during the pontificates of Julius II and Leo X than he did in the period before 1500. He did so, moreover, less through his own buildings than through the influence he exerted on Raphael, Antonio da Sangallo, Jacopo Sansovino and Michelangelo.

Raphael (1483–1520)

Born in 1483, the son of Urbino's court painter, poet and chronicler Giovanni Santi, Raphael had been brought up at the court in Urbino. From his father he must have precociously imbibed the principles of ancient architecture, so splendidly exemplified by the buildings of Francesco di Giorgio in his hometown. Giovanni commemorated Francesco in his rhyming chronicle and accorded him greater praise than most other contemporaries. Apprenticed as a boy to Perugino, Raphael speedily became his prize pupil. In his earliest painted architectural backgrounds he took over from Perugino the characteristic vaulted halls with lesenes that break through the surrounding impost cornice or entablature, as in Francesco di Giorgio. In the *Crowning of Enea Silvio Piccolomini as Poet*, designed for Pinturicchio's fresco decoration of the Libreria in Siena Cathedral in 1502, he came even closer to Francesco di Giorgio than he did to Perugino. He thus based the loggia of the upper storey on that of the valley façade of the Palazzo Ducale in Urbino (fig. 89) and linked its pilasters with the lesenes of the ground floor with a dwarf order. Inspired by Francesco's central-plan buildings, he transformed the octagonal temple of Perugino's *Sposalizio* into his own sixteen-sided version with surrounding peristyle and hence into one of the finest central-plan buildings of the time. Francesco's influence can be followed right down to Raphael's Roman years. Raphael thus produced a variation on Urbino Cathedral (fig. 93) in his design for *Christ in the Temple* in 1509.

Yet far more decisive was to be the influence of his kinsman Bramante. Indeed, the barrel-vaulted hall of the *School of Athens* of 1509 is the first and most immediate reaction to Bramante's Julian plan for St Peter's. Though the series of domical bays of the basilica in the *Expulsion of Heliodorus* of 1511/12 is still reminiscent of Francesco's Osservanza in Siena (fig. 90), they are now supported by columns of a giant Corinthian order as in Bramante's red-chalk plan for St Peter's. Thus, soon after his arrival in Rome in the summer of 1508, Raphael became Bramante's one congenial disciple.

Stables of the Farnesina

The rich banker Agostino Chigi gave him his first opportunity to translate his ideas into stone in *c.*1511/12. In the now largely destroyed stable block of the Villa Farnesina in Rome he invested the still-shallow Quattrocentesque wall relief of Peruzzi's adjacent Farnesina with greater plastic depth and more normative proportions. He gave a robust Doric order to the actual stables on the ground floor, and a more decorative *Corinthia* to the *foresteria* on the first floor.

In this he followed the arrangement of the orders in the Cortile del Belvedere and Bramante's Vatican Logge (fig. 139). But in the paired pilasters and the high balcony windows of the *piano nobile* he also harked back to Bramante's Palazzo Caprini and its dynamic hierarchy (fig. 136). At the same time he remained faithful to the functionally founded tradition of reducing the upper storeys (figs 65, 71, 83). To the subordinate function of the attic storey he assigned plain lesenes, which have no capitals and rise to the lower profiles of the upper cornice. As already in the *School of Athens*, the wall relief was denser than in the Palazzo Caprini; the paired pilasters are placed closer together and little space is left between the relief and the windows: Bramante opened up the wall, Raphael closed it. He did not articulate the side walls and thus treated the façade not as the side of a three-dimensional body set in space, but as a continuous pictorial surface, and thus in the last analysis as a painter.

Yet, almost as if to counter such a criticism, he painted in 1513 the papal palace in the background of his *Fire in the Borgo* in the Stanze as a three-dimensional volume. He stacked the discrete blocks of the three storeys one on top of the other and, with masterly foreshortening, showed how the entablature of the upper floor continues round the corner, into space. The blessing Pope Leo IV is distinguished by a triumphal *serliana*; the *piano nobile* predominates even more clearly over the rusticated podium than in the Palazzo Caprini. The pattern of the rustication, however, is no longer tectonically determined (as it is in the Palazzo Caprini): the radiating voussoirs are purely ornamental and focus the eye on the pope. The third storey is once again wholly subordinate. Also in this scene Raphael ingeniously contrasts the austerity of the papal palace and the old basilica with the magnificent columnar orders and material splendour of the ancient temple.

Cappella Chigi

Not long afterwards Raphael succeeded in one of his most brilliant inventions (fig. 162). When seen from the portal of Santa Maria del Popolo, the richly decorated arcade and the square pillars of the *Corinthia* remind us of the Pantheon pronaos. The order continues under the massive inner arcade and leads us into the octagonal chapel. As in Bramante's project for St Peter's (figs 147, 148), Raphael diagonally splays the four pillars and lets the pendentives expand above them. These massive pillars, with the pilaster order angled at the corners, relieve the four arches and permit a dome whose diameter of over 7 m (23 ft) exceeds the vaulted ceilings of the adjacent Quattrocento chapels. The square windows surrounding the drum illuminate the rich figural programme. Raphael thus created monumentality out of the smallest of spaces and proved himself a legitimate successor of the ageing Bramante. In the detail of the order and the festoon-decorated frieze between the capitals he came even closer to the Corinthian splendour of the Pantheon. In the iconography of the chapel Raphael fused Christian and pagan ideas. He alluded to the salvation of the soul in the statues of *Jonah* and *Elijah* and in the bronze relief *Jesus and the Woman of Samaria*. In the pyramids of the two funerary monuments he alluded not only to Egyptian pyramids and obelisks, but even to purgatory in the flames of the lower zone of their fire-red marble. The pyramids direct the eye upwards to the dome, from whose fictive *oculus* God the Father is

calling the souls to him. Through the golden ribs we see the angels moving the universe and guiding the gods of the seven planets. As in Dante's *Paradiso*, pagan gods rule the heavenly spheres. The archer Apollo and his sister Diana preside over the presumed tombs of Agostino Chigi and his wife below. In the floor Bernini's skeleton of death with the hourglass counters this hope in the ascension of the soul with a baroque *memento mori*. Thus the Cappella Chigi is a coherent ensemble of architecture, painting, sculpture and mosaic decoration: it was designed by one artist, and is the first real *Gesamtkunstwerk* of the Renaissance.

Sant'Eligio degli Orefici

Raphael's Sant'Eligio degli Orefici, the little guild church of the goldsmiths situated on the banks of the Tiber, has only survived in fragments (fig. 163). Presumably Raphael had designed it before 1514, in response to the wish of a friend, the head of the guild Antonio da San Marino. But in order to adjust it to the altered urban situation after 1514 (with the laying out of the side streets of the Via Giulia),

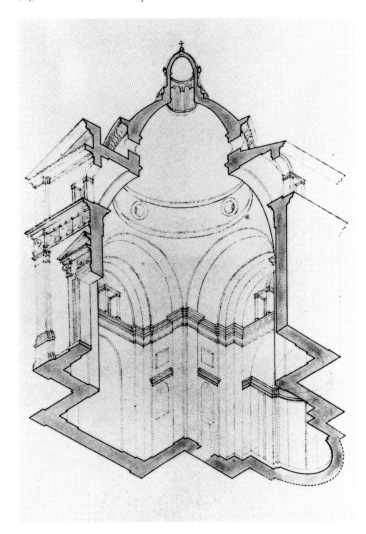

and his own altered ideas, Raphael reduced the closed block-like exterior, articulated with paired pilasters, to a Greek cross and articulated the single façade with bundled pilasters similar to those in the Palazzo Jacopo da Brescia (fig. 164). In this way he came closer, also in the exterior, to the type of central-plan church erected by Giuliano da Sangallo in the Madonna delle Carceri in Prato (figs 75, 76), which he must have admired during his Florentine years. Presumably he preferred the closed walls of the Greek-cross plan even to Bramante's quincunx system. The closed arms of the cross were in any case better suited to the assembly room of the goldsmiths.

As with Bramante's San Celso, economic reasons may have forced the articulation of the interior to be limited to lesenes and a surrounding impost cornice in stuccoed peperino. The interior in any case is unusually sober. From San Celso Raphael also took over the narrow splaying of the pillars supporting the dome, the low drum and the hemispherical dome. This creative synthesis of motifs from Bramante and Giuliano shows how little Raphael was satisfied with mere imitation and continued to seek his own way in the combination of the types and motifs familiar to him.

On the exterior he made the attic, once again articulated with lesenes, correspond to the zone of the barrel vaults, and the pediment to the roof. By closing the walls, by paying even closer attention to the correspondence between interior and exterior, and by coming closer to the *Dorica* of the norm of Vitruvius and Alberti, he created a type that lent itself more readily to imitation than San Celso; indeed the model of Sant'Eligio was widely copied and disseminated.

Palazzo Jacopo da Brescia

In 1515 Raphael was asked to erect a palazzetto for the papal physician Jacopo da Brescia not far from St Peter's (fig. 164). The pope and Cardinal Raffaele Riario, who was responsible for town planning, may have personally insisted that this exposed site at the mouth of the Via Sistina on the Via Alessandrina (close to St Peter's) be distinguished by an imposing building and perhaps even persuaded Raphael to design it. Raphael must in any case have found it challenging to reduce the scheme of a palazzetto to the extremely cramped and narrow site and invest it with all the allure of a grand patrician house in the classical style. Before the laying out of the Via della Conciliazione and the relocation of the building to its present site, the five windows of the *piano nobile* overlooked the prominent Via Alessandrina.

In deference to the patron's limited resources, Raphael also had to be satisfied with cheap materials like fine bricks and peperino, to which some semblance of the travertine of ancient monuments would have been given by stucco facing. Again he followed the traditional scheme of a palace with a vaulted ground floor, flat-ceilinged *piano nobile* and squat upper storey.

The differences from Bramante's Palazzo Caprini are even more striking than they are in the papal loggia of the *Fire in the Borgo*. The basement podium, containing shops topped by mezzanine windows, is layered with banded cushion-shaped rusticated courses without joints; only the keystones betray their origin from separated blocks. This emphasis on the horizontal forces is countered, on the *piano nobile*, by the vertical impulses of the pedimented window-aedicules

bay onwards. The result is that, when seen from St Peter's Square, the building, in its original position, must have seemed longer than it actually was; a perspective effect heightened by the strong parallel shadow lines cast by the banded rustication and the robust entablature.

The narrow side front, which formerly overlooked the crossroads and beyond it St Peter's Square, was dominated by a large blind triumphal-arch-like aedicule, with segmental pediment rising into the attic. It contained the huge marble coat of arms of the reigning pope and Jacopo's prominent inscription in the entablature. The close-set bundled pilasters at the corners lent further hierarchical emphasis to the blind central bay. But they also invested the wall with a dynamic inner unrest, only paralleled beforehand in the *Dorica* of Bramante's choir of St Peter's (fig. 147) and the slightly later background architecture in Raphael's *Coronation of Charlemagne*.

Façade of San Lorenzo

Raphael's competing project for the façade of San Lorenzo in Florence dates to the winter of 1515/16 (fig. 165); we know it only from a workshop sketch, presumably from the hand of the young Giulio Romano. Raphael takes as his starting point Giuliano da Sangallo's earliest façade projects, but he derived inspiration for the broad central bay in the ambulatories of St Peter's (fig. 159) and continued this rhythm in the narrower side bays and in the upper storey. He thus transformed the system into what was no doubt the most progressive of these years.

165 *Raphael, among many others, produced a design for the Medici church of San Lorenzo, 1515/16. This sketch is probably drawn by his pupil Giulio Romano.*

164 *Palazzo (or 'Palazzetto') Jacopo da Brescia, 1515. Here Raphael endows a relatively modest building with all the grandeur of the full classical style.*

and bundled pilasters inspired by the Cortile del Belvedere. The upward movement of the façade continues right up to the pronouncedly jutting entablature, terminating under the deep-shadowing eaves. These dynamic contrasts are neutralized in the high attic. By separating the *piano nobile* even more sharply from the other storeys, and continuing his aediculated windows almost right up to the entablature, he gave added emphasis to the patron's prestige.

Raphael's growing predilection for dynamic rhythms is also suggested by the perspectival foreshortening of this façade. Five triglyphs of the Doric entablature correspond to the first bay, on the corner, while only three correspond to the following four bays. The metopes, moreover, become progressively narrower from the second

Palazzo Alberini

Already in 1512, so just a few years after the planning of San Celso, Giulio Alberini, a young patrician who combined astuteness in business with connoisseurship in art, had begun a palazzo to serve as an apartment block on the corner opposite San Celso (fig. 166). He hoped to cover its costs at least in part by high rents. Probably the planning was entrusted to Raphael right from the start, and the basement system goes back to this first building phase of c.1512. Raphael there translated the rusticated courses of the Palazzo Caprini (fig. 136) into a less robust, more regular, refined and decorative language of smooth ashlars; the single blocks seem merely incised on the surface of the podium. After 1515, when Alberini had already rented some shops and an apartment to two Florentine bankers, Raphael and his pupil Giulio Romano altered the two upper storeys. But it was probably only after Raphael's death that Giulio added the fragmentary courtyard and the narrow but well-proportioned staircase. The building was completed by the Roman architect Antonio Sarti from 1864 onwards.

The Palazzo Alberini was conceived as a block of rented apartments, rather than as a patrician residence, and so Raphael did not return to the pretentious orders of recent patrician palaces. Nevertheless he succeeded in making the area of the residential quarters predominate even more commandingly over the basement podium than in his previous façades. In his articulation of the two upper floors Raphael recurred to the abstracted attic of the Palazzo Jacopo da Brescia (fig. 164). He replaced, however, the stuccoed peperino of the lesenes and blind panels with travertine for the mouldings and used small ochre-coloured bricks for the intervening walls. The *piano nobile* is only divided by its relatively shallow entablature from the third storey. Both storeys are so clearly segregated from the *basamento* and the attic that they grow together as a formal unity, as a single *piano nobile* with two rows of windows (none of them pedimented); this also conformed with the building's intended purpose.

The bases of the lower than normative shafts, raised over the continuous pediment zone of the *piano nobile*, suggest a *Tuscanica*. But since they possess no capitals and are projected only over the architrave of the abbreviated entablature, they are revealed as members of the kind of abstracted lesene orders that Francesco di Giorgio had helped to promote (figs 91, 93, 97). Rising from the same cornice as the pilasters are the mouldings that stretch up to the small oblong mezzanine windows and, in a more decorative form than blind panels, lend added emphasis to the windows. This system, which leaves the corners naked, is further abstracted in the upper storey, where the lesenes are transformed into oblong panels and the windows and their square frames seem to float over the flat surface.

These two residential storeys end in a widely projecting and deeply shadow-creating cornice. But, as in the Palazzo Rucellai (fig. 35), a squat attic follows above it. The alternating pillars and colonnades take up the rhythm of the lower storeys and recall the third courtyard storey of the Cortile del Belvedere.

Using the most restrained, primarily decorative forms, Raphael thus created new methods for the articulation of a residential building. His system for the Palazzo Alberini conformed to the

166 *The Palazzo Alberini, 1512–20, by Raphael and Giulio, was not a patrician palace but an apartment block with shops on the ground floor, built for profit.*

requirements of social differentiation, and lent even greater emphasis to the residential area than ever before.

Palazzo Branconio dell'Aquila

Long demolished and known only in graphic form, the Palazzo Branconio was begun by Raphael in the summer of 1518 for a close friend, the papal chamberlain Giovanbattista Branconio, who added to his name that of his hometown, Aquila (fig. 167). It was considerably smaller than the Palazzo Alberini, but its magnificently decorated façade made it immediately recognizable as the patron's house. Rather like the Palazzo Jacopo da Brescia which stood diagonally opposite it, it was intended to distinguish the mouth of the Via

167 *The Palazzo Branconio dell'Aquila of 1518 showed Raphael at his most self-consciously decorative, drawing special attention to the* piano nobile.

Alessandrina, now enlarged to form a piazza. The building site was somewhat broader and considerably deeper.

The basement podium consisted not of a rusticated arcade, but of five theatre motifs. The central archway led into *andito* and court-yard. The other four arches framed the shops. The *piano nobile* was significantly higher than that of the Palazzo Jacopo da Brescia and distinguished by Pantheon-type window-aedicules with alternating triangular and segmental pediments, separated by statue niches. The small oblong windows above the pediments formed a separate mez-zanine zone decorated with festoons, medallions and culminating in the central cartouche with tiara, keys and the papal arms. As in the Palazzo Alberini, the upper storey was separated from the *piano nobile* only by a shallow cornice and was knitted closely together with it by the continuation of the windows which alternate with decorated blind panels. Once again the residential quarters predominated in the façade. The marble-white surface was relieved by the polychrome accents of the coat of arms, marble doorframe and frescoes of the third storey. A terminating balustrade that first appeared in the Berlin perspective panel further underlined the dominance of the hori-zontal forces (fig. 72), though the monotony of its baluster row is relieved by being interspersed with short upright members. Raphael did everything possible not to degrade the *piano nobile* into a transition zone of the vertical forces. The wall apertures, decreasing in size from bottom to top, form pyramids, but these are separated, or rather counteracted, by the inverted pyramids that rise from the engaged columns of the basement to the niches, festoons and fresco panels of the attic.

Not only the Pantheon-aedicules and the Doric theatre motifs, but also the characteristic detail of the guttae-decorated architrave of the abbreviated Doric entablature had already appeared several years previously in the Palazzo Farnese (fig. 192). Its architect, Antonio da Sangallo the Younger, had been called in the autumn of 1516 to deputize for Raphael as second architect of St Peter's, and seems to have exerted an increasing influence on him. *All'antica* motifs, which

already belonged to Sangallo's repertoire, were, after the summer of 1518, thus to play an ever more important role also in Raphael's pro-jects for St Peter's, the Villa Madama and San Giovanni dei Fiorentini. Through close partnership with Sangallo he seems to have found an even more direct access to antiquity. But in his love for decorative richness, figural ornamentation and lavish materials he undoubtedly stood closer to Antonio's uncle Giuliano.

In the Palazzo Branconio, moreover, Raphael clearly went beyond Sangallo's paratactical composition. Like Bramante in his Palazzo Caprini, he opened up the aedicules into balconies and, as in the Pantheon, bound them to the wall by the abstracted entablature. He also derived inspiration from the Markets of Trajan in his alterna-tion of aediculated windows and niches, and from triumphal arches and mausolea in his festoons and medallions.

A project drawn by his prize pupil Giulio Romano has been pre-served for the low rear wing of the small courtyard, where it seems that Giulio was given a freer hand. Indeed, the complex corner pillars of the loggia or the vertical alignments of the orders and windows come closer to Giulio's slightly later Villa Lante than to the façade or to others of Raphael's buildings.

Palazzo Pandolfini in Florence

The design for the enlargement of the Florentine garden-palace of another prominent friend, the bishop Giannozzo Pandolfini, who had especially made a name for himself as a buffoon of the papal court, a burlesque companion of Julius II, presumably dates to the following year, 1519. The year 1520 is cited in the posthumous inscription and marks the onset of the work. After Pandolfini had died in 1525 and the building supervisor Giovanfrancesco da San-gallo in 1530, the building was abruptly terminated. Neither the irregular ground plan and asymmetrical façade nor most of its details can be associated with contemporary inventions of Raphael. The rusticated quoining and arched portal are reminiscent of the Palazzo Farnese (fig. 190); the window-aedicules of the ground floor, of San Salvatore al Monte (fig. 86); and the massive outward-jutting upper cornice, of the Palazzo Strozzi. Like the portal, all this could have been designed by Giovanfrancesco.

The *piano nobile* is only slightly higher than the closed ground floor, which also served as a residential storey for Pandolfini and con-tained a *vestibulum*, a study and a chapel. The main salon, however, is situated on the *piano nobile*, which is once again distinguished by monumental Pantheon-aedicules with continuous entablature; their proportions and details correspond roughly to those of the Palazzo Branconio. An alternation of similar aedicules joined by the abstracted entablature, with blind panels, occurs in Raphael's designs for a stage set and for the funerary monument of Francesco Gonzaga, so perhaps only this area of the *piano nobile* goes back to his project. When Baccio d'Agnolo transferred it to the middle of the three floors of his Palazzo Bartolini, he robbed it, however, of its monumental effect.

Raphael's palazzo on the Via Giulia

Raphael died only a few weeks after producing what was to be his last design for a building: it was to be his own house (fig. 168). Early in

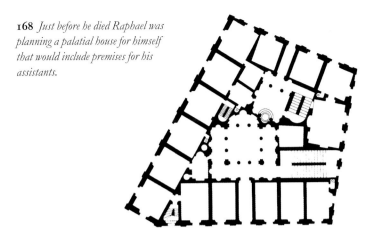

168 *Just before he died Raphael was planning a palatial house for himself that would include premises for his assistants.*

1520 he had purchased a trapeze-shaped piece of ground opposite San Giovanni dei Fiorentini, the national church of the Florentines, begun shortly before. Instead of using the whole site for an ambitious palazzo, he intended to divide it into a larger house for himself and a smaller one, separated from his own quarters and provided with its own workshops which perhaps was designed for Giulio Romano and Giovan Francesco Penni, his leading assistants. Raphael made do with a relatively narrow courtyard. It was to be surrounded by columnar porticoes, opening into a fountain-exedra to the rear,

with a comfortable but in no way princely flight of steps and relatively modest suite of rooms. On the other hand he laid the greatest value on the several workshops on the ground floor, a long enfilade of rooms in the favourably lit north wing of the *piano nobile*, harmonious proportions, and living quarters comprising a *studiolo*, bathroom with hot and cold running water, separate toilets and two side stairs, in other words an apartment suited to modern tastes. He ingeniously used every corner of the irregular site and amalgamated the rooms into a harmonious organism similar to his first project for the Villa Madama. Only the colossal order of the exterior, which was to span the two main storeys, would have given more decided expression to the prestige of the much-courted master, to whom, according to Vasari, the pope had even held out the prospect of a place in the Sacred College.

Villa Madama

The pope had bought the nucleus of the terrain for the building of a villa on Monte Mario on the outskirts of Rome in 1517. But it was only in the summer of the following year, when all the plans for papal residences on the Piazza Navona or in Florence had been abandoned, that the work on the villa began (figs 169–72). Raphael presumably completed his first project for the site shortly before

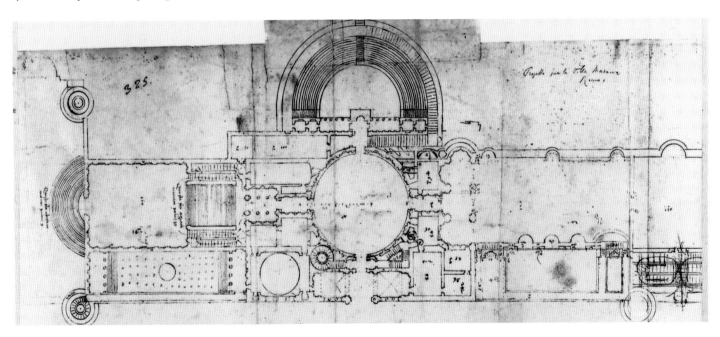

169 *Raphael and Antonio da Sangallo the Younger's second proposal for the Villa Madama. Its main features were a circular court and a theatre. The entrance from the Ponte Milvio was from the north-east (bottom of the plan), but a more monumental entrance from the Vatican via a staircase would have been from the south-east (left on plan).*

170 *Model of the north-east elevation, as planned. Only the right-hand half was ever begun.*

171 *The north-western loggia, opening into the terraced garden, built* c.*1519–20.*

172 *The fishpond, backed by three large exedras, serves as substructure of the terrace garden (right part of the plan).*

that. Cardinal Giulio de' Medici, appointed vice-chancellor in the previous year, now emerged as the official patron. The two cousins clearly wanted a villa with central loggia and several garden terraces that would open onto the gardens and the landscape, in the way that Alberti had prescribed and their great-uncle Giovanni had erected on the slopes of Fiesole (figs 51, 52). Raphael now adjusted this type to the papal requirements and his own ideas. He thus gave a similar form to both loggias as in Bramante's 'Nymphaeum' in Genazzano (figs 154, 155), and followed the model of the Vitruvian house in the sequence of *vestibulum*, *atrium* and *peristylium*.

Rather like Pliny the Younger, he described the villa in a detailed letter to Baldassare Castiglione. In the footsteps of the ancient authors and Alberti, he gave special attention to the villa's approach roads, its functions, its amenities (including its hippodrome and its baths), its views and its climatic conditions. Only *en passant* does he mention its form. Coming from the Vatican, one would have approached the villa axially on a gently ascending road and entered it through a portal flanked by round towers. The villa's longitudinal axis would then have led through a forecourt almost 50 m (164 ft) deep into a vestibule, atrium and thence into the inner courtyard. The latter is described as round by Raphael in his letter, but in his first project it is still oblong in shape, and has the same dimensions as the forecourt. Probably it would have been articulated by the same colossal *Ionica* as the exterior.

The transverse axis, reached from the Ponte Milvio, led to the central portal of the basement podium, so that, as Raphael's letter proudly remarks, one could have almost believed that the bridge had been built especially for the villa. In their breadth and axial alignment these approach roads would have been nearly as wide as the Via Giulia and would have invested the journey thither with a ceremonial pomp of a kind quite new for a villa. As he made his ascent the visitor would have admired a series of oval, round and square garden terraces, for which a project in Raphael's own hand has survived.

A hippodrome and stables for four hundred horses were planned in front of the some 200 m (650 ft) long valley front of the villa. The *vestibulum* of the basement podium was to be flanked to the left by a monumental bathhouse comprising a *tepidarium,* a *caldarium* and a *frigidarium* with a swimming pool, and to the right by the kitchens. The executed fragment of the elongated *vestibulum*, comprising a semicircular exedra, is still reminiscent of the loggia of the 'Nymphaeum' in Genazzano (figs 154, 155) and gives some idea of Raphael's first project. From this a double-ramp staircase for mounting on horseback would have ascended to the inner courtyard, ending in a nymphaeum at the centre of the rear wall. The central loggia overlooking the valley was placed over the *vestibulum*. It would have corresponded to it in plan and led into the large salon. As in Genazzano its impressive hemispherical dome rising over pendentives would have been flanked by two groin-vaulted bays. The summer apartment, the only one executed, is aligned north-east. It comprises only a *sala*, an antechamber and the cardinal's living room, from whose two corner windows he could enjoy the view over the Tiber valley on the one side and an exterior swimming pool on the other. From the antechamber one enters the large loggia opening onto an oblong garden terrace that continues behind a partition wall with Ionic portals. Thus the longitudinal axis would have been even deeper in extension than that of the Cortile del Belvedere. The *xystus*, as Raphael called the first garden, is supported by the rear wall of the pool; the wall was to end in a corner tower with the villa's only chapel, which is reminiscent of Bramante's Tempietto.

The left side of the salon would have continued in the five rooms of the winter apartment, a sheltered orange garden and the panoramic *dietha*, or observation tower. The semicircular auditorium of an open-air theatre was to be hewn into the steeply ascending slope to the back of the inner courtyard.

In no other project are the dreams, aspirations and inventions of the Renaissance so concretely expressed; in none are they so directly conceived for a re-creation of ancient villa life. The pope, the cardinal and their guests wanted to dine in the open air; bathe, perspire and be massaged in the baths; exercise themselves and be entertained by races in the hippodrome and by classical plays or comedies in the theatre. They wanted to stroll for their pleasure in extensive gardens and have at their disposal loggias, living rooms and bedrooms suited to every season in the year – a utopia in which Raphael fused the villas in Fiesole and Poggio a Caiano, the Cortile del Belvedere and Bramante's 'Nymphaeum' with everything described about the suburban villa by the ancient authors and Alberti.

Already during the winter of 1518/19, as work was proceeding on the basement floor, a radical change of plan was prompted by the need to consolidate the sloping and unstable terrain. This was entrusted to Raphael's assistant, Antonio da Sangallo the Younger. Partly because of the problem of the terrain, the rectangular courtyard was now replaced by a smaller circular court and the rear wall over the slope more efficiently buttressed by the theatre. The hand of the experienced engineer can also be felt in the static use of exedras, round towers, stables and garden terraces, or in the more rational staircase ramps of the forecourt. Sangallo's preparatory studies suggest that the round court and the reduction of the winter apartment, which had disturbed the symmetry of the façade, are attributable to him. They also show that in designing the theatre he held even more canonically to Vitruvian norms.

Yet Raphael still retained overall control of the architectural form. To be able to combine the circular court and loggias with the parts already executed before the change in plan, he even accepted the asymmetry of the garden loggia. The system of axes and the distribution of the rooms remained largely unchanged; indeed, the executed parts are far closer in style to him and Giulio than to Sangallo.

Before Raphael's death in April 1520, however, the only executed part of the *piano nobile* had been the shell of the garden loggia (fig. 171). It is perhaps the most impressive secular interior of the whole Renaissance. It differs from its prototype in Genazzano not only in its more monumental dimensions and rear exedras, inspired by the *caldarium* of the Baths of Caracalla, but also by much the same characteristics that had already differentiated Raphael's first architectural inventions from Bramante. The proportions are thus less steep, the walls hermetically closed, and a more continuous and rapid horizontal movement is determined by the dense succession of lesenes and niches. Raphael thus laid more emphasis on the horizontal rhythm of the pilaster order than on their load-bearing function. His unique art of suggesting spatial expanse – exemplified most potently in painting by the *School of Athens* – is more impressively expressed here than in his other buildings. The interior of the loggia does not branch out into adjoining rooms as in Bramante, but is firmly surrounded by the shell of the wall. In Bramante interior space is transparent; the walls are opened out; the eye is led, as in the Prevedari print (fig. 101), in various directions. In Raphael the richness and expansion of space are conjured out of a closed shell.

This spatial unity of the loggia has undoubtedly suffered from the fact that three different masters decorated it. Only the system used by Giulio in the decoration of the exedra adjacent to the summer apartment corresponds to Raphael's tectonic thinking.

The elevation of the valley façade was only executed after Raphael's death, under Giulio's supervision, and perhaps no longer corresponds in every detail to Raphael's project. No doubt it was intended to be as richly ornamented as the Palazzo Branconio (fig. 167). The colossal order of the *piano nobile* dominates the basement podium in a way anticipated only by Bramante's Palazzo dei Tribunali (fig. 150). As a place of *otium* and the preserve of the Muses, Raphael chose however an *Ionica* and reduced the rustication of the lower storey to the rusticated portal and the rusticated oblong windows.

On the *piano nobile* the central loggia is flanked on either side by two symmetrical triumphal-arch-like corner pavilions. The one on the left reflects the interior of the domed salon and is counterbalanced by the one on the right, where the huge Diocletian window is blind (fig. 170). Engaged columns carrying a projecting entablature flank the central arch of the loggia. In this arch, the only one that opens into a balcony, the horizontal and vertical forces intersect. It represents the Medici patrons even more magnificently than do the balcony windows of the Palazzo Caprini or Palazzo Branconio. The principle of correspondence of Francesco di Giorgio and Bramante is combined here with Bramante's hierarchical thinking and predilection for complex rhythms into a quite revolutionary dynamic that was not to be developed further till Vignola and Maderno.

The arcades of both side bays are also reminiscent of Francesco di Giorgio and the façade of Urbino Cathedral (fig. 93). Below the imposts the pillars are only differentiated from the Ionic pilasters by their Tuscan bases. They fuse with the wall above the imposts in a way reminiscent of the triumphal arch of Bramante's Canonica in Milan (fig. 113) and are more easily attributable to Giulio than Raphael.

The Villa Madama was one of the most influential buildings of the whole Renaissance and was repeatedly drawn and imitated by Genga, Serlio, Vignola and Palladio right down to Borromini, Robert Adam and Percier.

St Peter's

Bramante died in April 1514, just after he had begun work on both side ambulatories in St Peter's. Raphael's first sketches for the basilica date to the following months. Officially installed as the new architect on 1 August, he was to devote far more effort to St Peter's than to his other buildings. Yet his ideas can only be partially reconstructed. Most were discarded. Few demonstrably conduced to the progress of the building. The blame for this must mainly lie with Leo X, who had already commissioned Bramante to proceed to an unrealistic enlargement of the project in 1513/14.

Already in July 1514 Raphael proudly reported to his uncle in Urbino that the pope was consulting him and Fra Giocondo daily about St Peter's and wanted to spend 60,000 ducats on it annually, and altogether one million ducats; so a building period of over sixteen years was envisaged.

In his ground plan of 1514, as published by Serlio in his treatise, Raphael proposed, in essence, to complete Bramante's latest project with the quincunctial system of his first projects (figs 142, 143); this would have meant partially demolishing the just-completed chancel and rebuilding it to match the arms of the new transepts.

After his former partners Giuliano da Sangallo and Fra Giocondo had withdrawn from the building site in 1515, Raphael was given a freer rein in the planning of the new basilica. The second project of Raphael known to us dates to *c.*1518 and has been preserved in a precise copy (fig. 173). Like Giuliano da Sangallo in his last project (fig. 159), he now integrated Bramante's choir arm and articulated the exterior even more volumetrically than in 1514 by projecting square corner sacristies. He reduced the pillars of the ambulatories and expanded their colonnades. In doing so he altered the rhythm of Bramante's triumphal motifs, but at the same time opened up

173 *Elevation and section of Raphael's second project for St Peter's dating from about 1518.*

the ambulatories and condensed the corresponding articulation of the exterior.

The façade now reflected not only the triumphal rhythm of the nave and its colossal Corinthian order, but also the colonnades of the ambulatories, and thus corresponded even more closely to the interior than in any previous project. By opening it up in a two-storeyed colonnade Raphael went further than in his project for the façade of San Lorenzo (fig. 165). The relatively squat engaged columns of the giant order of the temple front, its Pantheon-aedicule projecting from the upper colonnade and the festoons of the towers resemble so closely the Palazzo Branconio (fig. 167) that the project may have been produced during the same months of the summer of 1518 and soon after his first project for the Villa Madama.

The lower colonnade, for which Raphael wanted to use columns from the old nave as in the ambulatories, continues round the whole exterior in the form of pilasters. But the upper colonnade is only continued in this way along the exterior of the eastern end of the aisles. By connecting temple front and triumphal arch, Raphael now sought inspiration from Alberti's Sant'Andrea (fig. 55), as Bramante had done when designing the nave.

The reduction of Bramante's order along the sides and the choir to less than half its height was dictated by the column shafts from old St Peter's that Raphael wanted to reuse; but it was unconvincing in form and immediately criticized by Antonio da Sangallo the Younger.

In Antonio's only ground-plan sketch, on which he remarked on Raphael's small order, he proposed a compromise. The order was now to reach up to the impost cornice of the arcades of the nave and with a shaft width of 9 *palmi* (*c.*2 m or 6½ ft) was to seek a middle way between Raphael's order of 5 *palmi* and Bramante's of 12 *palmi*. When constructing St Peter's, Bramante had laid the impost cornice of the nave at the level of the Sistine Chapel and the Sala Regia, in order to facilitate a future organic connection between the Basilica and the adjoining Papal Palace.

Sangallo's 9-*palmi* order, by respecting this connection and by being better coordinated with the interior of the basilica, was far more logical than Raphael's small one. The pope decided to adopt it, and presumably Raphael had himself been convinced by it in discussions with Sangallo. Execution of the south transept began shortly before his death: fragments of its apse can be seen in drawings by Heemskerck and a fresco by Vasari.

On the exterior engaged Doric columns of the 9-*palmi* order alternate with Doric aedicules, a paratactical succession that is more reminiscent of Sangallo's previous buildings than Raphael's. Yet Raphael's part in the project can be detected in the systematic way in which half-pilasters mediate between the engaged columns and the aedicules, and their linking together by a continuous entablature, as in the Palazzi Branconio and Pandolfini. The ideas of both masters seem to have been combined in a similar way as in the design of the circular court of the Villa Madama in the spring of 1519.

Raphael's corresponding project for the façade of St Peter's does not survive, indeed may not even have existed. It can only be inferred from Sangallo's contemporary projects (fig. 194). In these the bell-towers are eliminated and the colossal 12-*palmi* order and the 9-*palmi* order of the rest of the exterior are similarly joined together as on the choir façade of Santa Maria presso San Satiro (fig. 104).

San Giovanni dei Fiorentini

A drawing probably in the hand of Giulio Romano preserves Raphael's project for San Giovanni dei Fiorentini, the new national church of the Florentines facing onto the opening of the Villa Giulia on one side and the Tiber on the other. The temple pronaos with eight freestanding columns, the circular *cella* and the stepped dome follow the Pantheon. Yet, as in Raphael's second project for St Peter's, the temple front is flanked by two bell-towers, and the interior illuminated by a high drum, which only begins above the pediment. Indeed, the broad portico seems to be overpowered by the massive rotunda above it. The bell-towers are even slenderer and more elegant than those of St Peter's and their storeys exactly coordinated with the system of drum and dome. The interior of the rotunda was to have a diameter of *c.*100 *palmi* and a height of c.150 *palmi*. It is articulated with theatre motifs of a Doric order with engaged columns. In the main axes the arcades open into chapels reminiscent of the Cappella Chigi (fig. 162).

Seen from the Tiber the church would have had a similarly composite character as his project for St Peter's. Unconditioned by any previous building on the site, Raphael came closer here to the Pantheon than any of his predecessors and tried once again to fuse together the pagan temple with the Christian tradition.

Raphael's activity as an architect extends far beyond the relatively small number of his known buildings and projects. As papal architect he completed the *Loggie* of the Apostolic Palace and transformed their second storey into an all-encompassing *Gesamtkunstwerk* similar to the Cappella Chigi. The *Loggietta* and the bathroom of Cardinal Bibbiena on the fourth floor of the Vatican palace gave him the opportunity to come even closer to ancient decoration.

He also designed stage sets, was responsible together with Sangallo for town planning, and also assumed personal responsibility for

the preservation of the ancient monuments of Rome. To the study of the antique, indeed, he devoted quite special attention. He accordingly took into his house Fabio Calvo, a known humanist, to translate and help him to interpret Vitruvius. He was also commissioned by Pope Leo X to produce a topography of ancient Rome with surveys and reconstructions of the most important monuments, not least with the purpose of protecting them and erecting the foundations of the new Rome over those of the old. In the preface to this work written shortly before his death, he described to the pope this enterprise in great detail and the principles he intended to use in measuring and drawing the ancient structures. He placed it in the context of his ideas about the development of the history of art and architecture, as he had been able to reconstruct it by comparing the monuments with the ancient texts. These ideas are now much more concrete than those of Brunelleschi as described in Antonio Manetti's *vita* and go even beyond Alberti. The Greeks had – says Raphael – developed their 'rational' architecture from the careful balance between load and support in wooden buildings and basic geometric forms. They had followed the proportions of man, woman and girl in the invention of the Doric, Ionic and Corinthian orders (cf. Vitruvius Book VI). Only later had the 'Attic' order of quadrangular columns (*le colonne facte a quattro faccie*) and the more rarely used *Tuscanica* been added to the canon. Up to Diocletian and Constantine the Romans had built in a rational manner. But all this had been destroyed by the barbarians from the north. Thence the German 'manner' had also penetrated Italy (*la maniera dell'architectura tedesca*, i.e. Gothic): a manner that was equally based on the laws of nature, but that had been shown to be bizarre and less rational and enduring than ancient architecture. After this period of decline and fall, the Italians had then returned to the architecture of their forefathers in the third, modern age, as exemplified by the many fine works of Bramante, though without ever achieving its perfection. Raphael ends his foreword to the letter by expressing the hope that Leo X as prince of peace would preserve the ancient exempla, reawaken architecture to new life, and even surpass it.

Giulio Romano (1499?–1546)

Like his teacher Raphael, Giulio was a *Wunderkind*. He began his apprenticeship at the start of the pontificate of Leo X, when Raphael began to develop a more deliberately *all'antica* style and created his first *Gesamtkunstwerk*, the Cappella Chigi. So from the very beginning he was trained in all the visual media: no one, says Vasari, 'was better grounded, more bold, resolute, prolific and versatile'. Giulio learnt not only how to paint in fresco but also how 'to draw in perspective, take the measurements of buildings, and execute ground plans'. Already in the preparatory drawings for the *Fire in the Borgo* and the *Battle of Ostia* in the Vatican Stanze of 1513/14 his hand can be differentiated from that of his master. No matter whether he was only fourteen or some years older at the time, right from his debut he stood in the very forefront of European art.

For Raphael he sketched, probably in 1515/16, the façade of San Lorenzo (fig. 165) and in the late summer of 1518 he produced designs for San Giovanni dei Fiorentini, for the stage set of Ariosto's

Suppositi and for the fountain wall of the Palazzo Branconio court-yard. Raphael, indeed, left him considerable leeway in the articulation of that courtyard. A strong verticalism, very different from Raphael's façade of the same palazzo and perhaps inspired by Michelangelo's wooden model for the façade of San Lorenzo (fig. 240), was to remain a characteristic of Giulio's own independent Roman buildings.

His project for the elevation of the round court of the Villa Madama (in London) is still relatively close to Raphael's project for the ambulatories of St Peter's (fig. 173) and should therefore date to *c.*1520. The proportions of the round court, in part executed by Giulio, are considerably steeper. The prominent Ionic volutes that extend over the fireplace of the *salotto* of the villa betray the same hand as the windows of the Villa Lante. Giulio also went far beyond Raphael in the tendencies towards abstraction visible in the valley façade and in the asymmetries of the garden front.

Palazzo Adimari-Salviati

In May 1520 – so soon after Raphael's death and the start of the Palazzo Pandolfini – Filippo Adimari, like Pandolfini a bishop and Florentine patrician, had a similar suburban garden-palace erected for himself on the Via della Lungara (figs 174, 175). That it was Giulio's first completely self-designed building is confirmed by a surviving sketch. But it never progressed beyond the ground floor during his Roman years, and was revamped and completed by Nanni di Baccio Bigio for the Salviati after 1550.

Even if the building largely coincided in length and height with the Palazzo Pandolfini, its spirit is completely different. Giulio works with flat wall layers and allows the three-bayed centrepiece, repre-

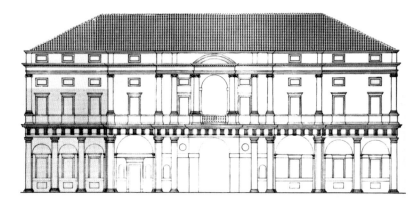

175 *Elevation of the Palazzo Adimari's garden front, which is wilfully asymmetrical.*

senting the large entrance hall and the *sala*, to clearly dominate the corner blocks with the master's rooms – a system that had been inspired by Bramante's Palazzo dei Tribunali, but which was not very widespread before Giulio. The surviving parts of the ground floor surpass even Sangallo's exemplary stonework in the elegant interplay of rusticated quoining, rusticated window-arches, ornamental brick-work and *opus reticulatum*. The *piano nobile* of the centrepiece was no doubt intended to be opened in a triumphal arch, as in the Palazzo Farnese. Giulio's on the whole more decorative and less monumental style would have especially determined the garden front. Its rhythm was even more dynamic than the valley façade of the Villa Madama and he used the irregular site to produce a dissonant asymmetry. In contrast to Raphael's palaces, the *piano nobile* would have been considerably squatter than the ground floor. The *Doric* order of slender pilasters that articulated the ground floor would have been superimposed by a delicate *Ionic* pilaster order, topped by a mezzanine which continued on the façade.

Villa Turini-Lante

At about the same time he designed a suburban villa on the brow of the Janiculum for the papal datary Baldassarre Turini da Pescia, an intimate confidant of Leo X and friend of Raphael (one of the executors of the artist's will) (fig. 176). The villa is built over ancient foundations, thought at the time to be those of Martial's villa: an inscription with an apposite quotation from the poet is walled into the loggia: '*Hinc totam licet aestimare Romam*' ('From here one can appreciate all Rome'). Such a rebuilding of an antique villa corresponded exactly to Raphael's ideas of the new Rome.

Not only the villa's extraordinary situation, but also its small number of rooms and its loggia, recall the Villa Medici in Fiesole (figs 51, 52). It must have been similarly intended as the meeting place for a cultivated circle of friends: not by chance did Giulio portray the rediscovery of ancient texts in a fresco in the *sala* and Raphael as a poet together with Dante, Petrarch and Politian in one of the adjacent rooms. The service rooms and the frescoed bath-room were installed in the basement podium built into the steep slope of the hill. On the main floor, a central corridor flanked by cubic living rooms leads into the cube-shaped, eccentrically situated *sala* and the loggia to the back, commanding panoramic views over

174 *Giulio Romano designed his first building in 1520, the Palazzo Adimari, Rome. Only parts of the ground storey were completed in his lifetime.*

176 *Model of the Villa Turini-Lante. Though heavily changed, it still stands on the brow of the Janiculum overlooking Rome.*

The arches of the loggia prevented Giulio from placing the pilasters of the second floor axially over the columns; so they are slightly displaced out of axis, in one case (the arch to the far left of the loggia façade) even further than necessary. Once again necessity tempted Giulio into a dissonant, even provocative charm. Moreover, the way that the arches of the *serliane* cut through into the upper storey robs the entablature of its structural effect and makes it purely ornamental. Rather as composers since the Romantic period countered excessive tonality with deliberate dissonance, the heir of Bramante and Raphael began to enliven the monotony of normative orders with irregularities.

The interior of the loggia is not articulated with the kind of exedras and niches that Bramante and his Raphael had privileged. Instead, the steep *serliane*, which are mirrored on the back wall, cut at right angles into the richly stuccoed barrel vault. The *serliana* motif is even repeated in blind form on the two short walls.

Palazzo Stati-Maccarani

Only after Leo X and his sister-in-law Alfonsina Orsini had died, and the plans of the Medici for the renewal of the Piazza Sant'Eustachio had foundered, did the young Roman patrician Cristoforo Stati dare to commission Giulio to design his family palace on the piazza (figs 177, 178). Perhaps the patron at first could afford to build only the three bays to the right of the façade; this would explain the eccentric situation of the inner courtyard. Two engravings in Windsor with three-bayed elevations, even closer in type to that of the Palazzo Caprini (fig. 136), possibly transmit Giulio's alternative projects. In one of these, the paired half-columns are coupled with blind arcades to form theatre motifs – a system on which Sangallo, Sanmicheli (fig. 224) and Jacopo Sansovino would later produce variations. In a third print the façade is enlarged to five bays and three storeys, decreasing in height from bottom to top, and thus directly prepares for the executed version.

In this preparatory version, Giulio follows the Palazzo Alberini (fig. 166) by separating the upper storeys only by a thin entablature and fusing them together into a unified system. Here the order of the *piano nobile* is furnished with full pilasters and steeper window-aedicules exclusively topped with triangular pediments that take up the whole height of the blind panels. The rusticated portal-aedicule, pressed between (and with its triangular pediment overlapping) the rusticated pillars of the ground floor, is still missing.

The executed façade follows the Windsor print in combining the robust rusticated basement plinth with the more delicate relief of the two upper storeys. The *piano nobile* is now as high as the ground floor and its bays are wider and articulated with paired lesenes. The slight broadening of the central bay and the alternation of triangular with segmental pediments help to counteract the vertical impulse. As in the Villa Turini-Lante, the plasticity is gradually flattened, and the vertical dynamic reduced, before ebbing away completely in the abstracted panels of the attic storey. The top cornice is limited to a few mouldings. The return to three storeys and the *descrescendo* of their articulation rob the *piano nobile* of the dominance with which Raphael had gradually invested it – as if Giulio were questioning the self-assurance of the previous decade. As in Francesco di Giorgio,

the whole of Rome. The vaulted ceilings of all the rooms are projected deep into the upper storey; that explains why several of its windows are blind. Giulio succeeded in a masterly way in combining rooms of different heights within the same interior and masking the disparities by a symmetrical exterior.

In contrast to the Villa Medici, the exterior is systematically articulated right round by similar slender decorative orders as in the Palazzo Adimari. In the *Dorica* of the ground floor Giulio combined the lower courtyard order of the Palazzo Branconio with the abbreviated entablature of its façade (fig. 167). As in his design for the fountain wall of the Palazzo Branconio, the full columns of the portal-aedicule grow out of half-columns, and as in the Palazzo Jacopo da Brescia (fig. 164) its segmental pediment breaks through the trabeation and stretches up into the upper floor.

In the ever-changing rhythm and subtle modulation of the exterior articulation Giulio goes far beyond Raphael. The pilasters on the corners are perceptibly broader and only doubled on the corners of both side fronts. On the corners of the loggia front they are fused together with half-columns, as in the courtyard loggia of the Palazzo Branconio. The relatively powerful and stocky pilasters of the *Dorica*, with its deep shadow-creating mouldings, are dissolved on the Ionic floor into shallow decorative stucco pilasters, as thin as pasteboard, and into the even shallower panels in the mezzanine frieze. The shafts of the *Ionica* are decorated with four flutes on the main façade, and with only three or even two on the valley front. Their delicate volutes seem flattened by the pressure of the architrave, and are continued by the volutes that curve out from the top of the window frames.

177 *Exterior of the Palazzo Stati-Maccarani, Rome, by Giulio Romano: the* piano nobile *is losing the predominance it had gained with Bramante and Raphael.*

178 *In the narrow but highly elegant courtyard Giulio again plays with vertical continuity and partial asymmetry.*

the order becomes ever more actively and integrally a part of the wall, though without reflecting the actual structure of the building.

The use of travertine is restricted to the mouldings, while the masonry is a conglomerate of bricks and tufa (as in the Villa Madama) but formerly stuccoed to resemble travertine. As in the Palazzo Caprini (fig. 136), the massive-looking rustication of the basement podium is not what it seems.

In the interior layout Giulio shows much the same mastery he had displayed in the Villa Turini-Lante. The central pedimented portal of the façade admits to a steep narrow barrel-vaulted *andito*, which leads as eccentrically into the left bay of the arcaded loggia of the court-yard, as the corridor of the Villa Turini-Lante into the *sala*. From the other end of the loggia the ingeniously placed staircase ascends to the upper floor. It is lit only from the courtyard, and the windows of its first landing thus cut through the abbreviated entablature of the order of its ground floor. This asymmetry is mirrored on the other side wall and compensated by the doubling of the pilasters between the second and third bay. The intercolumniations are clad in smooth continuous stuccoed ashlars; only on the back wall are narrow blind panels placed between the pilasters and the ashlared courses. The *piano nobile* of the courtyard is even higher than that of the façade and its Ionic order taller and slenderer than the Doric one beneath. The abbreviated entablature projects above the pilasters. Over the loggia of the ground floor stand the columns of the never-completed portico through which the salon and the main living rooms were to be reached. Like the façade of the Palazzo Alberini (fig. 166), the window-aedicules, unconnected by any cornice, seem to float in the wall. As on the ground floor, they are topped by mezzanine windows

– a system repeated later on many façades. The flat window-frames, profiled on the sides with half-balusters, were to inspire Peruzzi, Michelangelo, Alessi and many others.

Giulio's Roman house

Giulio inherited his parents' house on the Macel de' Corvi (near Trajan's Column) in 1524, the last of his Roman years. The house no longer exists but its façade can be reconstructed on the basis of some Cinquecento drawings (fig. 179). Giulio was bound to the height of its storeys and the width of its bays. These constraints inspired him to one of his most original inventions. The narrow two-bayed frontage was invested with all the dignity of a Renaissance town palace. Once again the ground floor predominated over the *piano nobile* and the entrance bay over the side bay. The rusticated pillars of the portal were not topped by a pediment as in the Palazzo Stati, but by an arch of long radiating voussoirs, of which the central keystone breaks through into the abbreviated entablature. The Ionic columns of the first-floor Pantheon-aedicule, protected by a closed balcony, were banded with square blocks, while a smaller version of the radiating voussoirs of the Stati portal was placed between the architrave and the triangular pediment. By repeating these wall apertures in a simplified form in the narrow side bay and by continuing the rustica-

179 *Model of Giulio Romano's Roman house, which he inherited and altered in 1524.*

tion uniformly, he created a certain balance within this utterly asymmetrical façade.

With this sequence of five buildings and a few other later-destroyed smaller architectural commissions, including the Loggia dei Trombetti in the Vatican and two rusticated garden portals, Giulio, by far the youngest of all Italian architects, succeeded in continuing Raphael's achievements at the highest level. But at the same time he altered them; indeed, by daring departures from his master's teachings, he even travestied them. By introducing the *serliana* in series (as in the Villa Turini-Lante loggia) and the abstracted order, by raising stucco rustication into a vogue, by developing the 'pictorial' qualities of architectural surfaces, by making asymmetry socially acceptable and by violating the metric regularity of the Renaissance, he not only paved the way for the following generations, but also showed Michelangelo the way to new inventions.

Palazzo Te

Like Bramante in Rome, so Giulio in Mantua introduced a new era in architecture: for the first time since Alberti and Bramante the focal point of architecture once again returned to northern Italy. Giulio's fame had spread rapidly beyond Rome and the Papal State. Already by the end of 1522 (when Giulio was still in his early twenties) Federico Gonzaga, the young margrave of Mantua, seems to have commissioned him to transform into a villa the destroyed castle of Marmirolo near Mantua. This was followed, in October 1524, by an invitation to Giulio to settle in Mantua. Shortly afterwards he began his designs for Sant'Andrea (fig. 54) and the Palazzo Te (figs 180–83).

At first he simply rebuilt an older stable block, situated just outside the town walls, and transformed it into what is now the north wing of the Palazzo. The decision to proceed to the erection of a four-winged complex must have been taken in 1526. It was conceived not so much as a villa as one of those suburban, garden-surrounded, princely residences which had already existed in Ferrara and were then coming into vogue: part of the transformation of feudal into courtly lifestyle. The Palazzo Te was just a few minutes from one of the Gonzaga town residences, the Palazzo San Sebastiano, and seems to have had a ceremonial as well as a residential function: not by chance did Federico receive there the Emperor, who had come to Mantua in 1530 to invest him with the title of duke; the Emperor paid a second visit in 1532.

As in the Villa Turini-Lante, Giulio started out with a square ground plan and its subdivision into smaller squares. As in his Roman house, he rusticated the walls all over and again made use of economical stuccoed bricks rather than masonry (suitable quarries were lacking in the vicinity). He articulated the one-and-a-half storeyed building – a ground-floor *piano nobile* and an upper mezzanine – with a Doric order with triglyph frieze and thus recognized the single-storeyed character of the ancient house, rather as Bramante had done in his 'Nymphaeum' at Genazzano (fig. 154).

The approach road, which Giulio wanted to adorn with a magnificent rusticated triumphal-arch-like town gate, led to the older north wing. Since Giulio was conditioned here by the pre-existing wing, the bay widths are adjusted accordingly and the pilasters of the paratactical system are only doubled at the corners. The double vestibule at its

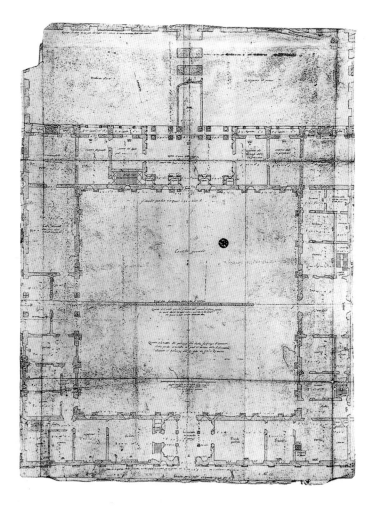

faces topped by blind panels recur at the corners of the wing, forming Bramantesque pilaster triads.

As in the Palazzo Farnese (figs 190, 191), the entrance of this main axis leads into a three-aisled atrium, its rusticated columnar order giving the impression of something deliberately left incomplete, and thence into the square courtyard, the *cavaedium* and *peristylium*. There the pilasters of the exterior are transformed into plastic half-columns with decorated capital necks, again as in the courtyard of the Palazzo Farnese (fig. 192). The portals and the windows are here topped by triangular pediments. On the west and east sides Giulio continued the triumphal-arch motif of the portal, but abandoned any correspondence with the interior layout. On the side wings he only slightly varied the rhythm of the exterior. So the courtyard predominates over the exterior, the longitudinal axis over the transverse axis and hence over the centralizing effect of the square.

At the same time Giulio indulged in a taste for caprice; indeed, put all previous *capricci* in the shade. The irregular rustication of the walls, with its part rough, part smooth surfaces, its arbitrary gaps, seems more deliberate than unfinished. The voussoir-like entablature blocks at the centre of each bay on the west and east sides slip downwards as if the entablature were not yet finished. In a preparatory design for the courtyard Giulio even wanted to give the impression that the building was like some earthquake-shattered ancient monument in danger of collapsing. Similarly, the (fictive) downward-tumbling dome in the adjacent Sala dei Giganti seems about to engulf the visitor. Such effects are both playful and unsettling: Giulio wanted both to terrify and amuse.

The longitudinal axis leads to the imposing garden loggia. Its basic scheme is that of the Villa Turini-Lante, but is on a far grander scale: its Doric order is more monumental and the *serliane* are supported by groups of four columns as in the ambulatories of St Peter's (fig. 159). A bridge leads into the secret garden to the rear; only from

180 *The Palazzo Te, outside Mantua, was begun when Giulio Romano was still a young man in his twenties.*

centre leads into the huge inner court. However, the main (longitudinal) axis of the Palazzo Te, which was established only in the second enlarged project, runs from west to east; this ambivalence of the axes must have been to Giulio's liking. The main entrance was distinguished by a portal at the centre of the west façade in the shape of a triumphal-arch. Its narrower side bays with niches hewn into their

181–83 *In his Mantuan masterpiece, the suburban palazzo-villa of young Federico Gonzaga, Giulio assembled all his Roman experiences in the capricious manner of the mid-1520s.*

there could the garden front and its reflections in the fishpond be properly enjoyed. Its rusticated basement is sunk in the water. The triple-arched loggia forms the slightly projecting centrepiece of the rear façade. It is flanked on either side by four small *serliane* that protect the rooms and their balcony windows from the sun. In the small colonnades of the squat attic storey, demolished in the eighteenth century, the rhythm was even more capricious.

The main reception room, the Sala dei Cavalli, was part of the older north wing. It leads through the Saletta di Amor e Psiche, Federico's living room and the Anticamera dei Venti into the smaller Camera delle Aquile, perhaps his *studiolo*. The latter is particularly magnificent in decoration and is connected with the servant's room in the mezzanine. On particularly hot days the duke could retreat to the garden grotto situated on the edge of the garden.

In the Palazzo Te Giulio created what was in effect Europe's first entirely courtly residence. Its ceremonial splendour, its spaciousness, its comfort, its lavish decoration, and not least its numerous *capricci*, differentiate it from all previous princely residences. Giulio's concern was not so much to create the conditions for life in the antique style, as Raphael had tried in the Villa Madama, as to pander to the luxury and changing moods of a sophisticated modern prince.

La Rustica

It was not until 1538/39 that Giulio found the opportunity to take his taste for caprice, his bold and playful spirit, even further in a two-storeyed gallery known as La Rustica (fig. 184). It connects two wings of the Cortile della Mostra in the Palazzo Ducale. Three of the depressed rusticated arches of its squat basement plinth open into a grotto, whose rock-faced rustication is, like that of the arches, again not of actual rock but of stuccoed brick, yet it arouses an even more rough-hewn, amorphous and tottering impression. Over this arcade rises the *piano nobile* with smoother, smaller and more regular rustication; Giulio's exploration of the potentialities of rustication for surface texturing is unmatched in his age. The columns of its *Dorica* rest on pedestals and they in turn on brackets, as in the *ricetto* of Michelangelo's earlier Laurenziana (fig. 243). A large diamond-pointed rusticated block is placed at the centre of the

intercolumniation between the pedestals. With their spirals the columns ape those in the choir of Old St Peter's and seem aggressively screwed into the wall mass. Their capitals are continued into projecting fragments of a normative entablature with triglyph frieze. On both sides of the windows, every second quoin projects from the wall surface. The windowsill-cornice seems to be threaded through the columns, and the fragile lintel is relieved by a depressed arch. The system as a whole is simpler than that of the Palazzo Te and the rhythm more relaxed. Here Giulio emphasized instead the chiaroscuro structure and patterning of surfaces and made the horizontal forces even more dominant.

Giulio's Mantuan house

Giulio bought a house in the town in 1538. Some two years later he began partially renovating it. Particularly revealing for his late style is its façade (fig. 185), for which a design has survived in Giulio's own hand. Its horizontal emphasis, squat proportions, decorative rustication, broad apertures and grainy light-sensitive surfaces are reminiscent of La Rustica, yet here he eschewed the kind of courtly *capricci* he had cultivated in the Palazzo Te. The inventive, or parodic, elements at work are more subtle and learned. The basement plinth is once again squat, pierced by square grated windows and dominated by the portal arch cut asymmetrically in the third of seven bays. The smooth continuous impost cornice separates the aperture from the blind lunette and the pillars between the windows from the two upper layers of rustication. The arch and the slightly projecting voussoirs of the portal's segmental arch echo the basement windows at pavement level. As in the Baths of Diocletian, the pediment over the portal arch is produced by the simple expedient of angling the cornice upwards. The pediment projects deep into the central blind arch of the *piano nobile*, with its shell niche containing a statue of Mercury. This predominance of the central bay continues in the central arch of the *piano nobile* with its statue niche. The window-aedicules are recessed within blind arches too, whose fine-grained rustication is pleasingly contrasted with the rougher rustication of the basement podium. The Ionic entablature seems supported not by an order but by the central, slightly outward-jutting keystones of the

184 *Giulio's late buildings such as La Rustica, a two-storeyed gallery in the ducal palace of Mantua enclosing an open court for equestrian shows, are distinguished by his sensibility for light and shadow and the contrasting surfaces of the structures.*

185 *The façade of Giulio's own house at Mantua, 1540, is a masterpiece of complex and innovative articulation with economic use of materials.*

186 *In 1540 Giulio modernized the abbey church of San Benedetto Po with an arcade of giant* serliane *along both sides of the nave.*

arches. Its frieze is pierced by tiny keyhole-like mezzanine windows and decorated with festoons and rams' heads. To this Ionic character also correspond the stucco ornaments of the lunettes and the flat strap-like window frames patterned with double wave scrolls, which continue into the architraves of the triangular pediments placed directly over the lintels. Notwithstanding the simplified design and economical articulation, every detail of this masterpiece betrays its antique origin and is at the same time transformed into a highly original, provocative and sophisticated language.

Giulio also adopted a rusticated arcade system in the Porta della Cittadella, begun in 1542. But here, with a rigour unusual for him, he recurred to a normative repertoire. Here the vibrancy and vitality of his first Mantuan years are reclaimed by a flatter, more composed style; again the emphasis is placed more on the variation of surface textures than on dynamic rhythms.

San Benedetto Po

Similar tendencies can be detected in San Benedetto Po, a Gothic Benedictine church situated close to Mantua (fig. 186). Giulio was commissioned to modernize it in 1540. He showed great ingenuity in transforming the irregularities and archaisms of the existing structure into an innovative and modern interior. The transverse arches over the nave retain their pointed form but rest on the projecting entablature of the colossal Composite pilaster order that separates the five bays, its domical vaults reminiscent of Peruzzi's designs for

San Domenico in Siena (fig. 215). Giulio made a virtue of the pointed-arch lunettes over the entablature, pierced them with *oculi*, and decorated the vaults with polygonal coffering developing out of a central octagon – a system of decoration less convincing in the steep dome over the crossing.

Only the first three bays of the nave are opened in *serliane*, supported by the squat columns of the pre-existing church. The walls of the two following bays, corresponding to the sanctuary and high altar, remain closed. The *serliane* are repeated on the outer wall of the aisles where their arcades open into the side chapels. By cutting into both sides of the barrel vaults of the aisles, these arcades create cross-vaults. This virtuoso system is at its most effective in the ambulatory of the choir, where pilasters replace the squat antique columns. With its five outward-projecting exedra-shaped chapels, the ambulatory is even reminiscent of the Santissima Annunziata in Florence (figs 31, 32).

Giulio was forced by the irregularities of the ground plan to progressively reduce the chapels of the left aisle in size, especially the two further towards the choir. The rhythm of the chapels of the right aisle and their corresponding side front is, on the contrary, only slightly disturbed by the varying depth of the nave bays. The vestibule is opened in three triumphal arches which would have been even more recognizable as such by a pedimented attic before the later alterations. In relation to the broad apertures of the arches, the pillars

between them, articulated with fluted Composite pilasters and hollowed out by steep doors, seem fragile. At the left corner the narrow pilaster-flanked bays are doubled; at the right, where the chapels are broader and project beyond the vestibule side, they are tripled. The rhythm of the right side front is even more complex. From left to right the pillars become progressively larger. Only the last two pillars become smaller again, though without producing a symmetry comparable to the north wing of the Palazzo Te.

Mantua Cathedral

The medieval cathedral had been gutted by fire on 1 April 1545. Giulio was commissioned to rebuild it (fig. 187). He had to incorporate a part of the old exterior walls and chapels in the new building, but otherwise was given a free hand to create a totally new interior. At his death in 1546, most of the columns had been installed and the new chapels had reached an advanced stage, but the crossing and choir were not completed till the later sixteenth century and do not correspond to Giulio's ideas.

Evidently Cardinal Ercole Gonzaga, the reform-minded brother and successor of the dead duke, wanted a building of the type of Old St Peter's. When he was still in Rome, in 1523, Giulio had translated

187 *The old cathedral of Mantua burnt down in 1545 and Giulio's replacement was another surprise: a modern version of an Early Christian basilica.*

the basilica in his *Donation of Constantine* fresco into the normative language of the columnar orders. He may also have been familiar with Peruzzi's comparable projects (fig. 213). Now he was able to translate the type into the reality of a trabeated columnar basilica with a nave and double aisles. He may even have considered continuing the inner aisles into an ambulatory, as in San Benedetto Po and in the Early Christian basilica of San Sebastiano in Rome. Unlike the latter, he eschewed arcades, and held fast to colonnades with straight entablature. But he seems also to have derived inspiration from Brunelleschi's basilicas in the use of a colossal order in the crossing, in the dimensions of the nave and inner aisles, in the relation of the width of the nave to its height of 1:2, in its flat-coffered ceiling and in the broad intercolumniations (figs 10, 11, 18, 19).

In contrast to Old St Peter's and the other Early Christian basilicas, but like Peruzzi's late projects, Giulio separated the nave and four aisles with relatively squat columns of one and the same Corinthian order and thus created a broad hall whose space freely expands into the chapels. With the help of relieving arches, he broadened the intercolumniations to *c*.3.40 m (11 ft 2 ins), i.e. a good deal broader than the norm prescribed by Vitruvius or exemplified by late antique prototypes such as Santa Maria Maggiore. He furnished the columns with Ionic bases. But only in the nave did he top them with a complete entablature and decorate its frieze with festoons and figural reliefs. The *Corinthia* of the clerestory, whose pilasters alternate with monumental window-aedicules, is placed over pedestals and therefore exceeds in height even that of the lower columnar order. The pillars of the crossing are splayed in the Bramantesque mode, but the diameter of the dome is actually less than the width of the nave. In this too he comes closer to Brunelleschi and the late Peruzzi than to Bramante and Raphael.

Since the mid-fifteenth century the aisles of Roman columnar basilicas had been vaulted. Giulio followed suit, and raised coffered barrel vaults over the architrave of the inner aisles. These are continuous but he divided their complex coffering by transverse arches that continue the vertical thrust of the columns. The outer aisles, by contrast, have flat coffered ceilings; here he formed square cells by the flat entablature without frieze that connects the columns with the pilasters of the side walls.

In spite of all the rich *all'antica* detail Giulio did not blindly classicize an Early Christian ancient basilica, but strove – like Brunelleschi, Alberti and Bramante before him – to adapt it to the functions and aesthetic predilections of his age and to fuse it together with elements of Brunelleschi and Peruzzi. Here, too, however, as also in his religious painting, Giulio's profane spirit gained the upper hand, as in the magnificently shaped fluted columns, in the lavish décor and in the brilliant lighting of the nave. The success of Mantua Cathedral may have contributed to the fact that shortly before his death in the autumn of 1546 he was called by Paul III to succeed Sangallo as the architect-in-chief of St Peter's, as Vasari tells us. Only afterwards did the pope call Michelangelo.

In spite of his heroic efforts, and epoch-making achievements, Giulio never again achieved the inexhaustible richness that makes the Palazzo Te the most important of his early masterpieces. All the artistic dreams that he had been unable to realize in his relatively modest

Roman commissions flowed together in that enterprise. In Mantua he became the standard-bearer of Rome, the missionary of true architecture, which had hardly spread in northern Italy beyond the level of the late Quattrocento. He was now in the privileged position of being able to fulfil himself for two decades in a far more unhindered way than other masters. But there he lacked the competition with his equals. His art thus ran the danger of degenerating into a courtly manner and adventuring less and less into new territory.

Antonio da Sangallo the Younger (1485–1546)

No earlier architect of the Renaissance had received such a solid and comprehensive education as did Antonio the Younger from both his uncles and from Bramante. None had such an opportunity to plan and build in so central a position for almost thirty-five years. If he was seldom esteemed as much as his merits deserved, this was due especially to a certain coarseness and monotony of his vocabulary and types. At the same time few if any were so totally, to the tips of their fingers, an architect. Few could similarly shape an architectural organism or express in it the same reciprocity of form, function and structure that is the basic principle of all architecture.

In a draft of his foreword to a projected commentary on Vitruvius, he reports he had come to Rome at the beginning of the pontificate of Julius II and had worked under Bramante. His earliest surviving drawings must in fact date from 1503–05: they include designs for a funerary monument, a mausoleum and a triumphal arch and surveys of the Colosseum and the Baths of Diocletian. In the precision of these drawings he clearly surpassed his uncle Giuliano. In *c*.1509 he became Bramante's most important assistant and as such played a decisive role in the building and further planning of the new St Peter's.

Sangallo's earliest architectural works go back to the last years of Julius II. They include his fireplace in the Sala di Costantino in the Vatican, and possibly also the papal loggia and inner keep of the fortress of Civita Castellana, which still follow the style of his uncle Antonio the Elder (fig. 133). In 1511/12 he rebuilt for Cardinal Alessandro Farnese the castle of Capodimonte on Lake Bolsena, perhaps his earliest independent building. Both in the stereometric compactness of the octagonal exterior and in the squat theatre motifs and the simplified detail of the Doric order of the courtyard he is still closer to Antonio the Elder than to Giuliano or Bramante.

Palazzo Ricci and Palazzo Baldassini

With the town house for the humanist 'Fedra' Inghirami, the palazzetto on Piazza dei Ricci, Sangallo prepared the way for both his early masterpieces, the Palazzo Baldassini and the more famous Palazzo Farnese. The three bare storeys of the Palazzetto Ricci elevation, decreasing in height from bottom to top, belong to a Roman tradition that goes back to the Palazzo Venezia (fig. 65) and the Palazzo della Valle, and to which Sangallo would remain faithful even in later buildings. The portal is also reminiscent of the north portal of the Palazzo Venezia, while Giuliano's influence can be felt in the volute-supported aedicules of the ground floor, the columnar arcades of the courtyard and its exaggeratedly high entablature (fig. 84). The Florentine motif of emphasizing the corners of the exterior with rusticated quoins, introduced by Michelozzo in the garden wing of the Palazzo Medici in Florence, had already been used by Antonio the Elder in the Rocca of Civita Castellana and in the Porta San Pietro. As in the courtyards of the castles of Capodimonte and Veiano or in the Palazzo Fieschi in Rome whose *piano nobile* he seems to have completed in *c*.1512, Sangallo still used here the windows of the Cancelleria type (fig. 130). They show how long he held fast to the style of the late Roman Quattrocento and that of his two uncles.

It was not until around 1513 that he embraced the more systematic and *all'antica* world of Bramante in the Palazzo Baldassini. He thus gave a more monumental format to the ground-floor aedicules and linked them with a cornice continuous with the windowsills – rather as Bramante had probably done shortly beforehand in the ground floor of the Palazzo Fieschi. In the loggia and in the three blind walls of the courtyard, as also in the arrangement of the rooms he probably followed the model of Bramante's Palazzo Caprini, the prototype of the Roman Renaissance palazzetto (fig. 136). The rooms progress from the *andito* to the entrance loggia and the broad staircase to the salon and Baldassini's apartment in the façade wing of the *piano nobile*. In the superimposition as also in the detail of both orders of the courtyard he derived inspiration instead from the Cortile del Belvedere (figs 139, 140) and from the older parts of the Palazzo Fieschi.

Sant'Egidio in Cellere

Sangallo also seems to have been under the influence of Bramante in what was his earliest church (fig. 188). The occasion for the building of this pilgrimage church was the betrothal of the elder son of Cardinal Alessandro Farnese, Pierluigi, to Girolama Orsini, a distant kinswoman of Leo X, in the summer of 1513 and the contemporaneous confirmation of the Farnese estates in the area of the Lago di Bolsena in northern Lazio. Sant'Egidio, dedicated to a saint known as a protec-

188 *Axonometry of Sant'Egidio in Cellere, the earliest church of Antonio da Sangallo the Younger, 1513: a Greek cross with three temple-like façades and concave pillars.*

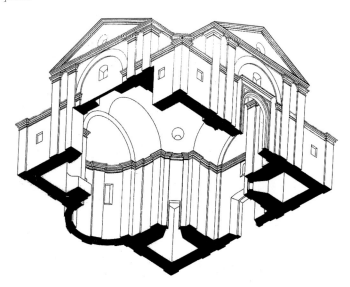

tor against fever, belongs to a particular type of isolated pilgrimage church like those built in Cortona and Todi (figs 97, 134).

In the Greek cross, with small sacristy-like rooms placed in the four angles, Antonio produced a simple but ingenious solution to a perennial problem: how to design a central-plan church. Even more systematically than Alberti in San Sebastiano and Bramante in Roccaverano (figs 55, 153), he continued the *cella*-like crossing in short arms, whose exterior can be recognized as a simplified temple front. On the rear side it is combined with the projecting semicircular apse. Like Bramante in Roccaverano, the arcade of the triumphal arch corresponds to the barrel-vaulted arms of the cross. The paired pilasters that flank the arches are reduced to a small order in the squat corner chambers. Sangallo presumably planned a fenestrated drum under the dome. In the interior the splaying of the pillars of the crossing is as broad as in St Peter's and in the Chigi Chapel (figs 148, 162). In a preceding project it is even concave in profile: a device aimed at forming the transition from pillars to pendentives as seamlessly as possible.

Palazzo Farnese

The experiences of the not yet thirty-year-old architect now flowed together into a far more monumental project: the Roman palace of Cardinal Alessandro Farnese (figs 189–92). Scion of a family of noble *condottieri* from northern Lazio, Alessandro had been educated

189 *Plan of the Palazzo Farnese, Rome. The original scheme was a sequence of spaces from the entrance (bottom of plan) through the courtyard to a rear façade which probably was to look on the Via Giulia and an intermediate square.*

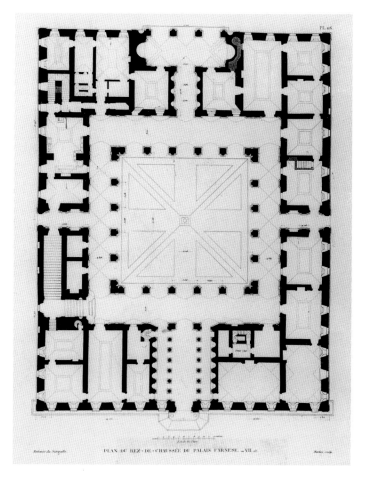

190 *The monumental façade of the Palazzo Farnese. Work progressed slowly; the upper part of the top storey and cornice were only added by Michelangelo.*

191 *The atrium follows the pronaos of the Pantheon with its colonnade supporting a barrel vault.*

by the humanist Pomponio Leto and had spent some time at the court of Lorenzo the Magnificent in Florence. His sister, the mistress of Alexander VI, helped him precociously to obtain a cardinal's hat in 1493, and already under Julius II he had risen to become one of the most influential members of the Sacred College. Leo X showered him with lucrative benefices, which encouraged him to commission Sangallo to rebuild his Quattrocento palazzo between the Via Arenula and the Via Giulia.

Like the Palazzetto Ricci and Palazzo Baldassini, but in contrast to the Cancelleria and the palaces of Bramante and Raphael, the Palazzo Farnese has no single façade, but like some of the earlier Florentine palaces (figs 37, 71–74) is a freestanding rectangular block, isolated from the urban fabric. Its Tiber front was probably supposed to overlook a piazza-like extension of the new Via Giulia; perhaps it was even intended as the main entrance front. What is now the main façade on the piazza can hardly compete with the Cancelleria (fig. 131) either in length or in material and formal

192 *The courtyard of the Palazzo Farnese underwent major changes. The windows in the lateral wings of the second storey and the top storey were added by Michelangelo.*

splendour, but each of its three storeys is higher. The rusticated portal follows the type of Bramante's Vatican portals and is matched by the rusticated quoins at the corners of the block. The window-aedicules of the ground floor with their two pairs of high volute-brackets recall those of Giuliano's contemporary Palazzo Medici-Lante.

Like the Rocca of Civita Castellana, this austere exterior, less a cardinal's palace than the seat of a rising dynasty, conceals a classicizing interior. Here one can feel the influence of the Roman house as Vitruvius had described it (Book VI.3) and as Giuliano and Fra Giocondo had reconstructed and perhaps even discussed it with the cardinal himself. Both *atrium* and *peristylium* come far closer to the ancient prototypes than in any building of Bramante or Raphael. Sangallo adopted as visual model of the *atrium* the three-aisled pronaos of the Pantheon with its central coffered barrel vault, the flat ceiling of its aisles and the abbreviated entablature, but made it deeper and more basilica-like. On the side walls he even surpassed Bramante in the robustly three-dimensional alternation of engaged columns and statue niches. By continuing the entablature of the *atrium* above the

pillars of the courtyard, he doubled their impost zone and produced the kind of horizontal continuity to which Bramante had accorded even higher value than Alberti and Francesco di Giorgio.

As in the Colosseum, and as Bramante no doubt had planned in the Palazzo dei Tribunali, he wanted to adorn the arcades of all three courtyard storeys with orders of half-columns in classical super-imposition. And as in the Theatre of Marcellus, the frieze of the Doric entablature is adorned with a triglyph frieze and the cornice with dentils. The trophy-decorated metopes of the courtyard allude, as does the exterior, to the cardinal's military, rather than ecclesiastical, ambitions. Much more volumetrically than Bramante in the upper garden of the Cortile del Belvedere, Sangallo in the corner-triads amalgamated two engaged columns with the fragment of a quadrangular one. The ground floor with its slender proportions and *all'antica* detail is far more accomplished than that of the Palazzo Baldassini and Sangallo's first project for this courtyard, so that its planning must have dragged on into 1515 if not beyond.

The staircase that axially ascends from the courtyard loggia was originally planned to turn towards the main façade. It took as its immediate precedent Bramante's (?) slightly earlier staircase in the Castel Sant'Angelo. Thanks to its width, its comfortable steps, and the splayed pillars and statue niches of its landings, it surpassed those of Urbino and the Cancelleria (fig. 130). Sangallo ingeniously adjusted the height of the vaulting to provide lighting for the landings: the consummate integration of the staircase windows into the exterior for the first time avoids any asymmetry in the fenestration.

Owing to the cardinal's limited finances, and to his numerous other enterprises, the building made slow progress. In *c.*1520 Antonio started to unify the two upper storeys with a colossal order inspired by that of the Palazzo dei Tribunali (fig. 150). But this meant that he had to reduce the top storey and eliminate the upper courtyard loggia. There may also have been economic reasons for the reduction in height. The actual execution never progressed beyond parts of the *piano nobile* before 1540.

Antonio was to surpass his design for the Palazzo Farnese in his project for the papal palace of Leo X on the Piazza Navona in *c.*1515. There the central aisle of the *atrium* continues axially into a central portico that separates two similar courtyards and into a rearward *andito*. The latter was to provide access to the garden to the rear of the palazzo and to be flanked by the two diverging staircase ramps that were to join at halfway height. The upper part of the staircase would thus have led axially into the upper portico, and this in turn to the portal of the huge salon at the centre of the façade wing. He articulated these ideas even more monumentally after 1527 in an ambitious project for a princely residence, perhaps intended for Charles V, comprising no fewer than five courtyards. He thus prepared the way, as no other architect of these decades did, for the spectacular axial interior layouts of the Baroque.

St Peter's, Santa Maria di Monserrato and San Giovanni dei Fiorentini (1518–21)

After having left Bramante's service in *c.*1513, Sangallo participated only indirectly in the planning of St Peter's. He was, however, undoubtedly involved by Giuliano in all discussions, and succeeded him as second architect of St Peter's in the autumn of 1516. In his earliest projects for St Peter's he combines the megalomaniac extension, octagonal sacristies, projecting ambulatories and bell-towers of Giuliano's projects (fig. 159) with motifs of Raphael's projects for St Peter's and the Villa Madama of the summer of 1518 (figs 169, 173). He considered eliminating the ambulatories and lengthening and punctuating the long narrow tunnel-like nave with secondary light-admitting cupolas. Shortly afterwards, he liberated himself from the ideas of Bramante, Giuliano and Raphael and reduced the nave to three bays which was more in keeping with his style.

He had already used a comparable flat articulation of the wall in Sant'Egidio (fig. 188), and was to do so again in his projects for the Spanish national church of Santa Maria di Monserrato dating to early 1518. This type of church with an unaisled nave and three chapels on either side can be traced back to the Badia in Fiesole (figs 48, 50) and to Giuliano's demolished church of Santa Caterina della Cavallerote in Rome (1508). But he gave to it a formulation that was to hold its own for generations. He himself was to vary this type in his designs for the churches of San Marcello, San Marco and Santo Spirito in Sassia in Rome during the following years.

In his designs for San Giovanni dei Fiorentini (fig. 193), the flat wall relief of most of his previous buildings was to be abandoned for

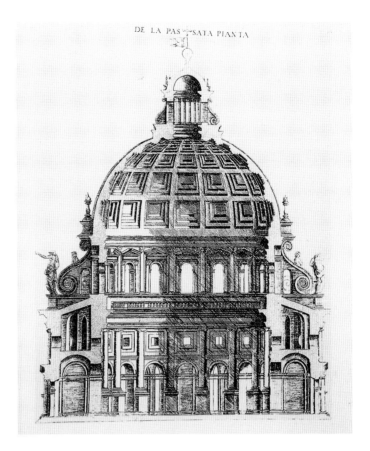

193 *Section of Antonio da Sangallo's design for San Giovanni dei Fiorentini. He made numerous alternative versions, none of them built.*

a more plastic idiom, closer to the courtyard of the Palazzo Farnese. His numerous alternative projects for this church range from three-bayed basilicas without transepts and five-bayed versions with transepts and ambulatory round the choir, to Pantheon-like rotundas with or without columnar colonnade – a range of types that the school of Bramante had been the first to develop. Sangallo's central-plan project for San Giovanni presupposes knowledge of Raphael's project for the church and so may postdate September 1518. In the reduction of the temple front to a wall block, in the elimination of bell-towers and large chapels, and in the combination of the buttressing system with a ring of small chapels, he sought a more pragmatic and functional solution than Raphael's. He opted instead for a cylindrical exterior, and therefore risked a certain monotony. He now articulated not only the interior but also the exterior by engaged columns, alternated with Pantheon-aedicules, as in his contemporary projects for the circular court of the Villa Madama and for St Peter's (figs 169, 194). His projects for San Marcello, San Giacomo Scossacavalli and San Marco, dating to the same period around 1519/20, also differ from those for Santa Maria in Monserrato in their more plastic wall relief.

During the second half of 1518, it seems Sangallo and Raphael had reached agreement on a style that was not only more plastic, but also more paratactical than that of Raphael's previous projects and that thus came far closer to the ancient prototypes.

In April 1520 Sangallo succeeded Raphael as papal architect in chief, while Peruzzi was promoted as his deputy. In the *Memoriale* he

194 *One of Antonio da Sangallo's designs for St Peters during the period 1518–20, showing him at his most fertile and inventive.*

195 *The entrance front of Antonio's papal Mint, later the Banco di Santo Spirito, 1525, incorporates a triumphal arch above a rusticated basement.*

196 *Antonio da Sangallo's project for the Villa of Cardinal del Monte (right) consisted of a large garden centred upon a curved casino.*

now addressed to the pope, Sangallo summed up the criticisms of the projects of Bramante and Raphael that hitherto he had only been able to articulate in counter-proposals. He complained that the ground plan was confused and its continuation in ambulatories inorganic; that the nave was too high, too long and too dark; that there was a lack of large chapels; that static problems were posed by the dome; and that the proportions and detail of the orders were not canonical. Corresponding projects and a wooden model (only known from drawings copied from it) suggest that he was only partially successful with this critique. Though he was now able to shorten the nave to three bays and expand its central bay into a second domed space, he was forced to retain the ambulatories and the old floor level.

Sangallo's numerous projects from the period 1518–21 are among the most accomplished and pregnant with ideas of the whole Renaissance (fig. 194). They show how freely, how creatively, how independently, he reacted to the proposals of Bramante, Giuliano and Raphael. Seldom has so high a level in architectural fertility been attained as that inspired by the rivalry between the many talents then active in Rome.

Designs for palaces and villas: 1516–28

Sangallo also came closer to Raphael in his projects for secular buildings during these years. The town house he began in *c.*1516 for Bartolommeo Ferratini, an influential curial official responsible for supervising the building site of St Peter's, in his hometown of Amelia, is thus adorned with window-aedicules similar to those of the Palazzo Jacopo da Brescia (fig. 164). He used a similar *Dorica* in his project for the tower he had to add to Cardinal Antonio del Monte's palazzo on the Piazza Navona in 1517. In the papal Zecca or mint, the later Banco di Santo Spirito completed for the Holy Year in 1525, he varied the side front of the Palazzo Jacopo da Brescia (fig. 195). Without altering the inner layout of the rooms, he made the

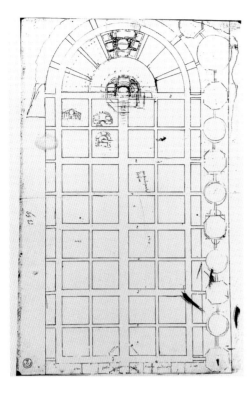

triumphal arch glorifying Leo's cousin and successor Clement VII even more predominant, and the basement podium still squatter. To the stone-built façade he lent something of the festive spirit of an ephemeral decoration. With its concave curve, the first of its kind, the façade catches the eye at the end of the present Via Santo Spirito. Sangallo retained the triumphal-arch system, though without the concave curve, in his projects for his own house on the Via Giulia and for the Zecca in Castro, both postdating 1530.

Giulio Romano's influence is apparent in the compact rusticated courses of its podium, the abstract panels of the side bays of the *piano nobile* and in the segmental arches of the mezzanine windows of the fragmentary Palazzo Cesi of *c.*1523 which was to be situated on the same square as the Palazzo dei Tribunali, or in the vertical ashlared courses of the ground floor of the Palazzo Ferrari, begun in *c.*1527.

In his project for the villa of Cardinal del Monte, the later Villa Giulia, begun by Jacopo Sansovino in *c.*1526, he envisaged a huge garden, whose longitudinal axis, as in Giuliano's Medici project, would have led the visitor to a garden pavilion placed on a higher level (figs 161, 196). In what is doubtless the last in a series of alternative versions, the casino has a concave façade, while its convex rear front dovetails neatly with the exedra-shaped end of the garden – a daring, eminently volumetric invention that looks back to the concave façade of the Zecca and heralds the ideas of Borromini and Bernini.

Once Pope Clement VII had fled to Orvieto after the Sack of Rome in May 1527 and building activity in the Papal State had ground to a halt, Sangallo evidently found time to reflect on the principles of architecture, and more especially to devote himself more actively to the study of the antique. The influence of Vitruvius is patent in his projects dating to *c.*1529 for the Palazzo Pucci in Orvieto, in the way he opens the façade wing in a *vestibulum*, as at Poggio a Caiano (fig. 77), and continues it axially in a square *atrium*, supported by four columns,

and in the *cavaedium* and *peristylium* of the courtyard. Two matching staircases and a 24 m (79 ft) broad colonnade overlooking the landscape in the rear wing also distinguish this project as one of the most progressive and classicizing of the first half of the century: it directly prepares the way for Peruzzi's Palazzo Massimo and the palaces of Sanmicheli, Sansovino and Palladio.

St Peter's under Clement VII and Paul III (1531–46)

Though the papal finances slowly recovered after 1530, the Sack of Rome had administered such a shock to the Church that the building of the new basilica had been brought to a standstill. In 1531, after returning to Rome, Clement VII ordered his two architects to reduce the project even more drastically than in 1521. Sangallo therefore proposed an unaisled three-bayed nave with side chapels and jettisoned both the quincunx system and the ambulatories.

Clement's successor, Paul III Farnese (1534–49), had been Sangallo's most important patron. He confirmed Sangallo as architect-in-chief but appointed Peruzzi as his equal and partner. Right from the start the pope, who was apparently *au fait* with Bramante's projects, wanted to return to a centralized quincunx system, as Sangallo and Peruzzi had already proposed under Leo X. Not until 1538, two years after Peruzzi's death, did Sangallo present a functionally feasible project, which, at the insistence of the Commission of the Fabbrica di San Pietro, had to be translated into a costly wooden model (the largest extant wooden model of the Renaissance) (figs

197 *Façade of Antonio's wooden model of his St Peter's, a design which, although worked out in considerable detail, was severely criticized by Michelangelo.*

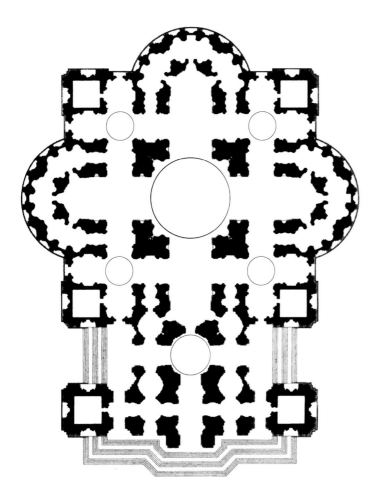

198 *The plan of Antonio's model of St Peter's, essentially combining Bramante's centralized design, Raphael's choir and a huge vestibule with the Loggia delle Benedizioni.*

197–98). Its ground plan differs from earlier projects in its raising of the floor level by over 3 m (10 ft), thus proportioning the colossal order of the interior in a more normative way. This made the closure of the ambulatories necessary. The basilica was to be preceded by a voluminous *atrium* topped by the Loggia delle Benedizioni, which was to be directly linked with the adjacent Papal Palace, and flanked by ten-storeyed bell-towers. No doubt for static reasons, he gave the interior of the dome a profile nearly as steep as the *cupolone* of Florence Cathedral, but held firm to its coffering. The interior of the basilica would have differed from Michelangelo's project (fig. 248), especially in the corner chapels, the system of the apses and in the lighting, which Sangallo wanted to concentrate on the large windows of the cross-arms, the arcaded windows on two storeys of the drum and the enormous lantern.

The exterior shows even more clearly how fundamentally Sangallo's style had altered since Raphael's death. Evidently Paul III and Sangallo agreed that the exterior articulation begun under Leo X be continued also in the upper storeys. As in the Colosseum, Sangallo combined a Doric order on the ground floor with an upper *Ionica*, both with engaged columns. In order to reach roof level, he separated both storeys with a lesene-articulated attic. This corresponded to the vaulted zone of the aisles and chapels and helped to improve the lighting of the interior. Such an attic had hitherto been used only

as a building's upper termination (fig. 163), but would soon catch on as an intermediate storey. In the two storeys of the immense drum of the dome itself Sangallo repeated the superimposition of *Dorica* and *Ionica*, and coordinated the bell-towers with all these different storeys. He was bound to so complex an articulation by the fact that the ground floor had already been begun, by his wish that the exterior should correspond to the interior, and by his deference to the Renaissance principle of superimposition. At the same time he remained true to his Florentine origins and did everything possible to articulate the building in closed, stereometric volumes that would, like the Colosseum, have had an especially impressive effect when seen from afar. Even the façade itself he dissolved into a hierarchical system of plastic volumes. The rhythm of vertical blocks, generated by the steep bell-towers, the projecting pedimented centre with its enormous, deeply-shadowed arcades on two levels and the intermediate bays with their paired Doric columns flanking the side portals, would undoubtedly have had a far grander and more volumetric effect than Maderno's existing façade. This project, in its vertical thrust, would meet with a particular resonance in France.

Castro

The numerous commissions with which Paul III overburdened his architect also included the transformation of Castro into the residence of a miniature duchy that the pope had presented in 1537 as a fief to his one surviving son, Pierluigi. The terrain of the strategically situated little hill-town in the far north-west of Lazio falls steeply away on all sides. The existing settlement precluded a more ambitious urban renovation and its transformation into a miniature new town, comparable to Pius's II's transformation of Pienza. Nonetheless, Sangallo was able, in the space of a few years, before Pierluigi was raised to the duchy of Parma and Piacenza in 1545, to lay out an elongated piazza with large loggia and mint. The Franciscan convent and its unassuming church never progressed much beyond their foundations.

Three alternative projects give some idea of how Sangallo intended to design Pierluigi's Palazzo Ducale. With its modest length of only *c.*30 m (100 ft) it could only have been intended for shorter visits. In one version he flanks the three rusticated storeys with a colossal Corinthian order and terminates the façade with a balustrade and statues. In another he surmounts a squat basement podium with a dominating *piano nobile* articulated by the blind arcades of monumental theatre motifs, balcony and mezzanine windows and a continuous balustrade. Paul III and Pierluigi seem to have opted, instead, for a third, more conventional version, closer to the Palazzo Farnese, with rusticated basement, corner pillars carrying projecting entablature fragments, Pantheon-aedicules, dominating central loggia, unbalustraded attic storey, and a courtyard with plain pillar-supported arcades.

Sangallo's most influential contribution to the new town was in the form of his designs for relatively small patrician houses. In these he fused together a Vitruvian sequence of rooms with villa elements such as the indirectly lit salon on the ground floor and the rear loggia overlooking a garden. He also planned a comfortable staircase and several water closets.

Sala Regia and Cappella Paolina

Sangallo had already renovated the Sala Ducale in c.1521. In 1538, slightly before his final project for St Peter's, he was commissioned to do the same for the two adjacent ceremonial rooms in the Vatican. He vaulted what was the main papal audience hall at the time, the Sala Regia, with a coffered and lavishly decorated barrel vault, as at Poggio a Caiano, improved its lighting by two enormous Diocletian windows in the lunettes, and framed its portals with Ionic marble aedicules (fig. 199). In short, he transformed it into what could justly claim to be at the time the most sumptuous reception room in Europe. It responded to the growing needs of the popes to present themselves in public, and to conduct the affairs of Church and state in suitably magnificent settings. He continued it axially into the similarly magnificent Pauline Chapel, the new Chapel of the Holy Sacrament and of the Conclave. All its four walls follow the triumphal rhythm of the *serliana*. The chapel was originally lit by three Diocletian windows. The central panels of the walls below the lunettes of the side walls were apparently intended right from the start to be decorated with Michelangelo's frescoes.

199 *The Sala Regia, the most sumptuously decorated ceremonial room in the Vatican palace.*

Palazzo Farnese under Paul III

Just a few weeks after his election Paul had a large piazza laid out in front of his still unfinished cardinal's palace, larger than in front of any earlier patrician or cardinal's residence in Rome (figs 189, 190). Sangallo, however, only began his remodelling of the Palazzo Farnese in c.1540. Evidently the planning of St Peter's, the Vatican and Castro had priority. In order to secure it as the residence of his heirs, Paul III transferred its ownership to Pierluigi, though in the foundation medals he still appeared as the patron. Vasari reported, indeed, that Antonio had transformed the former cardinal's residence into a palace fit for a pope.

After the Via Giulia and the Tiber front of Palazzo Farnese had lost their original importance, the Tiber wing was to be opened into a loggia overlooking a rear garden: a suitable feature for the residence of a ruling prince. In order to create a two-storeyed salon in the entrance wing with two rows of 3 x 5 windows, Sangallo transferred the two upper staircase ramps to the left side wing. He gave the steps a slightly upward-tilted profile and made them lower and deeper to secure an even more comfortable and solemn ascent than before. In individual forms he held still more exactly to Vitruvius than before. He thus tapered the Doric aedicules of the ground floor of the

200 *Detail of the Farnese Palace courtyard showing a portico on the ground floor with a Porta Dorica.*

courtyard loggia and the rear front, furnished them with shoulders, and gave them the double frames that he had already introduced into the Ionic windows of the Vatican Sala Ducale in 1521 and that were also sanctioned by ancient prototypes (fig. 200). Like the whole type of the Palazzo Farnese, these aedicules were to be adopted and varied innumerable times right down to the eighteenth century.

In the Ionic window-aedicules of the upper façade storey, he was inspired – as formerly Rossellino in Pienza Cathedral (figs 61, 62) – by the niches of the *natatio* of the Baths of Diocletian. As his cousin Giovanfrancesco had already proposed in the Palazzetto Ferrari before the Sack of Rome, the narrow arches break through the entablature. But now they rest on a pedestal zone with abstract blind panels flanked by paired volutes with abstracted surface. He also approached more closely to Vitruvian norms in the Ionic courtyard order; its frieze would only later be decorated by Michelangelo with masks and festoons. The Palazzo Farnese clearly remains Antonio da Sangallo the Younger's masterpiece, even though Michelangelo would add the massive top cornice to the façade and wholly alter the upper courtyard storey.

Sangallo's epoch-making achievements in architecture also include his numerous fortress layouts. The finest of these are the Fortezza da Basso in Florence and the Rocca Paolina in Perugia. Both are distinguished by their technical and functional innovations and their corporeal grandeur.

Sangallo was also one of the finest archaeologists of his day. In numerous drawings he succeeded in coming closer to the secrets of Vit-ruvius and the antique than most of his predecessors and successors. However, only two temple-like projects in his hand give a more immediate expression to his utopian vision of a new classicizing architecture.

His planned commentary on Vitruvius never progressed beyond its foreword and a corpus of hundreds of drawings by himself, his brother Giovanbattista and his cousin Giovanfrancesco with accompanying commentaries of varying degrees of detail. Yet, together with other experienced architects, he did found a Vitruvian academy in 1543. It was the answer to the Vitruvian academy, mainly formed of aristocratic and erudite laymen, that Cardinal Alessandro Farnese had established in 1538.

Antonio da Sangallo the Elder: 1502–34

After the death of Alexander VI in August 1492, Giuliano's younger brother and pupil returned to Florence. In 1502 he began to transform the church of Santissima Annunziata in Arezzo into a three-aisled basilica; as in the courtyard of the Rocca of Civita Castellana, he was still under the influence of Cronaca's spartan, heavy and lapidary style. But in the equally three-aisled, *serliane*-lit *vestibulum* that he added to the church in *c.*1515, the influence of Bramante and the Palazzo Farnese can already be felt.

In the same years Antonio was also active elsewhere. He may have contributed to two buildings designed by an important though unidentified architect from the inner circle of Giuliano. The first of these was the central-plan church of the Madonna della Consolazione at Todi, begun in 1508, and built round a miraculous icon of the Madonna (figs 134, 201). Still quite Florentine in character, it is

hardly attributable to its master builder Cola da Caprarola, who had already worked at Civita Castellana under Antonio the Elder. The building as a whole is complex in derivation and full of contradictions. In the parts below the vaulting executed in Antonio's lifetime, the interior is more coherent and progressive than the exterior. The combination of the colossal order of the crossing with two surrounding small orders is vaguely reminiscent of the system of Brunelleschi's San Lorenzo (fig. 14). The polygonal exterior of three of the four exedras and the four niches and the central portal of their interior recall the choir chapels of Florence Cathedral. The Ionic capitals of the interior are comparable with those of the courtyard of Civita Castellana (fig. 133), while the fluted variants of Doric and Corinthian capitals, the figurative capitals and the floating aedicules topped by pediments of the exterior are inspired by the pre-Roman period of Giuliano da Sangallo (figs 81, 84). The vertically continuous bands of pilasters which continue in rib-like transverse arches come closer to Francesco di Giorgio and Bramante (figs 97, 108). But Bramante's influence can most of all be felt in the direct connection of the crossing with the exedras to which the interior owes its particular spaciousness.

Another Bramantesque building in which Antonio the Elder may have had a hand is the Cappella Caracciolo in San Giovanni a Carbonara in Naples, built in c.1514–16. Here the rotunda and the triumphal arches of the Tempietto are combined with the plastic style of the late Bramante and the classicizing decorative style of the late Giuliano (fig. 160). The coarse detail and the ungainly proportions suggest, however, that the design should rather be attributed to a follower of Giuliano such as Antonio the Elder.

Antonio was so flexible, so chameleon-like, that he could succumb to Raphael's influence a few years later. In the palazzo he erected for Cardinal Antonio del Monte in his hometown of Monte San Savino he took over the *piano nobile* from Raphael's Palazzo Jacopo da Brescia (fig. 164), but eliminated the attic and remained steadfast to older prototypes in the rustication of the ground floor, in the window-aedicules and in the triadic corner pilasters. This is all the more striking as his nephew Antonio the Younger, at much the same time, was also inspired by the *piano nobile* of the Palazzo Jacopo da Brescia in his project for the tower of the same cardinal's palazzo on the Piazza Navona. Neither of the two had any real sense for Raphael's rhythm and dynamic. The ground plan of the palazzo in Monte San Savino, its courtyard and rear façade are equally old-fashioned.

In c.1518, however, Antonio the Elder combined these persistent late Quattrocento tendencies with the latest Roman inventions in his late masterpiece, the Madonna di San Biagio outside Montepulciano (fig. 202). Like Raphael in his project for San Giovanni dei Fiorentini, he wanted at first to precede the church with a Pantheon-like pronaos and thus to underline its likeness to a temple and its axis in depth. Once again he combined Quattrocentesque with more progressive elements by articulating the tried and tested type of Giuliano's Madonna delle Carceri (figs 75, 76) with the plastic forms of the courtyard of the Palazzo Farnese (fig. 192). His successful nephew's project for the tower of Cardinal del Monte seems even to have inspired the massing of engaged and square columns at the corners inside the church, though neither in the proportions nor in the detail did he achieve the same level as the Madonna di San Biagio.

201 *Antonio da Sangallo may have contributed to the church of the Madonna della Consolazione at Todi (left). Its exterior is shown in fig. 134.*

202 *The church of San Biagio outside Montepulciano is the masterpiece of Antonio da Sangallo the Elder.*

The *Dorica* of the exterior corresponds with the interior, but is reduced to two layers of flat corner pilasters. As in Sant'Eligio (fig. 163), an order of lesenes in the upper storey corresponds to the vaulted zone inside; the pediment grows out of the entablature projected above it: a system that recalls Pontelli's San Pietro in Montorio (fig. 127). The upper storey of the façade is otherwise articulated with five oblong blind panels, of a kind already found in Bramante's Milanese buildings (fig. 104). The aedicules combine Ionic capitals with a triglyph frieze, a *mescolanza* of two orders that Peruzzi had introduced in the portal of the Palazzo Fusconi, and may therefore be dated no earlier than 1523. Not only the belfry and dome, but also the drum with windows which funnel the light downwards in diagonal shafts as in the Medici Chapel, were only executed after Antonio's death; they do not reflect his design.

Baldassare Peruzzi (1481–1536)

Even if the career of the versatile Sienese artist Baldassare Peruzzi as an architect was less successful, and more intermittent, than that of Sangallo the Younger, he was a more refined architect. When he extended an older building near Siena into the villa of Sigismondo Chigi soon after 1500, he was still under the influence of his master Francesco di Giorgio (fig. 204). Its three-wing layout followed the tendencies of the early villas and villa-like buildings of central Italy (figs 48, 49, 129). In the arcades of the loggia he followed the niches of the Madonna del Calcinaio (fig. 97), but already differed there from Francesco's usually strong relief by his more delicate detail and the more normative archivolts.

The Farnesina and contemporary projects
Peruzzi presumably moved to Rome in the summer of 1503 in order to study the antiquities. He was at this time pre-eminently a painter and probably an assistant of Jacopo Ripanda, with whom he may have worked in the decoration of the courtyard loggias of the castle of Civita Castellana and later in that of the apse of Sant'Onofrio. His drawings during these years betray, in their mode of representation and in the character of their accompanying commentaries, the immediate influence of Giuliano and Cronaca, to whom they were long attributed. Peruzzi's intensive engagement with the architecture of Giuliano and Cronaca, but above all with the Cancelleria in Rome (figs 130–32), explains the considerable difference between the Farnesina and the typologically comparable Villa alle Volte.

203 *The Farnesina, Rome, built soon after 1505, stands opposite the Palazzo Farnese on the other side of the Tiber. It was designed and largely decorated by Baldassare Peruzzi as the rich banker Agostino Chigi's residence in Rome.*

204 *The Villa delle Volte near Siena was built by Peruzzi for Chigi's brother and foreshadows the Farnesina.*

Agostino Chigi, a Sienese banker and Sigismondo's elder brother, purchased a site on the banks of the Tiber outside the Porta Settignana in 1505 (fig. 203). The beginning of the Via della Lungara, on which it was situated, had been straightened under Alexander VI and had already permitted Cardinal Farnese to lay out a summerhouse with a large garden on an adjacent site. Chigi, however, under the influence of Alberti, wanted to combine the amenities of a villa with the comforts of an inner-city residence. In this combination, and in this wish to create the semblance of *rus in urbe*, he went even further than the suburban Palazzo Scala or Palazzo Pitti in Florence (figs 37, 70). Peruzzi shifted the building back from the street, surrounded it with gardens and a forecourt that was only separated from the garden by low walls, and opened the central of the three wings in the five-bayed arcaded entrance loggia of the *vestibulum*. A few steps led down to the platform between both projecting side wings which also served as a theatrical stage. To the right one entered the antechamber

of Chigi's combined living and bedroom, situated in the corner room facing towards the street. The longitudinal axis led into the dining room, whence the staircase ascended to the salon on the *piano nobile* and to the rooms of the family, while a short flight of steps led down to the secret garden to the back. A door in the left wall of the entrance loggia led into a second loggia, and above the roof a belvedere of the same size overlooked the large garden that descended to the banks of the Tiber. The service rooms were situated in the basement, while accommodation for servants and less prominent guests was provided in two low-ceilinged mezzanine floors over the flat ceilings of the two main floors.

The over thirty rooms of the Farnesina, which fulfilled all the needs of an urban palazzo, were enclosed, as in the Cancelleria, in a geometrically shaped block. Its height is proportioned to the depth as the depth to the width ($1:\sqrt{2}:2$) and the exterior thus follows a geometrical sequence that had already been used in the Middle Ages. As in the Cancelleria, the storeys are linked together on all sides by two similar paratactic pilaster orders. Their capitals are perhaps to be understood as Tuscan: an *aedes tuscanica* would have alluded to Chigi's Tuscan roots. As in the upper storey of the Cancelleria, the window-aedicules are rectangular, topped by mezzanine windows and amalgamated with the pedestals of the order into a coherent socle-zone. In the upper storey the mezzanine windows, as in the Villa alle Volte, are incorporated into the frieze of the upper entablature.

The largely destroyed decoration of the exterior was comparable with Giuliano's project for the Loggia dei Trombettieri in the Vatican of 1505 (fig. 157). The faux-marble allegories in the spandrels of the arcades, as also the *panischi*, theatrical masks, festoons and mythological scenes between the pilasters, only took on three dimensional form in the classicizing stucco frieze with putti, festoons and candelabra, they too originally as white as marble.

Bramante's influence cannot be felt any earlier than in the portico that was intended to surround the whole amphitheatre of the Piazza del Campo in Siena and which Peruzzi designed (but never built) in

205 *In 1508 Peruzzi provided designs in Bramante's style for a portico to surround the whole of the Piazza del Campo in his native Siena; it was never built.*

the summer of 1508 (fig. 205). The theatre motifs are now articulated with plastic engaged columns of a Doric order on tall pedestals and topped by an entablature with a triglyph frieze. The order is clearly inspired by Bramante's Palazzo Caprini and Cortile del Belvedere (figs 136, 139). The masterly perspective and the space-creating chiaroscuro of this first surviving architectural project by Peruzzi had already distinguished one of his previous drawings after the antique and recalls Bramante's Prevedari engraving (fig. 101). Bramante's influence is also unmistakable in the roughly contemporary project for San Sebastiano in Vallepiatta near Siena.

The years 1511–27

In 1513 Alberto Pio, lord of Carpi, and imperial ambassador in Rome from 1512 to 1519, commissioned Peruzzi to design a brick façade for the old cathedral (fig. 206). Pio had sacrificed its front half to the enlargement of his adjacent castle. Like Bramante in Roccaverano (fig. 153), Peruzzi framed the central arch, which corresponds to the nave, with a giant pedestal-raised 'attic' order. It supports the low and shallow triangular pediment. The outer corners of the matching smaller side bays are accentuated with pilasters of a small Composite order. The section of the medieval church forced him to adopt slenderer proportions, but he emphasized these verticalizing forces by the two slender orders which, as in the façades of the cathedrals of Pienza and Urbino (figs 61, 62, 93), break through the entablature and through the corners of the pediments. As in the façade of Urbino

207 *Peruzzi's interior of Carpi Cathedral also reflects Bramante's projects for St Peter's.*

206 *The façade of Peruzzi's cathedral of Carpi. Like Bramante, he expressed the nave and aisles externally.*

Cathedral, the triumphal grandeur of the central arch is diminished by the continuation of the entablature of the small order across the whole façade.

In the new cathedral, which dominates the narrow end of the huge piazza, Peruzzi started out from Bramante's 1506 project for St Peter's (fig. 147). The convex pillars supporting the dome (fig. 207) are no doubt inspired by Bramante too and by ancient prototypes such as the Oratorium Santa Crucis in Rome. Before the nineteenth-century remodelling they were articulated by a colossal pilaster order which supported the entablature of the drum. Here Peruzzi realized for the first time an idea that Bramante had proposed in his large red-chalk plan for St Peter's (fig. 146) and that had been taken up by Raphael in the background of the *Expulsion of Heliodorus*. But the fact that he replaced the triumphal arches of the nave by simple theatre motifs, eliminated the entablature projections and their continuation in broad transverse arches, and flanked the choir with octagonal sacristies on either side, shows that in many respects he was still closer in manner to Giuliano da Sangallo (fig. 159).

Of all his buildings in Carpi, Peruzzi's talent is shown most impressively in the nave of the Franciscan church of San Niccolò. When he prolonged its domed Greek-cross layout, reminiscent of Bramante's Milanese phase, and dating to the 1490s, by the addition of three bays with saucer domes in *c.*1518, he brilliantly took over almost all its forms and measurements and only allowed his Roman provenance to be recognized in the *serliane* of the lunette-windows and the strong relief of the blind arches in the aisles.

Ever since the Villa alle Volte and the Farnesina, Peruzzi had repeatedly adjusted his style to new developments. But he had neither ventured into new territory like Raphael, nor developed for himself a wholly personal manner. As also in his numerous figurative works, however, an unusually high level of proficiency and an astonishing ability to absorb the innovations of others distinguished him as an architect. This attitude would only slowly alter before the Sack of Rome in 1527.

Thus in designing a double palazzo in the Baths of Agrippa for two Orsini brothers in c.1517/18, he followed Raphael's efforts to save the ancient monuments from destruction by incorporating them as living entities in the new Rome. Like Giuliano in the Palazzo Medici-Lante in 1514, he too long held fast in his courtyards to the old-fashioned columnar arcades that the Younger Sangallo had already banned from his repertoire in c.1513 and that Raphael had proposed in none of his projects. Columnar arcades can also be found in the roughly contemporary Palazzo Ossoli-Missini (fig. 211), in which presumably Peruzzi varied the new palazzetto type of the Palazzo Caprini (fig. 136) and Palazzo Baldassini. As in his buildings in Carpi, he combined there the flat and static wall relief of the Farnesina with Sangallesque and Raphaelesque motifs. In the windows of the courtyard he was even inspired by those planned in 1518 for the rear wall of the courtyard of the Palazzo Branconio.

Peruzzi had already tried to come close to Raphael in the Cappella Ponzetti of c.1516. He succeeded in doing so most convincingly in the painted illusionistic architecture of the Sala delle Prospettive in the Farnesina in c.1519. There he remained faithful to the character of a *palazzo suburbano* by opening up fictive views of the townscape of Rome through the *trompe-l'oeil* colonnades. As in the Pantheon and in the ambulatories of Leo's projects for St Peter's (figs 3, 159), the colonnades are represented as alternating with wall blocks, into which statue niches are hewn. Peruzzi followed Raphael's ideal of a *Gesamtkunstwerk* also by decorating this fictive hall with polychrome marble incrustation, a mythological frieze and faux-marble statues of deities in the side niches, contrasted with the living deities placed in recumbent poses over the wall openings.

After 1519, Peruzzi succumbed increasingly to Sangallo's influence. The palazzo and the adjoining stables that he began for Gian Corrado Orsini in Bomarzo in late 1519 thus differ from Sangallo's buildings mainly in their more antique detail. Sangallo's influence is also detectible in his roughly contemporary central-plan projects for San Giovanni dei Fiorentini (fig. 208). The façade thus rises as a flat block out of the cylindrical building, and the chapels are as if hewn out of the massive circuit of walls. Peruzzi, however, reduces Sangallo's sixteen bays to twelve and replaces the theatre motif by the more complex and larger triumphal arches, which frame the high altar, entrance hall and diagonal chapels, but not the transversal axis, thus underlining the continuity of the interior cylinder. The lateral bays of the triumphal motifs lead into larger chapels, whose ground plan he varied in many different ways, from polygonal to round and even oval, one of the first in post-Antique architecture. In an alternative project (fig. 209) he started from a square exterior and an octagonal interior, both articulated by engaged columns. He used the intermediate area for hexagonal chapels with alternating niches which are accessible through double *serliane*. It can be felt how, in continuous engagement with the innovations of Bramante, Raphael and Sangallo, he now overcame all archaisms and began himself to conquer new territory.

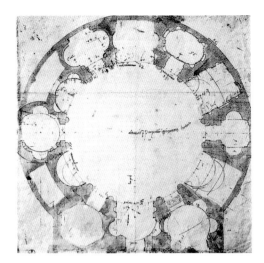

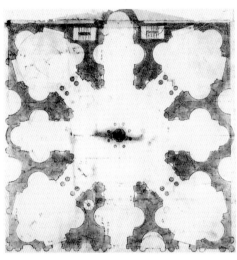

208, 209 *Two plans by Peruzzi for the much-debated church of San Giovanni dei Fiorentini in Rome. Both are variants of the centralized plan, showing to the full his ability to digest the ideas of his contemporaries.*

210 *Peruzzi was one of several architects who submitted designs for the unfinished church of San Petronio in Bologna. Respecting 'conformity', he tries to combine Renaissance space with a partially Gothic vocabulary.*

In his central-plan project for St Peter's of 1521 Peruzzi limited himself however to the simplification and harmonization of the previous projects. In the drawings for San Petronio dating to his Bolognese stay in 1522, he tried to obey the principle of conformity by combining the Gothic vocabulary of the old church with the dome of Florence Cathedral and the tectonic principles of the Vitruvian orders (fig. 210). In his contemporary projects for the Palazzo Lambertini in Bologna he explicitly espoused the Vitruvian principle of not combining columns with arches, but only with an entablature.

Following his return to Rome from Bologna in the summer of 1522, Peruzzi lost no time in coming to terms with the revolutionary innovations of Giulio Romano. In the window-aedicules of the Palazzo Fusconi he thus combined the Doric triglyph frieze with Ionic corner volutes into a mixture of two orders. Such a *mescolanza* had already been experimented with in antiquity and coincided with the spirit of caprice that characterized these years.

In the exterior of the little villa of Cardinal Fieschi on the river Salone east of Rome he also took over Giulio's Palazzo Stati in the reduction of the pilasters to vertical and the entablature to horizontal wall strips (fig. 212). Thus the façade is not so much articulated with an order as divided into a grid of abstract panels – an extremely economical principle of articulation that even outstripped the tendency towards abstraction that we have seen in the Villa Madama (fig. 170) and that soon met with the widest dissemination. At the same time he remained faithful to the type of the richly decorated triumphal arch in his numerous designs for portals, funerary monuments, altars and comparable miniature architectures; in this too he proved himself an heir to the legacy of Giuliano da Sangallo.

Only after fleeing from the Sack of Rome in 1527, and returning to his hometown of Siena, did Peruzzi find time, like Sangallo, to

211 *In Peruzzi's Palazzo Ossoli-Missini of about 1517/18 the paratactic articulation of the façade and the columnar arcades of the courtyard are combined with the vocabulary of Raphael and Sangallo the Younger.*

212 *In the villa he built for Cardinal Fieschi on the river Salone Peruzzi abandoned the orders altogether and relied on Giulio's bare abstract pattern.*

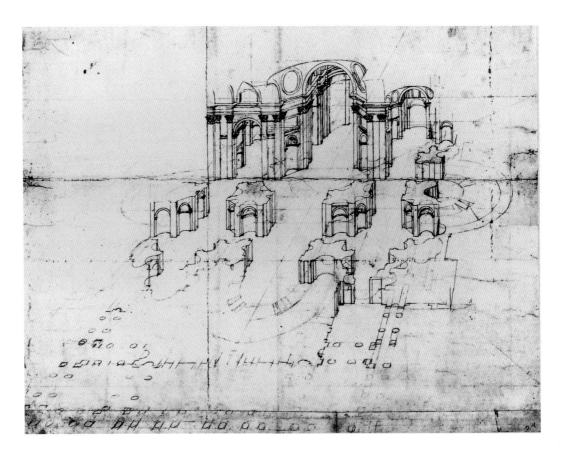

213 *For St Peter's Peruzzi returned to a centralized plan but with Raphael's piers, ambulatories and vestibule which opens in colonnades.*

214 *One of his last projects for a Sienese church shows Peruzzi's dependence on the column, perhaps an indication of his interest in both Vitruvian and Early Christian buildings.*

reflect on the basic principles of architecture. This allowed him to achieve his full maturity. In 1532 he proposed a series of alternative projects for the interior of the fire-gutted Dominican church in Siena. They range from a *Dorica* of colossal half-columns framing Pantheon-aedicules to full columns placed in front of the wall to a sequence of saucer-domed bays which would have transformed the

nave and the transept into spacious halls (fig. 215). For this wealth of motifs, and especially for the courage to express it on a monumental scale, he was indebted especially to Bramante, Raphael and the antique. Through his sense for proportion, harmony, balance, spaciousness, flowing transitions and the virtuoso play of light and shadow, Peruzzi imbued these projects with a magic that had been anticipated only by the garden loggia of the Villa Madama (fig. 171) and that contrasts with Sangallo's far simpler, more austere, static and angular interiors.

Similar qualities also distinguish others of Peruzzi's late designs. In the interior of some longitudinal projects for St Peter's he continued the system of the ambulatories into the aisles and replaced Bramante's and Raphael's arches with smaller colonnades. In the façades of his late central-plan projects for the basilica he recurred to the system of the temple front exclusively supported by columns (fig. 213). There he continued Raphael's and Sangallo's order of *c*.2 m (6½ ft) shafts in the four-column groups of the façade, knitted these together by quadrangular columns and continued this system along the lateral walls. Deep shadow-creating blocks of columns would thus have replaced the dense wall architecture of Raphael and Sangallo.

The column now assumed an even greater importance than it had had for Brunelleschi, Giuliano and the late Bramante. It comes into its own in its purest sense in several projects for churches in Siena, in which Peruzzi reflected on the origins of Christian architecture, no doubt inspired by the spirit of incipient Reform (fig. 214). He held fast to the system of the dome over the crossing of Brunelleschi's basilicas, but took a decisive step closer to Vitruvius by once again replacing the simple columnar arcades with groups of columns with straight entablature and by reducing the lighting to a mystical half-light.

215 *In 1532 Peruzzi proposed a series of alternative ways of restoring the fire-gutted Dominican church in Siena, e.g. a sequence of saucer-domed bays with a highly classicizing articulation of the walls.*

Palazzo Massimo alle Colonne

At much the same time as the projects for San Domenico, Peruzzi designed a palazzo in the centre of Rome for Pietro Massimo, a patrician whose family home had been burnt down during the Sack of Rome (figs 216–18). At the same time Pietro's two younger brothers also decided to erect houses for themselves on the site: Angelo commissioned Giovanni Mangone to build his town residence directly to the left of the Palazzo Massimo, while Luca commissioned Sangallo to erect his on the opposite side of the Via Papale. Peruzzi must have been especially challenged by this project, not least because he was able to replace the medieval façade portico, from which the former Palazzo Massimo had derived its epithet 'alle Colonne', with an *all'antica* colonnade. Such a *vestibulum* had been sanctioned by the Lateran Baptistery and Santa Costanza and anticipated by Giuliano's villa at Poggio a Caiano (fig. 77) and Sangallo's project for the Palazzo Pucci.

The entrance axis was determined by the considerably narrower left wing of the original (and partially preserved) old Palazzo Massimo. On the left corner of this wing the street, there only some 4.70 m (15½ ft) broad, was slightly curved. In Peruzzi's less costly alternative project, not only the courtyard, but also the façade would have been asymmetrical. The executed version was only possible because Angelo ceded a part of his plot of land to his brother (the part represented by the two bays to the left of the ground-floor colonnade). By eliminating the triglyph frieze of the alternative project, Peruzzi was no longer bound by a rigid rhythm. This meant that he was able to open the middle of the façade in a colonnade, flank it with bays of equal width, and give it a slightly convex front to adjust it to the curve of the street – a convex curve that Sangallo had anticipated in his project for the villa of Cardinal del Monte (fig. 196).

The curvature of the central bays lends flexibility to the rustication: the hard stone seems to bend like some malleable substance.

Only on closer inspection does the palazzo reveal its derivation from Raphael's Palazzo Branconio del'Aquila (fig. 167). Peruzzi eliminated the non-Vitruvian arcades and niches, doubled the columns and freed the central ones from the wall. He simplified the cornices and the rich decoration. So the continuous rustication is not interrupted and the residential area of the three upper floors is even more unified than in Raphael's Palazzo Alberini (fig. 166). The ground-floor colonnade is subordinated to, even crushed by, the top-heavy coherence of the upper part. Peruzzi, by renouncing the use of any order on the upper storeys, did not emphasize the vertical axes as Raphael had done in the façade of the Palazzo Branconio: only the central window on the *piano nobile* is situated over the broader intercolumniation at the centre of the ground-floor colonnade; all the others stand partially over members of the order. The windows of the *piano nobile*, moreover, are now smaller than the monumental Pantheon-aedicules privileged by Raphael and Sangallo. The presence of the patron in the façade is correspondingly downplayed.

In the windows of the *piano nobile* as also in the portal of the vestibule, Peruzzi continued the long tradition of the *Porta Ionica*, which can be traced back through his own previous attempts in the Palazzo Orsini at Bomarzo, to the Porta Santa of St Peter's (1524), to the portal of San Michele in Bosco in Bologna (1522), to the early attempts of Sangallo and the portal of Bramante's Tempietto (fig. 137), to Alberti's portals (figs 35, 44), and ultimately to the ancient prototypes and prescriptions of Vitruvius on which they are based. In the lower mezzanine windows, framed by abstracted volutes, the influence of Giulio's Palazzo Stati (fig. 178) can be felt, while the

216–18 *Peruzzi's most famous building is the Palazzo Massimo in Rome. Its façade (opposite above) is unusual in being curved. The ground-floor colonnade (below left) forms a vestibule leading to an inner court (below right) of which all four sides are different. Here we are looking towards the two-storeyed Doric and Ionic loggia.*

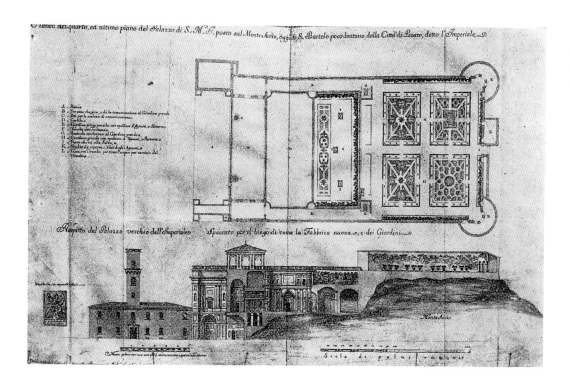

and, as in the Vatican, both buildings are connected by a corridor. Its large façade suggests a spacious and representative interior, but does not provide any princely apartment and is not even accessible by a ceremonial staircase. Instead it comprises a courtyard with grottos, two architectural gardens and a belvedere – a luxurious theatre for feasts and *otium* when the climate permitted (figs 220–22). Francesco Maria and his wife lived in the Quattrocento villa beneath and commissioned the fresco decoration of its rooms. Vasari was evidently including the old villa in commending not only the Villa Imperiale's unusual combination of 'colonnades, courts, loggias, fountains, and most delightful gardens', but also its 'apartments'.

Genga conceived the main façade of the villa as asymmetrical: the corridor at its right side is hidden by the older building and thus the projecting bay on the left seems to be balanced by a symmetrically projecting bay to the right. Giulio's buildings may have encouraged him to do so. The influence of the Villa Madama can also be felt in the abstract articulation of both the squat ground floor with its shadowy openings and the paired pilasters of the slender *Ionica* in the dominating *piano nobile*.

From the corridor one has to pass through two small rooms and a narrow door before reaching the steep and elongated *vestibulum* in the central wing. It is terminated by semicircular exedras like the *vestibulum* in the basement floor of the Villa Madama and continues in an *atrium* with five aisles separated by Ionic colonnades. The axial sequence continues in the symmetrical *cavaedium*. Its rear wing cuts into the slope of the hill and contains a grotto and baths. The complex rhythm of its order, and the deliberate contrast between different wall surfaces and textures, are directly inspired by Giulio and the valley façade of the Villa Madama (fig. 170). As in the garden court of the Palazzo Ducale in Urbino, the long staircase that leads up to the two gardens is hidden behind the convex corners of the courtyard. The only apartment is located in the squat upper storey; its small rooms are all of much the same size and shape.

In the Villa Imperiale Genga thus tried to revive aspects of the ancient house, to which Raphael too had alluded in his description of the Villa Madama. In spite of the astonishing flexibility and innovative dexterity with which the forty-nine-year-old master from the provinces sought inspiration from the inventions of Raphael and Giulio, the essentially inorganic interior layout and the somehow archaic proportions of the orders show how hard he found it to assimilate the new style and to fuse all these different ideas into a coherent whole.

In 1537 Francesco Maria decided to build his funerary church in Pesaro, but died in the following year. It was only in 1543 that his son Guidobaldo II laid the foundation stone. The project (though later altered) is, again, attributable to Genga. After his death in 1551 its execution was continued by his son Bartolommeo.

The single nave is flanked by three chapels on either side, roofed with a bare barrel vault and only illuminated through the *serliana* of the lunette. Obviously under Giulio's influence it is articulated with a completely abstract system of alternating arches, niches and wall panels. As in San Bernardino in Urbino (fig. 94), the centralized choir was presumably intended for the duke's funerary monument. Its four arches are supported by paired columns which were probably to be continued in a second order which would have reached the height of the impost of the nave. Neither the executed arches of the octagonal chancel, which are strangely super-elevated, nor the dome can correspond to Genga's design.

He articulated the ground floor of the façade with abstract arches, reminiscent of Francesco di Giorgio's Urbino Cathedral (fig. 93) and intended to clad it with marble incrustation. In the upper storey, which is executed only in brick, he varied Raphael's project for the façade of San Lorenzo (fig. 165). He connected the recessed sides of the nave with the façade and the transept by concave pillars – a proto-Borrominesque solution, quite unique for these years. Genga here too, as in the Villa Imperiale, combined innovation with archaism.

Michele Sanmicheli (1484–1559)

The only leading northern Italian exponent of the school of Bramante, Michele Sanmicheli was trained as a stonemason in Verona and moved to Central Italy at an early age. His presence is documented at Rieti in June 1512 and in Orvieto, where he was long active, from November 1512 onwards. In his magnificent altar for the Cappella dei Re Magi in Orvieto Cathedral he followed the model of Andrea Sansovino's tombs in Santa Maria del Popolo and may even have been Sansovino's assistant in this enterprise. Presumably on Bramante's recommendation, he was appointed architect of Orvieto Cathedral and had to present his model for the completion of its façade to the Roman authorities in *c.*1513/14. In 1514 Antonio da Sangallo the Younger, one of the most experienced engineers of his time, was sent to him as technical consultant, and would soon exert a decisive influence on his architectural development.

In his earliest independent building, the Petrucci Chapel begun in 1516 in the crypt below the choir of San Domenico in Orvieto, Sanmicheli showed his indebtedness to Sangallo in his choice of chapel type, vocabulary and proportions. The over-slender aedicules of his slightly later Palazzo Petrucci in Orvieto are reminiscent, on the other hand, of those of the Palazzo del Monte, which Antonio the Elder was then building in nearby Monte Sansavino. In the cloister of Sant'Agostino in Bagnacavallo (*c.*1524) Sanmicheli combined octagonal pillars of Quattrocento type with doricizing capitals and continuous entablature. So it seems as if he had still not found any style of his own.

In 1526 he accompanied Antonio da Sangallo, who in his role as papal architect-in-chief had been commissioned to inspect fortresses in Emilia and Romagna. No doubt in the same year Sanmicheli returned to his hometown, after an absence of about fifteen years. He would then have had an opportunity to get to know Giulio Romano's buildings (or projects) in Mantua and Falconetto's in Padua: both would decisively contribute to his artistic breakthrough.

Giovanni Maria Falconetto (1468–1535) had attempted, even before Giulio, to introduce the achievements of the High Renaissance architecture of Central Italy into the Veneto. In the Loggia in Padua that he erected after 1524 for the Paduan humanist Alvise Cornaro he continued a *Dorica* with triglyph frieze into an *Ionica*, decorated it with antique masks and victories and incorporated the dominating window-aedicules of the *piano nobile* in the pedestal zone (as in the Cancelleria). In these buildings or in the triumphal arch-like Porta San Giovanni, erected in 1528, however, Falconetto followed not so much Bramante, Raphael or Peruzzi as sculptor-architects like Giuliano da Sangallo and Jacopo Sansovino. He, more than anyone, was instrumental in developing the Venetian predilection for rich sculptural decoration in the spandrels of the arcades, as in the central arch of the Loggia Cornaro. Sanmicheli, under this influence, now acquired a similar taste for comparably rich and plastic decoration.

Cappella Pellegrini

When Sanmicheli designed the circular funerary chapel annexed to San Bernardino, the earliest of his Veronese masterpieces (*c.*1527), he combined Falconetto's rich decoration with that of Giuliano da Sangallo and of the courtyard of Jacopo Sansovino's Palazzo Gaddi (fig. 230). He followed Bramante's Tempietto (fig. 137) in the domed rotunda and the encircling triumphal arches of the ground floor, while the balustrade that runs round the foot of the drum seems indebted to Giuliano da Sangallo's Madonna delle Carceri (fig. 76).

Even more decisive was Raphael's influence on the chapel interior. The deep entrance arch and the detail of the *Corinthia* are reminiscent of the Chigi Chapel (fig. 162), while the wall blocks alternating with the four-column groups of the drum are indebted to the ambulatories of St Peter's (fig. 173). Sanmicheli enriched the four arches on the ground floor, as in the Palazzo Branconio (fig. 167), with window-aedicules with triangular pediments. He also followed

223 *The Cappella Pellegrini, which Michele Sanmicheli added to the church of San Bernardino in Verona about 1527, ingeniously combines a whole host of earlier influences.*

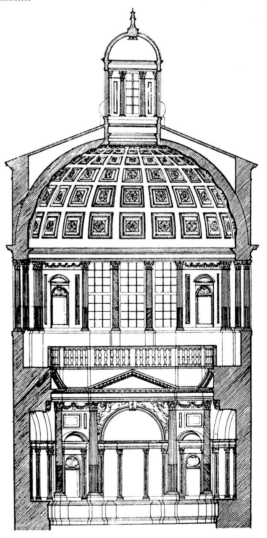

rusticated ground floor. The relatively small grated windows of the *basamento* are slightly recessed behind blind arcades in the wider bays. As in Peruzzi's Palazzo Fusconi, the triglyphs of the entablature are combined with deep consoles that support the cornice.

This façade once again demonstrates Sanmicheli's familiarity with the Roman monuments of his hometown, in particular the Porta de' Borsari which, like the Bevilacqua, alternates straight and spiral-fluted columns. It also evinces his decorative flair and inventiveness – in the splendid masks, the reclining victories in the spandrels, the festoons, the lion-headed volutes that support the windowsills of the arched windows or the magnificent acanthus frieze of the upper entablature. All this is displayed with even greater assurance than in the Cappella Pellegrini and is proof of his rapid assimilation of the Venetian tradition. The complex interplay of horizontal and vertical forces, and the more sculptural and classicizing decoration, seem to have inspired Sansovino's design for the Scuola Grande della Misericordia in Venice (fig. 231): proof, perhaps, that the Palazzo Bevilacqua had already been started by 1531.

Villa La Soranza near Castelfranco

The villa that Sanmicheli designed for the Venetian patrician Alvise Soranzo in c.1537–40 near Castelfranco, now largely demolished (fig. 227), consisted, in traditional fashion, of a central residential block only some 15 m (50 ft) high and was flanked by lower and narrower farm buildings. The tripartite complex was linked by a continuous

227 *The Villa La Soranza by Sanmicheli, c.1537–40, only partially survives. The central vestibule flanked by projecting wings recalls the Farnesina, but the arcaded barns on both sides demonstrate also the agricultural function characteristic of Venetian villas.*

wall with pedimented garden portals. By recurring to the ultimately antique type of portico-villa with projecting corner bays, Sanmicheli combined an old Venetian with a far more recent Tuscan and Roman tradition. As in the Farnesina, he flanked the central *vestibulum* with projecting wings (fig. 203), but was also inspired by Bramante's single-storeyed 'Nymphaeum' in Genazzano, which is recalled by the vestibule exedras (figs 154, 155). He came even closer to Giuliano da Sangallo's villa at Poggio a Caiano (figs 77, 78) by starting out from a basic grid of square apartments and rooms, raising the main storey over a *podium villae* and placing a staircase in front of the centre. The rusticated exterior was articulated by no order. The squat *basamento* with the tall windows of the service rooms is topped by the residential floor lit by tall narrow arcaded windows and a squat mezzanine.

Palazzo Lavezola Pompei

Sanmicheli may have planned the seven-bayed Palazzo Pompei as early as December 1536, when the Lavezola brothers purchased a building adjacent to their house in Verona. In its ground-plan type and courtyard, it is far closer to the Venetian tradition than the Palazzo Canossa. The central entrance hall and the similar salon on the *piano nobile* take up the whole depth of the entrance wing. The vault of the hallway rests on consoles and is as unassuming as the staircase that ascends from its rear corner. The façade is once again built of handsome honey-gold Veronese stone. Even more clearly than in the Villa La Soranza, Sanmicheli fused here Bramantesque prototypes with the picturesque and decorative tradition of Venice. The relief is deeper, the window arcades are more triumphal arch-like, the motifs and rhythms simpler than in the Palazzo Caprini (fig. 136) or in Sanmicheli's two previous Veronese palaces. Once again both floors open in arcaded windows. In the narrow bays of the *piano*

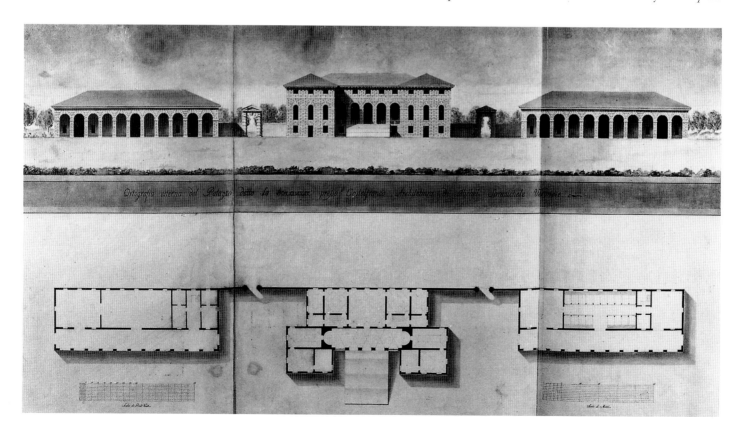

nobile they are extremely slender and alternate with single fluted columns on tall pedestals that are incorporated into the continuous balustrade. The central bay is hierarchically widened, and the corners are reinforced with quadrangular pillars. Sanmicheli used a normative vocabulary and his individual signature can be identified only in some details such as the abstract blocks of the pedestal zone or the huge masks above the upper window arcades.

City gates

Sanmicheli's fame rests not least on his magnificent city gates: they have, says Vasari, no equal. When he erected the Porta Nuova in *c.*1531/32–35, he must have been familiar with Giulio's project for the Porta Te: Giulio clearly inspired the rustication of the whole façade and its central temple-like front with its pediment rising into the attic. This central bay is projected outwards by a layer; and the bays by which it is flanked are in turn projected by a further layer from the lateral bays with the large portals and the projecting corner pillars. The effect is that of a *crescendo*, converging on the centre. The whole façade is as hierarchically organized as Serlio's Palazzo Zen in Venice, it too inspired by Genga's Villa Imperiale (fig. 220). On the other hand, such characteristic motifs as the combination of columns and pillars, or the relatively squat arcades, still seem influenced by the Sangallo. But Sanmicheli had the added advantage of being able to use here light honey-toned marble and invest his gateway with the Hellenic splendour of its glittering surface.

In its monotonous alternation of arcades and paired columns of a rusticated *Dorica*, its unbroken entablature and normative

details, the city front of another of Sanmicheli's city gates, the Porta Palio of 1547 (fig. 228), recalls, by contrast, the façade of the Palazzo Lavezola Pompei. With its fluted shafts, bases, escutcheons, epigraphs and masks, the outer façade of the gateway is much more complex, urbane and convincing. The columns are freed from the rustication. The arches are replaced by high pillars, which support a row of horizontal voussoirs. They create the rectangular recesses for the drawbridge of the central portal and for the lavish Ionic portals in the side bays. The exaggerated high frieze and elongated volutes of the side portals are directly inspired by a late-Antique portal in Spoleto and recur in the portal of his own house in Verona.

Madonna della Campagna

Presumably commissioned by Bishop Lippomano, Sanmicheli designed a round church in the vicinity of Verona in the summer of 1559, three months before his death. Built over a miraculous icon of the Madonna, it was his only independent church. Its execution, however, stretched into the following century and was accompanied by drastic alterations to his original project. Once again he started out from a Roman prototype, Sangallo's pilgrimage church of Santa Maria di Montemoro near Montefiascone. He underlined, however, the centrality of the octagonal interior by articulating it exclusively with rectangular niches. The arcade of the eight theatre motifs is decorated with a Composite pilaster order, and opened only into the three portals and the sanctuary area of the two main axes. In the diagonal axes the rectangular niches serve for further altars. To each theatre motif on the ground floor correspond three smaller bays on the drum storey; their pilasters remain separated at the corners as in Giuliano's sacristy of Santo Spirito. Each of the

228 *Sanmicheli was renowned as a military engineer. His Porta Palio of 1547 (below: the town side) was part of the defences of Verona.*

234 *The Venetian Mint (La Zecca) was built by Sansovino in 1536 in Giulio's rusticated fashion, but with the cool design of the born Florentine. He added the top storey in 1554.*

arcade and its keystones that project up to the cornice are once again reminiscent of the Palazzo Canossa (fig. 224). Also reminiscent of Sanmicheli is the grainy rustication. The *piano nobile*, with which the building originally terminated, is decorated with a *Dorica* with triglyph frieze. Abstracted rectangular aedicules with widely outward-projecting entablature are compressed between the banded shafts of the three-quarter columns. The façade thus possesses a compressed energy similar to the project for the Scuola Grande della Misericordia and the Palazzo Corner.

This tension is significantly slacker in the Ionic storey which Sansovino only added after 1554, when he prolonged the adjacent Library to align it with the elevation of the Zecca. There he supported the cornice by similarly projecting consoles as in the Palazzo Bevilaqua and used abstracted Ionic aedicules with ears, convex frieze and triangular pediments (fig. 226). As in the Palazzo Dolfin, he repeated the

façade system in the courtyard in simplified form; here too he is far closer to Sanmicheli than for instance to Giulio's Mantuan buildings.

In March 1537 Sansovino received a further commission from the Council of Ten: this time for the Libreria Marciana (fig. 235). It is by far the most magnificent library of the humanistic period. Originally the building was to comprise seventeen window-axes; it was extended to twenty-one axes in 1554. In contrast to the planned library of Julius II or Michelangelo's Laurenziana (fig. 244), it was situated on the most important piazza of the most powerful city-state of the day, and directly opposite its seat of government, the Palazzo Ducale. Sansovino seized the opportunity to transform the late-medieval piazza into a Vitruvian forum, as Brunelleschi and Francesco del Borgo had already tried to do (fig. 6). As in the Loggia delle Benedizioni of Pius II, both storeys are opened up in a sequence of pillared arcades with orders of engaged columns, while the ground floor is barrel-vaulted; even the original proportion of *c.*1:3 corresponds to that planned by Francesco del Borgo.

The theatre motifs, the Doric order and its engaged columns are inspired by the courtyard of the Palazzo Farnese (fig. 192). As in the

235 *With the Libreria Marciana, 1537, Sansovino translated Pius II's Loggia delle Benedizioni into the decorative richness of the Venetian Renaissance.*

portal of Palazzo Baldassini, their shafts are deepened into two-third columns in the recessed spandrels above the impost. In his opulent sculptural decoration Sansovino developed the taste he had expressed in his design for the façade of the Scuola Grande della Misericordia (fig. 231). But the windows are cut more deeply into the wall and framed by pairs of narrow columnar arches.

Sansovino devoted particular care to the articulation of the corners. As in the Basilica Aemilia, the columns in the round are here reinforced on the outside by powerful square columns which are somewhat broader than the engaged columns and closely bound to the pillars by the abstracted continuation of the base of the impost cornice. As in Bramante's cloister of Santa Maria della Pace (fig. 135), these abstract square columns are now faced with shallow pilasters that are just as broad as the round columns, but that project from the square columns by a further layer. This solution was criticized at the time, but Sansovino may have justified it because only thus could the

last triglyph be placed in axis. This tendency for axial continuity, however, did not conform to the tectonic orthodoxy of Vitruvius or Sangallo, which demanded that the triglyphs at the corners of the building should join: 'the triglyphs above the corner columns' – taught Vitruvius – 'are placed at their furthest edge, and not against the middle of the columns. Thus the metopes [placed] next to the corner triglyphs do not come out square but oblong by half the breadth of a triglyph' (Book IV.3). Moreover, by using thin pilaster facings he placed their three-dimensionality in question, and showed once again that the Vitruvian order had, ever since the imperial period, been reduced to a beautiful fiction. A section shows that the corner pillars are formed of ten different members of the order: a kind of amalgamation that cannot but remind us of the bundled piers of Gothic cathedrals.

With the normative *Corinthia* and the Pantheon-aedicules of the vestibule Sansovino responded to the revolutionary *ricetto* of Michelangelo's Laurenziana and tried to surpass all predecessors also in the décor of the staircase and in the large domed reading room.

Sansovino erected by far his most luxurious building at the foot of the Campanile (fig. 236). The Loggetta replaced a medieval predecessor that had served as a place of assembly for the patricians of Venice but had been destroyed by lightning in August 1537. As if he had finally found the opportunity to realize his early dreams, he recurred to a system of three triumphal arches, flanked by full columns carrying robustly projecting entablature blocks, and topped by a high balustraded attic. So inorganically did he join this triumphal front to the Bramantesque *serliane* of the recessed side walls that one feels his increasing danger of sacrificing tectonic systems to scenographic effects. The appeal of the Loggetta derives from the contrast between white and pink marble, the precious columns, the masterly bronze statues (sculpted by Sansovino himself) and the marble reliefs. The terrace is protected by a balustrade and the benches in front of it rest on triglyphed brackets. The Loggetta also enchanted contemporaries by its sculptural programme, which, like the whole piazza, pays tribute to the state, the arts and the sciences, here combined together in a quite unique way.

Villa Garzoni at Pontecasale

Sansovino's only villa (fig. 237) dates to almost exactly the same time as Sanmicheli's La Soranza (fig. 221). Like that, it was situated in the midst of one of those extensive estates with which the Venetian patriciate began to expand on the *terra firma*. Like La Soranza, it was flanked by the porticoes of auxiliary farm buildings. Its ground plan is similarly developed from the square, but its elevation is two-

236 *Sansovino's Loggetta at the foot of the Campanile, where Venetian noblemen assembled, is executed in polychrome marble.*

237 *About 1537 Sansovino built the Villa Garzoni for a Venetian patrician family on the* terra firma.

storeyed. Like La Soranza, it rises over a low basement, but the external staircase is now as wide as the five arches of the *vestibulum*. As in the Scuola Grande della Misericordia, Sansovino remained faithful to his origins and privileged stereometric building blocks and spaces. He thus comes closer to Sangallo than to Sanmicheli in the fully symmetrical interior layout of the rooms with the large reception rooms on the façade wing, in the surrounding courtyard loggias and the two-ramped interior staircase. In the façade he combined the five theatre motifs of the *vestibulum* and the loggia above it with the narrow arched windows of the Venetian patrician façade in the larger lateral bays. As in Sangallo and in the Palazzo Canossa, he continued the *vestibulum* in a *cavaedium*, a one-storeyed *peristylium* with splendid marble pavement and a rear garden. Both orders are inspired by the courtyard of the Palazzo Farnese (fig. 189), though their proportions are more composed, their entablatures and keystone volutes more ponderous and abstract. Following the long-consolidated Roman tradition, only column bases and capitals are of stone, the rest of stuccoed brick. And so the drastic simplification of the detail was also justified on economic grounds.

San Martino

In *c.*1540 Sansovino designed a suburban parish church in Venice and gave it a ground plan of a kind that had hardly been used since Alberti's San Sebastiano (fig. 46). However, he vaulted only the rectangular arms of the crossing and opened the walls in a way similar to Codussi's domed Greek-cross churches into square chapels with numerous windows (fig. 119). With this type of church, later much copied and varied, he not only came to terms with the constraints of the limited site, but also with the tendencies towards religious reform in the lagoon city. The interior articulation with slender corner pilasters of a Doric order is correspondingly spartan.

With the Palazzo Corner and his buildings in the Piazza San Marco Sansovino had achieved the high point of his creative potential. And although he remained active in Venice till 1570 and always highly esteemed, he built no further buildings of equal significance. Like Sangallo, Giulio and Sanmicheli, he created his masterpieces in the first half of his career. He too succeeded in creating a new architectural identity befitting his powerful patrons and in keeping with the spirit of his adopted city. That identity would continue to live on and exert its influence long after the Renaissance.

Sebastiano Serlio (1475?–1554?)

Sansovino's friends, supporters and propagators included Sebastiano Serlio, a Bolognese who had begun as a painter in the circle of Girolamo Cottignola, and had especially distinguished himself in his hometown by his virtuoso architectural backgrounds. It was in 1522 through his meeting with Peruzzi in Bologna that he became an architect. He assisted Peruzzi in his projects for San Petronio (fig. 210), and presumably joined him in Rome in *c.*1525. He then moved to Venice in 1527/28. In his dealings with the humanists in his hometown he had acquired the methodical and literary abilities on which his career was to be based. He speedily acquired a reputation as a connoisseur of the architecture of antiquity (in part culled from his master Peruzzi), published prints of the Doric, Ionic and Corinthian orders in 1528, and dubbed himself *professore di architettura*. His continuing dialogue with the resident artists and humanists of Venice, but above all his desire for a generally understandable and illustrated handbook to architecture, soon gave him the idea of compiling a treatise.

To the writing of that treatise, as well as to the few architectural commissions given to him during his later career in France, he devoted the rest of his life. He was perhaps already in his sixties when he published Book IV (the successive books did not appear in numerical order) on the columnar orders in 1537. In its foreword he thanked his master Peruzzi, with whose drawings he was evidently familiar. He also paid tribute to Sangallo, Sansovino, Titian, Michelangelo, Genga and an architect and theoretician by the name of Battista, no doubt Sangallo's younger brother. But he reserved his particular approbation for Raphael, Giulio Romano and Sanmicheli. Through all these masters and through numerous humanists and patrons, architecture – he claims – had reached a flowering only equalled by Latin architecture in the time of Caesar and Cicero. So not only did he confess his Latin identity, but he implied that the architecture of his time equalled, and even surpassed, that of ancient Rome.

Apart from the three illustrated in his prints of 1528, Serlio's five orders also comprise the *Tuscanica* and the *Composita*, the *Italica* that Alberti had already privileged, but that connoisseurs of Vitruvius like Sangallo had never accepted as a separate order. And since hardly any building of his heroes obeyed the rules of the five orders, he must have been conscious from the very start of the fundamental difference between normative rules and practical application. He illustrated each order through a series of elevations, which provide valuable insights into the ideas of his time. He laid special value on variety of rhythm, and varied all previous possibilities, ranging from single theatre or triumphal-arch motifs and *serliane* to their use in series or the combination of one motif with another. Some are inspired by Bramante, Raphael and especially by Giulio Romano, others by Sanmicheli or Sansovino. Sansovino, for instance, had anticipated the combination of Doric theatre motifs in the ground floor with Ionic *serliane* in the upper floor in his project for the Scuola Grande and developed it further in his project for the Libreria Marciana a few months before the publication of Serlio's book (figs 231, 235).

The Third Book, devoted to antique exempla, appeared in 1540. There he copied not only drawings after the antique, especially those of Antonio da Sangallo the Younger and Peruzzi, but also projects by Bramante (fig. 138), Raphael and Peruzzi, and classified them in hierarchical sequence according to function and type.

As a practising architect Serlio enjoyed little success and little opportunity. During his years in Venice he supervised the transformation of the Palazzo Zen from 1531 and, in doing so, was one of the first to introduce the principles of Roman secular architecture into the Serenissima. In the hierarchical layering of the walls he also derived inspiration from Genga's Villa Imperiale (figs 220, 221). But altogether he lacked the originality and energy that would help Sanmicheli and Sansovino to their speedy success.

After he had gone to Fontainebleau at the invitation of François I in 1541, he compiled the Sixth Book, dedicated to domestic architecture.

Following in the footsteps of Filarete and Francesco di Giorgio, he developed a social hierarchy of housing and differentiated between Italian and French versions. And while most leading architects in Italy at the time were reviving paratactical systems, he invented even more complex rhythms than before. With these inventions, however, he made little headway, either in his relations with the king or with his few other French patrons. Serlio's buildings at Ancy-le-Franc (fig. 238), Fontainebleau, Paris, Auxerre and Tournon are indeed far simpler in rhythm than many of his unexecuted projects during the same period. In the abstract panelling of the walls of his project for Saint-Élois des Orfèvres in Paris he followed Genga's San Giovanni Battista in Pesaro.

In France Serlio published three further books on geometry, perspective and church architecture. In the church designs of the Fifth Book he recurred far less to Venetian than to Roman proto-types and to Genga's tendency towards abstraction. He also tried to bring church architecture into conformity with what he took to be the principles of the ancient temple; he thus reduced central-plan projects of Raphael, Peruzzi and Sangallo to a single storey in his first seven examples.

In the Vienna version of the Sixth Book (c.1547) and the Munich version begun in c.1547–49 the French tradition progressively gained the upper hand. Despite this, it was never published during his lifetime. Likewise the Seventh Book, devoted to 'various accidents that may occur in building', the contingencies of architecture that had long bedevilled Serlio's career as a practising architect, appeared in print only after his death (Frankfurt, 1575). The Eighth Book, on military architecture, had to wait even longer – almost 450 years – before it was published. On the other hand, the *Libro straordinario*, published at the end of Serlio's life in 1551, enjoyed lasting success. Its bizarre inventions of various types of civic and triumphal gateways exactly met with the taste of the time. Lescot and Delorme, the real founders of the new French architecture, were heavily indebted to Serlio. He introduced them to the principles and inventiveness of the most recent developments in Italian architecture. Thanks to the proliferation of editions and translations of Serlio's treatise after his death, his influence lived on: the whole of Europe long continued to profit especially from Serlio's exposition of the columnar orders and the exempla of the Third and Fourth Books.

238 *Sebastiano Serlio is better known for his treatise on architecture than for his buildings. The most substantial is not in Italy but in France, the château of Ancy-le-Franc of 1546.*

11 Michelangelo (1475–1564)

Like the majority of leading Renaissance architects, Michelangelo began as a figurative artist and found his way to architecture slowly, indeed became an architect in the full sense of the term only in his old age. In his youth in Florence he could follow at close hand the efforts of Lorenzo de' Medici and Giuliano da Sangallo to revive the architecture of Antiquity and, after Lorenzo's death, the decline of Florentine and the rise of Roman architecture. Michelangelo lived in Rome from 1496 to 1501 and thus experienced at first hand Bramante's Roman exordium (figs 135, 136). Giuliano da Sangallo, deputy papal architect since early 1504, was no doubt largely instrumental in Julius II's calling back Michelangelo in February 1505 and commissioned him to sculpt his funerary monument. Soon afterwards Michelangelo must have reached agreement with the pope and his architects on the site of the funerary monument in the choir of the planned new building of St Peter's (fig. 143).

In his earliest surviving design for the tomb of Julius II, a wall monument of medium dimension, the pillared structure rhythmically tapers upwards from bottom to top, rather like the fictive architectural framework on the ceiling of the Sistine Chapel (*c.*1508). Comparable forms are previously found only in Bramante's Milanese fresco of the *Argo*, and so right from the beginning of his second Roman period Michelangelo seems to have succumbed to Bramante's influence. He was also inspired by Bramante in his later (1513) design for the monument itself. Here he allows the centre of the upper storey, where the sarcophagus is placed, to dominate hierarchically over the low ground floor, as in the Palazzo Caprini (fig. 136) and many of his own later projects.

The centre also dominates the tripartite window-aedicule in the Castel Sant'Angelo in 1514/15 (fig. 239). It frames a Quattrocento-type cruciform window on the exterior of the Chapel of Leo X. But now Michelangelo also derived inspiration from Giuliano da Sangallo's classicizing detail and from Antonio da Sangallo's tripartite projects for the portals of the Palazzo Baldassini and Palazzo Farnese of 1513/14. As there, the wider central pediment-topped bay is slightly projected outwards from the lateral bays with shell niches. Michelangelo protected the two apertures at ground level from prying eyes with bronze balustrade-like mullions and separated them with a central marble pillar, to which half-pillars correspond on either side. Such dwarf pillars, which continue above the impost cornice in a volute, had been used before only by Bramante in the gallery of the sacristy of Santa Maria presso San Satiro in Milan (fig. 106).

Façade of San Lorenzo

Michelangelo returned to Florence in the summer of 1516, embittered by the success of Raphael who was amassing all the great papal commissions. He now focused his attention on the competition for the façade of Brunelleschi's basilica of San Lorenzo and was finally

239 *After a brilliant career as a painter and sculptor, Michelangelo's earliest architectural commission (1514) was the façade of Leo X's chapel in the Castel Sant'Angelo in Rome.*

240 *Like many others, Michelangelo submitted a design for the façade of San Lorenzo in Florence; none were ever built.*

awarded the commission in 1518. He started out from Giuliano's designs of 1515/16, but made the triumphal central bay dominate the façade in a far more decided way. In the wooden model of 1518 he amalgamated all bays into a three-dimensional marble block (fig. 240). The vertical thrust of the central two-storeyed temple front is echoed by the projection of the narrow corner bays. Albeit with traditional forms and rhythms, Michelangelo tried to express the dominance of the central bay of the upper storey, much as Raphael had done in the valley façade of the Villa Madama (fig. 170). Both the central temple front and the corner bays project outwards from the level of the side portals not only by the entablature projected over the columns but also by a rear layer. Moreover, the wall surface is projected a further layer forwards between the columns of the temple front and of the side bays, so that the columns are embedded in niches. As in Alberti, they are both part of the wall and *primum ornamentum* (Book VI, c.13). At the same time they lose a part of the freedom that Brunelleschi, Giuliano and Bramante had reconquered. Michelangelo thus lends the wall a hitherto unprecedented dynamic, but also underlines the consubstantiality of wall and order and treats them in a way similar to the human body in his sculptures.

At the same time Michelangelo began to simplify and abstract the classicizing detail, as did Raphael and Giulio in the contemporary Palazzo Alberini (fig. 166) and Villa Madama. He stripped the brackets of the doors of any ornament and gave them a block-like form.

A similar abstraction is characteristic of the two pedimented window-aedicules with which he closed the corner loggia of the ground floor of the Palazzo Medici in *c.*1520 (fig. 29). There, by placing the volutes not below the cornice of the aedicule but below the projections of its abbreviated entablature, he subtly altered the Vitruvian syntax, though still without jeopardizing the logic of load and support.

Medici Chapel

Leo X's brother Giuliano had died in 1516 and his nephew Lorenzo, first-born male of the Medici, died in the spring of 1519. Michelangelo received the commission for the new funerary chapel for these two dukes and the two Magnifici, Lorenzo and Giuliano, even before the project for the façade of San Lorenzo had finally collapsed. It was to form the counterpart, even the twin, of Brunelleschi's Old Sacristy on the opposite side of San Lorenzo (figs 9–11). So Michelangelo had to conform to its type, dimensions and *pietra serena* members. At the same time, however, he must have wanted to surpass such splendid mausolea of the recent past as Raphael's Cappella Chigi (fig. 162). His original proposal to repeat Brunelleschi's altar wall and chapels on the three other walls, and place the funerary monuments in the three additional chapels, was rejected for various reasons, not least the restrictions of the site. That

241 *Michelangelo's New Sacristy of San Lorenzo, 1519, was conceived as a Medici mausoleum. It was his first chance to demonstrate his highly unorthodox version of the classical language.*

meant that he could only use the height, articulation and figurative décor for innovations (fig. 241). Not least to improve the lighting of the tombs, he added a second storey and large trapezoidal windows in the lunettes, which funnel the light diagonally down to the funerary monuments. As in the Old Sacristy, a Corinthian order carries the entablature, but recessed pillars without bases, flutes and capitals support the arches. Again the decorative function of the order takes precedence over its load-bearing role.

The arcaded wall opposite the entrance gives access to the square altar room, while the two lateral walls are devoted to the tombs of the dukes. Michelangelo divided each of the four walls into three bays. As in the exedra of the Pantheon, the central arch is projected into the upper storey. The lower, narrower bays on either side of the central arch contain doors (mostly blind) at ground level and pedimented aedicules above. Into these aedicules Michelangelo inserted what seem to be blind shouldered windows whose frames are suspended from the segmental pediments. Within these windows he cut a delicately framed, festoon-adorned rectangular niche, with a plinth as its base, but the niche is too shallow for a statue. The impression is thus created of three abstract blind frames of decreasing size being compressed, like Chinese boxes, into each other.

Rather as in the wooden model for San Lorenzo, the pedimented aedicules in the upper storey are reminiscent of Cronaca's San Francesco al Monte (fig. 86). In the detail of both orders, and especially in the abbreviated entablature of the upper one, Michelangelo revealed, on the other hand, knowledge of antique prototypes, which he had studied together with Giovanfrancesco da Sangallo and other interpreters of Vitruvius in the period around 1520. In his dome he again followed the model of the Pantheon (fig. 3).

The huge *pietra serena* windows of the lunettes are clearly inspired by the windows furnished with tapering apertures and double frames which Sangallo had introduced shortly before in the Vatican Sala Ducale (fig. 178). Yet Michelangelo loaded them with a heavy segmental pediment. As in the window-aedicules of the Palazzo Medici, he supported the pediment on the projections of the frieze and cornice. These projections are, however, supported in turn by the projecting upper part of the outer frame – a clear alienation of the ancient vocabulary. He designed the trapezoidal windows, tombs and marble aedicules only after a long intermission, in the spring of 1524, when the second Medici pope, Clement VII, resumed work on the chapel.

Michelangelo now developed a quite unmistakable style of his own. The two funerary monuments still correspond to a triumphal scheme similar to his projects for the tomb of Julius II. But the dukes are now flanked by narrow paired pilasters and enthroned in the broad central niche of the upper storey over the squat socle with the sarcophagi upon which recline the figures of Day and Night, Dawn and Dusk. One almost has the impression of a lord presenting himself on the central balcony of his palace: the hierarchical distinction of the prince is here invested with a meaning similar to the façades of the Villa Madama and St Peter's (figs 170, 173). In the capitals, volutes, half-balusters and in all the further décor he had planned, Michelangelo conducted himself as freely and as imaginatively as only Donatello had done before him (fig. 27).

The chapel was also intended to contain the double tomb of the Magnifici, Lorenzo and Giuliano, on the entrance wall, but of these only a few fragments survive. The sculpture of the tomb of the dukes was also left unfinished and Giovanni da Udine's decoration in stucco and painting of the dome is now lost. The frescoes Michelangelo had planned for the lunettes were never started. With all these decorations the chapel would have been far more magnificent and colourful in effect than it is now. It would only have achieved its full sense by the continuous masses for the souls of the dead celebrated there.

On the exterior of the chapel, too, Michelangelo went far beyond Brunelleschi by drawing a contrast between the hemispherical dome of the Medici Chapel and its elongated lantern. Echoing Brunelleschi's for the Old Sacristy, the lantern is encircled with a ring of slender freestanding columns with Composite capitals, placed in front of the small wall strips between the eight oblong windows. The projections of the entablature above the columns are topped by C-shaped volutes that form an attic pierced by round windows and support the lid-like helmet of the lantern with its faceted golden orb.

Biblioteca Laurenziana

In August 1524 Michelangelo began to build the library that the Medici pope Clement VII commissioned from him to the glory of his family, following the example of the Roman emperors and of his great-grandfather Cosimo. Since it was to be situated between the cloister of San Lorenzo, the Old Sacristy and the family chapel of the Medici, there was no room for a large ceremonial staircase in front, as became the fashion in these years (fig. 10). So Michelangelo ingeniously combined the spacious atrium, a type encountered in earlier Florentine palazzi and called a *ricetto*, with the staircase that rises to the entrance of the oblong reading room (figs 243, 244).

In the *ricetto* the upper storey once again dominates the low basement. Like a palace façade, it is distinguished by the paired columns of an abstract Corinthian order. Even if recessed in niches, the columns presumably allude to the four supports of the Vitruvian atrium (Book VI.3), which had been revived by the Sangallo dynasty, Fra Giocondo and Raphael. The original intention of lighting the room from above, like an *impluvium*, also alluded to the atrium. Even more clearly than in the façade of San Lorenzo, the columns are likened to statues in niches; they are both a part of the load-bearing system and *primum ornamentum* in the Albertian sense. Yet precisely because of their anthropomorphic quality, their hemmed-in position acts like a prison in which they are immured – a tendency also exemplified by Michelangelo's contemporary sculpture. The supporting function of the columns is visually, but not tectonically, emphasized by the paired volutes below, which are conspicuously separated from the column bases and so deprived of any load-bearing function. The walls, projecting outwards from the paired columns, were to continue in windows and therefore cannot have been the load-bearing structures; that function was evidently assigned to the columns. As in the courtyard of the Palazzo Farnese, round columns flank the quadrangular corner pillars (fig. 192). Their capitals are similarly abstracted in a way that only Alberti had anticipated (figs 36–38, 47), while the bases follow those of the Pantheon.

The floating aedicules topped with blind mezzanine windows between the paired columns further underline the more passive

242 *The* ricetto, *or vestibule, of the Biblioteca Laurenziana, 1524, rises above the adjoining cloister to provide light from two storeys of windows. Only the lower row was built in Michelangelo's lifetime. The upper was added after this photograph was taken.*

243 *The vestibule is Michelangelo's fullest statement of his personal style.*

nature of the projecting walls. Their fluted downward-tapering pilaster frames support, like herms, an abbreviated entablature and alternating pediments. Their Doric capitals are narrower than their shafts, but underlined by fragments of a Doric architrave with the *guttae* of triglyphs, while the shoulders of the delicate frames that surround the mezzanine windows are linked by festoons. Probably under the influence of Peruzzi's Palazzo Fusconi of *c*.1523, Michelangelo approximated the consoles to triglyphs: increasingly he tended to isolate the elements of the classical order, alienate them from their tectonic function and transform them into mere ornament.

The two portals far exceed in licence and invention the marble aedicules of the Medici Chapel. The inner frame of the portal leading to the reading room is relatively fragile; the many profiles of its architrave are contracted and it has no frieze. But it is projected from a far more monumental portal-aedicule whose vigorously outward-jutting broken triangular pediment is supported by two lesenes and fragments of a reduced entablature. Its corners overlap the flanking columns. This overlapping of several frames, which began with the marble aedicules of the Medici Chapel, is even more complex in the portal leading from the reading room to the *ricetto*. The inner frame is even more fragile; it is projected from a second block-like layer with triangular pediment with a fragmentary entablature. The barely

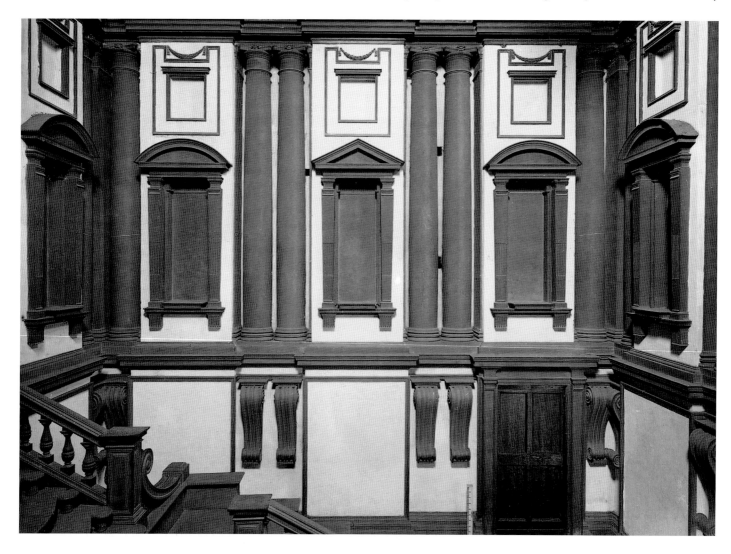

articulated second frame intersects the full order and segmental pediment of a third layer. Only fragments of this layer are visible; its entablature continues the fragmentary entablature of the second layer and seems to alienate it from its original context. So the overlapping layers are no longer boxed into each other but grow consubstantially together. By multiplying, overlapping and complicating their frames, Michelangelo made the portals not only more imposing, but also more puzzling – even disconcerting for the trained Vitruvian, who must have noticed the disintegration of the orders into decorative fragments.

None of the daring alternatives for the staircase, transmitted in Michelangelo's sketches, in large part inspired by Bramante's Cortile del Belvedere (figs 139, 140), was to be executed. The existing, widely spreading staircase follows a design of 1550, when Michelangelo had found his monumental late style. But it was executed and altered by Ammanati and others in his absence.

On the walls of the elongated reading room Michelangelo reduced the complex system of the *ricetto* to a *Dorica* with abbreviated entablature. It only begins above a bare socle at the height of the reading desks. Its simple Doric pilasters alternate in rapid rhythm

with the Ionic window-aedicules and a central portal and thus reverse the *mescolanza* of the two orders of the vestibule. As in the Palazzo Alberini (fig. 158), the aedicules are surrounded by profiled frames; their shoulders are now directly supported by volutes. The blind mezzanine windows are flanked with balusters, as in the courtyard of Giulio Romano's slightly earlier Palazzo Stati-Maccarani (fig. 178). In spite of all these Roman motifs, Michelangelo distanced himself here from the Bramante school by dispensing with the horizontal linking of the windows and complex rhythms.

In the coffered ceiling and in the matching inlaid floor, he incorporated ovals into the oblong fields of the broad central band, decorated them with festoons and rams' heads and enriched them in the pavement with the Medici balls.

Once again under the influence of the Palazzo Stati-Maccarani (fig. 177), he reduced the order of the lower floor on the external wall to blind panels, simplified the Ionic aedicules, topped them with depressed segmental pediments and combined the projecting frieze and the brackets into similar inverted and abstract U-shaped forms as on the lunette windows of the adjacent chapel (fig. 242).

Michelangelo intended to terminate the longitudinal axis in a triangular rare-book room, which was never built. With its splayed corners, his design for this room is a marvel of ingenuity and heralds the advances of library science of modern times: its inner walls are

244 *The reading room of the Biblioteca Laurenziana. Michelangelo planned a triangular rare-book room through the door at the end.*

hewn with alternating rectangular and hemispherical niches, and the interlocking triangular bookstacks are controlled by a circular desk at the centre.

Vasari ends his description of the Medici Chapel by thanking Michelangelo for having freed artists from the compulsion of blindly following Vitruvius and the antique: 'he broke the bonds and chains of a way of working that had become habitual by common usage.' Though hardly any of his predecessors had in fact literally followed the rules of Vitruvius, Michelangelo was the first to alter and enrich the context of the forms in a way no longer determined by the logic of load and support but by personal licence.

Although Michelangelo had not seen Rome since 1518, he must have been singularly well informed about Sangallo's, Peruzzi's and especially Giulio's latest innovations, and indeed the radical transformation of his style around 1524 cannot be separated from them. What was not much more than caprice and playfulness in Giulio, he transformed into new, pregnant and lasting forms. Yet there is no doubt that Giulio's rebellious streak helped Michelangelo to find a quite novel architectural style of his own: in this sense, Vasari's observation on Michelangelo's emancipating licence needs to be modified. He satisfied the growing need for capricious inventions that Giulio had awakened and that the artists at the beginning of the pontificate of Clement VII had further developed.

After Giulio had abandoned Rome, this trend gradually weakened: a reaction set in and this is also reflected in Michelangelo's contemporary architecture such as the portal of Sant'Appolonia in Florence of c.1526 and his reliquary tribune of San Lorenzo of 1530/31. In spite of a similar vocabulary, they are simpler and more classical in composure than the Library.

Palazzo Farnese

Up till the death of Clement VII in 1534 Michelangelo mainly lived in Florence and worked on the Medici Chapel. When the imperial forces besieged Florence in 1527, he designed bastions. The fortifications in his surviving drawings resemble a loose arrangement of polymorphic forms. Many of them were executed, and their technical efficiency and grasp of military requirements led to his

245 *Michelangelo's designs for bastions to defend Florence in 1527 are evidence of a fluent imagination and efficiency.*

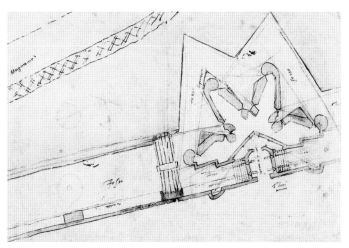

nomination as governor of the Florentine fortifications (fig. 245). They seem to combine an aggressive with a defensive attitude.

After his election in the autumn of 1534, Pope Paul III Farnese lost little time in calling Michelangelo back to Rome. He not only commissioned from him the *Last Judgement* in the Sistine Chapel and the frescoes in the Cappella Paolina, but also appointed him palace architect. Alongside the frescoes, Michelangelo tried to complete the funerary monument for Julius II. In c.1532, when the tomb was transferred to San Pietro in Vincoli, he had still held firm to the (in part) executed triumphal-arch system of the tomb started in 1513. In 1542, he remodelled its upper storey completely and provided it with an articulation that heralds his mature style (fig. 246). The thinness of the wall of the right transept of the church and the deep niches also forced him to differentiate for the first time between the skeleton of the supporting pillars and the shallow wall of the niches. He split up the wall in different layers, from the herm-like pilasters to the recessed niches of his sculptures and linked its members together by different cornices.

Even before Sangallo's death in September of 1546, Paul III had given preference to Michelangelo's design for the top cornice of the

Palazzo Farnese (fig. 190). Here Michelangelo recurred to the most famous Florentine prototype, Cronaca's cornice of the Palazzo Strozzi. He decorated the frieze with Farnese lilies and acanthus blossoms and increased its distance from the windows of the second floor. The blind arch of the *serliana*, with which Sangallo had distinguished the central balcony of the *piano nobile*, he replaced by a straight entablature and a colossal upper cartouche with the pope's coat of arms.

His interventions in the courtyard are far more characteristic (figs 192, 247). Sangallo had already begun its Ionic loggia. Michelangelo now proposed alterations that were soon to prove influential. In the *piano nobile* of the front and rear wings he thus began the barrel vaults of the loggias only above the arcades. Though depressed, they reach up into the pedestal zone of the second floor. This meant that the second floor could no longer be opened in arcades. The narrower side wings of the *piano nobile* were also closed and provided with low barrel vaults. A mezzanine could thus be installed above them and lit through the pedestal zone of the second floor. Lastly he proposed – evidently without success – that the depth of the rear wing be reduced so that its loggia would have overlooked the court on one side and the garden on the other, and approximated the garden front to a portico-villa with projecting corner bays. The longitudinal axis of the garden was to be accentuated by a fountain incorporating the colossal group of the *Farnese Bull* (now in Naples) and was to continue over a new bridge to the Farnese vineyard on the other side of the Tiber, 'so that it might be possible' – said Vasari – 'to go from the palace to another palace and gardens that the Farnese possessed

in Trastevere, and also to see at one glance in a straight line from the principal door which faces the Campo di Fiore, the court, the fountain, the Strada Giulia, the bridge, and the beauties of the other garden, even to the other door which opened on the Strada di Trastevere'.

Michelangelo had now been living in Rome continuously for twelve years, so it is no wonder that he once again moved closer in his forms to the antique and the Bramante school. As in the courtyard of Palazzo Gaddi (fig. 230), he decorated the frieze of the Ionic storey with masks and sumptuous festoons and lent so normative a form to the aedicules, their triglyph-fluted consoles and their balusters that they were long attributed to Vignola. In the upper floor he once again drew on Bramante and continued the theatre motifs of the *piano nobile* with bundled pilasters, as in the Cortile del Belvedere (fig. 140). But he provided all three pilasters with bases and placed them – since his storey was relatively high – on high plinths, as in the upper storey of the Colosseum. The abbreviated entablature is projected only over the vigorous central pilaster, as in some of Giuliano's and Bramante's buildings (figs 70, 77), and only up to the top cornice. He decorated both fascias of the architrave and cornice with masks and, as in the Laurenziana, mixed the orders by decorating the consoles with triglyphs.

In the windows he took even further the fragmentation, ornamentalization and intermixture of the classical vocabulary. They hang in a similarly free and top-heavy way in the walls as in the lunettes of the Medici Chapel or on the outside of the Laurenziana, and their pediments are supported by fragments of the Doric architrave similar to the aedicules of the Laurenziana *ricetto*. The triglyphed brackets and their supporting fillets are pressed downwards by lion-heads with rings and thus relieved of their tectonic meaning. The morphological closeness to the Laurenziana can also be felt in the festoons set into the tympana.

The upper floor of the courtyard continues Sangallo's system as inorganically as the marble aedicules and lunette windows continue the more traditional *pietra serena* skeleton of the Medici Chapel, but connects the individual inventions now in a much more systematic way.

St Peter's

During the last three years of Paul III's pontificate, Michelangelo also subjected Sangallo's project for St Peter's to a drastic revision (figs 197, 198). He had famously inspected Sangallo's wooden model and found it wanting: he said that it lacked windows, 'that it had on the exterior too many ranges of columns one above another, and that, with its innumerable projections, pinnacles and subdivisions of members, it was more akin to the German [i.e. Gothic] manner than to the good method of the ancients' (Vasari).

After extensive preparations, Michelangelo began the lateral arms of the cross in 1550 and the drum in 1554 (figs 248–50). He eliminated the ambulatories of Sangallo's model that had already been begun by Bramante and Raphael, the cross-arms of the secondary (auxiliary) domed areas, and the porch with the upper Loggia delle Benedizioni. In essential aspects of the exterior he returned to the executive project of Julius II in 1506 (fig. 147). As there, twin

248 *When Michelangelo took over the design of St Peter's in 1547 he simplified Sangallo's centralized interior, eliminated his vestibule and returned to Bramante's giant order.*

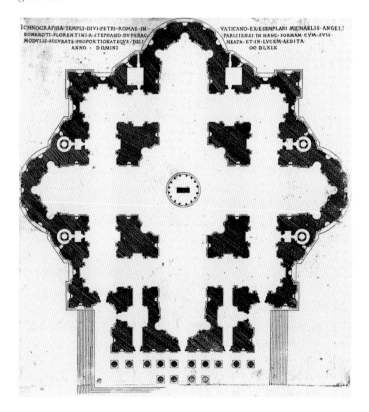

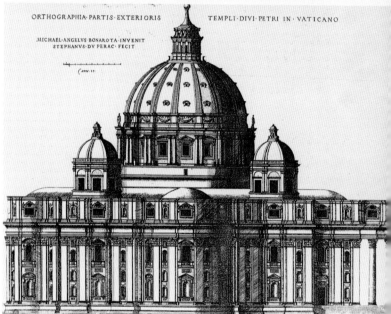

249, 250 *Section and elevation of Michelangelo's St Peter's, corresponding to the plan (left). Engravings by Dupérac.*

pilasters of a colossal order, separated by niches stacked one on top of the other, articulate the pillars that alternate in a triumphal rhythm with fenestrated bays. A single drum storey is topped by a hemispherical dome. The façade would probably have opened in a colonnaded temple front, and the squat deep-arched windows of the attic storey would, as in Bramante's 1506 plan, have originally funnelled the light down to the lower parts of the interior. In a letter to Ammannati, Michelangelo wrote that whoever distanced himself from Bramante's project, abandoned the truth.

But the Corinthian colossal order is now much more normatively formed, the correspondence of the exterior with the interior even more exact and the distinction between the load-bearing and non-load-bearing parts of the wall even clearer. In contrast to Bramante, the pillars are more massive and articulated as an abstract order with reduced bases and capitals which reappears even between the twin pilasters.

The four counter-pillars on the corners of the building block, which correspond to the splayed pillars of Bramante's crossing, are accentuated by triads of pilasters, which look like square columns. Between these and the apses diagonally splayed pillars create a smooth transition and amalgamate the different parts of the building into a coherent and continuous plastic body. They represent perhaps the most important innovation of the exterior. They correspond to the splayed pillars of Bramante's crossing and act as their counterweight. Another peculiarity of the corner blocks is the way the entablature is layered and twice projected over them: above the two pilasters and above the pillars. In contrast to Bramante, the order thus resembles an applied décor that could be stripped without damaging the structure.

So the eye finds rest only in the corner-pillars, while the fragmentation of the other triumphal motifs creates a restless movement that can be detected in none of Michelangelo's earlier buildings and that corresponded in some way to the religious fervour of these years; it would later be absorbed in Borromini's San Carlino.

251, 252 *Only on the exterior, in the apses (below) and in the cupola of St Peter's (right), was Michelangelo able to adopt his highly personal style. He split the wall into layers, but never abandoned the classical language and concentrated his capricious inventions on windows and niches.*

The window-aedicules are similar to Sangallo's classicizing aedicules in the upper storey of the Palazzo Farnese façade (fig 190), as if the *capricci* Michelangelo himself had dared in the courtyard of this palace were less appropriate in the church of the Prince of the Apostles. As in triumphal arches, he supported the pediments of the aedicules by a keystone volute. Only in some details, such as the triglyph-shaped brackets of the niche-aedicules or the garlanded decoration of the tympana, did he recur to his earlier repertoire. But he now integrated the various components in a more tectonic system. Thus he continued the arcade of the windows in a delicate layer, hardly visible from afar, up to the richly decorated tympanum. By keeping the window bays much narrower than Bramante, and by giving the same pediments to the aedicules of both windows and niches, he underlined even further the strong vertical impulse.

Michelangelo had executed a plain attic with deep arcaded windows. Perhaps inspired by Michelangelo's sketches after his death,

Pirro Ligorio articulated it in an eclectic manner and considerably reduced the window apertures.

The drum and the dome that rise above it are by contrast all the more majestic in effect. Indeed, they can, in many respects, be regarded as Michelangelo's most impressive architectural achievement. Even more strikingly than earlier architects, he separated the mighty pillars supporting the dome construction from the non-load-bearing window zones. He projected the pillars far outwards and reinforced their corners with the paired columns of a Corinthian order. They support massive projecting entablature blocks and are now nearly freed from the wall. Half-pilasters mediate between them and the wall. Neither the order nor the floating aedicules are abbreviated, abstracted or alienated from their normative forms as so often in his previous buildings. The cornice and the alternating pediments of the windows rest on brackets projecting from the naked wall, while the architrave-like window frames cut deeply into it.

The triumphal character of the columns is continued in the high, festoon-decorated attic of the drum. In Dupérac's engravings of Michelangelo's project (figs 249, 250), statues even stand on the entablature fragments placed over the paired columns, silhouetted against the lesene-pillars that articulate the attic. There, too, the exterior dome is still hemispherical, the lantern squatter and the profile of the ribs flatter than in Giacomo della Porta's executed version. Michelangelo was cleared inspired in his dome by Brunelleschi's *cupolone* for Florence Cathedral (fig. 4). Its load-bearing ribs are shaped like the slices of a melon and clad by an outer and inner shell.

The effect that Michelangelo intended in the interior can best be gauged in the cross-arms and in the dome. Although neither the proportions nor the order fundamentally differ from those of Sangallo's project, the space is far lighter and brighter. This is due to the alterations made to the upper two-thirds of the apses, to the drum and the dome. As on the exterior, the colossal order of the apses is now reduced to mere decoration of the muscular pillars that appear above the aedicules of the altars. As on the exterior, they are defined as an abstract order by their reduced capitals. Their projected entablature is continued into the relieving arches of the vault and that of the pilasters into the broad ribs. Michelangelo eliminated the pediments from Sangallo's altar-aedicules and linked them by the projection of their entablature with the aedicules of the window zone. These seem to abut onto the deeply recessed rectangular niches between the pillars. This reduction of the wall between the pillars is reminiscent of the tomb of Julius (fig. 246) and improves the lighting considerably.

The inside of the drum is articulated only by the relatively delicate paired pilasters of a normative Corinthian order. Their projecting entablature is continued into the ribs of the dome. The interior apertures of the sixteen windows are lower than their exterior, so that light is again funnelled through the relatively thin wall diagonally to the papal altar. The vertical impulses, weighed down by no mass and channelled upwards by converging lines, clearly predominate. They were to culminate in a lantern with deliberately reduced lighting. In contrast to the powerful and triumphal exterior of the drum, the interior of the dome thus gains a floating, indeed metaphysical and anagogical character, entirely in keeping with the spirit of these years.

San Giovanni dei Fiorentini

In 1559 the Florentines made a further effort to complete their national church on the Tiber in Rome. Their duke, Cosimo, succeeded in winning over the eighty-four-year-old Michelangelo to the project. After Sansovino's abortive plan, Sangallo had begun the execution of a basilica system. Michelangelo, in his numerous projects, jettisoned this system and recurred to antique prototypes such as the Pantheon, Santo Stefano Rotondo and Santa Costanza, with entrance portico, interior colonnades, exedras and a hemispherical dome as already planned by Raphael, Sangallo and Peruzzi (fig. 253). In his final project he articulated the inner rotunda with eight triumphal-arch motifs. In the main axes they open up to four rectangular vestibules and in the diagonal axes doors lead to four oval chapels.

As in the Pantheon, the arcades cut into the upper storey, but their arches rest on pillars as in the Medici Chapel. The Ionic columns of the upper order are thus aligned with the Tuscan ones of the lower order. In the ground floor Michelangelo opened the wall in semicircular niches and between the upper columns in windows: once again the light is channelled down diagonally in shafts. As in St Peter's, he drew a clear distinction between load and support by projecting the entablature above both columnar orders and continuing their line with unprecedented dynamic vertical thrust directly into the ribs of the hemispherical dome. As in St Peter's, the massive walls between the secondary rooms were to support the whole weight of the dome. Columns and ribs were to be the visible expression of the building's structural forces. As there, too, the aedicules and niches float freely in the wall surface and the orders are horizontally connected not only with each other, but also with the chapels by continuous cornices and entablatures. As before only in Santo Stefano Rotondo, the altar was to be situated in the centre. The oval chapels were to contain the many funerary altars of Florentine donors.

The exterior of Michelangelo's final plan is enlivened by the contrast between the dominating drum-raised dome and the squat

253 *Engraving of the model made by Michelangelo for the proposed church of San Giovanni dei Fiorentini, in Rome; not built.*

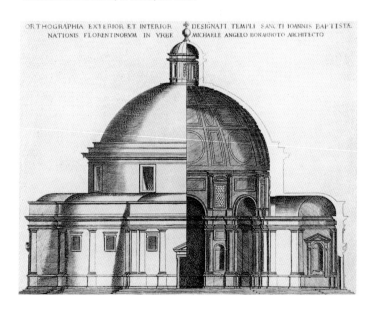

chapels. As in St Peter's, their walls are amalgamated into a continuous shell. The pilasters of the Tuscan order continue those of the interior. In a preliminary stage of the planning process Michelangelo even planned to open up the entrance porch in a colonnade. As in St Peter's (figs 249, 250), triads accentuate the corners. All arches are eliminated from the exterior and all that remains of the triumphal-arch motifs is the widening of the central bay pilaster. A smooth attic above the entablature was to conceal the vaults of the chapels. Seen from the Via Giulia, the dome would have disappeared behind the *c.*14 m (46 ft) high entrance porch, and the visitor would have been confronted with an exterior of extreme sobriety. With its bare cylindrical drum and its diameter of *c.*30 m (98 ft), the Pantheon-dome would however have held a commanding position over the banks of the Tiber. In Primaticcio's never-finished Rotonde des Valois at St Denis Michelangelo's project found an immediate successor.

Cappella Sforza

Despite its modest dimensions, the funerary chapel that Michelangelo designed in Santa Maria Maggiore for a nephew of Paul III, Cardinal Ascanio Sforza, in 1560, belongs to his most complex inventions (fig. 254). In his early designs Michelangelo had used the roughly square site for a centralized plan. But in the building as executed he separated the baldachin of the real mausoleum from the rectangular annex of the relatively conventional altar room. He connected both by a Composite order: full columns under the baldachin and pilasters in the exedras into which it extends, as well as in the altar room and on the entrance wall. The entrance itself was originally much wider: so, from the portal, the central baldachin and its lateral exedras with the cardinal's tomb would have been more clearly visible. To the baldachin, indeed, its splendid Composite capitals no less classicizing than any of Raphael, Sangallo, Peruzzi or Palladio, is displaced the chapels centre of gravity. With its splayed columns (following the precedents of late-Antique mausolea such as the Chapel of San Zeno in the nearby church of Santa Prassede) and saucer dome, it is hierarchically distinguished and visually more important than the altar room with the Holy Sacrament to the rear.

At the same time the splayed columns and polygonal pillars create a smooth transition from the central baldachin area to the flat lateral exedras. Since bases and capitals of the pillars remain just as reduced as the walls of the entrance and altar areas, they are once again to be understood both as part of the wall and as an abstracted order. As in the imperial *thermae* or in Bramante's churches, their form is the result of the different spaces on which they border (figs 143, 146). Towards the exedras they are symmetrically flanked by other columns of the same order supporting their own arch. Thus the weight of the vaults is equally distributed between the eight columns and the four intermediate pillars. This system of load and support exemplifies a transformation in Michelangelo's architectural thinking. While the engaged columns of his earlier works had become full columns embedded in niches in the model for the façade of San Lorenzo, and pairs of full columns imprisoned in the wall in the Laurenziana *ricetto*, here in the Cappella Sforza the columns are now freed from the wall and become the most evident load-bearing part of the order. The shallow exedras are articulated by the

254 *Towards the end of his life Michelangelo designed the Cappella Sforza in Santa Maria Maggiore, Rome, 1560, a tiny chapel that shows how he succeeded in combining the column with the muscular energy of the supporting pillar.*

triumphal rhythm of pilasters and were illuminated by a window in the vault of the central bay and smaller windows under the entablature of the side bays.

All the more puzzling, then, is the contrast with the short entrance bay. It was formerly distinguished by an exterior triumphal façade, which continues in the deeper altar chapel. This box-like room seems to intersect the baldachin and is articulated by the same flat triumphal triad.

Santa Maria degli Angeli

Immediately after he became Pius IV in 1559, Gian Angelo Medici, inspired by a Sicilian priest, Antonio del Duca, who for years had been trying to establish a cult of the seven angels on the site, asked Michelangelo to transform the well-preserved *frigidarium* of the Baths of Diocletian into his funeral church. It was the first step towards a reorganization of this area which included the Strada Pia and Porta Pia (both named after the same pope). Michelangelo elevated the floor of the Roman imperial hall by *c.*2 m (6½ ft), but did not change its structure, forms and two main axes forming a cross. With Pius IV's tomb presumably intended to be placed in the centre, surrounded by the chapels of cardinals of his family, the *frigidarium* would have become not only one of the most impressive papal mausolea but, after the Pantheon, also the most monumental Christianization of a pagan interior.

Porta Pia

Two years later Michelangelo transformed the inner façade of the Porta Pia into the terminating prospect of the new Strada Pia (fig. 255). It had become Rome's most elegant street, ennobled not by palaces or churches but by Europe's most splendid patrician gardens and villas and their rusticated portals. Michelangelo combined the type of rusticated garden portal as designed by Giulio Romano and Sebastiano Serlio with that of the two-storeyed Tuscan city gate. This combination of two particular types shows once again how impossible it is to deduce a whole stylistic phase from a single building.

In the Porta Pia the dominance of the central bay over the lower side bays is taken to its conclusion. The central bay is pierced by the colossal pedimented portal and was to have been topped by an unusually tall temple front with paired pilasters of a normative Corinthian order. By contrast the side bays are only sparingly articulated with corner lesenes and small isolated travertine windows. It may have been Michelangelo's intention to cover the irregular bricks by a layer of stucco, which would have added a kind of surface homogeneity to the whole ensemble. The attic is crowned with merlons in the form of Ionic capitals with the Medici balls of Pius IV's coat of arms. Its horizontal rhythm is penetrated and broken through by the verticalizing and hierarchically predominant centrepiece – in a way comparable to the two intersecting spaces of the

255 *The Porta Pia, Rome, of 1561, can only be understood as point de vue of the newly traced Strada Pia. The pediment of the upper storey was added much later.*

Sforza chapel (fig. 254). The enormous contrast in size makes the lateral aedicules look even smaller. The portal appears like a gigantic mask.

In contrast to the portals of the Laurenziana (figs 243, 244), the different layers of the portal are much more clearly divided and tectonically motivated. Two rusticated pillars support radial and polygonally cut voussoirs and are decorated by a fluted order. The naked capitals represent at the same time fragments of an architrave and its Doric guttae seem pressed out of it by the weight of the pediments. The fragments of the frieze are disproportionately raised in height and flank a relieving arch in the form of a blind Diocletian window. Placed in front of it is a bearded mask. The fragments of the broken pediment above are rolled at their ends into metallic spirals with even more convolutions than in the sarcophagi of the Medici Chapel (fig. 241) and joined by a laurel festoon suspended below the dedicatory inscription of the patron, Pope Pius IV. The pillars without rustication continue behind the fluted pilasters and re-emerge on either side. Their line is continued above the impost without capitals but with guttae into the projection of the pediment. These abstracted pillars are repeated in a second shadow-like layer at a deeper level. They develop, above the entablature, flat volutes in profile, supporting a huge triangular pediment which doubles the fragmentary segmental one.

Michelangelo was now concerned to exploit the potential of the various light-sensitive surfaces of smooth, rusticated and fluted travertine. Between the capitals and the entablature he made the forces of load and support interact far more dynamically than in the Laurenziana. Thus in spite of the isolation, fragmentation and alienation of heterogeneous antique motifs, Michelangelo here again is the genuine architect he had become in the 1540s. He wrested the antique vocabulary from its Vitruvian context, fragmented and reassembled it in daring new forms. In the upper storey he wanted to counterbalance it with a temple front in the same classicizing forms he had used in the Cappella Sforza and on the Capitoline Hill. It was to enshrine the two angels supporting Gian Angelo de' Medici's elaborate coat of arms. The simplified capitals and entablature and the baroque-like pediment of the upper storey, as we see it today, were only added in the later nineteenth century.

Capitoline Hill

When the bronze equestrian statue of Marcus Aurelius was transferred from the Lateran to the Capitoline Hill in 1538 and Michelangelo had finished its socle, he may already have been thinking of placing it at the centre of a symmetrically laid-out piazza. Neither then nor in the 1540s, when he designed the Palazzo del Senatore's twin-ramped staircase, does he seem, however, to have produced any concrete plans for the buildings.

The executed project can only be related to the last years of his life. Work on the Palazzo dei Conservatori only began in 1563. When Michelangelo died in the spring of 1564 the first bays had been completed (figs 256–258). Almost a century was to elapse before the other two buildings facing onto the piazza were to be completed, but only the façade of the Palazzo del Senatore is fundamentally different from Michelangelo's design.

256, 257 *Michelangelo replanned the Roman Capitol in his last years, but it was not finished until long after his death. Two symmetrical palaces which were to house the communal council prepare for the hierarchically dominant seat of the* Senatore, *while the geometrical pavement gives the space cohesion.*

Ever since the Middle Ages the Capitoline Hill had been the communal centre of Rome and symbol of republican independence, and hence a kind of weaker antithesis to the Vatican. The complex of buildings on the Capitol had been renewed in the fifteenth century, especially by Nicholas V. The popes tried increasingly to gain control over the Campidoglio, curb its republican aspirations and absorb it into papal rule over the city. This is also quite clear from the inscriptions on the socle of the Marcus Aurelius statue in which Paul III identifies himself with the emperor.

Michelangelo's most difficult task was to integrate the late-medieval Palazzo dei Conservatori, in which the patricians held their council meetings, and the fortress-like Palazzo del Senatore, seat of the leading communal official and magistrate, into a piazza that would be worthy of the ancient Capitol. He planned new façades for both the Palazzo del Senatore and the Palazzo dei Conservatori without destroying the older ceremonial rooms. Engravings of 1567 and 1569 suggest that he wanted to erect a symmetrical pendant to the Palazzo dei Conservatori on the left side of the piazza. In such a concept he went far beyond not only the piazza of Pienza (figs 60, 62) or the ideal piazzas of the panels of Urbino and Baltimore, where no exact symmetry is created between the sides (figs 72–74), but also those of Vigevano and the Santissima Annunziata in Florence with their monotonous repetition of arcades.

In Dupérac's engraving a broad ramp leads axially up to the Palazzo del Senatore, which dominates the Capitoline Hill. The two flanking palaces create a court of honour, protected by the broad balustrade. The centre of the oval piazza is dominated by the wise emperor on horseback, but the eye is drawn further to the statue of Jupiter which Michelangelo had planned to place in the central niche of the double-ramped staircase. The splayed frontages of the flanking buildings have an anti-perspective effect and make the piazza

appear nearly square. Similarly the centripetal stellate pattern on the pavement makes the oval appear almost round.

The whole piazza is hierarchically concentrated on the Palazzo del Senatore. Like Bramante in his Palazzo dei Tribunali (fig. 150), Michelangelo combined the corner towers and rustication of the castle with the central bell-tower of the medieval *palazzi comunali* and the colossal order of the Palazzo di Parte Guelfa (fig. 24). With its paratactical succession of pilasters of a colossal Corinthian order, highly plastic wall relief, two rows of columnar window-aedicules and statue-crowned balustrade, the *piano nobile* would have risen even more commandingly over its squat rusticated basement podium and presented itself even more convincingly as the new symbol of communal government than Bramante's prototype. As in Vitruvius there are no arches.

The two flanking palaces are articulated by a colossal Corinthian order similar to that of the *piano nobile* of the Palazzo del Senatore but are clearly subordinated in situation and size. The broader window of the central bay and the second bay of the side fronts were only added later. As in the apses of St Peter's (fig. 251), the pilasters are placed against massive quadrangular pillars. These pillars are projected through the entablature of the colonnade and the continuous cornices of the windowsills. Rather as in one of Peruzzi's projects for St Peter's, a colonnade extends between the pillars and supports the Pantheon-aedicules of the *piano nobile*. Michelangelo, however, was not content with a two-dimensional colonnade: he lent it depth by answering the two columns of each bay with two corresponding columns to the rear of the portico. So four columns in each bay are combined into a three-dimensional coffered baldachin. Every rear column is embedded in niches formed by the protruding wall. Even here the column is less imprisoned than in Michelangelo's Laurentian Library (fig. 243). The wall-strips between them are now connected by an entablature with the pillars of the façade and support the partition walls of the ceremonial rooms on the upper floor. They are thus structurally motivated as load-bearing pillars. This identity of form and structure is the same as in the dome of St Peter's and goes beyond similar tendencies in Bramante, Sangallo and Peruzzi.

258 *The Palazzo dei Conservatori, with the ancient Roman statue of Marcus Aurelius in the foreground, is the most classicizing architecture of the Roman Renaissance. The central window was added by Giacomo della Porta.*

In the *piano nobile* the pillars are reduced to a flat travertine layer and the muscular forces transformed into grave splendour. In his consciousness of the ancient origins of the Capitol Michelangelo preferred a normative entablature to the broken and restless one of St Peter's. He restricted his personal idiosyncrasies to details such as the spreading trumpet-shaped capitals of the Ionic colonnade, or the window-aedicules: the gap between their projecting entablature and the window frames is unconventionally large, their Composite capitals are without leaves and their broken pediments are decorated by huge shells. Nevertheless, it is even more antique in spirit than Bramante's Tempietto or Peruzzi's Palazzo Massimo (figs 137, 216).

Until 1520 Michelangelo had used the language of Giuliano, Bramante, Raphael and Sangallo for his anti-conformist inventions. Then the late Raphael, Giulio Romano and Peruzzi inspired him to change his use of the ancient vocabulary in a way that would outlive all ephemeral fashions. He must have sensed the end of golden Latinity in architecture and succeeded in creating out of it a sort of new architectural *volgare*. This new language was characterized more by pregnant and innovative form than by Vitruvian logic and coherence. It was taken to the extreme of alienation. He struck a chord that resonated with younger masters like Vasari, Ammannati and Alessi. They were tired of the usually dogmatic diktat with which the Vitruvians tried to get their way, and of Sangallo's stale repetition of the same types and forms. They yearned for a liberation that only Michelangelo could offer them. But after having assumed late in 1546 the prestigious post of papal architect-in-chief formerly occupied by Bramante, Raphael, Peruzzi and Sangallo, he became more and more conscious of the Roman tradition. In none of his projects did he question the exemplary status of Antiquity. Like his predecessors, he strove to fuse the traditions, functions and impulses of the intermediate centuries with this legacy. In his mature buildings he was moved not so much by a further distancing from Vitruvian norms as by a growing understanding of the interrelation of function, structure and form.

Only in the upper storey of the funerary monument for Julius II did he begin to fuse the forms together into members of a three-dimensional organism that obey the laws of load and support. And only in his projects for St Peter's did he begin to give proof of his fuller understanding of systematic planning, complex rhythms, the virtuoso balancing of contrasting forces, and the correspondence between interior and exterior. Compared with the drum of St Peter's, the Cappella Sforza and his designs for San Giovanni dei Fiorentini, his previous buildings seem like a series of façades.

Astonishingly Michelangelo designed some of his most important projects after he had turned eighty. When he died he had wholly transformed the architectural scene, and not only in Central Italy. He had progressively enlarged his architectural scope to fortifications, piazza layouts and city gateways. He had continued the great tradition of the Roman school as architect-in-chief of St Peter's for almost twenty-eight years. The buildings of his last years are so various, so inventive, so heterogeneous that they cannot be reduced to a linear development.

12 Late Renaissance

Jacomo Barozzi da Vignola (1507–73)

Like the far older Serlio, Vignola began as a painter in Bologna and, like him, got to know Peruzzi in *c*.1522. He probably also followed Peruzzi to Rome as a studio assistant, and through him was inducted into architecture. Vignola's career developed slowly. Even in the late 1530s he was still mainly active as a draughtsman and surveyor of Roman antiquities and as assistant of Jacomo Meleghini, Peruzzi's successor as second architect of St Peter's. In 1541/42 Vignola was assisting Primaticcio to make moulds of the most famous sculptures in the Vatican Belvedere for François I. Primaticcio even took him to France as his assistant 'in order to make use of him in matters of architecture and to have his assistance in casting in bronze the above-mentioned statues' (Vasari). There Vignola spent two years. At that time he had already submitted a project, worked out in detail, for the villa of Cardinal Cervini near Montepulciano, in which he combined the ideas of Raphael, Peruzzi and Sangallo in a still relatively eclectic way. A little later he was appointed architect of San Petronio in Bologna and executed his first buildings there.

In the Palazzo Bocchi in Bologna, begun in 1545, Vignola also adopted a similarly eclectic manner. He combined a Sangallesque façade system with the windows of Giulio Romano's Roman house (fig. 179). He also incorporated motifs derived from Serlio, such as a portal reminiscent of that of the Grand Ferrare, which he had seen at Fontainebleau.

San Giovanni dei Fiorentini and Villa Giulia

Vignola's rise to be one of the leading architects of Europe began after he had passed the age of forty-three. That was when Julius III (1550–55) ascended the pontifical throne. Vignola began his service for the new pope in 1550 by submitting a project for San Giovanni dei Fiorentini. It differed from Sangallo's and Peruzzi's earlier central-plan designs for the church (figs 193, 208, 209) by its inclusion of an ambulatory, by the abstracted articulation of its drum, and especially by its oval ground plan. On the façade he framed the central portal-aedicule with a broad temple front; its low colonnade supports tall panels for figural reliefs and follows Peruzzi's designs for St Peter's.

Vignola began the Villa Giulia for the pope in the same year (figs 259–63). Its ground plan and elevation can be mainly attributed to him, although Vasari and Michelangelo may have contributed to the project's preparation. Vignola clearly started out from the fragmentary pre-existing building begun before 1527 for the pope's uncle by Jacopo Sansovino, who had given it a similar central section and a semicircular or even round court. According to Vignola's project, the two diagonal access roads were to converge in a semicircular square in front of the villa. Even more systematically than Raphael in the Villa Madama, Vignola tried to integrate his plan into the urban context. The villa's relatively modest façade is imbued with the spirit of Giulio and Serlio (fig. 174). It is distinguished by the dominance of the centrepiece with its rusticated and energetically projecting

triumphal-arch entrance and its continuation in the deep niches of the papal loggia above. The deeply recessed outer bays emphasize the three-dimensional quality of the building.

The repetition of the central triumphal-arch motif in the court and in the nymphaeum gives the longitudinal axis a visual emphasis

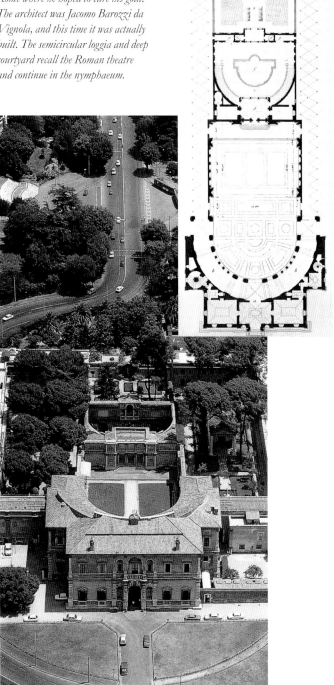

259, 260 *In 1550 a new pope, Julius III, commissioned a magnificent villa, the Villa Giulia, on the outskirts of Rome where he hoped to cure his gout. The architect was Jacomo Barozzi da Vignola, and this time it was actually built. The semicircular loggia and deep courtyard recall the Roman theatre and continue in the nymphaeum.*

261 *The entrance front of the Villa Giulia, combining triumphal arch and papal loggia, is influenced by Giulio's Palazzo Adimari.*

262 *The sunken pool of the nymphaeum, surrounded by a balustrade and supported by caryatids, was designed by Ammannati.*

only anticipated by Bramante's Cortile del Belvedere (figs 139, 140) and by Michelangelo's project for the Palazzo Farnese. In the ground floor of the courtyard columnar porticoes connect the triumphal arches. As in his project for San Giovanni dei Fiorentini and in Peruzzi's late projects for St Peter's, the barrel vaults of the loggia are concealed behind their high blind panels. The inside of the loggia is

one of Vignola's most successful creations. But the inconsistencies of the squat upper storey of the court show that he did not always find it easy to continue the inventions of his teacher.

In the dynamic rhythm of the back wall of the nymphaeum (fig. 262), inspired by the courtyard of the Villa Imperiale (fig. 221), Vignola's hand can once again be felt. After Easter 1552 it was continued in a rather inorganic way by Bartolommeo Ammannati. So here a partisan of Michelangelo had the last word.

263 *Looking back from the main courtyard to the semi-cylindrical entrance of the Villa Giulia.*

264 *In the small church of Sant'Andrea in Via Flaminia, a reduced version of the Pantheon, Vignola introduced an oval cupola.*

Sant'Andrea in Via Flaminia

More homogeneous in effect is the little central-plan church of Sant'Andrea, which served as the palace chapel of the Villa Giulia (fig. 264). It was begun in 1551. Like Sangallo in Santa Maria di Loreto in Rome, Vignola faced the rectangular brick mausoleum-like building with a flat single-storey temple front, articulated with a Corinthian order of pilasters, shell niches and pedimented Ionic portal. The attic storey, corresponding to the pendentive zone, supports the oval dome which can only be recognized as such by its stepped upper half – an ingenious paraphrase of the far larger Pantheon. In the exterior as a whole Vignola once again demonstrated his aptitude for composition in stereometric volumes. In the interior he topped four simplified triumphal motifs with Diocletian windows, as in Sangallo's Cappella Paolina, but differed from that model in his tendency to verticalism, abstraction and the splitting of the wall into different layers.

Palazzo Firenze-del Monte

In the summer of 1552 Balduino del Monte, the powerful brother of Julius III, bought the fifteenth-century Palazzo Cardelli and proceeded to renovate it. Inspired by the projects for the Palazzo Farnese (fig. 247), he had the inner courtyard closed by a rear wing, with a loggia overlooking a huge rear garden, thus making the building more resemble a princely residence. Baglione attributed its design to Vignola, who was undoubtedly responsible for its ground plan. In its trapezoidal rear wing, which fills the intermediate space between the courtyard and garden, the rooms are laid out with Raphaelesque virtuosity. The inside of the loggia, too, no doubt goes back to Vignola and not to Ammannati, who would soon replace him as the architect of the Palazzo del Monte.

Castello Farnese in Caprarola

After the death of Julius III, Vignola entered the service of the Farnese and took over the architectural supervision of their build-

265 *Air view of Vignola's most spectacular creation, the Castello Farnese at Caprarola, 1558. Its pentagonal shape is due to the foundations laid earlier by Sangallo and Peruzzi.*

266 *As in Sangallo's project, the inner court of the Castello Farnese is unexpectedly circular, with paired Ionic engaged columns supported by a rusticated basement.*

267 *The dominance of the Castello is emphasized by its axial approach via a long street, stepped terraces and symmetrical oval ramps.*

ings, including the Cancelleria, where the powerful Cardinal Alessandro resided (figs 130–32). In 1556 the cardinal commissioned him to complete and enlarge the castle in Caprarola, which Sangallo and Peruzzi had begun for his grandfather as a cardinal in 1520–25 (figs 265–67). It was a pentagon built round a circular central courtyard. Each of the five points of the pentagon had been fortified with a projecting bastion. Vignola was obliged to take these features over when he enlarged it into the dimensions of a huge cardinal's palace. The actual work did not begin till 1558 and continued even after Vignola's death.

In his layout of the access to the building Vignola was inspired by Michelangelo's project for the Palazzo Farnese. An axial road, carried over two bridges, was cut straight through the late-medieval village in northern Lazio. The perspective effect is such that the main façade of the castle rises ever more imposingly the closer we get to it. But only once we reach the end of this approach road do we realize its polygonal shape and the gulf – physical and hierarchical – that separates us from the building. So the castle was closely connected with the village and simultaneously separated from it. This paradox reflected the self-glorification of early absolutist princes. Uniquely comprising axial approach, perspective effect, fortification, architecture, fresco decoration and gardens, Vignola's composition proved influential. It would soon inspire the architects of Ippolito d'Este in the layout of his villa in Tivoli (fig. 268) and Tommaso Ghinucci, the architect of Giovanfrancesco Gambara, in the garden of the villa at Bagnaia – the first where the visual unity of the garden has become more important than architecture itself (fig. 269).

The castle could be entered by carriage – just then coming into fashion – by ascending two elliptical ramps to a kind of parade ground and then continuing to the foot of the large spiral staircase in the basement storey. Riders on horseback, on the other hand, could ascend by zigzag ramps from the parade ground to a small Braman-

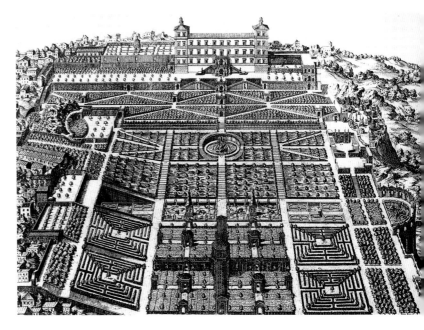

268 *When he laid out his famous garden at Tivoli, Ippolito d'Este combined the traditions of Roman, Ferrarese and Tuscan gardens with the axial symmetry of Caprarola.*

tesque oval staircase, which provided access to the drawbridge and to the rusticated main entrance.

As in the Cancelleria where the cardinal lived, the façade is flanked by projecting corner bays and only the two upper storeys are articulated by pilaster orders. The *piano nobile* is opened up into a central loggia of five arches; the blind outer arches are fenestrated

269 *The last work of Ippolito's garden architect Tommaso Ghinucci was the Villa Lante at Bagnaia, where the architecturally organized garden and its many fountains have become the main protagonists.*

and link up with the closed projecting corner wings. A horizontal crescendo is thus produced that intersects with the vertical crescendo rising from the steps and portal to the central portico. This composition, which focused on the centrepiece and on the person of the lord of the house, Alessandro Farnese, seems to have been directly inspired by a building that was then the property of the Farnese: the Villa Madama (fig. 170).

The *piano nobile* of the courtyard dominates the rusticated basement podium even more majestically than on the façade. It is articulated with an Ionic order of half-columns that alternate with an arcade and niches in the rhythm of eight triumphal-arch motifs. The pedestals are connected by an encircling balustrade that is repeated in the attic.

The large spiral staircase, supported on paired columns of a Doric order, flooded with light from three sides and culminating in a domed rotunda, surpasses in magnificence Bramante's famous spiral staircase in the Vatican (fig. 141). The two apartments on each of the two main storeys are in the latest courtly style. As in the Cancelleria, their rooms become ever more intimate the closer they approach the cardinal's room to the rear: the only room to be distinguished by a tower. It also has a *studiolo* and is linked by a secret staircase to a bathroom in the ground floor and by a drawbridge to the two gardens to the rear of the castle.

In detail, Giulio Romano's influence is largely superseded by that of Bramante, Peruzzi and Sangallo. Vignola was a champion of orthodoxy: he tried to defend Vitruvian norms from the licence of Michelangelo and his school. His style is expressed less in the invention of new motifs than in a predilection for dynamic longitudinal axes, crescendo effects, the vertical continuity of window bays, the layering of the wall and the abstraction of the forms.

In the Portico dei Banchi in Bologna, begun in 1560, he adopted a similar vocabulary. As in the central loggia of Caprarola, he faced the bare pillar arcade without archivolts with a pilaster order and topped it with triads of windows with dominant centre. In Bologna the order is a *Composita*. The arcade is squatter and not even furnished with imposts. The mezzanine floor is opened into a window triad. In the lower top floor Vignola replaced the order with blind panels as in Giulio Romano's Palazzo Stati (figs 177, 178), but topped it with an entablature similar to that of Caprarola. Also comparable with Caprarola are the Ionic aedicules crowned with amphorae and double volutes. Vignola's genuinely north Italian mentality appears here even more clearly in his predilection for composed proportions, horizontal rhythms, layering of wall surface, and ornamental decoration.

Palazzo Farnese in Piacenza

Francesco Paciotto (1521–91), the architect of Ottavio Farnese and a compatriot and pupil of Genga, had presented a plan for the new Farnese residence in Piacenza. But this fell through in 1558. The result was that, two years later, Vignola received what was doubtless the most splendid commission of his career (figs 270, 271). The real patron of the building was now Ottavio's wife, Margaret of Parma, the natural daughter of Charles V, who felt herself safer on the borders of imperial Lombardy than in Parma. Instead of terminating the exterior with projecting corner wings, as Paciotto had envisaged, Vignola accentuated the centre with a belfry, an old symbol of Italy's

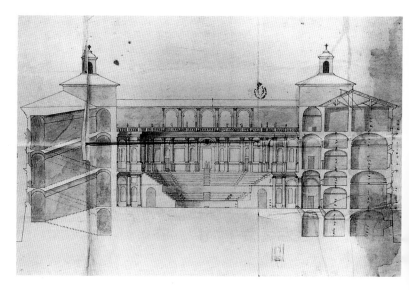

270 *When Vignola designed the Palazzo Farnese at Piacenza for Margaret of Parma he incorporated a theatre auditorium in the courtyard.*

palazzi comunali as also of Margaret's Flemish homeland. The three storeys of the palace were to culminate in the triumphal arches of the belfry. As in the Farnese family palaces in Rome and Caprarola, the corners of the brick building are reinforced with rusticated quoins. But as had become increasingly common since Giulio and Sangallo (fig. 178), each of the two main storeys is also lit by a second smaller row of windows. With its more conspicuous entablature and the segmental pediments of its windows, the *piano nobile* slightly predominates over the lower and upper storey.

As at Caprarola, Vignora devoted considerable attention to how the palace was to be approached: once again the visitor was to be inducted along an axial access road to the portal and thence into an

271 *The unfinished courtyard of the Palazzo Farnese in Piacenza based on the triumphal-arch motif and angled at the corners.*

oblong inner courtyard. Only on approaching the façade would he have become conscious of its unusual size. The 11 m (36 ft) height of its main storeys was never equalled in Roman palaces. The apartment of the duchess was situated in the right half, while that of the duke, who felt more comfortable in Parma, was never in fact executed. The summer apartments were intended to be opened in porticoes overlooking extensive gardens stretching to the banks of the Po. The winter apartments and the large ceremonial rooms were situated in the central storey.

Paciotto had already given the rear wing of the courtyard the form of an enormous exedra. Vignola developed this into the auditorium of an ancient theatre, of a kind familiar to Margaret from the designs for the Villa Madama (fig. 169). The courtyard itself was to serve as the stage.

The three courtyard loggias continue the triumphal-arch motifs of the tower. They are angled in the corners in such a way that the arcades continue in diagonal niches. Here Vignola came closer than ever before to the Vitruvian norms in his vocabulary and in the superimposition of half-columns of an *Ionica* and a *Corinthia*, which once again achieves the slight predominance of the upper floor. Vignola illustrated similar orders in his treatise, on which he was working at the same time.

This last and most magnificent princely residence of the Renaissance fundamentally differs from the one that Margaret's half-brother Philip II erected in the Escurial a little later. Philip, bowing to the spirit of the Counter-Reformation, combined his apartment not with a theatre but with a convent and his funerary chapel.

The Gesù

Of that spirit there is, in truth, little to be felt even in Vignola's designs for the Gesù (figs 272, 273). The planning of the Roman mother-church of the militant Jesuits goes back to the years following the foundation of the order by St Ignatius Loyola in 1540. But it was only when Cardinal Alessandro Farnese was afflicted by a serious illness in 1562 that he promised to finance the building, and may already then have intended it as the place of his burial. A bitter dispute had hitherto raged about whether the church should be oval or longitudinal; whether it should have a single nave or a nave and two aisles; and whether it should have a flat ceiling or be vaulted. Then in 1568 the cardinal got his way with his proposal for an aisleless nave with side chapels and hemispherical dome over the crossing. This was despite the Jesuits' preference for a church designed for preaching with an acoustically more suitable wooden ceiling; under a vaulted ceiling it was feared that the voice of the preacher would be lost because of the echo. The cardinal disputed this.

With its three short arms radiating from the crossing, drum-supported dome rising over splayed pillars, three-bayed nave, unbroken tunnel vault lit by clerestory windows and rhythmic

272 *Vignola's design for the façade of the Gesù in Rome was never built. Alessandro Farnese preferred the project of Giacomo della Porta which provided a higher and better-illuminated interior and a slenderer and more Michelangelesque façade.*

273 *In the nave of the Gesù deep side chapels replace aisles. The cardinal chose the Gesù as his burial church and insisted on a barrel vault and a crossing with cupola.*

alternation of pillar arches and paired pilasters, Vignola's interior comes closer to the nave of Bramante's 1506 project for St Peter's than any other building of the previous decades (fig. 147). In adopting such a plan Vignola no doubt responded to the wishes of the cardinal who in his dedicatory inscription on the entrance wall in any case made it plain that he was more concerned with his own glory than with humble service to the order. He was in fact buried in front of the high altar in 1589 – in the shadow of his grandfather, whose tomb was supposed to have stood near the dome of St Peter's.

As previously in his designs for Santa Maria in Traspontina and Santa Maria dell'Orto (in Trastevere, Rome), Vignola was inspired, in the dynamic crescendo of his façade project, by Raphael's and Sangallo's designs for St Peter's and the Villa Madama (figs 170, 173). But just as Julius III had ditched Vignola for Ammannati, so Cardinal Alessandro decided in 1570 to commission Giacomo della Porta for the façade of the Gesù. He elevated the drum, introduced an attic under the tunnel-vault of the nave, and thus had to heighten also the façade. He paired the columns, continued their line through both storeys, intensified the vertical thrust, and used Michelangelesque detail. Like the palace in Piacenza, Vignola's project for the Gesù stood at the end of the Renaissance: only through della Porta's alterations, especially the giant scroll buttresses, was it transformed into the prototype of innumerable Baroque churches.

If the buildings planned by Vignola for the Del Monte and Farnese families were warmly received mainly in the Catholic countries, his *Regola delle cinque ordini d'architettura*, published in 1562, was speedily disseminated throughout Europe. In this treatise he followed more limited, but also more precise, objectives than, for instance, Serlio. He confined himself to the orders and even commented on these sparingly. Vignola, however, surpassed Serlio in the precise illustration and the representation of simple rules of thumb that permitted orders to be transferred to walls of any height. Like Alberti and Serlio, he knew that the rules of a treatise did not necessarily coincide with building practice.

Pirro Ligorio (1513/14–1583)

Pirro Ligorio, who was slightly younger than Vignola and came from a noble Neapolitan family, also began as a painter. He too may have become an assistant of Peruzzi. His intensive study of the architecture of Antiquity soon took on encyclopaedic proportions. He migrated to Rome in c.1534, gaining a reputation for decorative paintings on the façades of Roman palaces, and entered the service of the powerful Cardinal Ippolito d'Este in 1549. First employed as the cardinal's antiquary, he assembled most of his rich collection of ancient sculpture, a great part of which was distributed through the gardens of the Quirinal and the cardinal's country house, at the Villa d'Este at Tivoli (fig. 268). Under the impression of the Palazzo dei Senatori he planned Ippolito's country house. Already in 1557 Paul IV appointed him architect of the Papal Palaces. During the following years he erected not only the great tower-like Nicchione and the southern exedra of the Cortile del Belvedere, but also his masterpiece, Pius IV's Casino to the west of the Cortile del Belvedere (fig. 140).

Casino of Pius IV

Probably planned by the ailing Paul IV as a single-storeyed *ritiro* in late 1558, this elaborate garden-house was only completed by his successor in 1562 (figs 274, 275). Its façade is aligned north-east and bears no axial relation to the Papal Palace. Coming from the old Papal Palace or from the northern gardens, the visitor entered the Casino through the transverse axis. Two small vestibules provided access to the oval court, surrounded by low walls with stone benches. The Casino is thus far more systematically connected with its adjacent buildings than in Peruzzi's project for the Villa Trivulzio near Tivoli and even in Vignola's suburban buildings. The Casino is entered through the colonnade of the *vestibulum*, which provides access to the summer apartment of the pope with its some 11 m (36 ft) long *sala*, antechamber and bedroom. From the antechamber the staircase ascends to the flat-roofed upper storey designed for the cooler seasons of the year, where the *vestibulum* is replaced by a *galleria*: an early example of a room-type imported from France. From the upper antechamber a spiral staircase ascends to the tower-like belvedere. Only when viewed frontally does the building appear symmetrical. The picturesque asymmetry of the other sides is

274 *The Casino of Pius IV, in the Vatican garden, is situated in the immediate neighbourhood of the Papal Palace and thus much smaller than the Villa Giulia. It opens in a loggia on an oval court which is mirrored by a loggia on the opposite side, from where one could admire the architectural garden.*

reminiscent of Giulio Romano and was particularly influential in the early nineteenth century. Ligorio was to play even more boldly with asymmetrical dissonances and diverging axes in his design for the palazzetto for the Borromeo brothers on the Via Flaminia in 1561.

The façade of the Casino astonishes by its height, three-storeyed elevation and over-lavish decoration. As on the loggia opposite, its Doric colonnade follows the triumphal rhythm. The outer columns are flanked by broad pilasters that are repeated on both sides of the building. Thus the broad central bay dominates the narrow side bays even more pronouncedly than in previous buildings. In the relation of the *piano nobile* to the squat basement podium, the top-heaviness of his teacher Peruzzi's Palazzo Massimo (fig. 216) is taken to the point of grotesqueness, as if Ligorio wanted to parody the hierarchical principle here. Both the vaulted zone of the ground floor and the windowsills of the upper storey are concealed behind the blind intermediate attic, which is therefore higher than the ground floor and articulated with niches and blind shouldered windows filled with decoration as if it were a separate storey of its own. Richly decorated strap-like panels connect it with the similar second floor, whose shouldered windows open onto the gallery and are accompanied by blind mezzanine windows. This system is continued on the sides of the entrance wing, but is reduced to smooth ashlared courses in the

275 *Pius IV's Casino was originally to comprise only the ground floor. When Ligorio added the upper one he covered the façade with stucco statues.*

rear wings. Caryatids, Pantheon-aedicules and reliefs with spiral columns continue the rhythm of the ground floor in the upper floor of the opposite loggia.

No previous architect of the Renaissance had used the ancient vocabulary so playfully. But Ligorio could permit himself such licence because he was designing what, after all, was a pleasure-house. In his study of ancient villas such as Hadrian's Villa (itself the apotheosis of the ludic principle), he had no doubt observed that the columnar orders remain concentrated on porticoes or wall-apertures, but that closed exterior walls were often articulated by no more than stuccoed ashlars or decorative motifs and that strict axiality and symmetry played a far lesser role than in the villas of his own time.

In architectural detail Ligorio is close to Raphael and Peruzzi, but not to Michelangelo. In his exaggerated hierarchy, vertical continuity, abstraction and alienation of the orders and windows, on the other hand, he follows the tendencies of his own time. Indeed he may even have been familiar with such a recent building as Vasari's Uffizi (fig. 279). In the Casino's rich decoration with ancient and stucco statues and reliefs he followed the tradition already set by the Palazzo Branconio (fig. 167) and the Palazzo Capodiferro or the antiques-garden of the Palazzo della Valle in Rome. But none of the numerous villas of the following period can vie with the Casino of Pius IV.

In the plans of both the Villa d'Este and the suburban palace of the Borromeo brothers near the Villa Giulia, Ligorio showed his interest in asymmetrical compositions. In 1566 he planned, together with Sallustio Peruzzi, Baldassare's son, the transformation of the Palazzo del Sant'Uffizio in the Vatican and the Casale of Pius V near Via Aurelia Antica, whose access and austere articulation are reminiscent of the Villa d'Este.

Bartolommeo Ammannati (1511–91)

Villa Giulia and Palazzo del Monte-Firenze

If Vignola remained true to the Bramante school throughout his life, two Florentine architects of the same generation soon after 1550 embraced the school of Michelangelo. Ammannati was a sculptor, a pupil of Bandinelli. Already as an eighteen-year-old he was so fascinated by Michelangelo that he stole drawings from him. When the theft was discovered, he was forced to leave Florence and it was only years later that he could contact the revered master again and return to his hometown. He then worked under Sansovino in Venice and designed a garden portal in the triumphal style of Sanmicheli for the celebrated jurist Benavides in Padua in about 1544. In *c.*1550 he settled in Rome, and replaced Vignola as the architect in charge of the Villa Giulia and the Palazzo Firenze, perhaps with Michelangelo's support, in 1552.

At first he decorated the corner of the road that turns off from the Via Flaminia and leads to the Villa Giulia with a concave fountain wall, whose aedicule still betrays Sangallo's influence. Michelangelo's influence is already unmistakable in the nymphaeum of the Villa Giulia (fig. 262). The layout had been largely planned by Vignola: Ammannati had to accept it, but was able to convince the pope to use his own contribution, especially his rich decoration of columns, statues and reliefs and the sculptural detail of his orders and portals. In the upper loggia of the nymphaeum he compressed the Ionic half-columns and portals closely together. In the triglyph-decorated consoles or the abstracted order of the portals he varied the inventions of Michelangelo in his own quite peculiar way, but eschewed any organic link with the already existing parts. Similar brackets recur in the central window of the courtyard façade (fig. 263). Ammannati is at his most convincing in the sunken ground-floor centre of the nymphaeum, which, like the whole villa, follows the ground plan of an ancient theatre and is surrounded by an elegant curvilinear balustrade. In the recessed exedra-like grotto the balustrade is supported by four naked caryatids.

The *Ionica*, with which Ammanati decorated the side walls of the large court, recurs in quite similar form in both façades of the loggia of the Palazzo Firenze, where Vignola was replaced by Ammannati presumably at the same time (fig. 277). The Sangallesque language of its garden front with its superimposition of three-quarter columns clearly differs fundamentally from the courtyard front that Ammannati enriched for the Medici, presumably in *c.*1572.

Palazzo Griffoni

After he was able to return to Florence through Vasari's mediation, Ammannati began to build the Palazzo Griffoni for the secretary of Cosimo I at the corner of the Piazza Santissima Annunziata in 1557. It is a square block with five by five bays, but follows the model of the Palazzo Farnese (fig. 190) in its three storeys, rusticated quoining, rusticated portals, volute-supported aedicules, central *serliana* and brick-clad walls: like so many later architects Ammannati combined Sangallo's types with Michelangelo's forms. He lent even greater emphasis to the widened central bay and once again expressed his architectural

skill especially in sculptural detail. He topped the ground floor with a Doric, the *piano nobile* with an Ionic and the upper floor with a reduced Corinthian entablature, and thus developed a simplified superimposition of the orders. While the windows of the two upper floors or the beautiful ram-headed consoles of the *andito* are decidedly Michelangelesque, the ornament in the attic of the portal on the Via dei Servi is derived from Bandinelli. Ammannati, indeed, always ran the danger of losing sight of the whole in his pursuit of eclectic decoration. In the asymmetrical courtyard he limited himself to archaizing columnar arcades topped with entablature fragments.

Palazzo Pitti

The success of the Palazzo Griffoni and Florentine predilection for sculptural detail no doubt led to Ammannati being awarded the contract in 1560 for the transformation of the Palazzo Pitti and its huge garden into the new grand-ducal residence – a measure that is inseparable from Duke Cosimo's political successes (fig. 276). Perhaps even in deference to the old republican ideals, Cosimo and his architect eschewed on the exterior the kind of characteristic symbols of absolute rule that Paciotto and Vignola had proposed to the Farnese. He thus limited himself to enriching the rear façade of the Quattrocento Palazzo Pitti with the monumental window-aedicules of the ground floor. In their upper triglyph-consoles Michelangelo's influence is as clearly to be felt as in the Palazzo Griffoni. But Ammannati

276 *The garden side of the Palazzo Pitti, Florence. Ammannati combined the façade of Palazzo Farnese with Giulio's rustication.*

followed his own bent in the magnificent crowned lion's head between the brackets. To the Quattrocento façade he added two unrusticated wings which were stepped back from the alignment of the façade not just once as in the Villa Giulia, but twice, and which flanked the building like towers. Rather as Guglielmo della Porta was to propose for the Palazzo Farnese, he closed the three surrounding courtyard loggias with a single-storey back wing. He varied the design of the Palazzo Farnese courtyard (fig. 192) by rusticating both the half-columns and the arcades and thus conformed to the growing fashion for rustication promoted by Giulio, Sanmicheli, Sansovino and Vignola. As he had previously done in the Palazzo Griffoni, he opened up the broadened central bay of the entrance wing in *serliane*, from which the ducal pair could watch theatrical performances in the courtyard and enjoy the view of the fountain wing and the Boboli Gardens rising up the hillside beyond. Yet here the broadening of the central bay is unmediated: one misses Vignola's ability to prepare the dominating centre by flanking bays.

Palazzo Firenze and Villa Medici

In 1572 Ammannati received the commission to transform the Palazzo Firenze in Rome into the residence of the twenty-three-year-old Cardinal Ferdinando de' Medici (fig. 277). The rear wall of the courtyard, on which the glance of the visitor first falls, was with its Vitruvian orders no longer in keeping with the fashion for lavish decoration that distinguished this period, and so Ammannati enriched it with magnificent individual forms such as the ram's-head consoles of the portal, Michelangelesque mezzanine windows, a central *serliana* and the double frame of the niches in the upper storey.

277 *The front side of the rear wing of Palazzo Firenze, Rome, in a language strongly influenced by Michelangelo.*

278 *When Ammannati had to remodel the Villa Medici in Rome, he transformed the garden side into a richly decorated* court d'honneur.

In 1576 Ferdinando bought the villa of Cardinal Ricci, which Sangallo's long-standing companion Nanni di Baccio Bigio had begun to build on the Pincio in Rome, and once again entrusted its enlargement to Ammannati. This was the Villa Medici. On its façade overlooking the Pincio Ammannati's hands were tied: he had to limit himself to the columnar portal, the balcony window and the staircase at the right side. But by adding belvedere-towers he gave it a more volumetric form and helped it achieve a more prominent position in the skyline of Rome, in a way that only the Villa Imperiale in Pesaro had previously achieved (fig. 220).

The main entrance was shifted to the Via di Porta Pinciana so that the courtyard in front of the garden loggia could now be reached by coach (fig. 278). Gardens were acquiring an ever more central role in princely residences (figs 268, 269) and consequently the garden façade was now lavishly decorated. The precedent for such a scheme had already been set by Ammannati himself in the rear façade of the grand-ducal apartment of the Palazzo Pitti overlooking the court-yard and garden. Clearly inspired by Vasari's Uffizi (fig. 279), he transformed Nanni's loggia into a triumphal *serliana* supported by paired columns. This broad central part is flanked by two square and slightly projecting lateral wings with lower storeys; their alignment is staggered in a syncopated manner. The predominance of the *serliana*-opened loggia is underlined by the flanking towers as in the façade of the Palazzo Pitti. In this daring interplay of *volumina* Ammannati went far beyond Pirro Ligorio, by whose Casino of Pius IV the lavish deco-ration with ancient statues and reliefs was clearly inspired (fig. 275).

Giorgio Vasari (1511–74)

The precocious Vasari was only thirteen when the Medici brought him from his birthplace of Arezzo to Florence. There he was apprenticed to Andrea del Sarto, Rosso Fiorentino and for a short time even to Michelangelo. Already in 1535–37 he imitated the volutes of the Lau-renziana *ricetto* in his organ loft of the cathedral of Arezzo. Up till 1550 he was especially famous as a painter and pioneering chronicler of art history. But thereafter he belonged with Vignola and Ammannati to the group of new talents who were first to prove themselves as archi-tects under Pope Julius III. In 1550 he received the commission for the funerary chapel of the Del Monte family in the Roman church of San Pietro in Montorio, in the planning of which the pope later involved Michelangelo and Ammannati too. He also claims to have made a deci-sive contribution to the planning of the Villa Giulia (figs 259–63).

In was not until 1555, after his return to Florence, however, that Vasari emerged as an architect in his own right. In that year he assumed overall responsibility for the artistic enterprises of the grand duke. At first he worked on the transformation of the Palazzo Vecchio into a princely residence and especially helped its great reception hall, the Sala dei Cinquecento, to achieve a grander effect.

The Uffizi

In 1559, at the same time that Cosimo asked Ammannati to trans-form the Palazzo Pitti into his future residence, Vasari received the commission to gather together all the state offices scattered over the city into a single administrative building, and thus to give architec-tural expression to the comprehensive administrative reform to which Cosimo devoted himself after the stabilization of the political situation (fig. 279). The building was also conceived as part of the long overhead corridor that was to connect it with the new residence in the Palazzo Pitti on the other side of the river. Vasari followed Bra-mante in type, not so much in his functionally comparable Palazzo dei Tribunali (fig. 150) as in the Cortile del Belvedere (figs 139, 140). Two nearly identical wings of a long three-storeyed building flanked a new street, or rather elongated piazza, leading from the Palazzo Vecchio to the Arno.

So, while Grand Duke Cosimo de' Medici shut himself up in his suburban palazzo on the Oltr'Arno, with its powerful rustication and rather forbidding façade, he gave to the centre of the city an adminis-trative building that was quite unparalleled in the Europe of the time, and that was intended to impress on its citizens the benefits, rigour, rationality and transparency of his *buongoverno*.

Vasari was now faced by the task of combining his prototype with administrative rooms (the *uffizi* from which the building takes its name). In the lower colonnade he combines the third storey of the lower court of the Cortile del Belvedere, whose colonnades were also separated by pillars, with the projecting walls of Michelangelo's *ricetto* (fig. 243). The pillars represent a caesura between the individual offices, while the colonnades open up into passageways. These are lighted by mezzanine windows which cut into the barrel vault as in the courtyard of Peruzzi's Palazzo Massimo (fig. 218) and are divided by consoles on the façade.

Triads of large balcony windows with alternating triangular and segmental pediments pierce the *piano nobile*, its order abstracted into even flatter wall panels than that of the Laurenziana (fig. 242). The plain colonnades of the upper floor are lower in height and clearly subordinated. This long repetitive row of identical elements is broken by the vertical continuity of the pillars. As in the Laurenziana *ricetto*, they are considerably broader than the column shafts and have statue niches hewn into their faces. There is, however, no ambiguity about their load-bearing function. Their vertical thrust is continued into the projecting entablature above their abstracted capital, and thence into the double volutes of the mezzanine floor. At the same time the pillars are hierarchically subordinated to the colonnade by their abstracted bases and capitals. Though Vasari's language is much more Michelangelesque than that of Ammannati, the tectonic skele-ton thus produced is still similar to that of the Cortile del Belvedere: as there, the horizontal and vertical forces are clearly distinguished and intersect in the pillars.

Both wings are connected by a scenic arcaded loggia on the banks of the Arno: a double *serliana* opens up views of the Uffizi looking towards the Piazza Signoria on the one side and of the river and its opposite bank on the other. Its central arch rests on paired columns and cuts into the mezzanine, as in the Medici Chapel (fig. 241). On the Arno front it was far harder to amalgamate the various elements into a satisfactory whole.

In his later buildings, too, such as the Cappella Vitelli in San Francesco in Città di Castello, the Badia delle Sante Flora e Lucilla and the Palazzo delle Logge in Arezzo, Vasari combined the types and the tectonic skeleton of the Bramante school far more systematically

279 *For Cosimo, duke of Florence, Giorgio Vasari built the most impressive administrative offices in Italy: the Uffizi, two parallel ranges ending with a* serliana *on the bank of the Arno.*

than Ammannati with the vocabulary of Michelangelo's Florentine buildings. These had transcended Brunelleschi's world and created a new Florentine identity.

Galeazzo Alessi (1512–72)

Born in Perugia, Alessi was only one year younger than Ligorio and one year older than Ammannati and Vasari. Like Vignola and Vasari, he began as a painter, in the shop of the Perugian painter and architect Giovan Battista Caporali. But Genga's Villa Imperiale outside Pesaro must also have been one of his earliest formative impressions (figs 220, 221). In the late 1530s Alessi came to Rome, and his architectural talent was discovered by Sangallo and the papal legate Tiberio Crispi in the early 1540s. This led to his being entrusted with the demanding task of supervising the building of the gigantic Rocca Paolina in Perugia.

He also designed other buildings in Perugia. In the Oratorio degli Angeli and the Loggia dei Priori he proved a faithful pupil of the Bramante circle. He comes closest to Sangallo in the Vitruvian orders of these buildings, and to Giulio Romano's Palazzo Stati-Maccarani (figs 177, 178) in the finely layered wall panelling and baluster-shaped window frames. His own idiosyncratic style appears even more clearly in the façade of Santa Maria del Popolo in Perugia in 1547. Here he repeats the Doric *serliana* of the portal on a second level with square columns and encloses both between entablature-projected wall blocks with doors, niches and abstracted order. The influence of Michelangelo's *ricetto* (fig. 243) can be felt even earlier than in

Ammannati. On the other hand, Genga's influence is unmistakable in the steep proportions and abstract articulation of the Oratory of Santa Giuliana designed in 1548.

Instead of returning to Rome, Alessi accepted an invitation to go to Genoa. He was invited thither by the papal protonotary Stefano Sauli, an influential and humanistically trained politician and descendant of an old banking family. The only exponent of the Roman school active in Genoa after the Sack of Rome had been Raphael's pupil Perino del Vaga (1501–47), and his decorative language was highly influential on Alessi's further work. Alessi left his stamp on the city; indeed he gave it an architectural character similar to that given to Mantua by Giulio, to Verona by Sanmicheli and to Venice by Sansovino.

Villa Cambiaso-Giustiniani in Genoa

Alessi produced a masterpiece in his very first Genoese building, the Villa Cambiaso-Giustiniani begun in 1548 (figs 280–83). This is a type of suburban villa with a *vestibulum* flanked by slightly projecting wings and opening to an atrium from which the staircase ascends. Its axial-symmetrical prototype goes back to Sangallo's projects for villas and the patrician houses in Castro. But Alessi showed himself quite un-Sangallesque by situating the loggia and terrace of the *piano nobile* in the rear wing and by preparing for it only partially by the walls of the ground floor. As in the Palazzo Farnese, the vault of the ground floor springs from the impost, whereas the vaults of the *piano nobile* only begin above the arcades and are projected deep into the roof. More systematically than Raphael in the Palazzo Branconio dell'Aquila (fig. 167), he extended the hierarchical principle to the whole building, though without jeopardizing its closed stereometric character.

As in Giulio's Villa Turini-Lante, he articulated the ground floor with a *Dorica* and the upper storey with fluted pilasters of a more

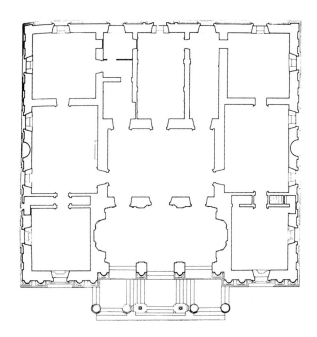

280–82 *In Genoa architecture was dominated by Galeazzo Alessi. The functional plan of his Villa Cambiaso-Giustiniani, begun in 1548, follows Sangallo's reconstruction of the ancient house. The two orders of the lavish main façade and the abstraction of the side fronts and the vestibule (below right) are, however, nearer to Raphael, Giulio and Pierin del Vaga.*

283 *Opposite: Alessi's Porta del Molo, 1553, is more aggressively rusticated.*

decorative order (fig. 176). But he came closer to Sansovino's Venetian buildings by using half-columns in the ground floor (fig. 235). The upper storey is distinguished as the *piano nobile* not only by its height, but also by its magnificent *Composita*, monumental balcony windows, grouped in a triad at the centre, and crowning balustrade. For Alessi, too, as for other architects of his generation, the Vitruvian orders meant especially *all'antica* decoration. He therefore preferred to render them in more abstract form, as Giulio had taught, on the three other sides of the exterior. In both loggias he attached an order to the pillars, which continue on the three closed walls and support the arches of the arcades and of the exedras. By following Genga in the abstracted detail of the exedras and portals, and Perino in the rich decoration of herm-shaped pilasters, festoons and volutes, Alessi fused together two antithetical worlds.

Alessi was so successful with his Villa Cambiaso that he drew on it as his model and varied it in ever-new ways in a series of other Genoese villas (delle Peschiere, Sauli and Grimaldi) in the following years. In the orders, as in the décor, he gradually distanced himself from Raphael and Sangallo, and sought inspiration instead in Perino, increasingly in Giulio Romano, even in Vignola. In the zigzag staircase ramps and terraces of the Villa delle Peschiere he rivalled Vignola's Caprarola (fig. 267).

Sangallo and Giulio also inspired one of his finest inventions, the Porta del Molo on the harbour, begun in 1553 (fig. 283). The stairway leads up to the Doric portal flanked by columns with banded

rustication. It is flanked in turn by huge segmental exedras hollowed out by niches; here the rusticated order continues in the flat pilasters of triumphal motifs.

Santa Maria di Carignano

In 1549 Alessi had also been commissioned by his Genoese patrons, the Sauli, to rebuild their funerary church (figs 284, 285). Each of the four chapels was destined for a member of the family. In a letter of 1569 Alessi expressed his wish to articulate the church like an ancient temple. The wooden model was completed in 1552. But during the long and wearisome execution he seems to have made radical alterations to his original design, influenced successively by the changing fashions and trends of the day. Once again he began from a Sangallesque prototype, the recently discarded wooden model for St Peter's (figs 197, 198). In its temple front flanked by corner towers and its drum articulated by triumphal-arch motifs, the church is also reminiscent of Raphael's project for San Giovanni dei Fiorentini, while Michelangelo's influence can be felt only in the interior of the drum and dome. Since the splaying of the pillars supporting the dome is narrower than in St Peter's and they are not articulated by members of the order as they are in Bramante, the crossing does not achieve a comparable sense of expanding space (fig. 148). The barrel vaults of the cross-arms open in lunette windows and once again stretch up into the roof. And since the roofline is coordinated with the pediments of the three temple fronts, Alessi was forced to make the pediments unusually high. The articulation of the wall is relatively flat and culminates hierarchically in a projecting triumphal temple front. During execution Alessi seems to have reduced in height the

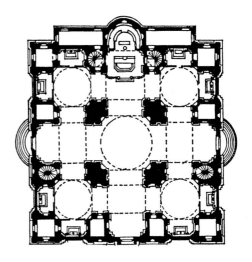

284, 285 *Alessi's Santa Maria di Carignano, Genoa, begun 1549, is an original variant of the centralized domed plan, this time square. The smaller domed spaces in the corners are funerary chapels of the Sauli family. The drum uses the triumphal-arch motif.*

pedestals originally planned in front of the high socle zone of the exterior. He thus weakened the predomination of the vertical forces, expressed most conspicuously in the upwards-expanding bell-towers and dome which majestically hold their own in the cityscape of Genoa.

Palazzo Marino in Milan

Even more eclectic in style is what is perhaps Alessi's most important palace, erected for Milan's most powerful banker in 1557/58 (figs 286, 287). The five central bays of the entrance front only reach up to the

286 *Alessi's vast and highly eclectic Palazzo Marino in Milan keeps the main entrance front (here on the left) low in order to light the courtyard.*

piano nobile. They ensure the good lighting of the inner courtyard and are flanked by tower-like lateral wings. In contrast to the Villa Cambiaso and other villas, Alessi weakened here the predominance of the *piano nobile* by topping it with a third storey of the same height. This upper storey comprises only one row of windows and is articulated with tapered herm-pilasters in the style of Perino. Their heads are wedged between brackets, which (as in Vignola) ascend in two superimposed rows, and support the deeply projecting, shadow-creating top cornice. In both lower storeys the smooth rustication is projected behind the windows by a delicate layer and, as in the Villa Imperiale (fig. 220), forms an additional support for the unprojected entablature.

Like Vignola and Palladio, Alessi used a variation of the windows of Giulio's Roman house on the ground floor (fig. 179). But Michelangelo's influence can be detected in the scale-decorated volutes that support the *Ionica*, and in the window frames of both upper storeys.

In the lavish atrium the *Dorica* is deployed even more systematically than in the Palazzo Farnese, continuing into the open staircase placed in the left wing. The arcaded courtyard loggia on the ground floor opens out into *serliane*. Paired lion-head consoles support the broad meander-decorated cornice that replaces the ground-floor entablature. There is only one upper storey: here Perino's influence is even more manifest. Instead of the *Ionica*, female herms, their fronts exposed down to the navel, their hair rolling out into lateral volutes, support the imposts, above which rectangular relief-decorated panels reach up to the Ionic entablature. Ornate balustrades, statue niches, swags and festoons add to the sumptuousness of the courtyard decoration. But as a pupil of Sangallo, even where he decoratively alienates the individual form, Alessi always holds fast to a coherent tectonic skeleton, far more systematically than for instance the more licentious Ligorio or Ammannati.

On the entrance axis one enters the enormous ground-floor *salone* (*c*.12 x 25.50 m/39 x 84 ft). It takes up the centre of the rear wing and can also be reached directly through the columnar portal of the longer side front. Its fenestrated vault rises deep into the *piano*

nobile and in its capricious Perino-inspired décor is without parallel in the architecture of the Cinquecento.

These characteristic examples of Alessi's enormous output may suffice to show how different his development was from that of his generation in Rome, Florence or Venice, even though he grew from roots similar to theirs. Alessi too held fast to the Vitruvian orders and the tried and tested ground-plan and elevation types of the Roman school. Yet he was concerned less with the complex rhythmic modulation or splitting up of the wall than with extravagant and ever more bizarre detail. It is no surprise that the mainly organic form of his decoration was enthusiastically rediscovered during the Liberty period (Italy's version of Art Nouveau). Like Giacomo della Porta in Rome, he exerted a powerful influence in Lombardy on important masters of the following generation such as Tebaldi, Seregni, Vittozzi, Domenico Fontana and Maderno, through whom the elements of his style then flowed back to Rome.

287 *The courtyard of the Palazzo Marino is even more bizarre than the exterior, comprising lion-head consoles, female herms, statues in niches, swags and festoons.*

13 Andrea Palladio (1508–80)

When Alessi was piling together the most bizarre forms of the previous decades in the Palazzo Marino in Milan, Palladio was intent on achieving a final revival of Antiquity in Vicenza, only some 200 km (125 miles) away. Son of a miller and married to a carpenter's daughter, Andrea di Pietro (his real name) was trained as a building worker. He had learnt the rudiments of his trade from a stonemason in his hometown of Padua, and soon after entered the famous workshop of the Pedimuro in Vicenza, to which he remained attached until he was well into his thirties. There portals, funerary monuments and altars in the style of Sanmicheli were produced, and there he may also have begun to practise as a draughtsman. In the mid-1530s he was discovered by the Vicentine count Giangiorgio Trissino, who took him under his wing and gave him the suitably classical name Palladio. This name had already graced a character in Trissino's heroic epic poem *L'Italia liberata dai Goti* who describes a classicizing palatial courtyard, expatiating on the proportions and details of its classical columns. Trissino, one of the leading literati and humanists of Italy, had spent many years at the courts of Leo X and Clement VII, and there must have come into close contact with architects and students of Vitruvius like Sangallo. Indeed Trissino could have sent Palladio to study under Sangallo even before 1540.

When Trissino built his villa in Cricoli near Vicenza in 1537/38, he no doubt drew on the services of his gifted young protégé. In comparison with own autograph designs, in which he had tried to reconstruct Vitruvius's Roman house, the ground plan of the villa at Criccoli seems significantly more functional and professional and already heralds Palladio's own villas. With its three theatre motifs flanked by fragments of the triumphal arch the loggia is reminiscent of Sangallo's loggia at the Castel Sant'Angelo. In his Third Book of 1540 Serlio used a similar façade system for the garden front of the Villa Madama, though he adjusted its proportions and detailing to his own style. As in Palladio's earliest façade designs, the window-aedicules follow the model of the Odeion that Falconetto had erected for Alvise Cornaro in Padua. Cornaro was another important humanist whom Palladio may already have got to know through Trissino. The sham corner towers of the rear side of the villa and the schematic spirals of the Ionic capitals reveal, however, the hand of the learned dilettante.

Early villa projects

It was presumably through Trissino that Palladio was given the commission for the Villa Godi in Lonedo in *c.*1537. With its symmetrical ground plan developed from a grid of rectangles, unadorned exterior, high *podium villae*, mezzanine-heightened *piano nobile*, recessed vestibule-loggia and flanking wings with the service quarters, it seems inspired by Sanmicheli's Villa La Soranza (fig. 227). Palladio may have learned from Sanmicheli how to design a villa with naked, clearly defined *volumina* intended to have an effect when seen from afar. Bramantesque and Sangallesque motifs such as the *serliana*, the rusticated portal or the lion's-paw-supported fireplaces already point, however,

to a direct knowledge of Roman prototypes. This Roman influence is even more manifest in the Casa Civena in Vicenza, begun in 1540.

In the summer of 1541 Palladio undertook a journey to Rome together with Trissino. The effect of this journey is to be deduced from numerous projects for villas, for which Palladio adopted more decidedly Roman motifs such as the open pediments of the imperial *thermae* or the window-aedicules of Giulio's Roman house (figs 179, 290).

Like Alvise Cornaro before them, Trissino and his protégé were motivated in the first place by the idea of reconstructing and reviving the ancient house with porch or *vestibulum*, its interior arrangement and its comforts. In 1556 Daniele Barbaro, in his Vitruvius commentary, was to describe the primeval house as the germ of all architecture (fig. 288). Palladio was to endorse the same opinion in 1570 in his own treatise *I quattro libri dell'architettura*, whose centre-piece is the second book devoted to the house. Whether as palace or villa, hospital or convent, the revival of the ancient house with porch remained thereafter the central theme of Palladio's forty-year activity. Alberti had already traced back the *vestibulum* of the ancient house and the porch of the temple to the primeval house and therefore topped both with a pediment (Book IX, c.3.f.). And while Giuliano da Sangallo had incorporated the pediment into the wall at Poggio a Caiano (fig. 77), Antonio da Sangallo the Younger, in his reconstruction of the Roman house, placed it as a part of self-contained column-supported portico in front of the façade, as in the Pantheon. In Barbaro's edition of Vitruvius Palladio's reconstruction of the ancient house is preceded by a monumental octastyle portico (fig. 289).

288 *For Daniele Barbaro's commentary on Vitruvius Palladio reconstructed the plan of an ancient Roman house, the source for many of his own palace and villa plans.*

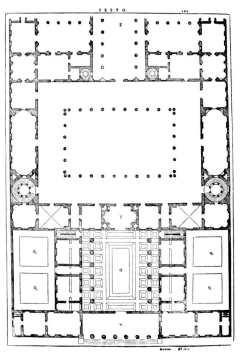

289 *Front elevation of Palladio's reconstructed Roman house. He gives it a temple-like portico, as he did many of his own houses. He thought that both the house and the temple originated from the primitive hut. Thus he distinguished also the ancient house with a portico and then repeated this motif on many of his mature villas.*

After initial experiments, Palladio opted for a single-storey villa type with mezzanine, dominant central *vestibulum* and projecting side wings, as anticipated by Bramante in his 'Nymphaeum' at Genazzano (figs 154, 155) and as adopted by Sanmicheli in his Villa La Soranza. Bramante had also been able significantly to reduce building costs by the simplification of the forms and the use of tufa, brick, stucco and limited amounts of hewn stone. Trissino and Palladio learnt from these economic techniques, and were able, not least for this reason, to persuade the nobility of Vicenzo, such as Valmarana,

Gazzotti, Pisani, Caldogno and Thiene, to build classical-style villas from 1541 on.

Palazzo Thiene

Palladio found the most understanding of his early patrons in Marcantonio and Adriano Thiene. In *c.*1542 they commissioned him with the brick-built Villa Thiene at Quinto, one of the most classicizing of his early period. With its paired pilasters of a Doric order, it clearly betrays its descent from Roman buildings such as Raphael's Chigi stables. By contrast, the influence of the Palazzo Te is to be felt in his first designs for the Palazzo Thiene in Vicenza.

In his final project for the palace Palladio adopted the same kind of economic rustication from roughened and stuccoed bricks that Giulio Romano had first developed (figs 291, 292). The *piano nobile* dominates the rusticated podium in a clearly Raphaelesque way, and finds its clearest parallel in the Villa Madama (fig. 169). Another model was Bramante's Palazzo Caprini (fig. 136): as there, the arcaded lateral bays of the rusticated ground floor of the main façade were to open in rectangular shops and blind lunettes with mezzanine windows. Palladio in fact uses exclusively Roman motifs in the Palazzo Thiene, including the rusticated windows of Giulio's Roman house (fig. 179). In the slender proportions, in detail, and in the paratactical rhythm of the order, which he doubled only in the corner bays, he followed once again Sangallo. Again the main façade was to culminate in the projecting centrepiece with the vestibule and a pediment-topped *piano nobile*. Rather as in Giulio's Palazzo Adimari (fig. 174), the centrepiece was to be complemented by projecting corner

290 *Projected plan and façade from the Villa Valmarana at Vigardolo.*

291 *Palladio's project for the Palazzo Thiene, Vicenza, from the* Quattro libri.

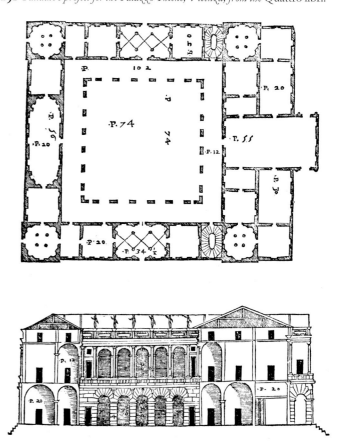

single large staircase: clearly the ceremonial entry to the *piano nobile* played a smaller role in Vicenza than in Rome.

Altogether Palladio revealed himself in the Palazzo Thiene for the first time as the real heir of the Roman school. As in the immediately preceding buildings of Sanmicheli and Sansovino (figs 224–26, 232–35), the effect lies not in complication, alienation, abstraction or bizarre décor, but in strict tectonic system, balanced composition and classical vocabulary. It is not by chance that comparable ground plans recur in Barbaro's reconstruction of the ancient house of 1556 and Palladio's own reconstruction of 1570.

Palazzo Iseppo Porto

During his next visits to Rome in 1545/46 and 1547 Palladio would have seen how, after Sangallo's death, a more decorative approach to architecture had come into fashion. In his designs for the façade of his next patrician palace of 1549, the Palazzo Iseppo Porto, he still recurred to a Bramantesque prototype and based his detail on the Palazzi Caprini, Farnese and Massimo (figs 136, 190, 216). And, as in the round court of the Villa Madama, he alternated the dominating Pantheon-aedicules of the *piano nobile* with simple Ionic half-columns. At the same time, he smoothed the rustication as in the Palazzo Canossa, decorated the façade with masks, victories and festoons, projected the entablature over the columns in triumphal-arch mode, and continued the line of the columns into the statue-decorated attic. There is thus a more Venetian feel to the façade, despite its Roman prototype. Like Sanmicheli and Sansovino, he used an ever-greater approximation to triumphal arches for the glorification of his patron.

In the atrium he amalgamated the columns with the corner pillars and raised a cross vault above them. In this way he approached the spaciousness of the Venetian *portego*. The courtyard loggias were to be given the form of a Corinthian colonnade. With a height of *c*.10.40m

293 *Classicizing, functional and economical projects such as the Villa Poiana provided Palladio already in the 1540s with many commissions in the neighbourhood of Vicenza.*

292 *Street elevation of the unfinished Palazzo Thiene, strongly influenced by Giulio Romano, though differing both in the slenderer proportions and the more normative detail.*

bays. Palladio thus formed a style of austere monumentality, of Roman grandeur, that was diametrically opposed to Giulio's late Mantuan buildings (figs 182–85).

The exact correspondence between courtyard and façade is also Roman: it finds its closest parallel in Lorenzetti's Palazzo Caffarelli. The unadorned arcades and the narrower corner bays of the *piano nobile* are still reminiscent of Trissino's villa and differ even more markedly in their steep proportions from Giulio's Mantuan buildings.

In the four-column atria with rusticated columns that imitate those of the Palazzo Te, in the octagonal corner rooms, oval staircases and gallery-like rooms of the rear wing, Palladio varied room forms of the imperial *thermae* in the way that Raphael had done in the Villa Madama. He followed Sangallo, on the other hand, in the rigorous axial symmetry of the ground plan; he even adopted two matching smaller staircases, in order to avoid the asymmetry of one

(34 ft 1½ ins) their massive columns would have been only *c.*2 m smaller than those of the pronaos of the Pantheon. Probably inspired by ancient prototypes, Palladio wanted to suspend the balcony of the *piano nobile* between these columns. The concealed courtyard of a small provincial town in northern Italy was thus a welcome opportunity for him to vie with the leading monuments of Roman Antiquity.

Projects of the Bramante circle and of Michelangelo must have gradually opened his eyes to the beauty and power of the column. In the fourth book of the *Quattro libri* he extols Bramante as the first to have rediscovered the good and beautiful architecture of the ancients. Michelangelo, Sansovino, Peruzzi, Sangallo, Sanmicheli, Serlio, Vasari, Vignola and Leone Leoni had then followed Bramante along the same path.

The Basilica

Trissino and other well-wishing patricians no doubt contributed to the fact that Palladio was commissioned in 1549 to clad the core of the late-medieval town hall of Vicenza with a surrounding screen of loggias in light-coloured limestone (fig. 294). In his first design of 1542 he once again followed a system of rustication of the kind made fashionable

by Giulio Romano. Then after his journey to Rome in 1545/46, he proposed a project that was far more similar to the Basilica as built. This he must have perfected still further after his later trip to Rome of 1547.

Palladio adopted a system of *serliane* on two storeys – the famous Palladio motif – to surround the town hall. By varying the width of the lateral bays of the *serliane*, he was able to adapt them to the wall openings of the old town hall and to hide the irregularities – in contrast to Giulio, who had used them to create dissonances on the garden front of the Palazzo Te. As in the upper story of the Libreria Marciana in Venice, he doubled the *serliane*, so that they fill the entire depth of the walls. And as in Serlio's Fourth Book, he separated them by narrow pillars against which he projected a big order of engaged columns, Doric on the ground floor, Ionic on the first. These engaged columns once again betray their derivation from the triumphal arch by carrying projecting segments of the entablature topped by statues. They counteract by their vertical impulse the

294 *An important early commission of Palladio's (1549) was the cladding of the old town hall of Vicenza with a classical screen. The* serliane *are wider than in Sansovino's Libreria Marciana and the columns used in a more structural way.*

horizontal movement of the *serliane*. In the corners the columns are compressed into Bramantesque triads. More than ever the detail follows Sangallo's courtyard of the Palazzo Farnese (fig. 246).

Palazzo Chiericati

In 1551 Palladio could further develop ideas with which he had already experimented in his early Palazzo Civena. As there, and as already in Sansovino's Palazzo Dolfin, Girolamo Chiericati was authorized to extend the front of his narrow building site using a piece of public ground provided it did not obstruct public passage (fig. 295). No doubt inspired by Peruzzi's Palazzo Massimo (fig. 216), Palladio opened the ground floor in a Doric trabeated colonnade to provide a through-way. He slightly projected the central five bays of the eleven-bay façade to form a centrepiece, and originally wanted to further distinguish this by a pediment. So he once again identified it with the *vestibulum* of the ancient house. As in his design for the

Palazzo Thiene, this dominant centrepiece also corresponds to the salon on the *piano nobile*. It is distinguished by large pedimented windows set behind a balcony-balustrade and topped by a row of small mezzanine windows above. The salon was reached once again by two astonishingly small staircases from the courtyard loggia. The magnificent façade as a whole brilliantly disguises the narrowness of the site. In the space of a few years Palladio, with the simplest materials and often unfavourable plots of land, succeeded in turning Vicenza into the most classicizing town in Europe.

Villa Rotonda

Not long afterwards Palladio combined the colonnade of the Palazzo Chiericati with the type, proportions and simple detail of his earlier villas and created his most successful invention, a villa with a classical temple portico in front. Like Alberti, he equated the *vestibulum* with the pedimented porch of a temple, believing that both derived from the pillar and roof of the primitive hut. He later produced a rich variation of this new type of villa with a temple front in his villas for Montagnana, Vancimuglio, Piombino Dese and Fratta Polesine. But it was in 1566 that he gave this type its most perfect form in the

295 *Façade of the Palazzo Chiericati, Vicenza, 1551. Here Palladio cleverly extended the building over the public way and opened the vestibule of the ground floor in a Doric colonnade.*

299 *Of the vast Palazzo Barbarano da Porto only two bays (out of seven) were ever built, featuring giant half-columns of a Composite order linked by festoons of fruit.*

300 *The Loggia del Capitanio was the seat of the Venetian governor. Planned to have five or seven bays, its side front is articulated in a very decorative way by a triumphal arch with small orders.*

and voussoirs of the rustication. They are hemmed in between pedestals like the over-slender balcony-windows between the powerful columns of the *piano nobile*, so that – contrary to the Palazzo Barbarano da Porto – greater emphasis is given to the verticals, not only in the columns, but also in the narrow intercolumniations. The decoration is once again concentrated on the ponderous festoons of the panels between the capitals. A deep atrium was to lead into the exedra-shaped courtyard, its ground floor articulated with a small Composite order.

Loggia del Capitanio

The seat of the military representative of the Republic of Venice in Vicenza was planned as a five- or seven-bayed loggia (fig. 300). Originally its fine brick was stuccoed white. The loggia on the ground floor, which served for public transactions, is opened with a pillared arcade over a stepped podium. The squatter *piano nobile* with the council hall is articulated with steep balcony windows. Both storeys of the piazza front are knitted together into a compact block and decorated with the colossal half-columns of a triumphal *Composita*. The balconies are supported by abstracted triglyph-consoles as in Michelangelo's *ricetto* (fig. 243). The ground floor of the side front is articulated by an independent small order. Its triumphal arch probably served as the main entrance. The projections of its abbreviated entablature support a broad balcony and statues. The centre of the upper floor opens in a triumphal *serliana* – perhaps the tribune on

which the Capitano was to show himself to the people. As in the side walls of the Redentore (figs 304–6), both the *serliana* and the windows of the piazza front cut through the terminating entablature. For the first time Palladio decorated the exterior of a building with a series of different triumphal motifs without any systematic tectonic connection between them; he thus dispensed with any horizontal continuity and renounced the fiction of a coherent load-bearing skeleton of the kind he had adopted in his previous buildings.

San Giorgio Maggiore in Venice

It was not until relatively late that Palladio succeeded in gaining a foothold in Venice. But he was to leave his indelible mark on the city with fragments of a monastery and two great churches.

His work for the rich Benedictines on the island of San Giorgio started with the monastery he erected in 1560 (figs 301–3). In the axial alignment of entrance vestibule, central staircase and doorway into the elongated oblong refectory, he was clearly inspired by the layout of Michelangelo's Laurenziana (fig. 10). On the other hand, the refectory's monumental proportions, barrel vault, Ionic aedicules and three enormous Diocletian windows are indebted to Sangallo's Cappella Paolina and Sala Regia in the Vatican (fig. 199) – a unique but characteristic case in which he combined elements of a Michelangelesque type with Sangallo's language.

301–3 *The abbey church of San Giorgio Maggiore was one of Palladio's major contributions to the architecture of Venice. The plan, a quincunx with an aisled nave, differs from Roman prototypes in the position of the presbytery. The high altar does not stand under the cupola, but in a typically Venetian square presbytery which continues in the deep choir of the monks. Palladio's project for the façade was probably changed by a follower.*

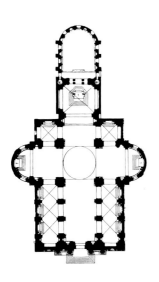

The courtyard of the convent of the Carità, which he started in 1561, is also Sangallesque. Here too he followed the layout of the antique house with its sequence of *vestibulum, atrium, cavaedium, peristylium* and *tablinum*. As in the villa of Cricoli and the courtyard of the Palazzo Thiene, the seven theatre motifs are flanked by the lateral bays of the triumphal arch. The system of superimposition and the engaged columns of the two lower floors follow the courtyard of Palazzo Farnese (fig. 192). But the frieze of the *Dorica* is decorated as if it were Ionic, a rare case of *mescolanza* in Palladio. And since there are no pedestals, the balustrade of the second floor stretches between the pillars. The articulation of the third floor is as simple as that in the courtyard of the Cancelleria (fig. 132). The columns of the three-aisled *atrium* would have been nearly as giant as those in the courtyard of the Palazzo Iseppe Porto.

Four years later he once again declared his fidelity to the Roman tradition in the church of the San Giorgio monastic complex. The Benedictine community could afford an imposing aisled basilica, drum-supported dome over the crossing, monumental pedimented façade and cladding with classical orders in gleaming white stone. But instead of basing his design on ancient temples, Palladio modelled himself on such prototypes as Sangallo's projects for San Giovanni dei Fiorentini or Peruzzi's new cathedral in Carpi (fig. 207). As there, the domed crossing is incorporated in a quincunx with apses and deep chancel; the weight of the barrel vault is distributed between pillar arcades with half-columns of a Composite order. As in the basilica, the twin pilasters of a small Corinthian order support the impost of the deep arcades. The dome pillars are reinforced by quadrangular columns, in a way anticipated only by the Madonna di San Biagio in Montepulciano (fig. 202). The connection of the entrance wall with the first pillars of the nave again recalls projects for St Peter's; and as in Sangallo's model for St Peter's (figs 197, 198), the barrel vaults are pierced by lunettes with Diocletian windows. The alternation of aedicules and niches in the chancel is reminiscent of the Palazzo Branconio dell'Aquila (fig. 167). The demarcation of the high altar space from the crossing, and its distinction by corner columns, are, however, a clear deference to Venetian models such as the Madonna dei Miracoli. Especially Venetian is the suffusion of the interior with light, which floods into the church on two levels and plays over its luminous sculptural relief and its white-stuccoed walls.

In 1562, in his prostyle temple-front façade of San Francesco della Vigna, Palladio had translated the system of Bramante's façade in Roccaverano (fig. 153) into the more magnificent and more sculptural styles of Sanmicheli, Sansovino and his own mature buildings. A surviving drawing shows that he planned for San Giorgio, by contrast, a temple front with large and small orders rising from the ground level.

The Redentore

Not until 1577 was Palladio able to fuse all these heterogeneous elements and motifs together with his own style and the Venetian tradition into an even more homogeneous church on the Giudecca (figs 304–06). The Senate had vowed its construction during a plague epidemic that had ravaged the city, and entrusted it to the Capuchins. The interior is simpler than that of San Giorgio. In the unaisled nave flanked by chapels, trilobate crossing with high altar and chancel, and also in the form of vaulting, Palladio combined two models of monastic church: Sansovino's San Francesco della Vigna and Genga's San Giovanni in Pesaro. Palladio, like Genga, furnished the crossing under the dome with lateral exedras, closed it off from the nave on the one side and the chancel on the other, splayed the pillars of the trefoil-shaped altar-room to support drum and dome, and hollowed out the pillars between the three rectangular chapels with niches. But he replaced the four circular sacristies that flank Genga's crossing with two slender minaret-like campanili with spiral staircases.

In the articulation of the interior, and in the variety of its spatial effects, however, he is far more sensuous and classicizing than Genga. He adopted more composed and monumental proportions, articulated the walls of the nave with triumphal-arch motifs, dispensed with pedestals, and symmetrically turned the articulation of engaged Corinthian columns and unbroken entablature round the four corners of the nave to culminate in the triumphal arch of the crossing. The light-flooded trefoil-shaped altar-room under the dome is at once closed off and expanded in space: an unbroken vista, unprecedented in sweep, is created through its rear apse to the semicircular screen of Corinthian columns leading into the choir.

The exterior, like Genga's San Giovanni, is reinforced on the sides by paired buttresses and was originally white-stuccoed (not red as it is now). It develops upwards from the marble temple front to the cylindrical drum and the lead-sheathed dome, which in conformity with the Venetian tradition of an exterior wooden coping is much higher than Roman domes of the Cinquecento. In contrast to the

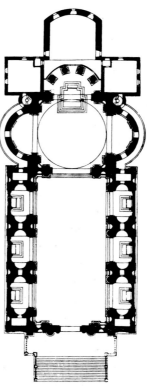

304–06 *When in 1577 Palladio built his Redentore for Capuchins, he was inspired by Genga's San Giovanni in Pesaro and influenced by the Counter-Reformation. He made the trefoiled room under the cupola coincide with the presbytery and opened its apse in a colonnade to the choir of the monks. The giant temple front of the façade penetrates a lower one which corresponds to the chapels.*

During the last years of his life Palladio came even closer to the ancient temple. He turned the little church of the villa of his friend Daniele Barbaro, who had since died, into a temple by giving it a richly orna-mented Corinthian pronaos with pyknostyle intercolumniations (fig. 307). The round *cella*, surrounded by four triumphal arches, the wall rhythm of its chapels and its balustrade betray its descent from San-micheli's Cappella Pellegrini (fig. 223). Palladio, however, eliminated the drum, the aedicules of the ground floor and entablature projec-tions. He thus freed the space from every vertical impulse. Perhaps even in deference to the tendencies of the Counter-Reformation, he combined the rotunda with a Greek cross; in his treatise he had already stressed the cruciform ground plan of San Giorgio. He distributed the weight of the dome over eight pillars and allowed the chapels to project in segments from the Greek cross of the exterior. From this the build-ing expands hierarchically upwards over the campanili to the lantern. As in the Redentore, Palladio stacked and compacted ever broader and higher layers, one behind the other in depth, into the façade.

307 *The church that Palladio built for the Villa Barbaro at Maser is a self-conscious miniature version of the Pantheon combined with a Greek cross.*

façades of Roccaverano and the old cathedral of Carpi, Palladio does not project the section of the interior on the façade, but reduces a temple pronaos to plastic relief. As in Roman antiquity the temple front is raised over a squat socle with a balustraded staircase. Two quadrangular corner columns and two inner engaged columns of a Composite order support the unbroken triangular pediment. Palladio alludes here to the triumphal-arch motif not only by broadening the central bay, but also by adding an attic rising behind the pediment; it is crowned with statues of the *Redentore* (Redeemer) and angels. As in the façade of the old Carpi Cathedral (fig. 206), this central temple front is intersected by a second lower and broader temple front, whose pediment fragments correspond to the roofs of the aisles. Its entabla-ture runs in abstracted form through the big temple front, and re-emerges in the central columnar portal-aedicule as a complete order. Behind this second layer rise the lateral buttresses of a third layer, abstract in articulation, but culminating in fragments of a pedi-ment and shown to be an integral part of the façade by their marble cladding. The small order reaches up to the top of the vaulting of the chapels, so that the Diocletian windows of the side walls intersect its entablature. This intricate play with hierarchy, orders and overlapping wall layers is more easily explained in scenographic than in rational or tectonic terms, in a way similar to the corner bays of the Palazzo Val-marana or the side front of the Loggia del Capitanio. The overall effect is of three temple fronts stacked and compacted together in depth.

308 *Palladio's last work was a theatre built for an academy of learned humanists of Vicenza, the Teatro Olimpico. Modelling his design on Vitruvius and on surviving Roman examples, Palladio compromises by placing it indoors under a roof.*

Teatro Olimpico

Shortly before his death Palladio was given the opportunity to erect a classical theatre for the theatre-loving patriciate of Vicenza (fig. 308). Raphael, Sangallo, Paciotto and Vignola had all showed an interest in theatre design, but their efforts never advanced beyond projects. Like Sangallo in his project for the Villa Madama, Palladio followed the Vitruvian construction of the Latin theatre (Book V.3), fixing the angles of the stage and the stepped auditorium by four equal-sided triangles contained in a circle. The Vitruvian theatre, like the classical theatre in general, was open. In order to incorporate it in an older building and to protect it from the elements by a roof, Palladio broadened the auditorium into half an oval, as Sangallo had already done in his reconstruction of the Theatre of Marcellus, and opened its terminating colonnade only in the lateral intercolumniations. This meant he had to keep the *scenae frons* considerably lower than in Barbaro's reconstruction of the Latin theatre: its upper order only slightly rises over the colonnade at the back of the auditorium. Execution had been begun but not completed on Palladio's death and only differs in detail from the right-hand alternative of his project. As in the Pantheon (fig. 3), a Corinthian order articulates the tall ground floor and squat upper storey of the *scenae frons*; its columns alternate with aedicules and its central arch cuts into the upper storey. Palladio, however, combined this system again with that of the triumphal arch. The columns are thus topped with projecting entablature fragments and, above them, with statues which are set against the engaged columns of the upper storey. The attic is adorned with another order of statues alternating with relief panels. The perspective stage sets are based on Scamozzi's and not Palladio's design: Palladio obeyed the ancient Roman principle of a fixed architectural proscenium and ignored the dynamic development of the pre-Baroque stages of Florence or Parma.

The Quattro libri

During their Roman stay in 1541 Trissino and Palladio must have met Sangallo, who knew the monuments and their relation to Vitruvius far more exactly than any earlier architect. In the same years the distinguished Accademia Vitruviana tried to elucidate the continuing philological and theoretical problems posed by the text of Vitruvius. So Trissino and his architect found ideal interlocutors in Rome. Palladio's drawings from the antique and his illustrations for Barbaro's commentary on Vitruvius (1556), as also his own treatise, *I quattri libri dell'architettura* (1570), suggest that Sangallo had given him access to his drawings – as he had already done before to Peruzzi, Serlio and Labacco. And even if Palladio could not vie with Sangallo's archaeological precision, he was the only one who did not just copy Sangallo, but developed his reflections and in many points even went beyond them. His collaboration with Barbaro in the early 1550s then gave him the opportunity to get to know Vitruvius even better than he had done through Trissino. At the same time he found patrons who enabled him to realize much that previous architects had merely dreamt of.

From building to building he could thus collect experiences in classicizing and columnar architecture that his precursors lacked. It is no wonder therefore that he felt compelled in his old age to transmit these experiences to future generations, all the more so at a time when anti-normative and Counter-Reformist tendencies were threatening the continuity of the great tradition. He himself confessed that only by measurement of the monuments of Rome had he ascertained how far their rules differed from those of Vitruvius and the authors who followed Alberti. He therefore intended the exempla of ancient monuments, as well as his own projects, as guidance to future architects. His treatise has a primarily empirical character, and is anything but systematic in its composition. In the First Book he first treats of materials, building techniques, vaults and staircases, and then of the orders. In their hierarchically ascending canon from the *Tuscanica* to the *Composita*, as also in their proportions, they differ only slightly from Vignola's earlier *Regola delli cinque ordini d'architettura* (1562/63). Admittedly Palladio uses richer decoration, but remains inferior to Serlio in the variety of the ancient capitals and their decorative forms that he adduces. Like Vitruvius and Alberti, he regards nature as the great teacher, derives all architecture from the primordial wooden hut, and castigates any violation of the law of load and support. Thus a broken pediment he regards as incompatible with the function of a roof. Although in his Second Book he wanted to introduce the types of residential buildings that Francesco di Giorgio and Serlio had proposed for the various social classes, he confined himself almost exclusively to illustrating the palaces of the nobility of Vicenza and the villas of landowners with similarly high social claims. In his exteriors he drew no fundamental distinction between palace and villa and mainly ignored the Vitruvian terminology. He thus described *vestibulum* and *atrium*, in spite of all his Vitruvian learning, simply as 'loggia' or 'entrance' in his drawings. Only from his reconstruction of Vitruvius's five different *atria* can it be inferred that he tried to approximate his residential buildings to the Roman house. Not one of his projects, however, is provided with a comparably large inner courtyard.

Like Alberti, but contrary to Serlio, Palladio avoids any fundamental division between ancient and modern buildings. In the Third Book on bridges, piazzas, basilicas and palestrae he merely mentions that the hall of his Basilica in Vicenza was situated on the upper floor, contrary to those of Antiquity, which were on the ground floor. Above all, however, the Fourth Book devoted to the temple shows how systematically he equated the church with the pagan temple. Admittedly he attributes symbolic meaning to the cruciform ground plan, but does not illustrate his own church of San Giorgio in the treatise. He sees the ideal form of the sacred building in the circle as an image of the universe, and thus includes Bramante's Tempietto as the one modern building in his series of exempla. Further books that he wanted to devote to baths and theatres he failed to finish before his death.

So, like Alberti, Palladio hoped to return to the architecture, and hence to the forms, of Antiquity. The influence of his rational, normative style, imbued with the spirit of humanism, at first remained limited to the Veneto and to the Protestant countries. In the Catholic countries it was not until the mid-seventeenth century that he gradually began to exert an influence through Bernini and the French Academicians.

Retrospect

The 160 or so years between Brunelleschi's first works and Palladio's death form a fairly coherent period in which Italian architects followed the example of Antiquity as closely as possible. The consciousness of a Latin identity, fundamentally different from that of other countries, and their responsibility to restore it to new life, is still present in Palladio. With unprejudiced rationality and instinctive certainty, architects during this period succeeded in replacing the medieval with the classical vocabulary. At the same time they fused the compositional methods, functional traditions and technical achievements of the later Middle Ages with those of Antiquity. They thus created what Kugler and Burckhardt called a 'derivative style' (*abgeleiteter Stil*) in contrast to the Greek temple and the Gothic cathedral which had followed their own laws. Through this synthesis they created, perhaps often without being conscious of the fact, works that, in spite of all their deference to, or imitation of, the models of the ancient world, would have been unthinkable in Antiquity. These medieval roots remain unmistakable even in the buildings of Bramante and Michelangelo, though without standing in the way of their allegiance to the Latin tradition. Even the attempts to preserve architecture from dogmatic and stereotyped repetition by deviating from the norm and violating the Vitruvian rules (sometimes provocatively so as in Giulio Romano and Michelangelo) in the period after 1520 continued to feed off the heritage of Antiquity and never placed in question its ultimate authority. It has to be said, too, that these unorthodox tendencies in the field of architecture were never combined into a coherent movement that followed the Renaissance and which would justify the separation of a stylistic phase in architecture that could, as in painting, be labelled Mannerism.

The 160 years of our period can be conveniently divided into two equal parts, one corresponding to the fifteenth and the other to the sixteenth century. Though this whole period is given an overall coherence by its allegiance to a single tradition, it was anything but continuous in development and is inseparable from all the conflicting or centrifugal forces and tendencies of the age. So all attempts to see Renaissance architecture as a coherent unilinear development are doomed to failure.

Indeed, without a series of sheer accidents, architecture in this period would never have followed so happy a course. As far as we know, Brunelleschi largely acted on his own impulses. He was born into a flourishing city-state and ever since his youth participated in its humanistic, artistic and political culture, which stood higher than elsewhere and aroused his enthusiasm for antiquity. He broke out of the narrow confines of his original profession and travelled to Rome. This voyage of discovery was comparable to that of the great navigators of his time who crossed the oceans to discover and explore new continents. He must soon have recognized that humanistic treatises, paintings or statues did not suffice to vie with Antiquity, and that this also demanded a renewal of architecture and the unification of all the arts. Brunelleschi was a devout, but probably at the same time sceptical, Christian and dedicated himself almost exclusively to religious

architecture. In his conversations with humanists he must have reflected on the origins of Christianity and hence on his own religious identity. He built no images of the heavenly Jerusalem, in the way the masters of the Gothic had done, but columnar basilicas 'made in the measure of man', in which the Florentines could gather and worship together. And even if his three central-plan buildings served as the mausolea of affluent patrons, he was anything but a courtier. Rather, he was the responsible representative and aesthetic conscience of his republican home. His dome of Florence Cathedral surpassed all previous constructions in the post-antique Western world and became the abiding symbol of Florentine self-confidence.

Through his tectonic, archaeological and optical studies Brunelleschi had developed architecture into a science that surpassed the technical skills of most architects of his time. So the first great accident in our period was the fact that the ban on the Alberti family was lifted in 1428 and Leon Battista was allowed to return to Florence. Only through the inspiration of Brunelleschi did he find his way to architecture. In his early treatise Alberti enlarged the focus of Vitruvius who had only described Hellenistic architecture, and tried to find rules that were also valid for the architecture of imperial Rome and of Brunelleschi. The wall, he taught, was the primary element of architecture and the column only its fragment and most beautiful ornament. The beauty of a building depended not so much on its ornaments as on its proportions. Thus architecture could be restricted to stereometric volumes, and wall and order could be merged, reduced and abstracted.

As a practising architect Alberti went far beyond his treatise and beyond Brunelleschi. While the latter had translated late-medieval types into golden Latinity, Alberti tried to revive ancient building types such as the temple and the triumphal arch and to merge both in an unheard-of way. Almost exclusively, he took on only those commissions that conformed, or approximated, to his ideas: commissions, in short, for triumphal façades or temples with pronaos and cella. For such commissions it was far harder to win over the pope or the republican communes than ambitious individuals, intent on perpetuating their own glory. With his triumphal monuments, directly inspired by the architecture of imperial Rome, Alberti expressed the ambitions of Florentine bankers or powerful lords like Sigismondo Malatesta, Alfonso of Aragon and Lodovico Gonzaga even more clearly than Brunelleschi, and so his buildings, and their incorporation of the triumphal-arch motif, were assured of a broad influence right from the start. They would soon be not only widely imitated, but also varied and further developed. Important patrons of the arts like Pius II, Paul II, Federico da Montefeltro, Lorenzo de' Medici or Lodovico Sforza found in followers of Alberti such as Bernardo Rossellino, Francesco del Borgo, Francesco di Giorgio, Giuliano da Sangallo and the Milanese Bramante the most suitable masters to satisfy their passion for building and to perpetuate their name. They thus prepared the ground for the second great phase of Renaissance architecture.

The Sforza were expelled from Milan in 1499, and as a result Bramante moved to Rome. This must be considered the second major accident that cannot, any more than the first, be derived from any continuous development. And hard upon it occurred yet a third accident that cannot be separated from it: Alexander VI suddenly died and Julius II ascended the papal throne in 1503. No prince of the Renaissance came closer to imperial power than Julius II: only he enabled Bramante to design truly imperial buildings, of the kind that Alberti had only dreamt of. The widely scattered achievements of the Quattrocento required a concentration of forces and no place was predestined to become it more than the Rome of Julius II.

Bramante (unlike Alberti) was no trained humanist, but he did know parts of the treatises of Vitruvius and Alberti and he grasped with extraordinary facility, and even more concretely than Alberti, the character of the ancient monuments. He came to Rome at a time when the immediate imitation of the antique had reached its maturity; none of his Milanese buildings give any presentiment that one day he would design a building like the Tempietto. This classicizing *tholos* was now accepted even by the Spanish kings as a *memoria* of the place of martyrdom of St Peter. Not long afterwards Pompeio Colonna commissioned Bramante to erect a villa in the style of the imperial baths near Genazzano. Bramante made the papal palace and St Peter's the very crucible of European architecture, and found in Raphael, Sangallo and Peruzzi pupils who perfected and enriched his legacy and disseminated it far beyond the borders of Italy. The place of origin of the most important prototypes had now become the home of the greatest architects of the day. They succeeded in inspiring patrons from the most varied social backgrounds to embrace bold and imaginative projects. Raphael created in the Cappella Chigi perhaps the most perfect *Gesamtkunstwerk* of the Renaissance and came even closer than Bramante to the forms, functions and spirit of Antiquity in his designs for the Villa Madama.

That Rome ceased to exert its centripetal force on architects soon after the deaths of Raphael and Leo X was due not only to a political, economic and religious crisis. Like Alberti before them, Michelangelo, Giulio Romano, Sansovino and Sanmicheli found more favourable conditions for work elsewhere in Italy even before the Sack of Rome in 1527. It was not until 1534 that the papacy re-emerged as a major source of patronage for architecture. Paul III made Sangallo the most powerful architect of the papal state, but his supremacy proved in the long run less innovative than the diaspora of Bramante's followers among the various centres of central and northern Italy.

The last major accident in our period was that Paul III, after the premature death of Sangallo and Giulio Romano in 1546, won Michelangelo, largely inexperienced in vault construction, as the architect of St Peter's. So the seventy-one-year-old master, tired of sculpting and fresco painting, devoted himself mainly to architecture for the last eighteen years of his life. He fundamentally and permanently renewed it in a way that none of the younger masters was able to do. He had designed a series of triumphal projects for Julius II and the Medici, and had developed an undogmatic *volgare* in his eighteen-year-long Florentine absence from Rome. Only after his return to Rome, and as a follower of Bramante, Raphael, Peruzzi and Sangallo as architect of St Peter's, did he become the guardian of tradition. He became an architect who concentrated no longer on wall relief and the individual form (as he had done in Florence), but on the reciprocity of form, function and construction, as in the drum of St Peter's, in the Sforza chapel and in his projects for the Campidoglio and San Giovanni dei Fiorentini, in the way that Vitruvius had already postulated. The imperial ambitions of Julius II had in the meantime been definitely buried, and so Michelangelo's monumental buildings could at most compensate for the inexorable loss of temporal power of the Church. In many respects they correspond better to the rise of absolute power in Europe than to the Tridentine spirit. Only in the restless exterior of St Peter's and the soaring interior of its great dome could he express the religious fervour of his last years.

Palladio and Vignola, the two most influential exponents of the younger generation, did not allow their faith in the ancient norms to be swayed by Michelangelo's sometimes unorthodox vocabulary. Yet both profited from Michelangelo's sense for volumetric building blocks, colossal proportions and dynamic axes. While Palladio was able to convince the patricians of the Veneto of his triumphant classicism and even approximated their villas to ancient temples, Vignola's powerful projects corresponded to the absolutist claims of the papal *nipoti*. It was only after the deaths of Michelangelo and of Pius IV that Roman architecture began to turn away from the ideals of the Renaissance and to adapt to the spirit of the Counter-Reformation. But even then the different artistic centres of Italy continued the manner of their architectural founding fathers. Architects like Giacomo della Porta, Mascarino, Domenico Fontana or Maderno tried to amalgamate the language of Michelangelo and Sangallo. Yet when Bernini, Borromini and Cortona after 1630 once again raised Rome to the unchallenged centre of European architecture, they rapidly bypassed the spirit of these teachers, by once again seeking immediate guidance from the models of Antiquity, Bramante, Raphael, Peruzzi, Michelangelo, Serlio, Vignola and Palladio, the same masters who also bulk large in the architectural books and guides of the following centuries as the fathers and precursors of the true architecture. From the mid-eighteenth century Cinquecentism in architecture gained ever-wider dissemination. It even survived the neo-medieval and neo-Baroque revivals of the nineteenth century. Many Italian towns returned to their Cinquecentesque identity. The columnar order maintained its authority right down to the early twentieth century: its influence can still be felt in great pioneers of the modern movement like Otto Wagner, Adolf Loos or Peter Behrens. Only about sixty years after the architects of the modern movement had finally liberated themselves from the columnar orders, the post-modern movement has returned to the heritage of the Renaissance: Aldo Rossi could even copy the courtyard of the Palazzo Farnese in a façade of the reunited Berlin.

Bibliography

In the following reference books on Renaissance architecture you will find exhaustive bibliographies and rich visual documentation.

L.H. Heydenreich and W. Lotz, *Architecture in Italy 1400 to 1600*, Harmondsworth 1974; revised edition of Heydenreich's part by P. Davies, New Haven 1996

Italian Renaissance Architecture from Brunelleschi to Michelangelo, ed. H. Millon, London: Thames & Hundson, 1994 (abridged paperback edition 1996)

Storia dell'architettura italiana: Il Quattrocento, ed. F. P. Fiore, Milano: Electa 1998

Storia dell'architettura italiana: Il primo Cinquecento, ed. A. Bruschi, Milano: Electa 2002

Storia dell'architettura italiana: Il secondo Cinquecento, ed. C. Conforti and R. Tuttle, Milano: Electa 2001

You will find further information and bibliographies in the following selection of books and essays published after the three above-cited Electa volumes (in chronological order).

General:

C.L. Frommel, *Architettura alla corte papale del Rinascimento*, Milano 2002

A. Hopkins, *Italian Architecture from Michelangelo to Borromini*, London 2002

C. Thoenes, *Opus incertum: italienische Studien aus drei Jahrzehnten*, München 2002

La chiesa a pianta centrale, ed. B. Adorni, Milano 2002

Architektur-Theorie von der Renaissance bis zur Gegenwart, ed. B. Evers, Köln 2003

G. Clark, *Roman House – Renaissance Palaces: Inventing Antiquity in Fifteenth-Century Italy*, Cambridge 2003

L'invention de la Renaissance. Proceedings of the conference, Tours 1994, ed. J. Guillaume, Paris 2003

A. Bruschi, *L'antico, la tradizione, il moderno, da Arnolfo a Peruzzi; saggi sull'architettura del Rinascimento*, ed. M. Ricci and P. Zampa, Milano 2004

G. Simoncini, *Topografia e urbanistica da Bonifacio IX ad Alessandro VI*, Firenze 2004

Andrea Palladio e la villa veneta da Palladio a Carlo Scarpa, ed. G. Beltramini and H. Burns, Venezia 2005

C. Conforti, *La città del tardo Rinascimento*, Bari 2005

Démeures d'éternité: églises et chapelles funéraires aux XV e XVI siècles, ed. J. Guillaume, Paris 2005

C.L. Frommel, *Architettura e committenti da Alberti a Bramante*, Firenze 2006

Brunelleschi:

P. Gärtner, *Filippo Brunelleschi 1377–1446*, Köln: Könemann 1998

Der Humanismus der Architektur in Florenz: Filippo Brunelleschi und Michelozzo di Bartolommeo, ed. W. von Löhneysen, Hildesheim 1999

S. Di Pasquale, *Brunelleschi: costruzione della cupola di Santa Maria del Fiore*, Venezia 2002

U. Schedler, *Filippo Brunelleschi: Synthese von Antike und Mittelalter in der Renaissance*, Petersberg 2004

Michelozzo:

Michelozzo: scultore e varchitetto nel suo tempo (1396–1472). Proceedings of the conference, Florence 1990, ed. G. Morolli, Firenze 1998

Alberti:

Leon Battista Alberti a Napoli: la corte aragonese e la lezione albertiana. Proceedings of the conference, ed. S. Borsi, Capri 1994

C. Syndikus, *Leon Battista Alberti: das Bauornament*, Münster 1996

V. Biermann, *Ornamentum: Studien zum Traktat 'De re aedificatoria' des Leon Battista Alberti*, Hildesheim 1997

R. Tavernor, *On Alberti and the Art of Building*, New Haven 1998

I. Lorch, *Die Kirchenfassaden in Italien 1450–1527: die Grundlagen durch Leon Battista Alberti und die Weiterentwicklung des basilikalen Fassadenspiegels bis zum Sacco di Roma*, Hildesheim 1999

A. Turchini, *Il Tempio Malatestiano, Sgismondo Malatesta e Leon Battista Alberti*, Cesena 2000

A. Grafton, *Leon Battista Alberti: Master Builder of the Italian Renaissance*, London 2001

L. Boschetto, *Leon Battista Alberti e Firenze*, Firenze 2001

Il principe architetto. Proceedings of the conference, Mantua 1999, ed. A. Calzona, F. P. Fiore and A. Tenenti, Firenze 2002

S. Borsi, *Leon Battista Alberti e Roma*, Firenze 2003

Domus et splendida palatia: residenze papali e cardinalizie a Roma fra XII e XV secolo. Proceedings of the conference, Pisa 2002, ed. A. Moncatti, Pisa 2004

S. Borsi, *Leon Battista Alberti e l'antichità di Roma*, Firenze 2004

D. Mazzini, *Villa Medici a Fiesole: Leon Battista Alberti e il prototipo della villa rinascimentale*, Firenze 2004

Leon Battista Alberti: umanisti, architetti, e artisti alla scoperta dell'antico nella città del Quattrocento. Catalogue of the exhibition, ed. F.P. Fiore with the collaboration of A. Nesselrath, Milano 2005

Leon Battista Alberti – Humanist, Kunsttheoretiker, Architekt. Proceedings of the conference, Münster 2004, ed. J. Poeschke, Münster 2005

Leon Battista Alberti: architettura e committenti. Proceedings of the conference, Florence, Rimini, Mantua 2004, ed. A. Calzona and F.P. Fiore, Firenze 2006

Il 'De re aedificatoria di Alberti'. Proceedings of the conference, Mantua 2003, ed. A Calzona and F.P. Fiore, Firenze 2006

C.L. Frommel, *Il Sant'Andrea a Mantova: Storia, ricostruzione, interpretazione*. Catalogue of the exhibition *Alberti a Mantova*, ed. A. Calzona and F.P. Fiore, Milan 2006

Architecture under Sixtus IV:

R. Samperi, *L'architettura di S. Agostino a Roma (1296–1483); una chiesa mendicante tra Medioevo e Rinascimento,* Roma 1999

Sisto IV: le arti a Roma nel primo Rinascimento. Proceedings of the conference, Rome 1997, ed. F. Benzi, Roma 2000

Luciano Laurana and Francesco di Giorgio Martini:

E.M. Wolf, *The Ecclesiastical Architecture of Francesco di Giorgio Martini,* Ann Arbor 1998

Francesco di Giorgio alla corte di Federico da Montefeltro. Proceedings of the conference, Urbino 2001, ed. F.P. Fiore, Firenze 2004

J. Höfler, *Der Palazzo Ducale in Urbino unter den Montefeltro (1376–1509),* Regensburg 2004

Baccio Pontelli:

F. Benelli, 'Baccio Pontelli, Giovanni della Rovere, il convento e la chiesa di S. Maria delle Grazie a Senigallia,' in *Quaderni dell'Istituto di Storia dell'Architettura* 31, 1998, pp. 13–26

Sangallo and Architecture under Pope Alexander VI:

Roma di fronte all'Europa al tempo di Alessandro VI. Proceedings of the conference, Città del Vaticano/Rome 1999, ed. M. Chiabò, S. Maddalo, M. Miglio and A.M. Oliva, 3 vols, Roma 2001

Le rocche alessandrine e la rocca di Civita Castellana. Proceedings of the conference, Viterbo 2001, ed. M. Chiabò and M. Gargano, Roma 2003

Bramante:

H. Bredekamp, *Sankt Peter und das Prinzip der produktiven Zerstörung,* Berlin 2000

Bramante e la sua cerchia a Milano e in Lombardia 1480–1500. Catalogue of the exhibition, Milan 2001, Milano 2001

Donato Bramante: ricerche, proposte, riletture, ed. F.P. Di Teodoro, Urbino 2001

Bramante milanese e l'architettura del Rinascimento lombardo, ed. C.L. Frommel, L. Giordano and R. Schofield, Milano 2002

J. Niebaum, 'Bramante und der Neubau von St. Peter: die Planungen vor dem "Ausführungsprojekt",' in *Römisches Jahrbuch der Bibliotheca Hertziana* 34, 2001–02 (2004), pp. 87–184

C. Thoenes, 'Il Tempietto di Bramante e la costruzione della "dorico genere aedis sacra",' in *Per Franco Barbieri: studi di storia dell'arte e dell'architettura,* ed. M.E. Avagnina and G. Beltramini, Venezia 2004, pp. 435–48

St. Peter's in the Vatican, ed. W. Tronzo, Cambridge 2005

Petros eni. Catalogue of the exhibition *Vatican City* 2006, ed. C. Carlo-Stella, Milan 2006

Raphael:

J. Shearman, *Raphael in Early Modern Sources (1483–1602),* New Haven 2003

F.P. Di Teodoro, *Raffaello, Baldassare Castiglione e la Lettera a Leone X,* Bologna 2003

P.N. Pagliara, 'Palazzo Pandolfini, Raffaello e Giovan Francesco da Sangallo,' in *Per Franco Barbieri: studi di storia dell'arte e dell'architettura,* ed. M.E. Avagnina and G. Beltramini, Venezia 2004, pp. 241–67

Antonio da Sangallo the Younger:

All'ombra di 'sa' gilio a celeri di farnesi'. Proceedings of the conference, Cellere 1999, ed. E. Gualdieri and R. Luzi, Cellere 2001

Peruzzi:

C.L. Frommel, F.T. Fagiliari Zeni, Buchicchio, 'Un'opera riscoperta di Baldassarre Peruzzi: il palazzo per Giovanni Corrado Orsini a Bomarzo,' in *Römisches Jahrbuch für Kunstgeschichte der Biblioteca Hertziana* 32, 1997–98 (2002), pp. 131ff.

S. Bettini, *Baldassarre Peruzzi e la cappella Ghisilardi: origine, occultamento e recupero di un'opera nella basilica di San Domenico a Bologna,* Milano 2003

Baldassarre Peruzzi 1481–1536. Proceedings of the seminar of CISA, Vicenza 2001, ed. C.L. Frommel, A. Bruschi, H. Burns, Venezia 2005

Genga:

M.L. Cannarsa, 'L'opera incompiuta: il San Giovanni Battista a Pesaro,' in *Annali di Architettura* 15, 2003 (2004), pp. 107–36

Sanmicheli:

P. Davies and D. Hemsoll, *Michele Sanmicheli,* Milano 2004

Serlio:

S. Frommel, *Sebastiano Serlio: Architect,* London 2003

Sebastiano Serlio à Lyon, ed. S. Deswartes, Lyon 2004

Michelangelo:

S. Krieg, 'Das Architekturdetail bei Michelangelo: Studien zu seiner Entwicklung bis 1534,' in *Römisches Jahrbuch für Kunstgeschichte der Biblioteca Hertziana* 33, 1999–2000 (2003), pp. 101–258

G. Maurer, *Michelangelo – die Architekturzeichnungen: Entwurfsprozess und Planungspraxis,* Regensburg 2004

G. Satzinger, 'Michelangelos Cappella Sforza,' in *Römisches Jahrbuch für Kunstgeschichte der Biblioteca Hertziana* 35, 2003–04 (2005), pp. 327–414

Vignola:

Jacopo Barozzi da Vignola, ed. R. Tuttle, B. Adorni, C.L. Frommel and C. Thoenes, Milano 2002

Vignola e i Farnese. Proceedings of the conference, Piacenza 2002, ed. C.L. Frommel and M. Ricci, Milano 2003

Palladio:

Andrea Palladio: atlante delle architetture, ed. H. Burns and G. Beltramini, Venezia 2002

L. Puppi, *Andrea Palladio,* Venezia 2005

Glossary

abacus: stone slab between capital and entablature

acanthus: formalized leaf of the *acanthus spinosus,* used as a decorative motif in Greek and Roman architecture, e.g. in the Corinthian capital

acroteria: ornament over the apex or at the ends of a classical pediment

aedicule: door or window aperture framed by a classical order, usually two columns or pilasters supporting an entablature and often topped by a pediment. The jambs can be formed by the vertical continuation of the architrave. An opening framed in this way can be described as *aediculated*

ambo, ambones: Early Christian pulpit or singing desk, like an open sarcophagus approached by steps or ladder; imitated by Brunelleschi and Donatello

andito: entrance passage

annulet: a circular moulding under the capital of a Doric column

apse: semicircular or polygonal recess in church or other building

arcade: a row of arches supported on columns, piers or pilasters, or an arched opening with its structural parts

architrave: the lowest partition of a classical entablature

archivolt: a curved architrave round an arch

astragal: a small semicircular moulding, often underneath a classical capital

atrium: the entrance hall or court of a Roman house

attic structure: upper part of triumphal arch; small storey placed above another of greater height

barrel vault: a continuous stone ceiling, either pointed or semicircular in section

basamento: the ground floor or basement plinth (above ground level) of a building

battered: of walls, slightly sloping as in fortifications

bay: division of wall or space between openings of a wall or members of an order

bifora: a double, or twin, window with colonnette in the middle

bottega: shop on the ground floor of Italian houses and palaces

braccio (Florentine): unit of measurement equivalent to 586 cm (23¼ ins)

bracket: flat-topped projection from wall serving as support

capital: topmost element of a column, marking the transition to what it supports; in classical architecture, one of the main feature by which the orders are defined

cavaedium: term used in Antiquity for the courtyard of a house

cella: the inner sanctum of an antique temple housing the image of the deity

coffer, coffering: sunken panels, usually circular, square or octagonal, in a vault or ceiling

colonnade: a row of columns supporting a flat entablature, not arches

column: a post, circular or quandrangular in section, topped by a capital, supporting an arch or entablature

Composite: one of the orders of classical architecture called Italic by Alberti, the capital being a combination of Corinthian and Ionic

console: a stone bracket in the form of a scroll

Corinthian: one of the orders of classical architecture, the capital based on acanthus

cornice: the uppermost part of a classical entablature, usually with a prominent overhang

cosmatesque: inlaid geometrically patterned decoration of architectural elements and floors consisting of marble, mosaic and coloured stones in the manner of the thirteenth-century Roman Cosmati family

crenellation: battlement, a row of merlons alternating with gaps

crossing: the centre of a cruciform church, where nave, transepts and chancel meet

dentil: literally, a tooth: a form of moulding consisting of a series of small rectangular blocks

Diocletian window: huge semicircular window divided into three lights by two mullions as in the Baths of Diocletain

Doric: one of the orders of classical architecture; the echinus capital is plain and in Greek Doric there is no base

drum: a cylindrical structure supporting a dome; another word for tambour

echinus: element of transition between the shaft of the column and the abacus of its capital; plain cushion-shaped in Greek Doric, but carved with egg-and-dart in Ionic

egg-and-dart: a classical decorative motif forming part of an entablature, archivolt or echinus, consisting of alternating ovals and arrowheads

engaged column: a column that is half, two-thirds or three-quarters buried in a wall

entablature: the whole horizontal lintel above a classical colonnade, including architrave, frieze and cornice. *Abbreviated entablature:* entablature without architrave or frieze

entasis: slight swelling in the middle or lower third of a classical column

exedra: a semicircular recess, much the same as an apse

fascia: simplified cornice in the form of a flat horizontal band

flute: semi-cylindrical vertical groove in column

frieze: the middle element of an entablature, often with decoration

foot (Roman): unit of measurement equivalent to 29.8 cm (11¾ ins)

Gesamtkunstwerk: work of art in which architecture, painting and sculpture are formally unified

groin: the meeting of two surfaces in a sharp edge

guilloche: a form of ornament consisting of overlapping or interlaced circles

guttae: drop-shaped ornaments of the Doric frieze

Hallenkirche: church with aisles of the same height as the nave

impost: springing of an arch or vault

intrados: the inner surface of a voussoir

intercolumniation: interval between members of an order

Ionic: one of the orders of classical architecture, the capital distinguished by volutes and egg-and-dart

jamb: the vertical part of a door or window frame

lantern: glazed opening at the apex of a dome to admit light

lesene: a flat vertical strip, like a pilaster without capital and mostly without base

loggia: a roofed or vaulted space with an open arcade on one or more sides

lunette: a semicircle cutting into a vault

merlon: the raised part of a crenellated battlement

mescolanza: mixture of classical orders

nymphaeum: an open-air structure, often semicircular in plan, incorporating a pool

octastyle: describes the eight columns of a *pronaos*

opus reticulatum: wall-facing consisting of small square stones set diagonally to form a diamond pattern

order: in classical architecture, a system of load and support consisting of a combination of columns or pilasters, capitals and entablature proportioned and decorated in accordance with one of the five orders: Tuscan, Doric, Ionic, Corinthian and Composite

palmo (Roman): unit of measurement equivalent to 22.34 cm (8¾ ins)

paratactical: a sequential principle of articulation of equal bays which are articulated by single elements

pedestal: a substructure placed under a column, consisting of a base or plinth, a dado and a cornice

pediment: a triangular or segmental feature crowning a portico or a whole building (corresponding to a gable) or, on a small scale, a door or window

pendentive: a triangular fragment of a sphere which forms the 'corner' between a square crossing and the bottom of a round dome

peristylium: colonnade of the antique courtyard

piano nobile: the main ceremonial storey of a palace usual**ly** situated above the ground floor

pietra serena: dark greenish-grey limestone from Fiesole

pilaster: flat projection of a column on a wall

pillar: support with round, square or polygonal section

plinth: lower square member of base of column or statue; projecting part of wall immediately above ground

podium: platform or base of a building; the *podium villae* is the ground floor of an antique villa

portego: entrance hall of Venetian palace or villa

portico: a roofed or vaulted space forming a porch in front of a classical building supported by a colonnade or arcade

pronaos: vestibule of a classical temple in front of the *cella* of an antique temple; usually the same as a portico

pulvinated: an architectural element with a convex pillow-like profile, especially a frieze

pyknostyle: a colonnade with narrow intercolumniation, the space between the columns being one-and-a-half column diameters

quincunx: architectural type of Byzantine origin where four minor vaulted rooms are set at the corners of a square whose centre is dominated by a main cupola

quoin: dressed stones articulating the corners of buildings, especially the dressed alternate header and stretcher stones at the corners of buildings, sometimes raised from the surface

revetment: facing of masonry or stone

rhythmic travée: see triumphal-arch motif

rustication: masonry consisting of or feigning rectangular blocks whose surface has been left rough and the mortar recessed

sacellum: small sanctuary or chapel

saucer dome: hemispherical cupola rising directly above pendentives

scenae frons: stage of antique theatre

serliana: a tripartite arrangement of openings or windows consisting of a central arch flanked by flat-topped openings

shouldered window: a projecting upper member, likened to an ear or shoulder, of a door or window frame

springing: the point where an arch meets a vertical plane (see impost)

stereometric: a readily measurable solid block-like form or volume

strigilation: decorative motif consisting of repeated incised elongated S-shapes; derived from the Roman *strigil*, an instrument like a sickle used by athletes to scrape their skin

studiolo: private study

stylobate: base or flat surface on which a classical colonnade rests

superimposition: placing one above the other of at least two of the five classical orders in hierarchical sequence (as in the Colosseum)

tabernacle: three-dimensional aedicule housing altar, tomb or statue

tambour: see drum

tectonic: principle of support of the entablature by columns, pilasters or brackets

temple front: front side of antique temple

theatre motifs: sequence of arcades supported by pillars and decorated with single members of an order, derived from the Tabularium, the Colosseum and other Roman theatres

thermae: Roman baths

thermal window: see Diocletian window

tholos: round temple with *cella*

tiburio: roofed polygonal or circular tambour-like exterior structure hiding a dome (or false dome)

trabeation: post-and-lintel system; see entablature

transept: either arm of transverse part of a cruciform church, or the arms on either side of the crossing

transverse arch: an arch at right angles to the longitudinal part of a building, usually articulating a barrel or groin vault

tribune: choir or elevated gallery

triglyph: ornament of the frieze in Doric order, consisting of block or tablet with vertical grooves, alternating with metopes

triumphal-arch motif: architectural scheme based on Roman triumphal arches consisting of a big central arch often flanked by two smaller ones, adorned by an order and topped by an attic; exemplified by the interior of Alberti's Sant'Andrea in Mantua where a series of large arches are each flanked by narrower bays. Called 'rhythmic travée' by Geymüller, it became one of the favourite motifs applied to the elevations of post-medieval architecture. Its triumphal effect is close to a *serliana*

tufa: soft volcanic stone

Tuscan: one of the orders of classical architecture, with simpler capital and base than Roman Doric and unfluted

vestibulum: first room of the Vitruvian house

voussoir: wedge-shaped stone forming part of an arch

Sources of Illustrations

Where not otherwise mentioned, the photographs have been kindly supplied by the Bibliotheca Hertziana, Rome

GDSU: Gabinetto dei Disegni e delle Stampe, Uffizi, Florence

2 Photo Alinari Archives, Florence
3 GDSU 164 A
4 Photo Alinari Archives, Florence
5 Saalman, *Filippo Brunelleschi, the Buildings*, p. 54
6 Photo Alinari Archives, Florence
7 Bruschi
8 Saalman, op. cit., p. 84
9 P. Sanpaolesi, *Brunellesco e Donatello nella Sacristia Vecchia di San Lorenzo,* Pisa, 1948
10 Plan from Paatz
11 Photo Alinari Archives, Florence
12 Saalman, op. cit., p. 129
13 Photo Scala, Florence
14 Photo Alinari Archives, Florence
15 Saalman, op. cit., p. 256
17 Drawing P.A. Rossi
18 Photo Alinari Archives, Florence
19 From W. and E. Paatz, *Die Kirchen von Florenz,* Frankfurt, 1952
20 Biblioteca Laurenziana, Florence, Cod. Ashburnham 1828, f. 85
21 Biblioteca Vaticana, Rome, Cod. Barberini 4424, fol. 15. Photo Courtauld Institute of Art, London
22, 23 From G.B. Montano, *Raccolta dei Tempii et Sepolcri, Rome,* 1638
25 Bruschi
26 Heydenreich and Lotz (see Bibliography), p. 9
27 Photo Alinari Archives, Florence
28 Photo Georgina Masson
29, 30 Photo Alinari Archives, Florence
31, 32 From M. Ferrara and F. Quinterio, *Michelozzo di Bartolomeo,* 1984
33 Photo Scala, Florence
34 C.L. Frommel
35 Photo Alinari Archives, Florence
37 Photo Alinari Archives, Florence
39 Photo Alinari Archives, Florence
40 Staatliche Museen Preussischer Kulturbesitz Münzkabinett
41, 42 Photo Alinari Archives, Florence
44 Photo Scala, Florence
46 From Calzona-Volpi-Gheradini, 1994
48 Alinari Archives, Florence, and V. Viti, *La Badia Fiesolana,* 1926
50, 51 Photo Alinari Archives, Florence
52 Mazzini (see Bibliography)
53 Biblioteca Laurenziana, Florence, Cod Ashburnham 1828, app., ff. 56v–57r
54 Borsi, *Leon Battista Alberti,* p. 171
55–57 Photo Alinari Archives, Florence
58 Drawing G. Diller. From F.P. Fiore, 1998
59 C.L. Frommel, R. Niccolo, *Leon Battista Alberti,* proceedings of the Münster conference, 2005
60 From Murray, *Architecture of the Italian Renaissance,* p. 82
61 From Stegmann and Geymüller, *Der Architektur der Renaissance in Toscana*
64 Drawing J. Friedrich. From F.P. Fiore, 1998

65 Photo Alinari Archives, Florence
69 From F. De Champagny and others, *Rome dans sa grandeur,* Paris, 1870
71 Photo Stefano Giraldi
72 Gemäldegalerie, Berlin
73 Palazzo Ducale, Urbino
74 Walters Art Gallery, Baltimore
76, 77 Photo Alinari Archives, Florence
78 Heydenreich and Lotz (see Bibliography), p. 134
79 GDSU 3963A
80 Biblioteca Apostolica Vaticana, Rome, Cod. Barb., Lat. 4424, f. 8v
81 Photo Alinari Archives, Florence
83–85 Photo Alinari Archives, Florence
87 Photo Georgina Masson
88 From Baldi, *Bianchini* 1724
89–92 Photo Alinari Archives, Florence
93 Tafuri, *Francesco di Giorgio*
94 Photo Scala, Florence
98 Photo Alinari Archives, Florence
99 Biblioteca Nazionale Centrale, Ord 312 II 1, 140c, 43r
100 Photo Alinari Archives, Florence
101 Civica Raccolta Stampe, Milan
103 From F. Cassina, *Le Fabbriche piu cospicue di Milano,* 1840. Photo Courtauld Institute of Art, London
104 Photo Alinari Archives, Florence
105 Photo Aragozzini
106 Photo Alinari Archives, Florence
107 Frommel, Schlimme
110 Photo Aragozzini
111, 112 Institute de France, Paris, MS 'B'. Photo Courtauld Institute of Art, London
115 Photo Alinari Archives, Florence
117 From O. Förster, *Bramante, Vienna and Munich,* 1956, by kind permission of Anton Schroll & Co
118 Soprintendenza ai Monumenti, Venice
119 Photo Ferruzzi
121–123 Photo Alinari Archives, Florence
125 Frommel, Schindler
131 Frommel, J. Kraus
132–135 Photo Alinari Archives, Florence
136 A. Lafrérie, RIBA, London
137 Photo Georgina Masson
138 From Sebastiano Serlio, *The Five Books of Architecture,* Book III, f. 18
139 Drawing G. Diller
140 M. Cartaro
141 Photo Alinari Archives, Florence
142 A. Bruschi, C.L. Frommel, et al, *San Pietro che non c'è,* Milan, 1996. Drawing P. Fölbach after GDSU, 1A
143 After GDSU 1A, drawing P. Fölbach. From H.A. Millon and V.M. Lampugnani, *The Renaissance from Brunelleschi to Michelangelo,* 1994
144 Biblioteca Vaticana, Rome
145 GDSU 8A
146 GDSU 20A

Index